Who Tracked Soccer Through the House?

A CLEATS Collection by Bill Hinds

**Andrews McMeel
Publishing**

Kansas City

04 05 06 07 08 BBG 10 9 8 7 6 5 4 3 2 1

ISBN: 0-7407-4138-1

Library of Congress Control Number: 2003111240

**To the people who give their
time so kids can play**

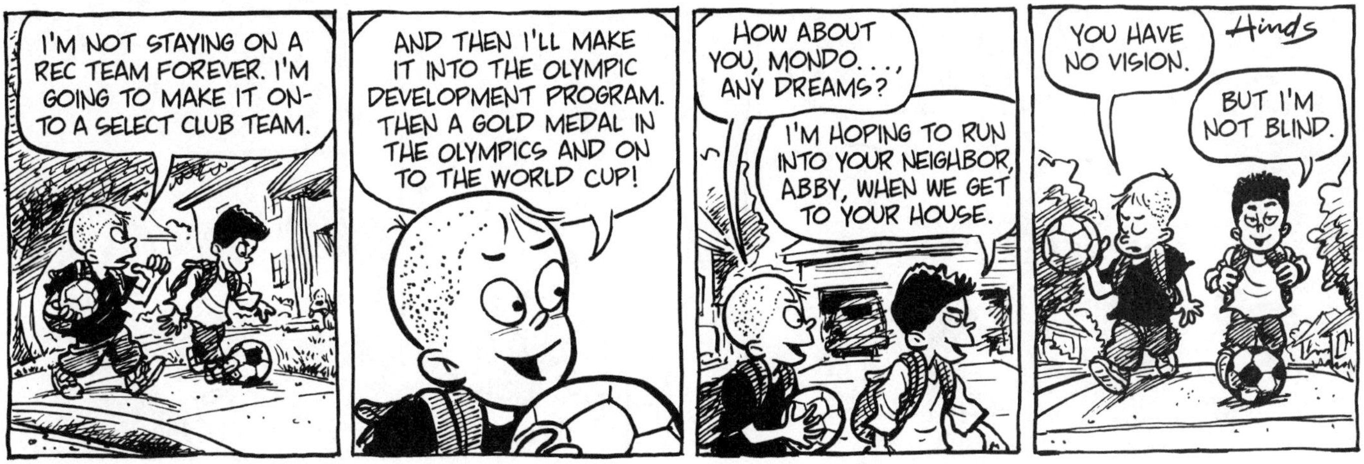
I'M NOT STAYING ON A REC TEAM FOREVER. I'M GOING TO MAKE IT ON-TO A SELECT CLUB TEAM.
AND THEN I'LL MAKE IT INTO THE OLYMPIC DEVELOPMENT PROGRAM. THEN A GOLD MEDAL IN THE OLYMPICS AND ON TO THE WORLD CUP!
HOW ABOUT YOU, MONDO. . . , ANY DREAMS?
I'M HOPING TO RUN INTO YOUR NEIGHBOR, ABBY, WHEN WE GET TO YOUR HOUSE.
Hinds
YOU HAVE NO VISION.
BUT I'M NOT BLIND.

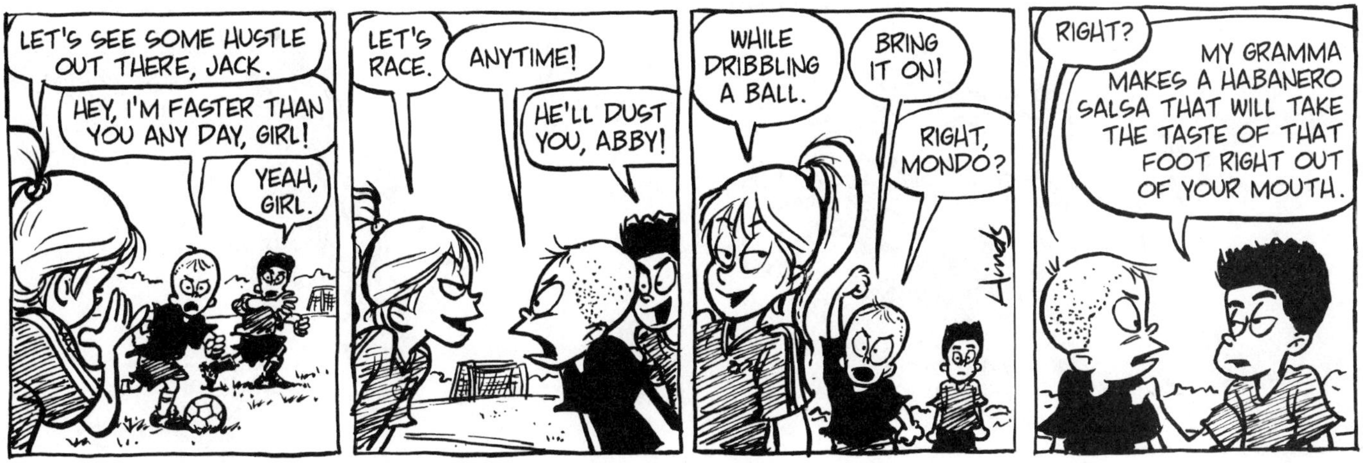
LET'S SEE SOME HUSTLE OUT THERE, JACK.
HEY, I'M FASTER THAN YOU ANY DAY, GIRL!
YEAH, GIRL.
LET'S RACE.
ANYTIME!
HE'LL DUST YOU, ABBY!
WHILE DRIBBLING A BALL.
BRING IT ON!
RIGHT, MONDO?
Hinds
RIGHT?
MY GRAMMA MAKES A HABANERO SALSA THAT WILL TAKE THE TASTE OF THAT FOOT RIGHT OUT OF YOUR MOUTH.

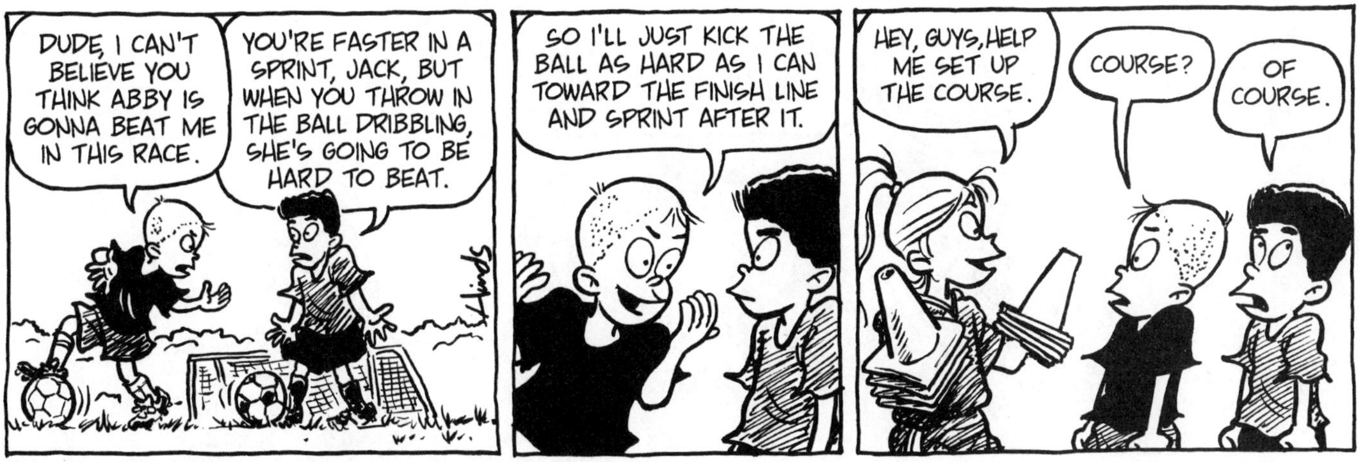
DUDE, I CAN'T BELIEVE YOU THINK ABBY IS GONNA BEAT ME IN THIS RACE.
YOU'RE FASTER IN A SPRINT, JACK, BUT WHEN YOU THROW IN THE BALL DRIBBLING, SHE'S GOING TO BE HARD TO BEAT.
Hinds
SO I'LL JUST KICK THE BALL AS HARD AS I CAN TOWARD THE FINISH LINE AND SPRINT AFTER IT.
HEY, GUYS, HELP ME SET UP THE COURSE.
COURSE?
OF COURSE.

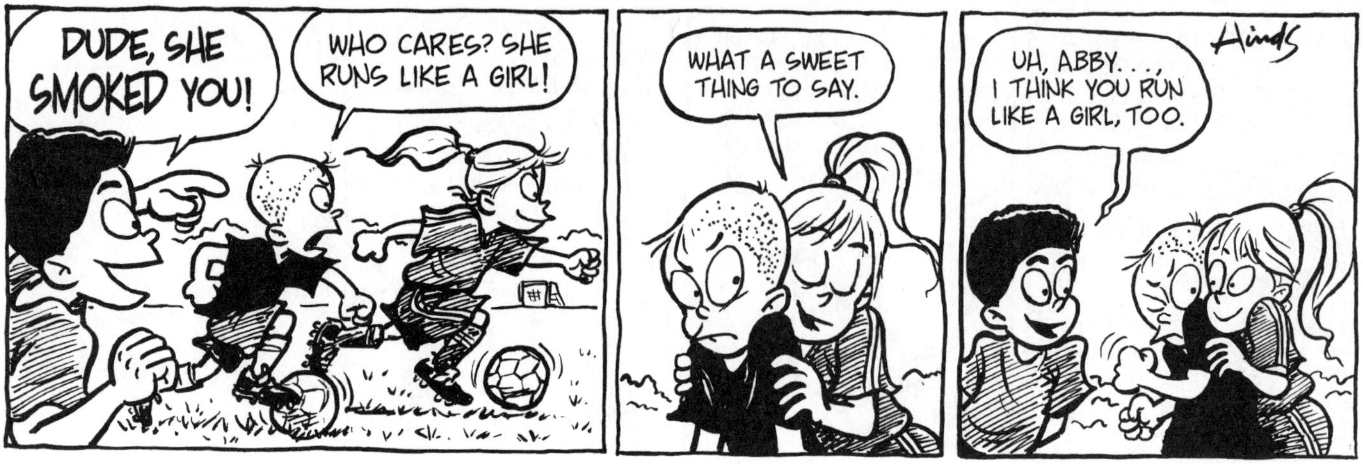
DUDE, SHE SMOKED YOU!
WHO CARES? SHE RUNS LIKE A GIRL!
WHAT A SWEET THING TO SAY.
UH, ABBY. . . , I THINK YOU RUN LIKE A GIRL, TOO.
Hinds

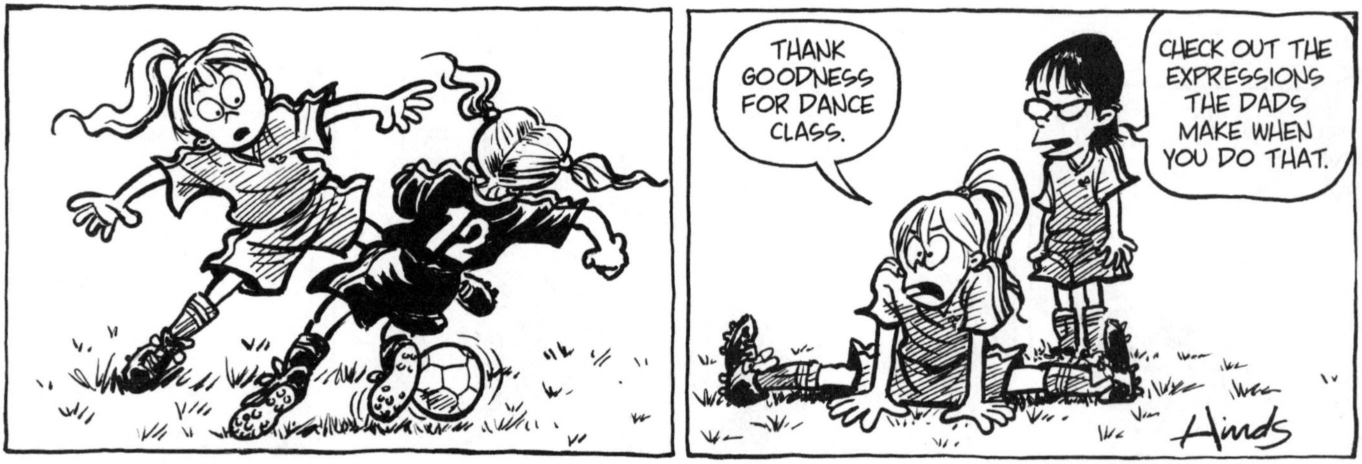
12
THANK GOODNESS FOR DANCE CLASS.
CHECK OUT THE EXPRESSIONS THE DADS MAKE WHEN YOU DO THAT.
Hinds

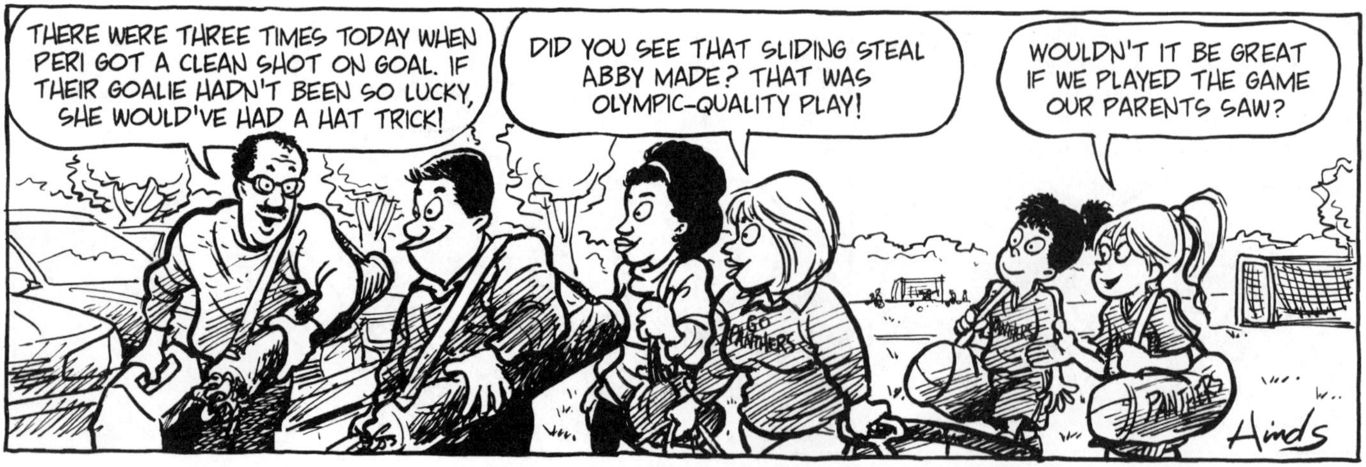
THERE WERE THREE TIMES TODAY WHEN PERI GOT A CLEAN SHOT ON GOAL. IF THEIR GOALIE HADN'T BEEN SO LUCKY, SHE WOULD'VE HAD A HAT TRICK!
DID YOU SEE THAT SLIDING STEAL ABBY MADE? THAT WAS OLYMPIC-QUALITY PLAY!
WOULDN'T IT BE GREAT IF WE PLAYED THE GAME OUR PARENTS SAW?
GO PANTHERS
PANTHERS
Hinds

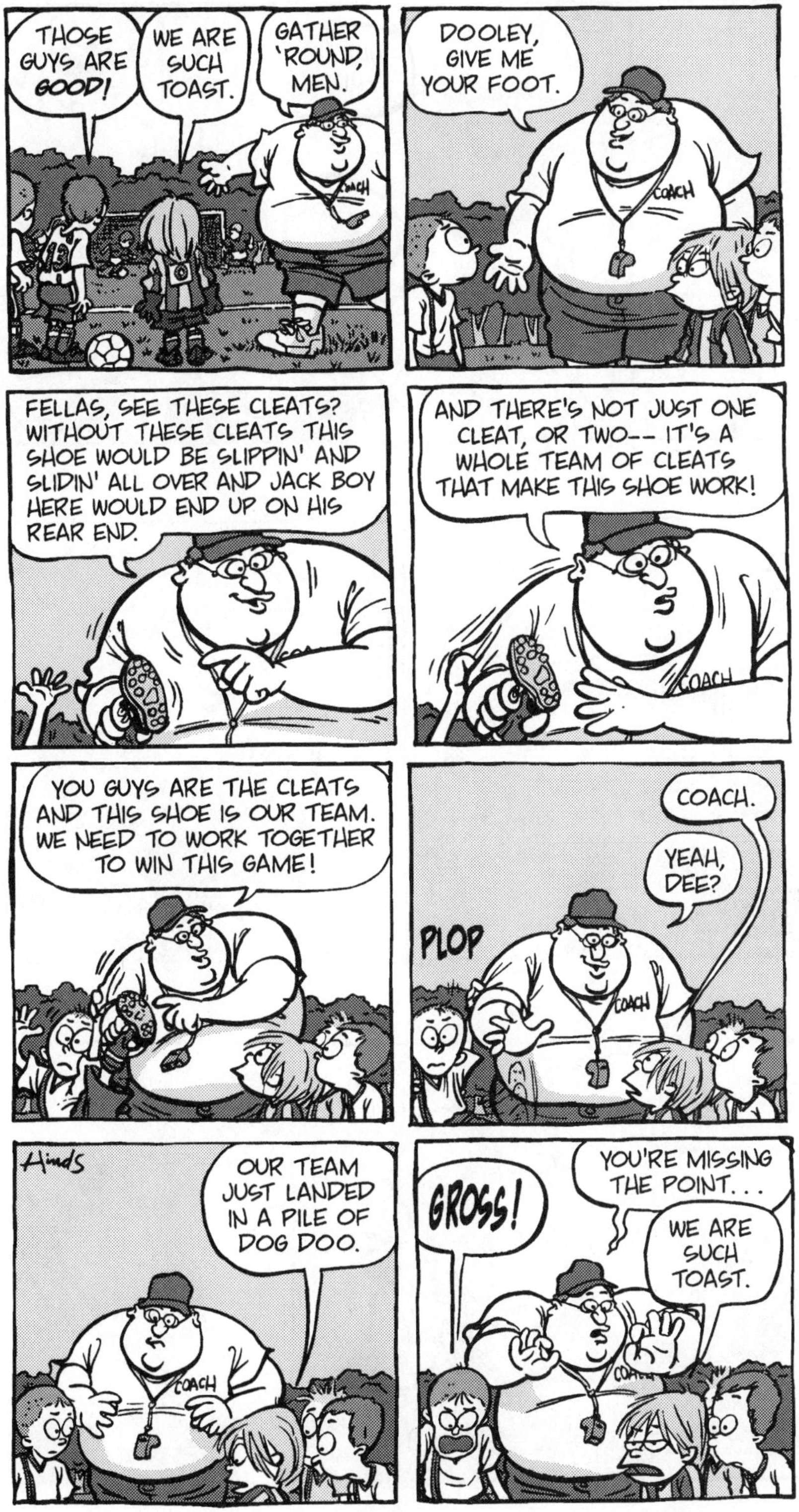
THOSE GUYS ARE GOOD!
WE ARE SUCH TOAST.
GATHER 'ROUND, MEN.
COACH
DOOLEY, GIVE ME YOUR FOOT.
COACH
FELLAS, SEE THESE CLEATS? WITHOUT THESE CLEATS THIS SHOE WOULD BE SLIPPIN' AND SLIDIN' ALL OVER AND JACK BOY HERE WOULD END UP ON HIS REAR END.
AND THERE'S NOT JUST ONE CLEAT, OR TWO-- IT'S A WHOLE TEAM OF CLEATS THAT MAKE THIS SHOE WORK!
COACH
YOU GUYS ARE THE CLEATS AND THIS SHOE IS OUR TEAM. WE NEED TO WORK TOGETHER TO WIN THIS GAME!
PLOP
COACH.
YEAH, DEE?
COACH
Hinds
OUR TEAM JUST LANDED IN A PILE OF DOG DOO.
COACH
GROSS!
YOU'RE MISSING THE POINT...
WE ARE SUCH TOAST.

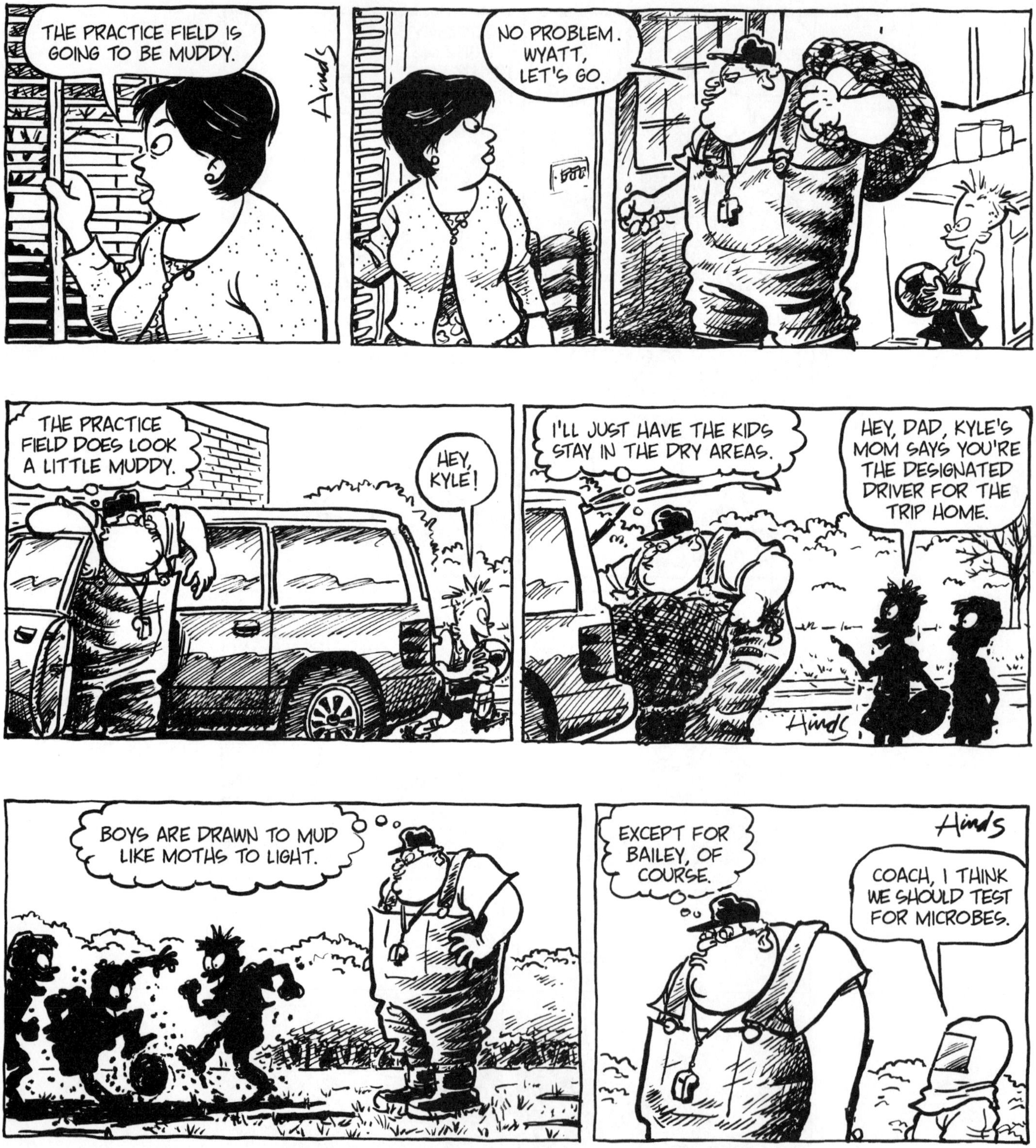
THE PRACTICE FIELD IS GOING TO BE MUDDY.
Hinds
NO PROBLEM. WYATT, LET'S GO.
THE PRACTICE FIELD DOES LOOK A LITTLE MUDDY.
HEY, KYLE!
I'LL JUST HAVE THE KIDS STAY IN THE DRY AREAS.
HEY, DAD, KYLE'S MOM SAYS YOU'RE THE DESIGNATED DRIVER FOR THE TRIP HOME.
Hinds
BOYS ARE DRAWN TO MUD LIKE MOTHS TO LIGHT.
EXCEPT FOR BAILEY, OF COURSE.
Hinds
COACH, I THINK WE SHOULD TEST FOR MICROBES.

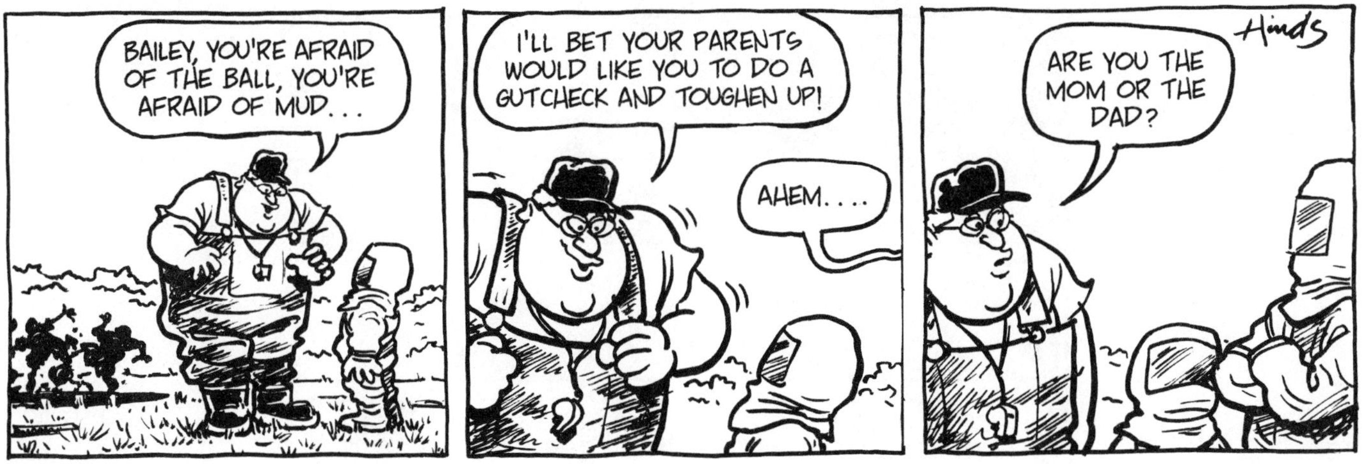
BAILEY, YOU'RE AFRAID OF THE BALL, YOU'RE AFRAID OF MUD...
I'LL BET YOUR PARENTS WOULD LIKE YOU TO DO A GUTCHECK AND TOUGHEN UP!
AHEM....
Hinds
ARE YOU THE MOM OR THE DAD?

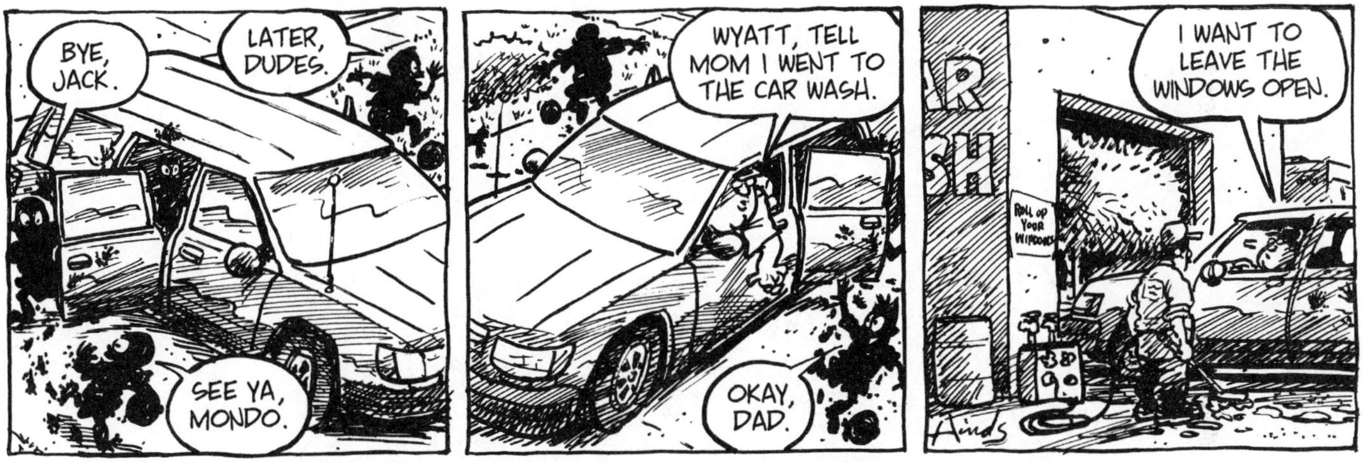
BYE, JACK.
LATER, DUDES.
SEE YA, MONDO.
WYATT, TELL MOM I WENT TO THE CAR WASH.
OKAY, DAD.
I WANT TO LEAVE THE WINDOWS OPEN.
Hinds

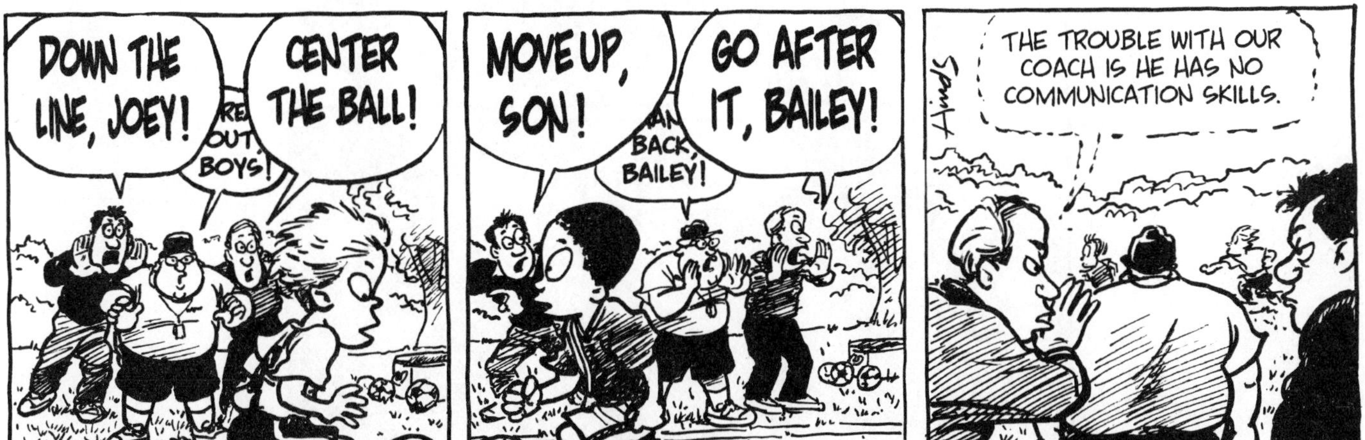
DOWN THE LINE, JOEY!
BOYS!
CENTER THE BALL!
MOVE UP, SON!
BACK, BAILEY!
GO AFTER IT, BAILEY!
Hinds
THE TROUBLE WITH OUR COACH IS HE HAS NO COMMUNICATION SKILLS.

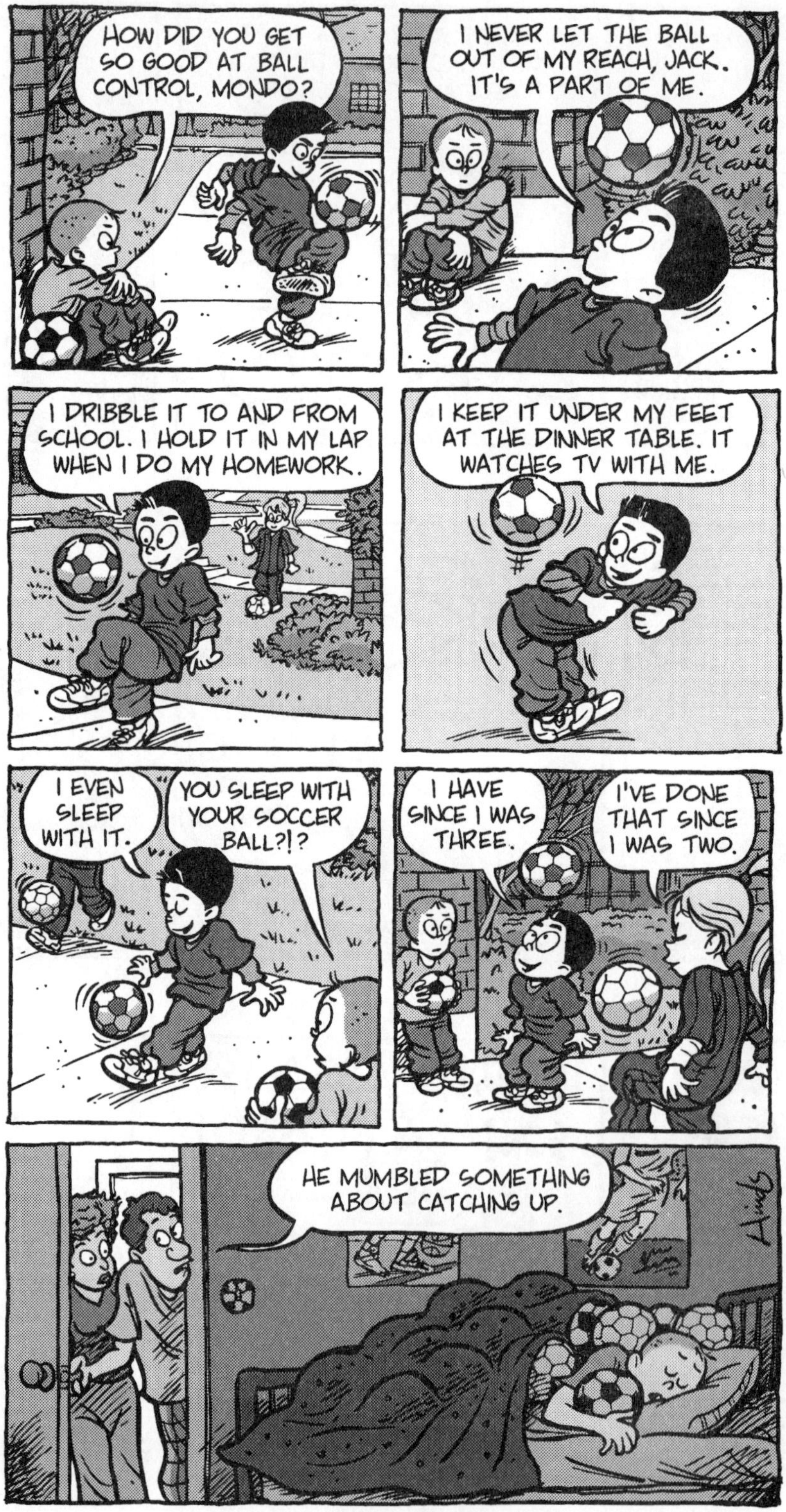
HOW DID YOU GET SO GOOD AT BALL CONTROL, MONDO?
I NEVER LET THE BALL OUT OF MY REACH, JACK. IT'S A PART OF ME.
I DRIBBLE IT TO AND FROM SCHOOL. I HOLD IT IN MY LAP WHEN I DO MY HOMEWORK.
I KEEP IT UNDER MY FEET AT THE DINNER TABLE. IT WATCHES TV WITH ME.
I EVEN SLEEP WITH IT.
YOU SLEEP WITH YOUR SOCCER BALL?!?
I HAVE SINCE I WAS THREE.
I'VE DONE THAT SINCE I WAS TWO.
HE MUMBLED SOMETHING ABOUT CATCHING UP.

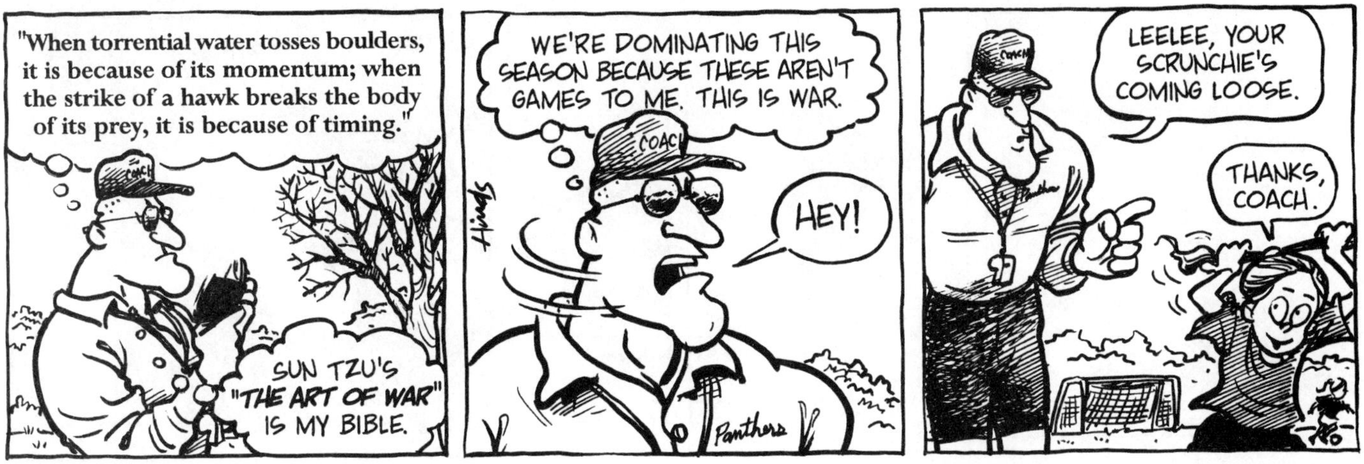
"When torrential water tosses boulders, it is because of its momentum; when the strike of a hawk breaks the body of its prey, it is because of timing."
SUN TZU'S "THE ART OF WAR" IS MY BIBLE.
WE'RE DOMINATING THIS SEASON BECAUSE THESE AREN'T GAMES TO ME. THIS IS WAR.
HEY!
LEELEE, YOUR SCRUNCHIE'S COMING LOOSE.
THANKS, COACH.

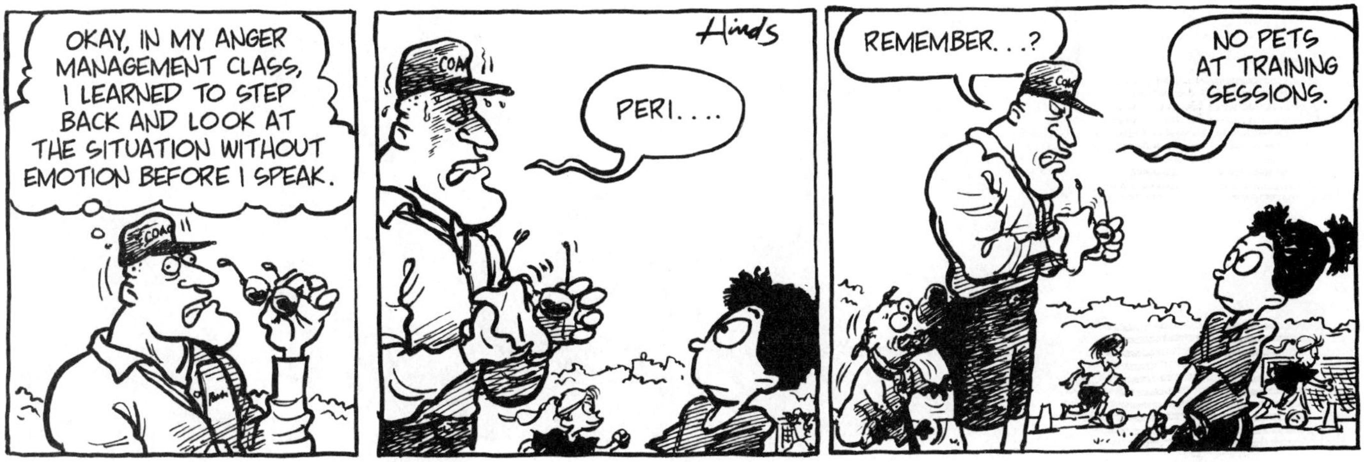
OKAY, IN MY ANGER MANAGEMENT CLASS, I LEARNED TO STEP BACK AND LOOK AT THE SITUATION WITHOUT EMOTION BEFORE I SPEAK.
PERI. . . .
REMEMBER. . .?
NO PETS AT TRAINING SESSIONS.

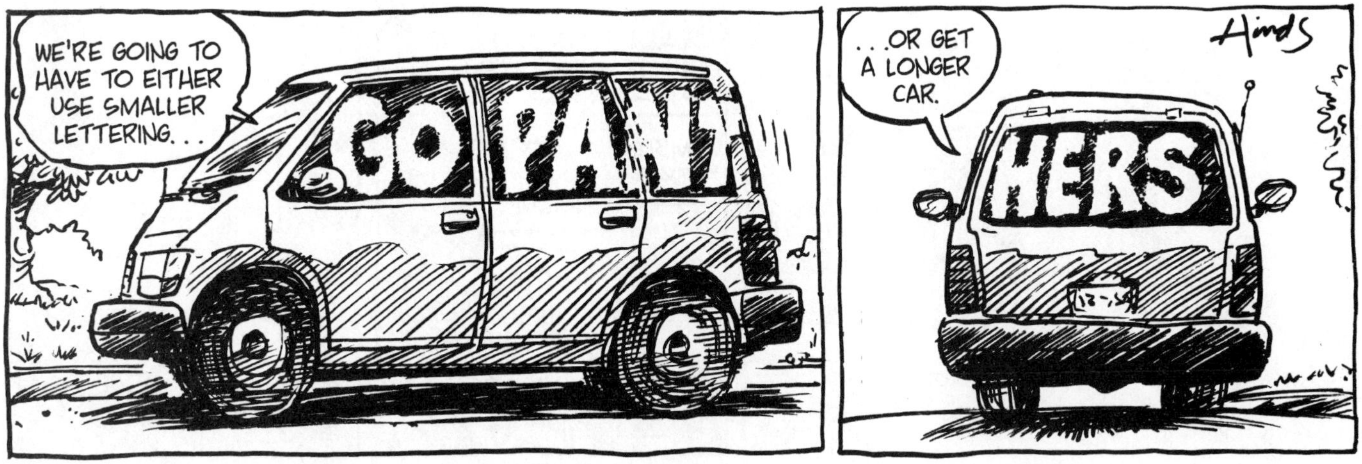
WE'RE GOING TO HAVE TO EITHER USE SMALLER LETTERING. . .
GO PANT
. . .OR GET A LONGER CAR.
HERS

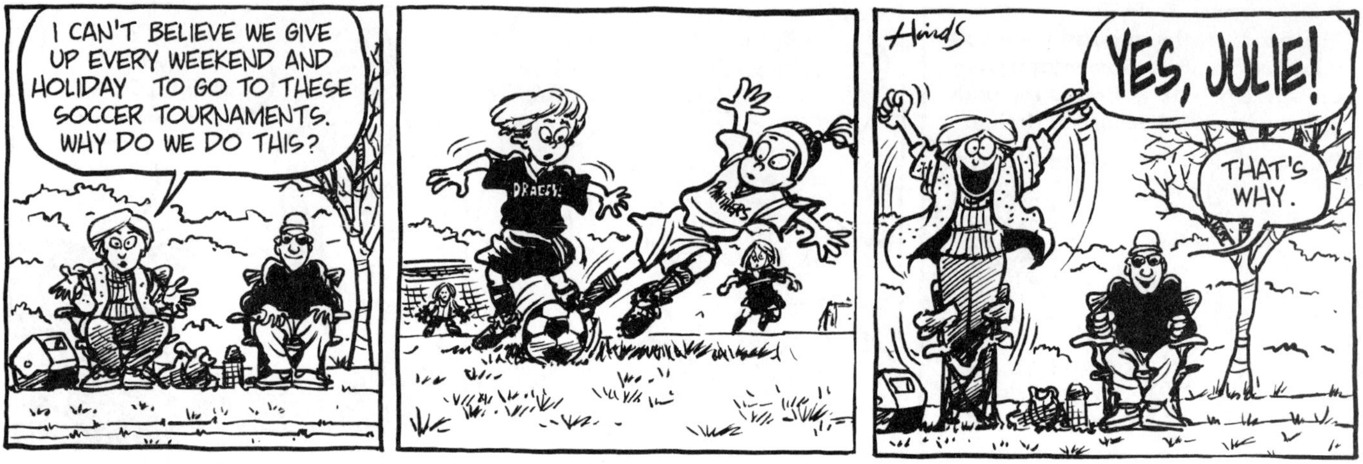
I CAN'T BELIEVE WE GIVE UP EVERY WEEKEND AND HOLIDAY TO GO TO THESE SOCCER TOURNAMENTS. WHY DO WE DO THIS?
Hinds
YES, JULIE!
THAT'S WHY.

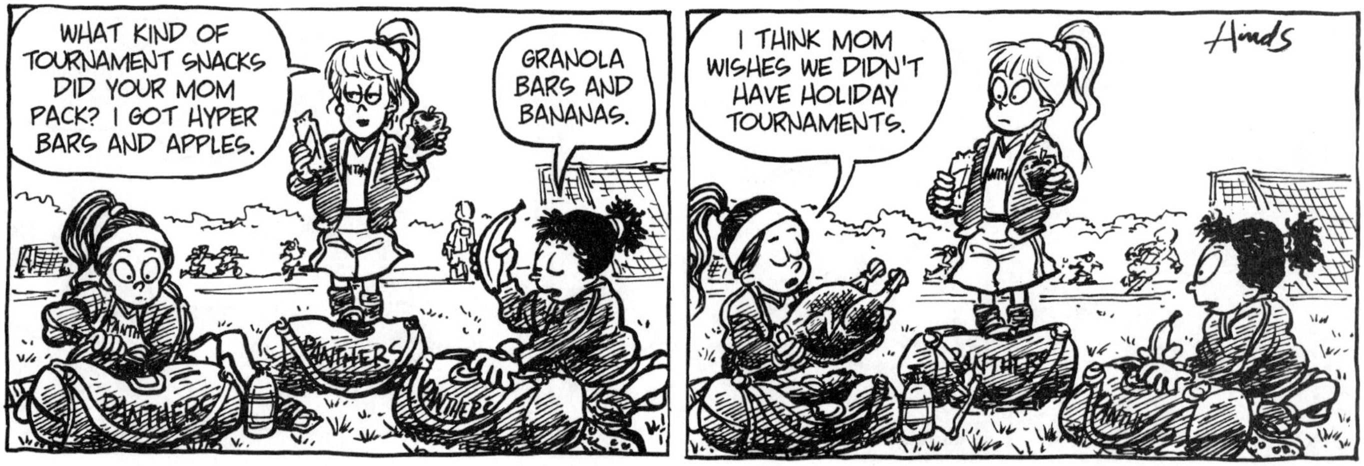
WHAT KIND OF TOURNAMENT SNACKS DID YOUR MOM PACK? I GOT HYPER BARS AND APPLES.
GRANOLA BARS AND BANANAS.
I THINK MOM WISHES WE DIDN'T HAVE HOLIDAY TOURNAMENTS.
Hinds

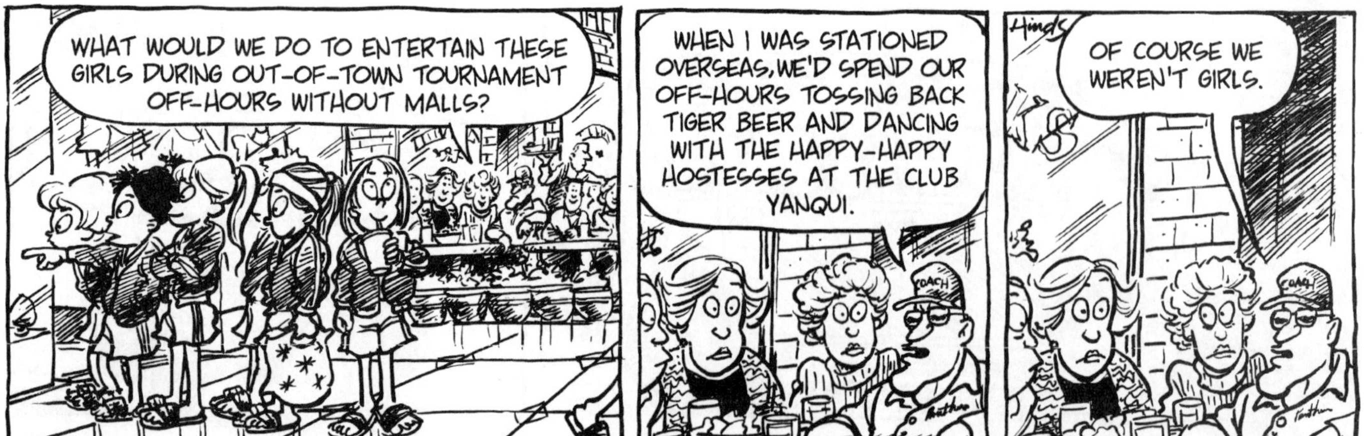
WHAT WOULD WE DO TO ENTERTAIN THESE GIRLS DURING OUT-OF-TOWN TOURNAMENT OFF-HOURS WITHOUT MALLS?
WHEN I WAS STATIONED OVERSEAS, WE'D SPEND OUR OFF-HOURS TOSSING BACK TIGER BEER AND DANCING WITH THE HAPPY-HAPPY HOSTESSES AT THE CLUB YANQUI.
Hinds
OF COURSE WE WEREN'T GIRLS.

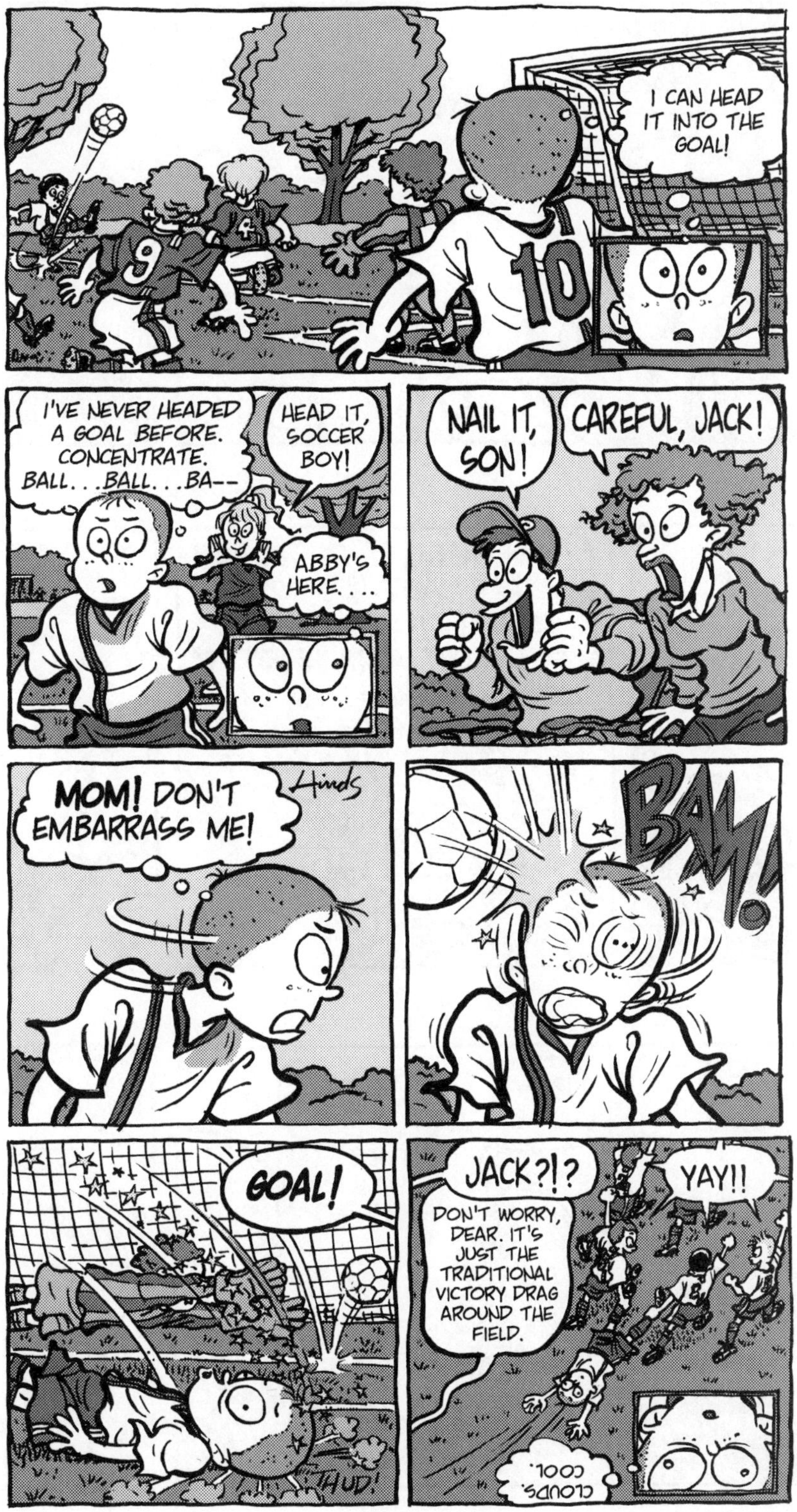
I CAN HEAD IT INTO THE GOAL!
I'VE NEVER HEADED A GOAL BEFORE. CONCENTRATE. BALL. . .BALL. . .BA--
HEAD IT, SOCCER BOY!
ABBY'S HERE. . .
NAIL IT, SON!
CAREFUL, JACK!
MOM! DON'T EMBARRASS ME!
Hinds
BAM!!
GOAL!
THUD!
JACK?!?
YAY!!
DON'T WORRY, DEAR. IT'S JUST THE TRADITIONAL VICTORY DRAG AROUND THE FIELD.
CLOUDS. COOL.

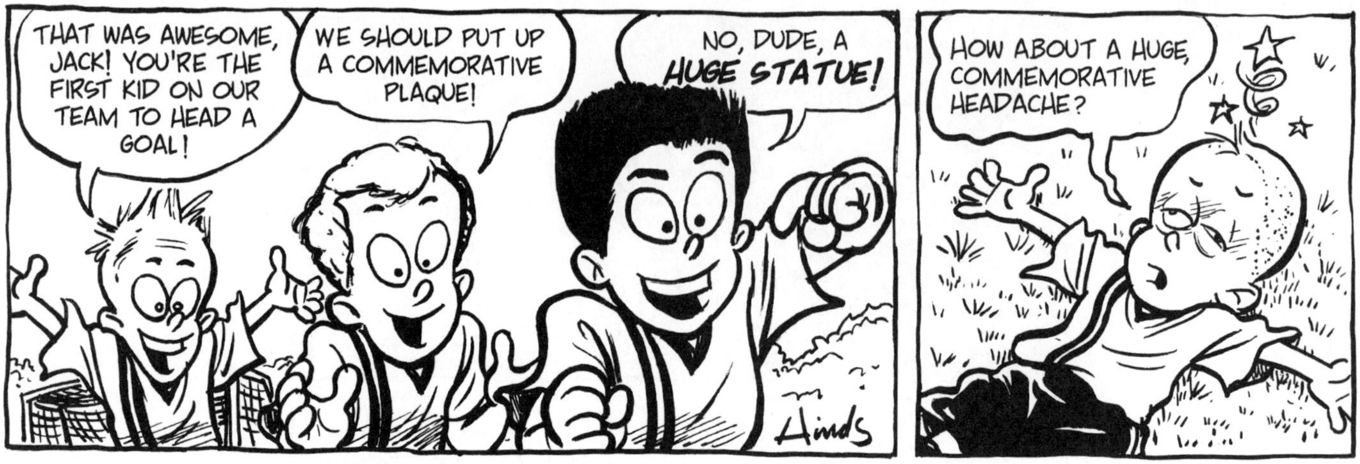
THAT WAS AWESOME, JACK! YOU'RE THE FIRST KID ON OUR TEAM TO HEAD A GOAL!
WE SHOULD PUT UP A COMMEMORATIVE PLAQUE!
NO, DUDE, A **HUGE STATUE!**
HOW ABOUT A HUGE, COMMEMORATIVE HEADACHE?
Hinds

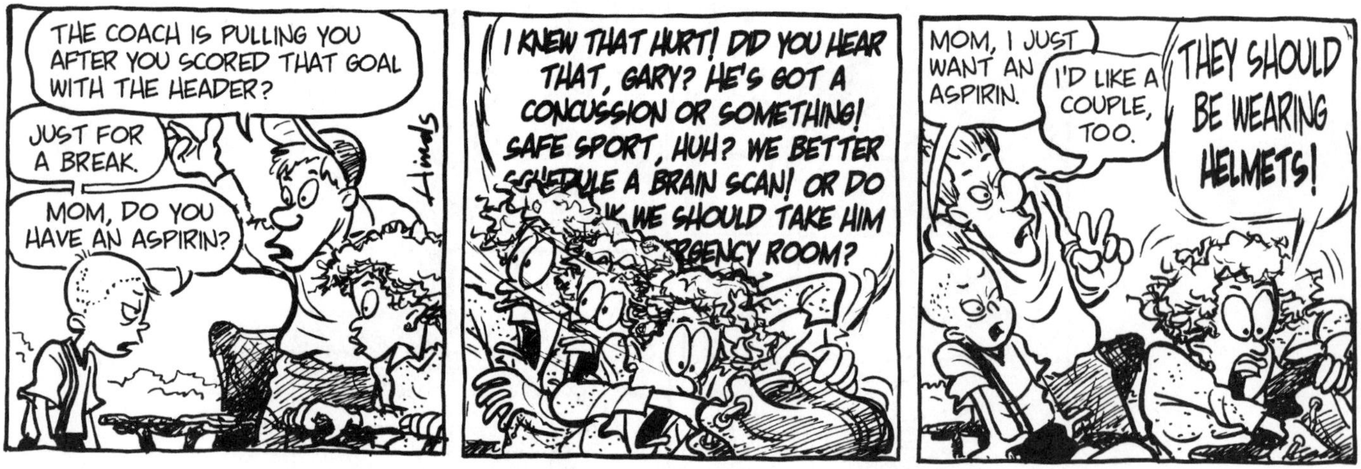
THE COACH IS PULLING YOU AFTER YOU SCORED THAT GOAL WITH THE HEADER?
JUST FOR A BREAK.
MOM, DO YOU HAVE AN ASPIRIN?
Hinds
I KNEW THAT HURT! DID YOU HEAR THAT, GARY? HE'S GOT A CONCUSSION OR SOMETHING! SAFE SPORT, HUH? WE BETTER
A BRAIN SCAN! OR DO
WE SHOULD TAKE HIM
ROOM?
MOM, I JUST WANT AN ASPIRIN.
I'D LIKE A COUPLE, TOO.
THEY SHOULD BE WEARING HELMETS!

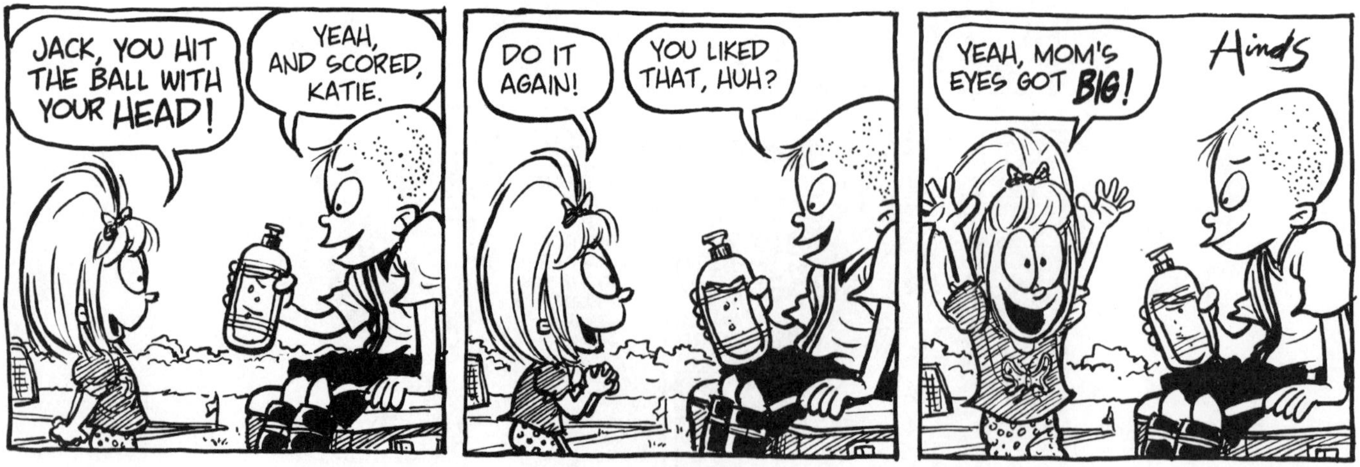
JACK, YOU HIT THE BALL WITH YOUR **HEAD!**
YEAH, AND SCORED, KATIE.
DO IT AGAIN!
YOU LIKED THAT, HUH?
YEAH, MOM'S EYES GOT **BIG!**
Hinds

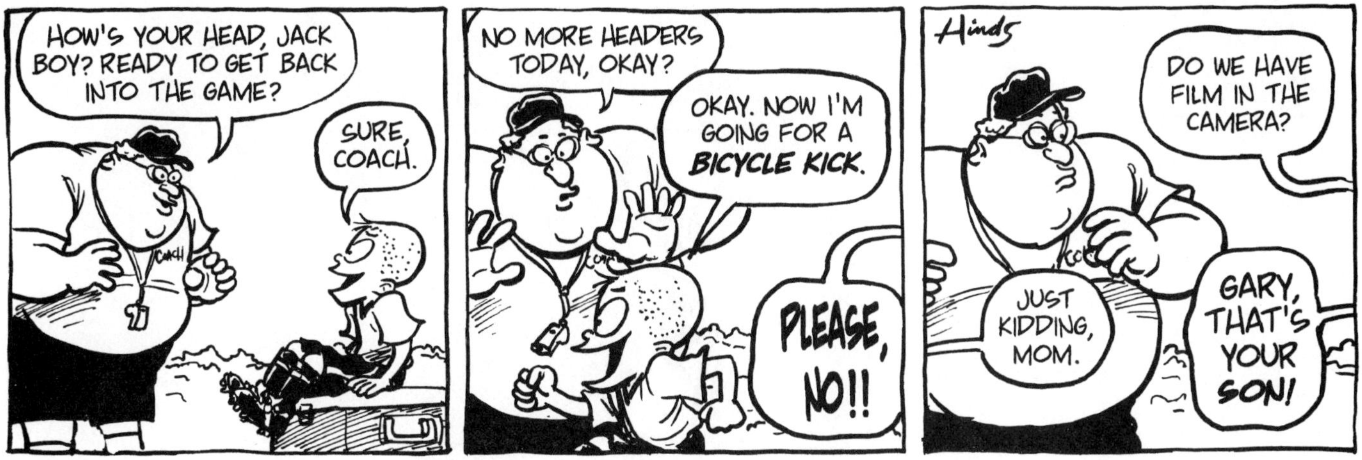
HOW'S YOUR HEAD, JACK BOY? READY TO GET BACK INTO THE GAME?
SURE, COACH.
NO MORE HEADERS TODAY, OKAY?
OKAY. NOW I'M GOING FOR A BICYCLE KICK.
PLEASE, NO!!
Hinds
DO WE HAVE FILM IN THE CAMERA?
JUST KIDDING, MOM.
GARY, THAT'S YOUR SON!

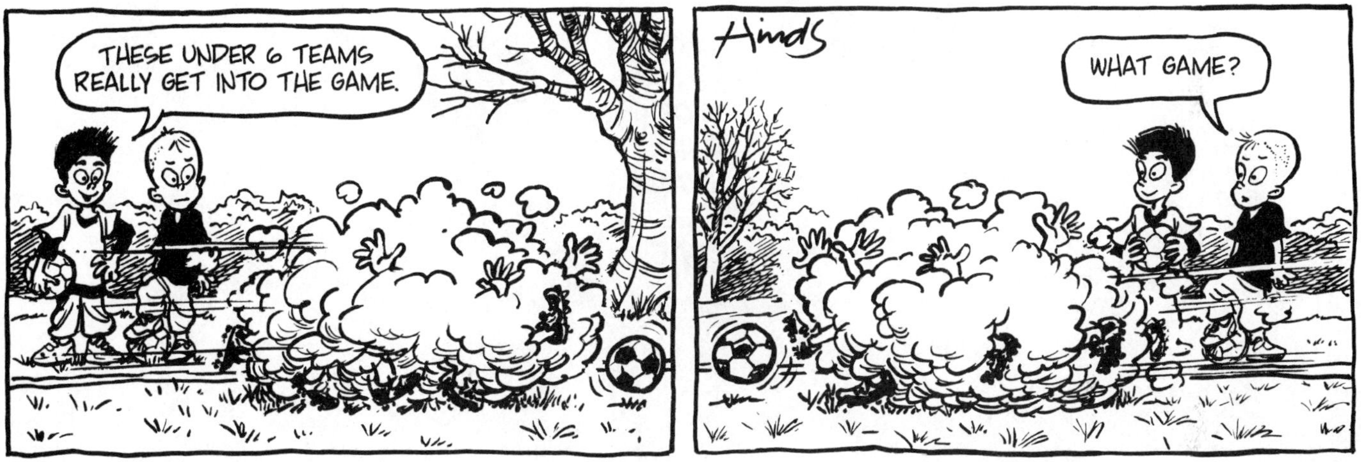
THESE UNDER 6 TEAMS REALLY GET INTO THE GAME.
Hinds
WHAT GAME?

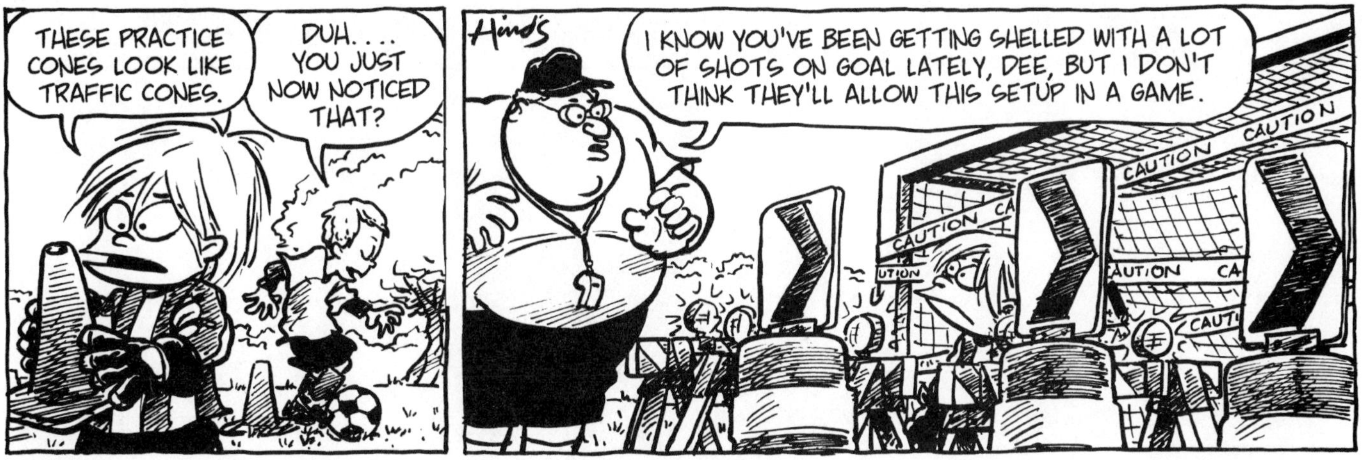
THESE PRACTICE CONES LOOK LIKE TRAFFIC CONES.
DUH. . . . YOU JUST NOW NOTICED THAT?
Hinds
I KNOW YOU'VE BEEN GETTING SHELLED WITH A LOT OF SHOTS ON GOAL LATELY, DEE, BUT I DON'T THINK THEY'LL ALLOW THIS SETUP IN A GAME.
CAUTION
CAUTION

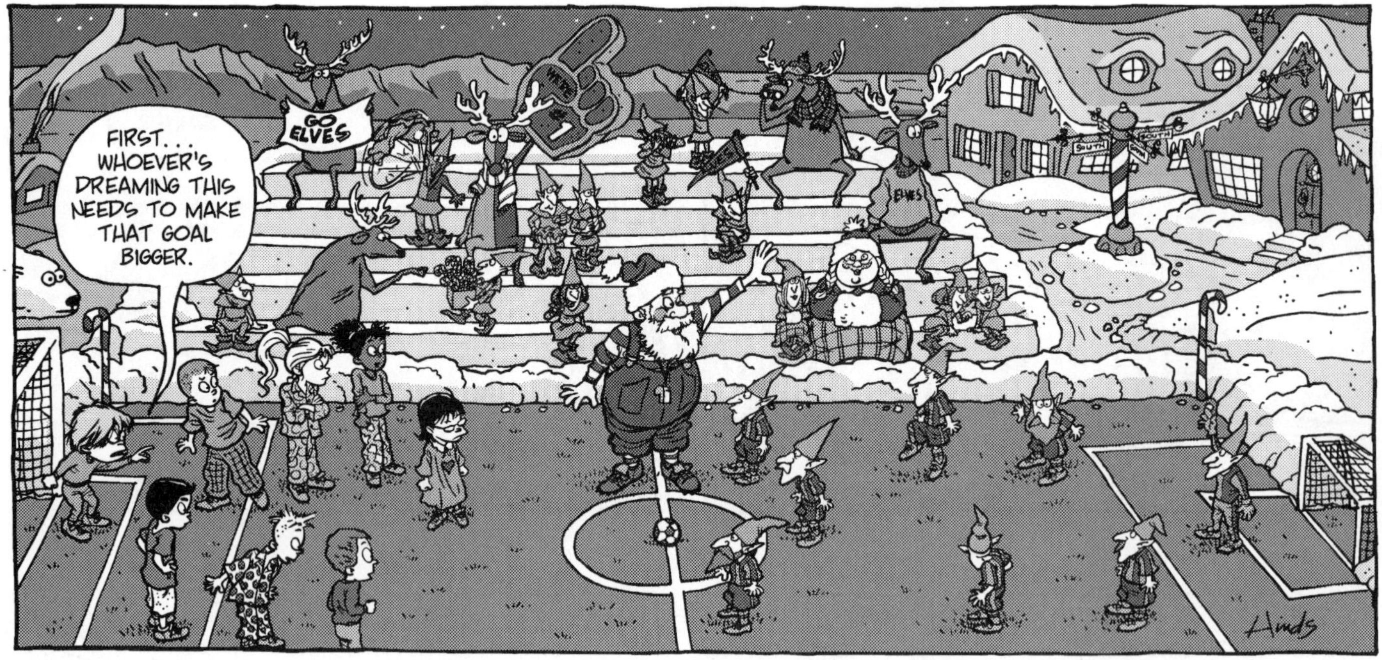
GO ELVES
WE'RE #1
SOUTH
SOUTH
ELVES
FIRST. . . WHOEVER'S DREAMING THIS NEEDS TO MAKE THAT GOAL BIGGER.
Hinds

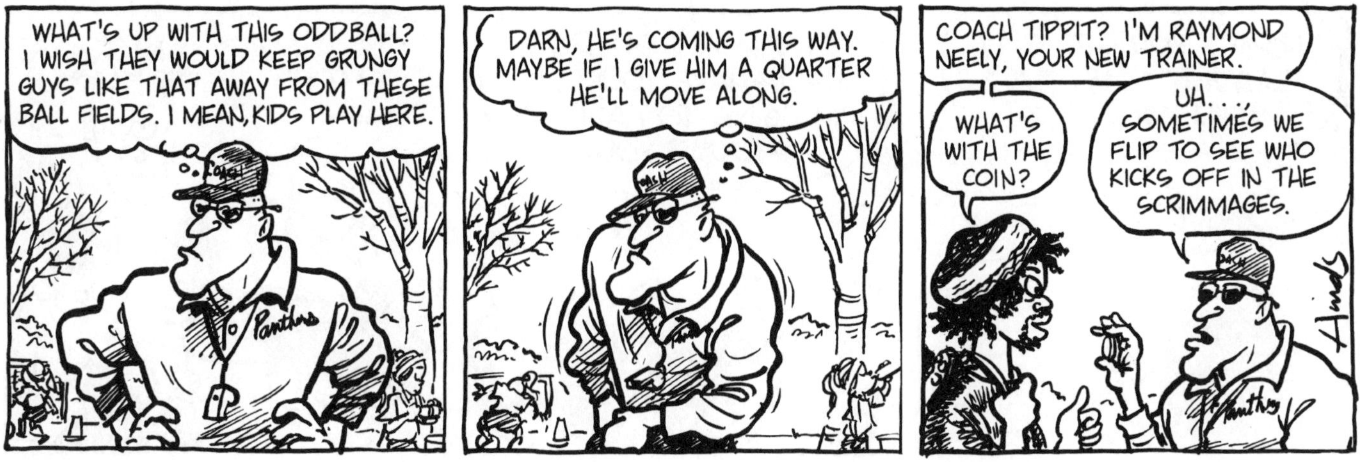
WHAT'S UP WITH THIS ODDBALL? I WISH THEY WOULD KEEP GRUNGY GUYS LIKE THAT AWAY FROM THESE BALL FIELDS. I MEAN, KIDS PLAY HERE.
DARN, HE'S COMING THIS WAY. MAYBE IF I GIVE HIM A QUARTER HE'LL MOVE ALONG.
COACH TIPPIT? I'M RAYMOND NEELY, YOUR NEW TRAINER.
WHAT'S WITH THE COIN?
UH. . ., SOMETIMES WE FLIP TO SEE WHO KICKS OFF IN THE SCRIMMAGES.

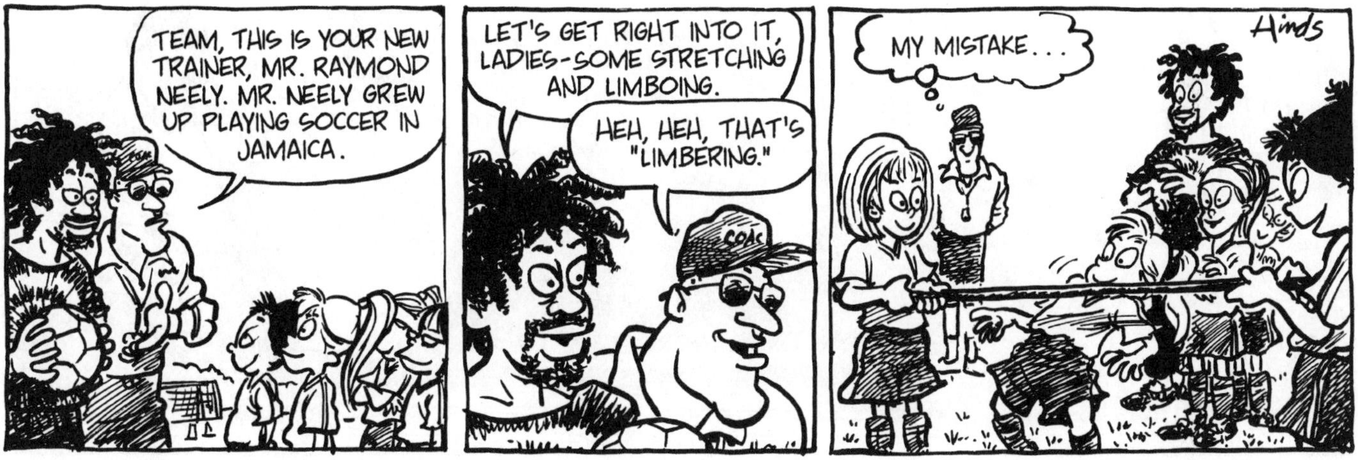
TEAM, THIS IS YOUR NEW TRAINER, MR. RAYMOND NEELY. MR. NEELY GREW UP PLAYING SOCCER IN JAMAICA.
LET'S GET RIGHT INTO IT, LADIES-SOME STRETCHING AND LIMBOING.
HEH, HEH, THAT'S "LIMBERING."
MY MISTAKE . . .

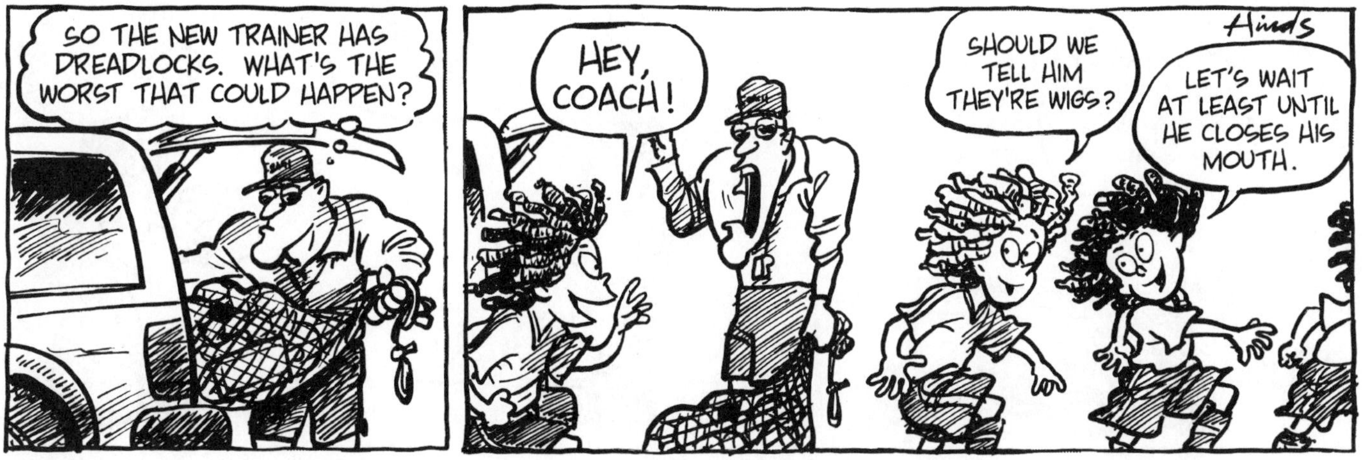
SO THE NEW TRAINER HAS DREADLOCKS. WHAT'S THE WORST THAT COULD HAPPEN?
HEY, COACH!
SHOULD WE TELL HIM THEY'RE WIGS?
LET'S WAIT AT LEAST UNTIL HE CLOSES HIS MOUTH.

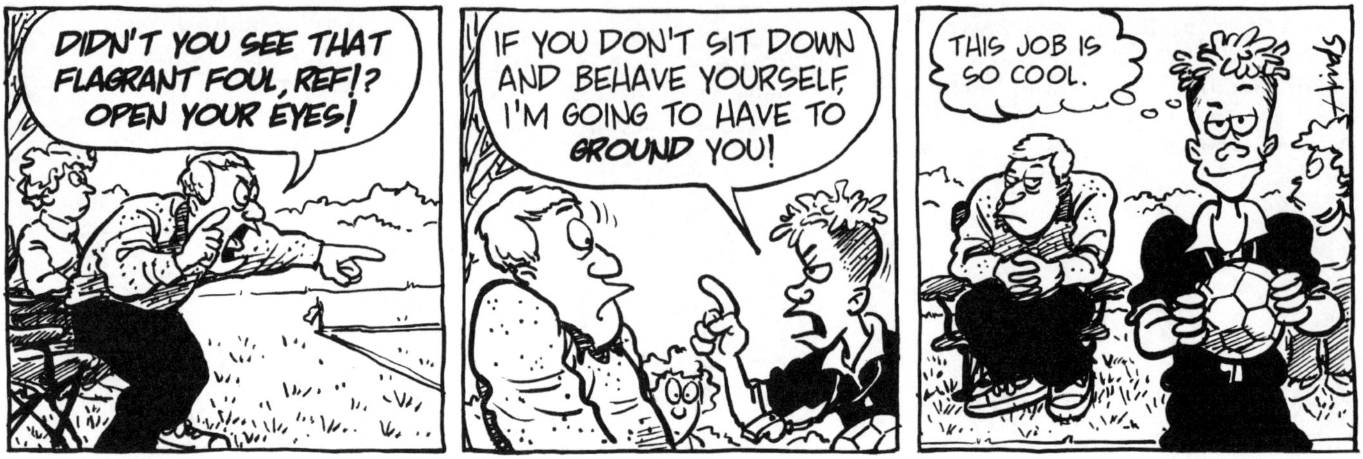
DIDN'T YOU SEE THAT FLAGRANT FOUL, REF!? OPEN YOUR EYES!
IF YOU DON'T SIT DOWN AND BEHAVE YOURSELF, I'M GOING TO HAVE TO GROUND YOU!
THIS JOB IS SO COOL.
Hinds

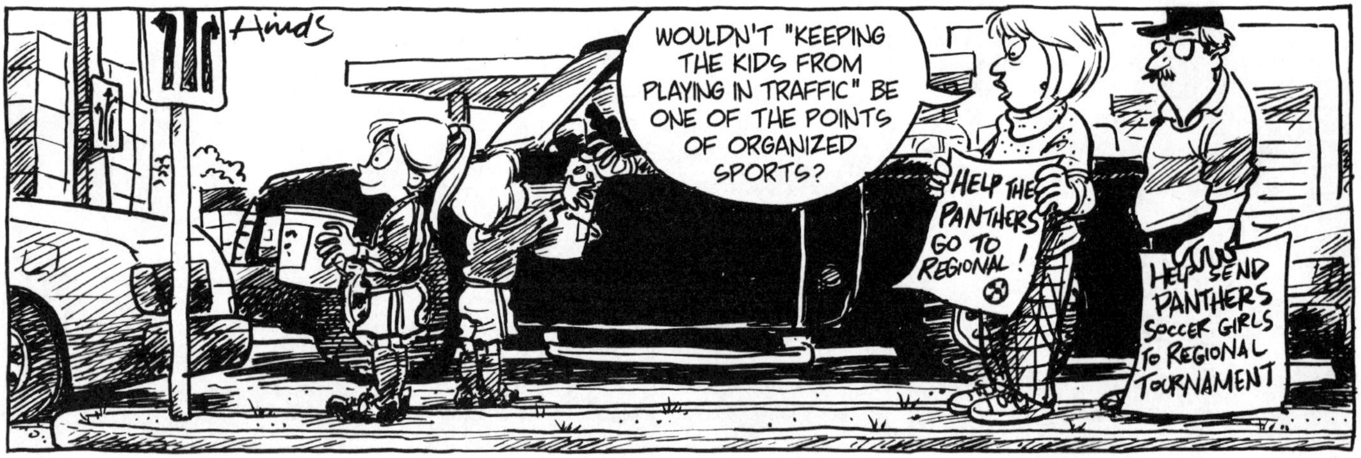
Hinds
WOULDN'T "KEEPING THE KIDS FROM PLAYING IN TRAFFIC" BE ONE OF THE POINTS OF ORGANIZED SPORTS?
HELP THE PANTHERS GO TO REGIONAL!
HELP SEND PANTHERS SOCCER GIRLS TO REGIONAL TOURNAMENT

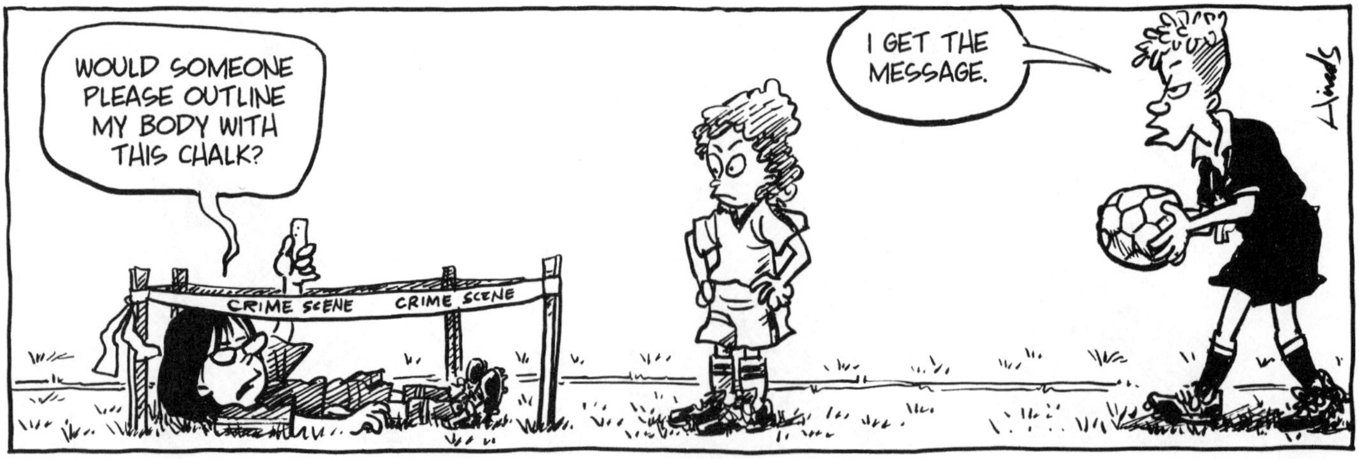
WOULD SOMEONE PLEASE OUTLINE MY BODY WITH THIS CHALK?
CRIME SCENE CRIME SCENE
I GET THE MESSAGE.
Hinds

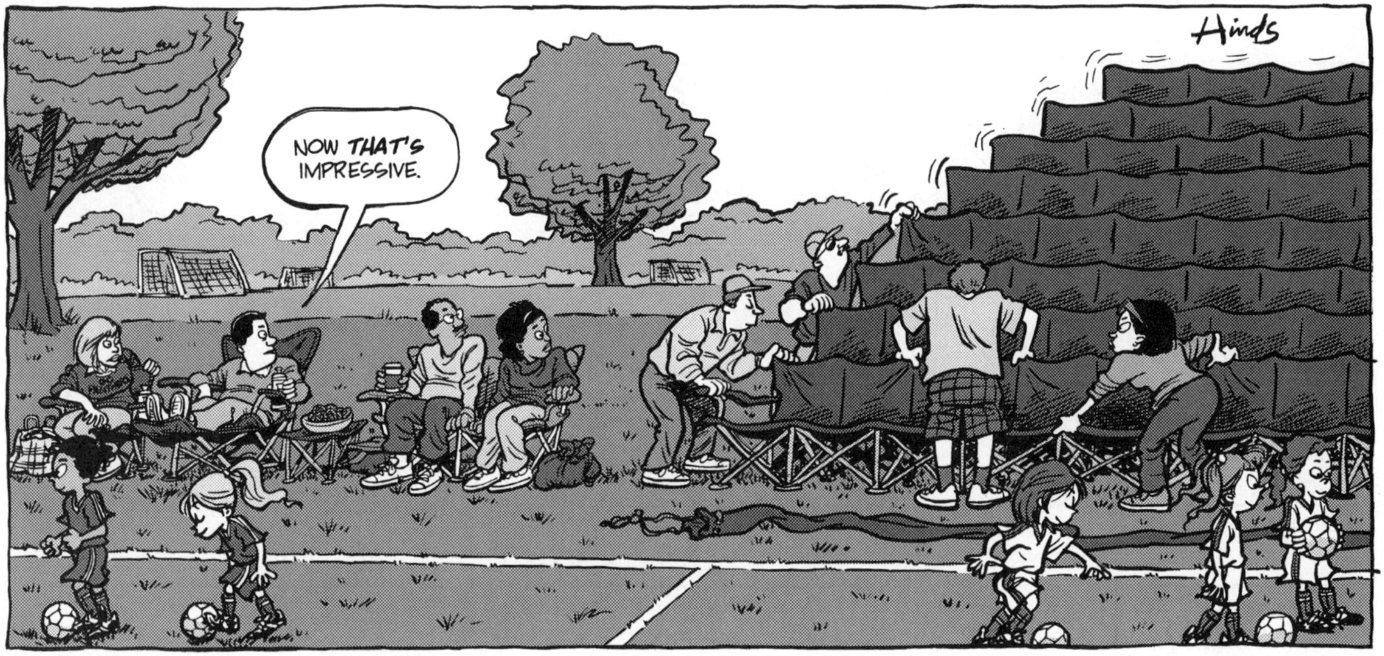
NOW THAT'S IMPRESSIVE.
Hinds

Panel 1: SO THIS IS A SOCCER COMPLEX.

LITTLE SISTER, ON ANY GIVEN WEEKEND YOU HAVE THE POPULATION OF A SMALL TOWN OUT HERE, HALF OF THEM WEARING CLEATS.

Panel 2: UNFORTUNATELY, IT'S A SMALL TOWN WITH ONE DRIVEWAY.

MEGAWOODS PARK
HOME OF MEGAWOODS SOCCER CLUB

Panel 3: THERE ARE A FEW RULES OF SIDELINE ETIQUETTE YOU SHOULD KNOW, BABY SISTER:

Panel 4: NO RUNNING UP AND DOWN THE SIDELINE. NO HANGING OUT BY THE GOAL. NO SHOUTING INSTRUCTIONS TO THE PLAYERS. DON'T SAY ANYTHING TO THE REFEREES.

I BET THOSE ARE TOUGH RULES FOR PARENTS.

Panel 5: TOUGHER FOR SOME.

HUL-LA.

Panel 6: YOUR TEAM HAS ITS OWN MEDIC?

AUGH!

JOAN'S AN **EMT**. SHE BRINGS HER FIRST AID KIT JUST IN CASE.

Panel 7: ARE THERE A LOT OF INJURIES AT THESE GAMES?

AUGH!

Panel 8: MOSTLY FAN MUSCLE PULLS.

AUGH!

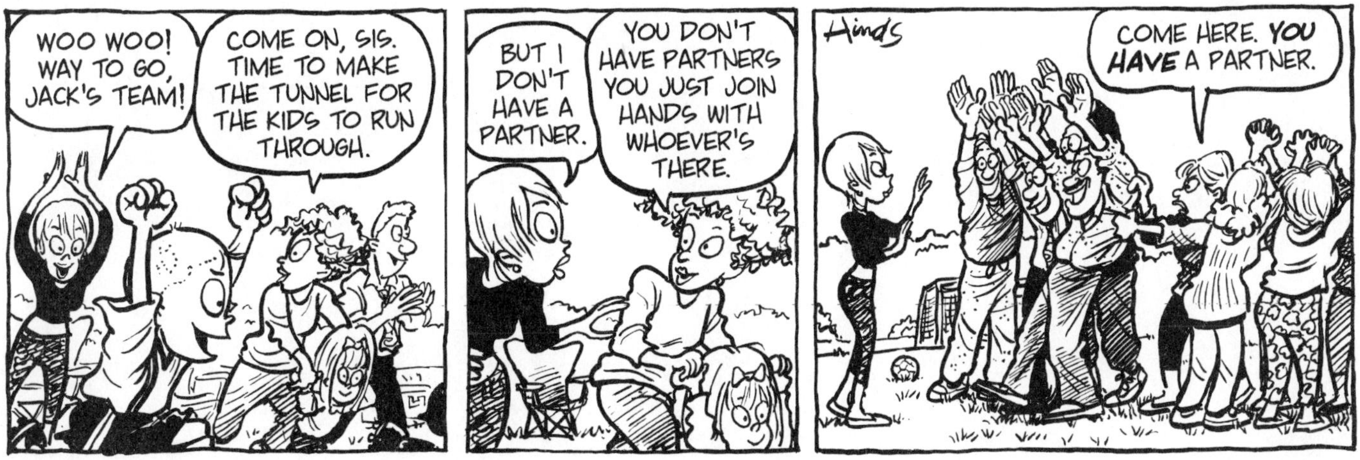
WOO WOO! WAY TO GO, JACK'S TEAM!
COME ON, SIS. TIME TO MAKE THE TUNNEL FOR THE KIDS TO RUN THROUGH.
BUT I DON'T HAVE A PARTNER.
YOU DON'T HAVE PARTNERS YOU JUST JOIN HANDS WITH WHOEVER'S THERE.
Hinds
COME HERE. **YOU HAVE** A PARTNER.

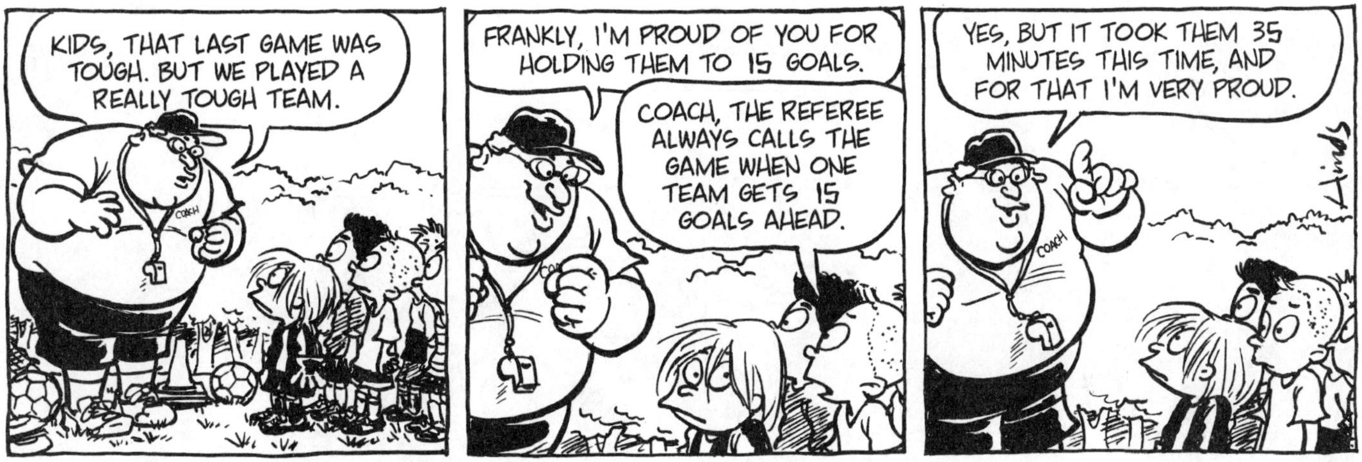
KIDS, THAT LAST GAME WAS TOUGH. BUT WE PLAYED A REALLY TOUGH TEAM.
COACH
FRANKLY, I'M PROUD OF YOU FOR HOLDING THEM TO 15 GOALS.
COACH, THE REFEREE ALWAYS CALLS THE GAME WHEN ONE TEAM GETS 15 GOALS AHEAD.
YES, BUT IT TOOK THEM 35 MINUTES THIS TIME, AND FOR THAT I'M VERY PROUD.
COACH
Hinds

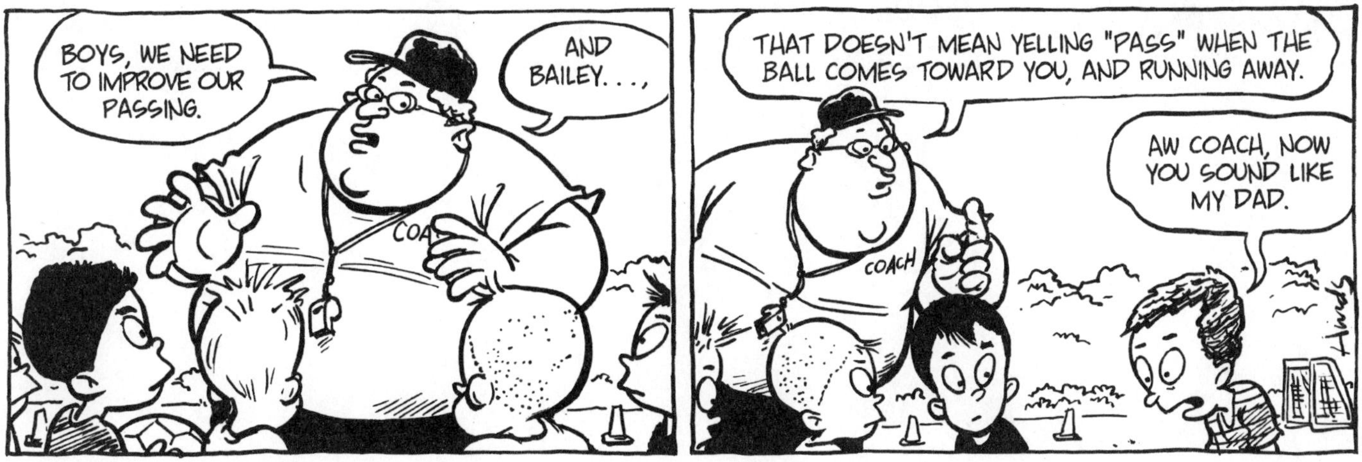
BOYS, WE NEED TO IMPROVE OUR PASSING.
AND BAILEY. . . ,
THAT DOESN'T MEAN YELLING "PASS" WHEN THE BALL COMES TOWARD YOU, AND RUNNING AWAY.
COACH
AW COACH, NOW YOU SOUND LIKE MY DAD.
Hinds

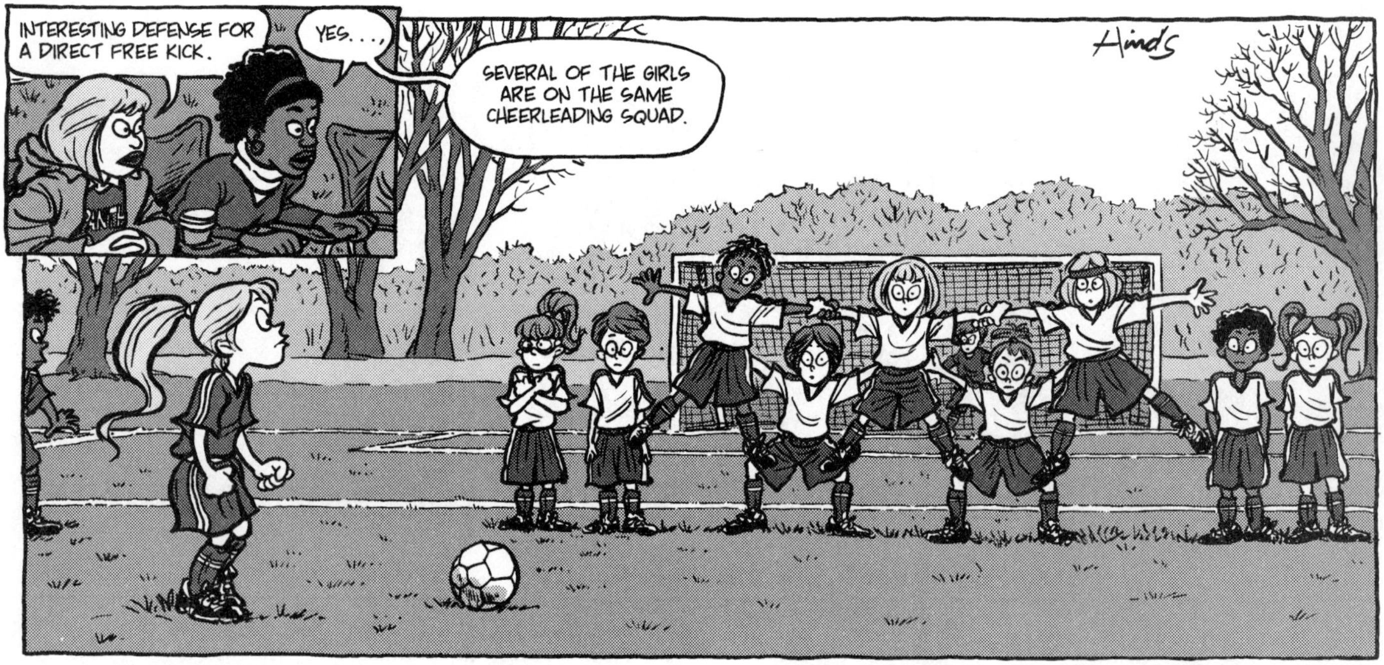
INTERESTING DEFENSE FOR A DIRECT FREE KICK.
YES. . . ,
SEVERAL OF THE GIRLS ARE ON THE SAME CHEERLEADING SQUAD.
Hinds

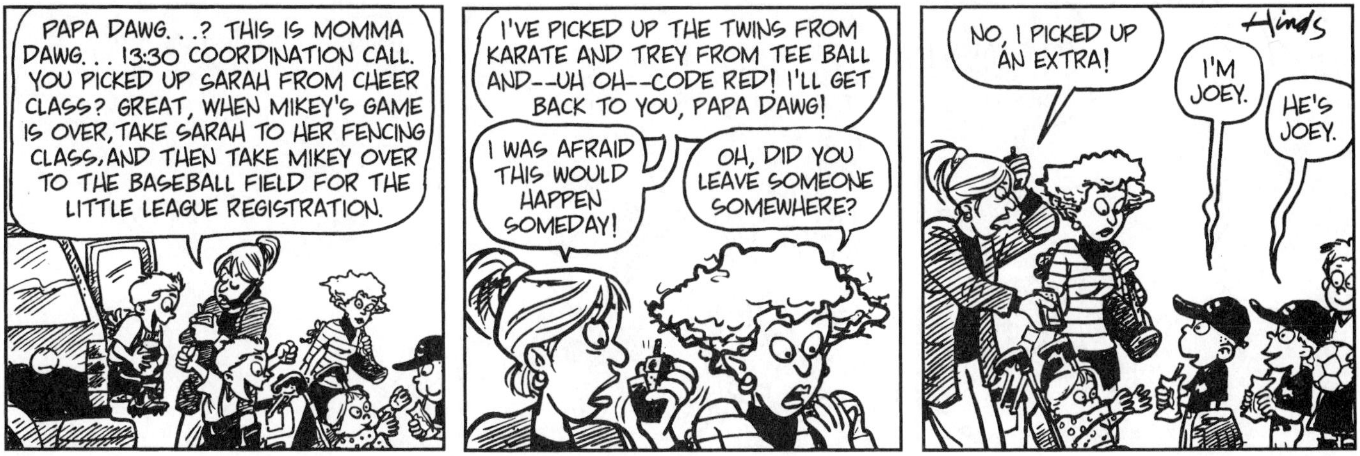
PAPA DAWG. . .? THIS IS MOMMA DAWG. . . 13:30 COORDINATION CALL. YOU PICKED UP SARAH FROM CHEER CLASS? GREAT, WHEN MIKEY'S GAME IS OVER, TAKE SARAH TO HER FENCING CLASS, AND THEN TAKE MIKEY OVER TO THE BASEBALL FIELD FOR THE LITTLE LEAGUE REGISTRATION.
I'VE PICKED UP THE TWINS FROM KARATE AND TREY FROM TEE BALL AND--UH OH--CODE RED! I'LL GET BACK TO YOU, PAPA DAWG!
I WAS AFRAID THIS WOULD HAPPEN SOMEDAY!
OH, DID YOU LEAVE SOMEONE SOMEWHERE?
Hinds
NO, I PICKED UP AN EXTRA!
I'M JOEY.
HE'S JOEY.

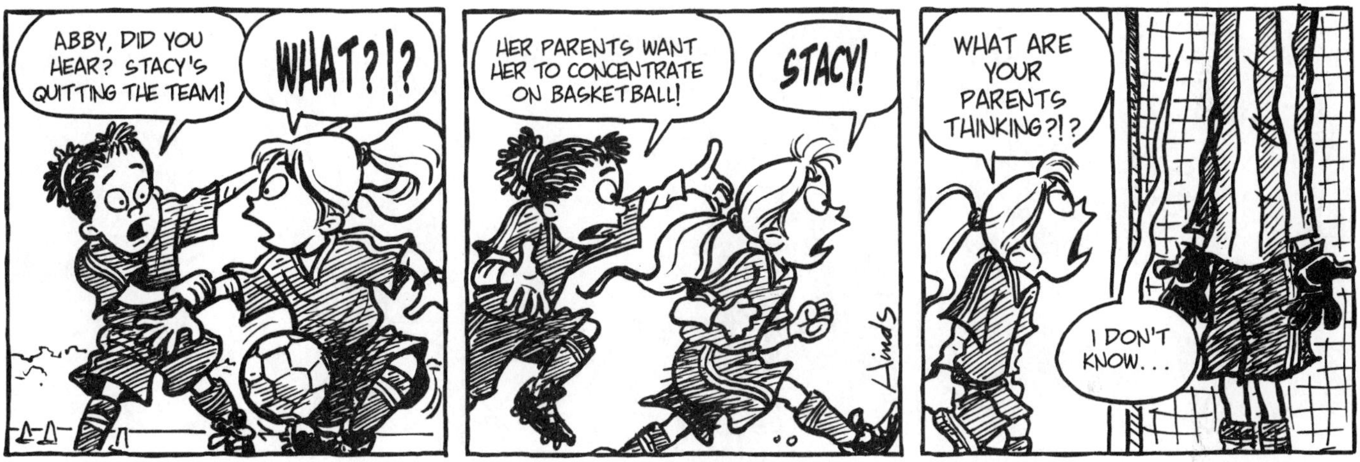
ABBY, DID YOU HEAR? STACY'S QUITTING THE TEAM!
WHAT?!?
HER PARENTS WANT HER TO CONCENTRATE ON BASKETBALL!
STACY!
Hinds
WHAT ARE YOUR PARENTS THINKING?!?
I DON'T KNOW. . .

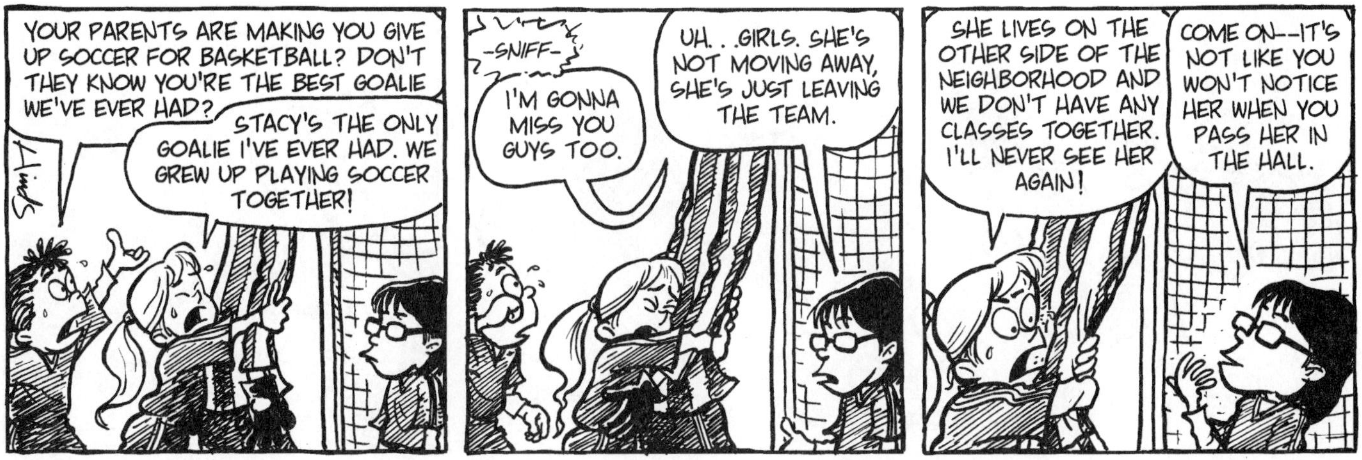
YOUR PARENTS ARE MAKING YOU GIVE UP SOCCER FOR BASKETBALL? DON'T THEY KNOW YOU'RE THE BEST GOALIE WE'VE EVER HAD?
STACY'S THE ONLY GOALIE I'VE EVER HAD. WE GREW UP PLAYING SOCCER TOGETHER!
Hinds
-SNIFF-
I'M GONNA MISS YOU GUYS TOO.
UH. . .GIRLS. SHE'S NOT MOVING AWAY, SHE'S JUST LEAVING THE TEAM.
SHE LIVES ON THE OTHER SIDE OF THE NEIGHBORHOOD AND WE DON'T HAVE ANY CLASSES TOGETHER. I'LL NEVER SEE HER AGAIN!
COME ON--IT'S NOT LIKE YOU WON'T NOTICE HER WHEN YOU PASS HER IN THE HALL.

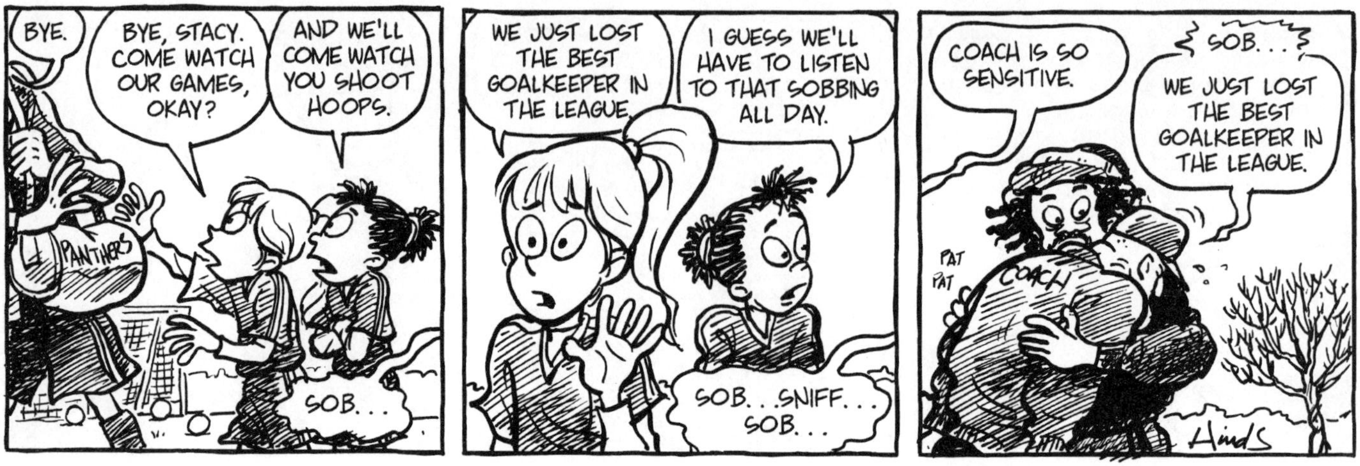
BYE.
BYE, STACY. COME WATCH OUR GAMES, OKAY?
AND WE'LL COME WATCH YOU SHOOT HOOPS.
PANTHERS
SOB...
WE JUST LOST THE BEST GOALKEEPER IN THE LEAGUE.
I GUESS WE'LL HAVE TO LISTEN TO THAT SOBBING ALL DAY.
SOB...SNIFF... SOB...
COACH IS SO SENSITIVE.
SOB...
WE JUST LOST THE BEST GOALKEEPER IN THE LEAGUE.
PAT
PAT
COACH
Hinds

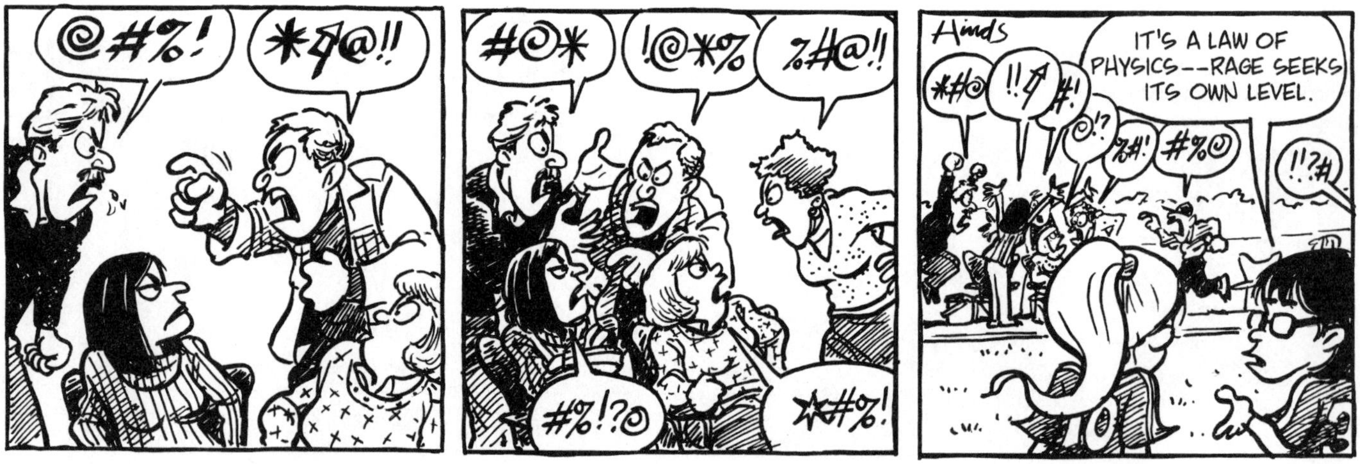
Hinds
IT'S A LAW OF PHYSICS--RAGE SEEKS ITS OWN LEVEL.

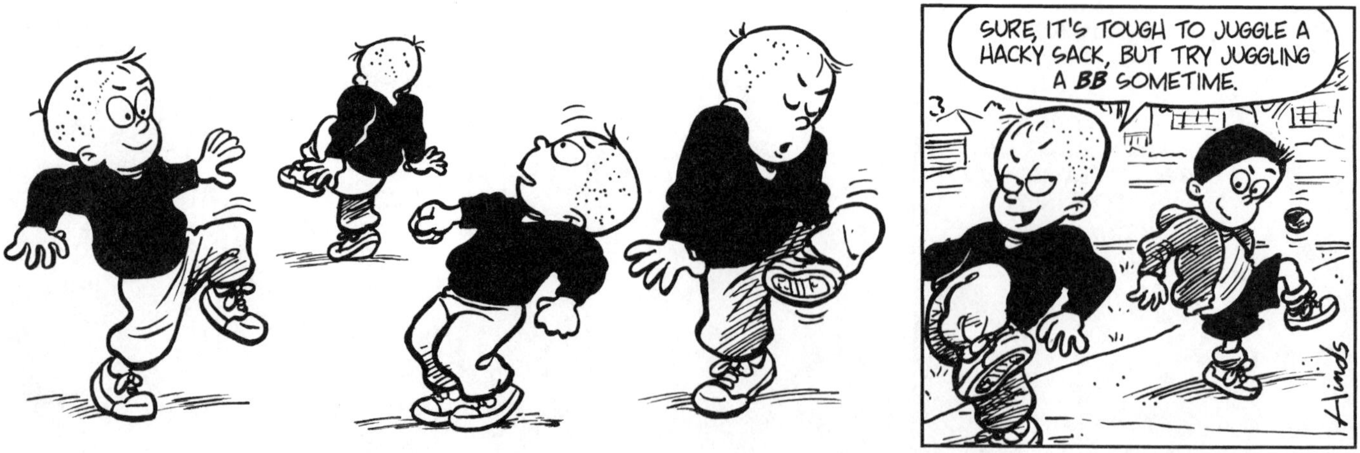
SURE, IT'S TOUGH TO JUGGLE A HACKY SACK, BUT TRY JUGGLING A ***BB*** SOMETIME.
Hinds

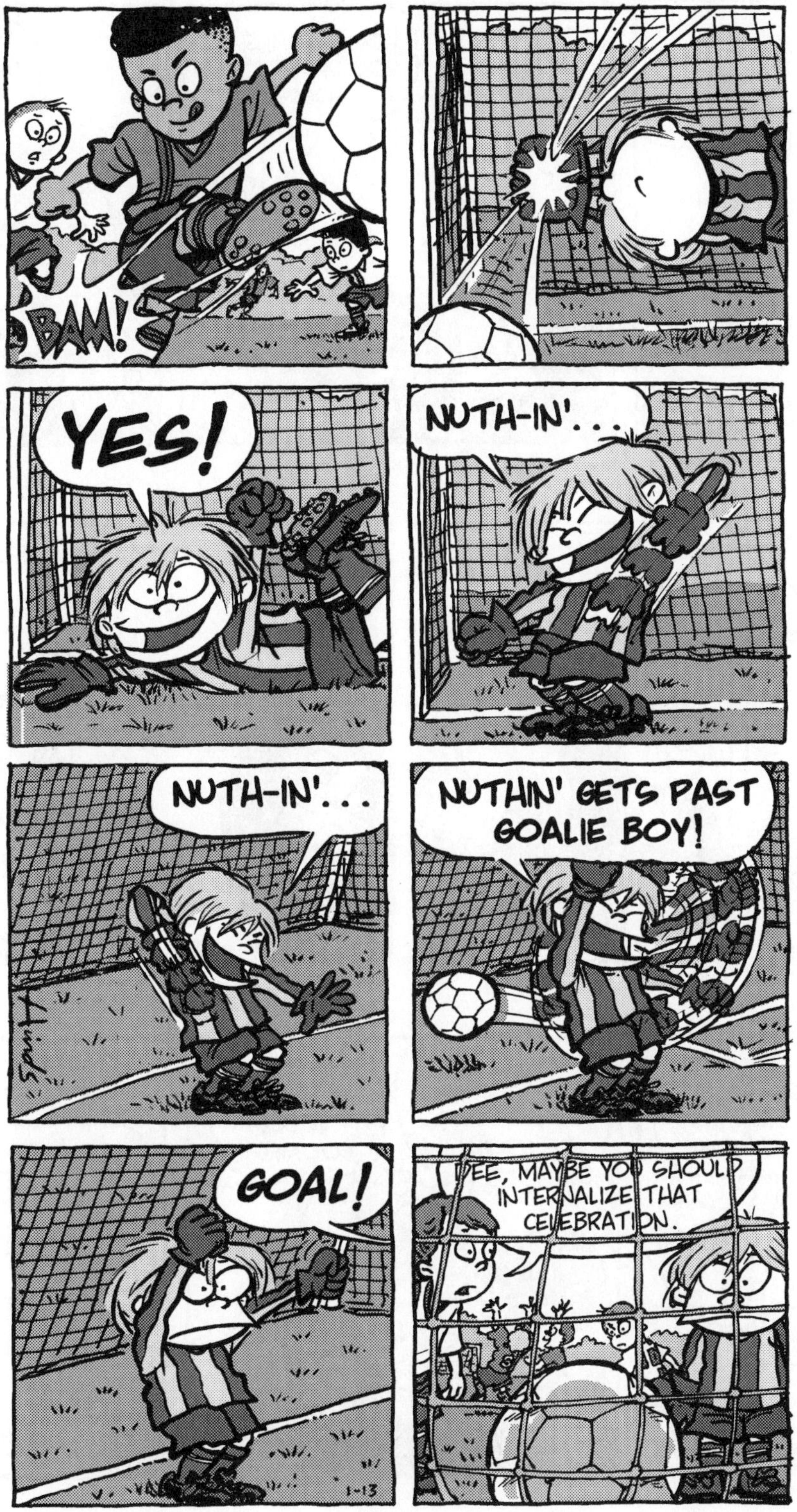
BAM!
YES!
NUTH-IN'. . .
NUTH-IN'. . .
NUTHIN' GETS PAST GOALIE BOY!
GOAL!
DEE, MAYBE YOU SHOULD INTERNALIZE THAT CELEBRATION.

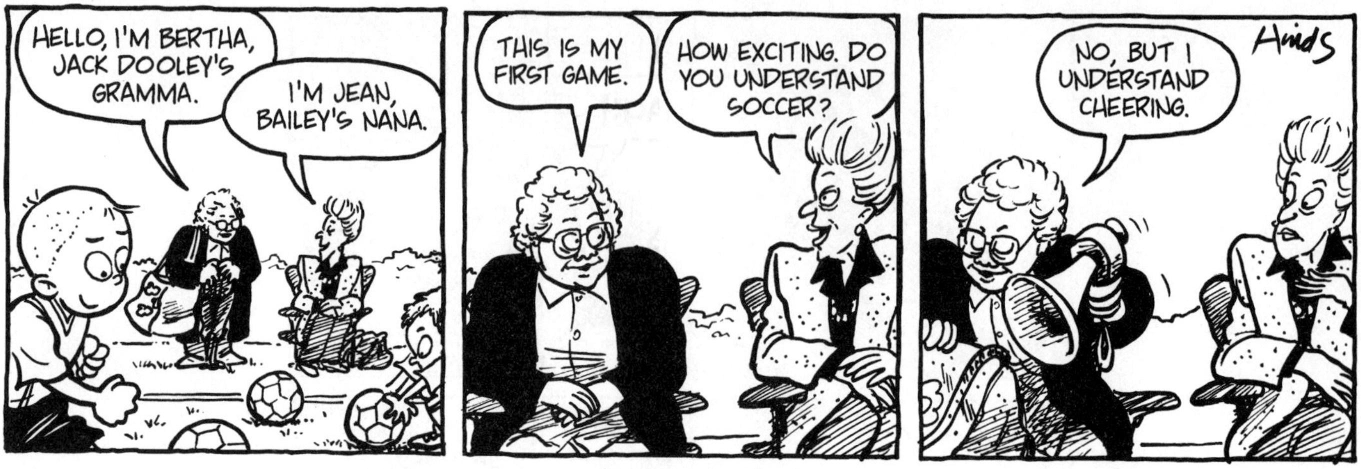
HELLO, I'M BERTHA, JACK DOOLEY'S GRAMMA.
I'M JEAN, BAILEY'S NANA.
THIS IS MY FIRST GAME.
HOW EXCITING. DO YOU UNDERSTAND SOCCER?
NO, BUT I UNDERSTAND CHEERING.
Hinds

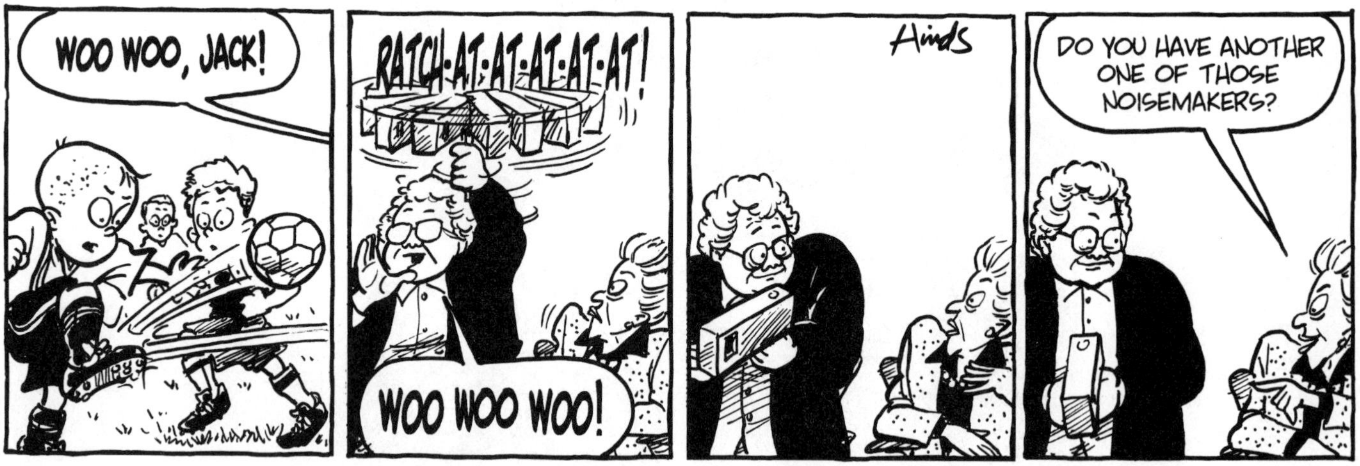
WOO WOO, JACK!
RATCH-AT-AT-AT-AT-AT!
WOO WOO WOO!
Hinds
DO YOU HAVE ANOTHER ONE OF THOSE NOISEMAKERS?

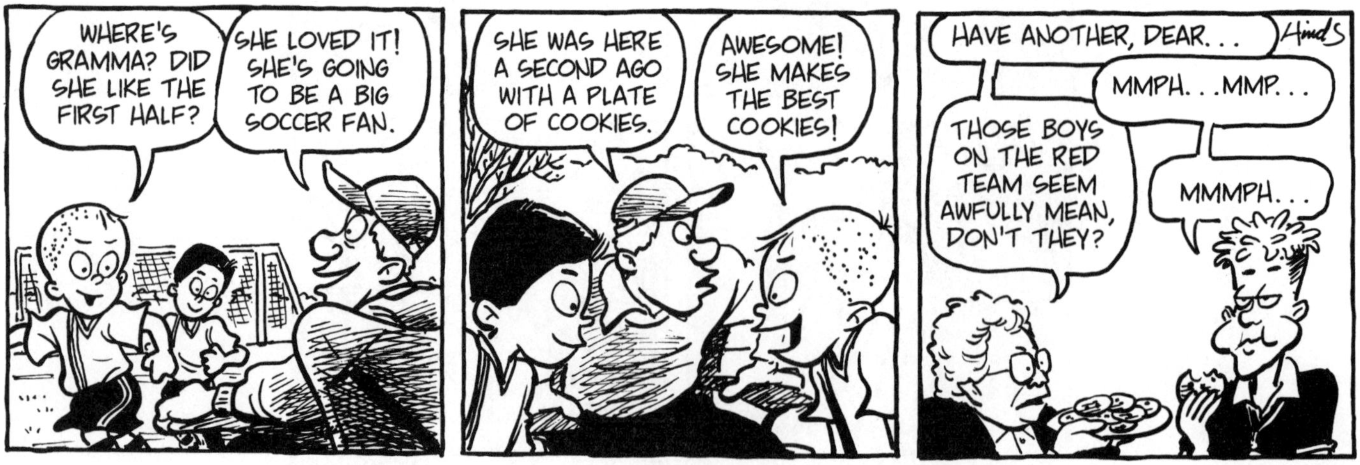
WHERE'S GRAMMA? DID SHE LIKE THE FIRST HALF?
SHE LOVED IT! SHE'S GOING TO BE A BIG SOCCER FAN.
SHE WAS HERE A SECOND AGO WITH A PLATE OF COOKIES.
AWESOME! SHE MAKES THE BEST COOKIES!
HAVE ANOTHER, DEAR...
Hinds
MMPH...MMP...
THOSE BOYS ON THE RED TEAM SEEM AWFULLY MEAN, DON'T THEY?
MMMPH...

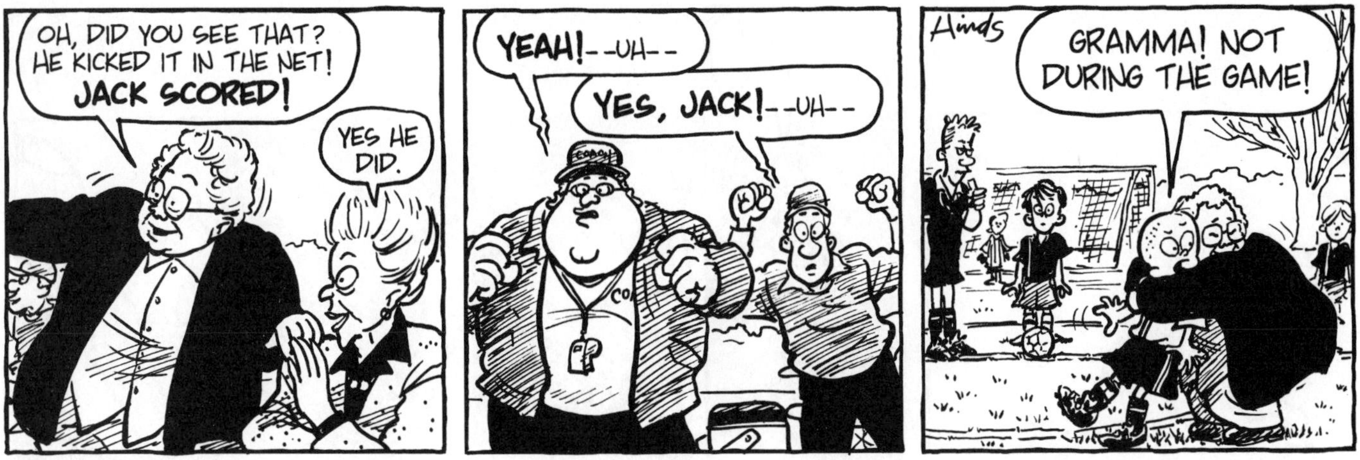
OH, DID YOU SEE THAT? HE KICKED IT IN THE NET! **JACK SCORED!**
YES HE DID.
YEAH!--UH--
YES, JACK!--UH--
Hinds
GRAMMA! NOT DURING THE GAME!

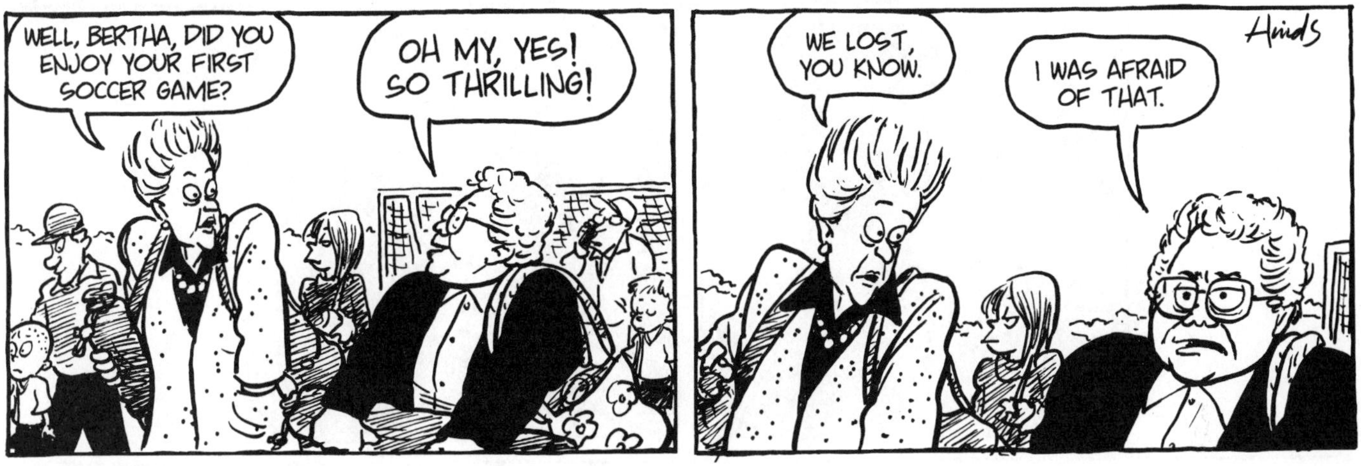
WELL, BERTHA, DID YOU ENJOY YOUR FIRST SOCCER GAME?
OH MY, YES! SO THRILLING!
Hinds
WE LOST, YOU KNOW.
I WAS AFRAID OF THAT.

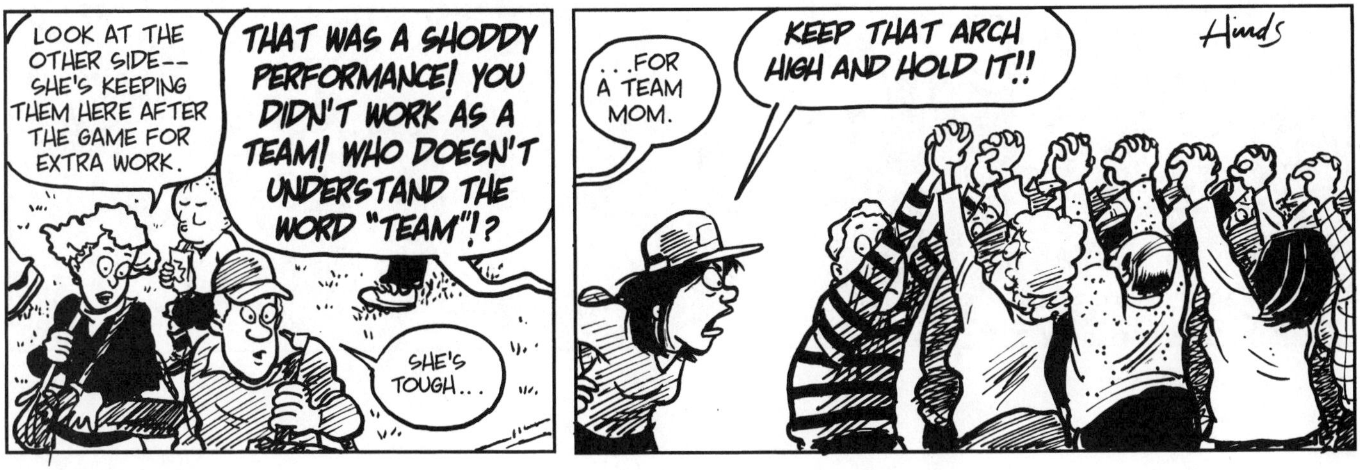
LOOK AT THE OTHER SIDE-- SHE'S KEEPING THEM HERE AFTER THE GAME FOR EXTRA WORK.
THAT WAS A SHODDY PERFORMANCE! YOU DIDN'T WORK AS A TEAM! WHO DOESN'T UNDERSTAND THE WORD "TEAM"!?
SHE'S TOUGH...
Hinds
...FOR A TEAM MOM.
KEEP THAT ARCH HIGH AND HOLD IT!!

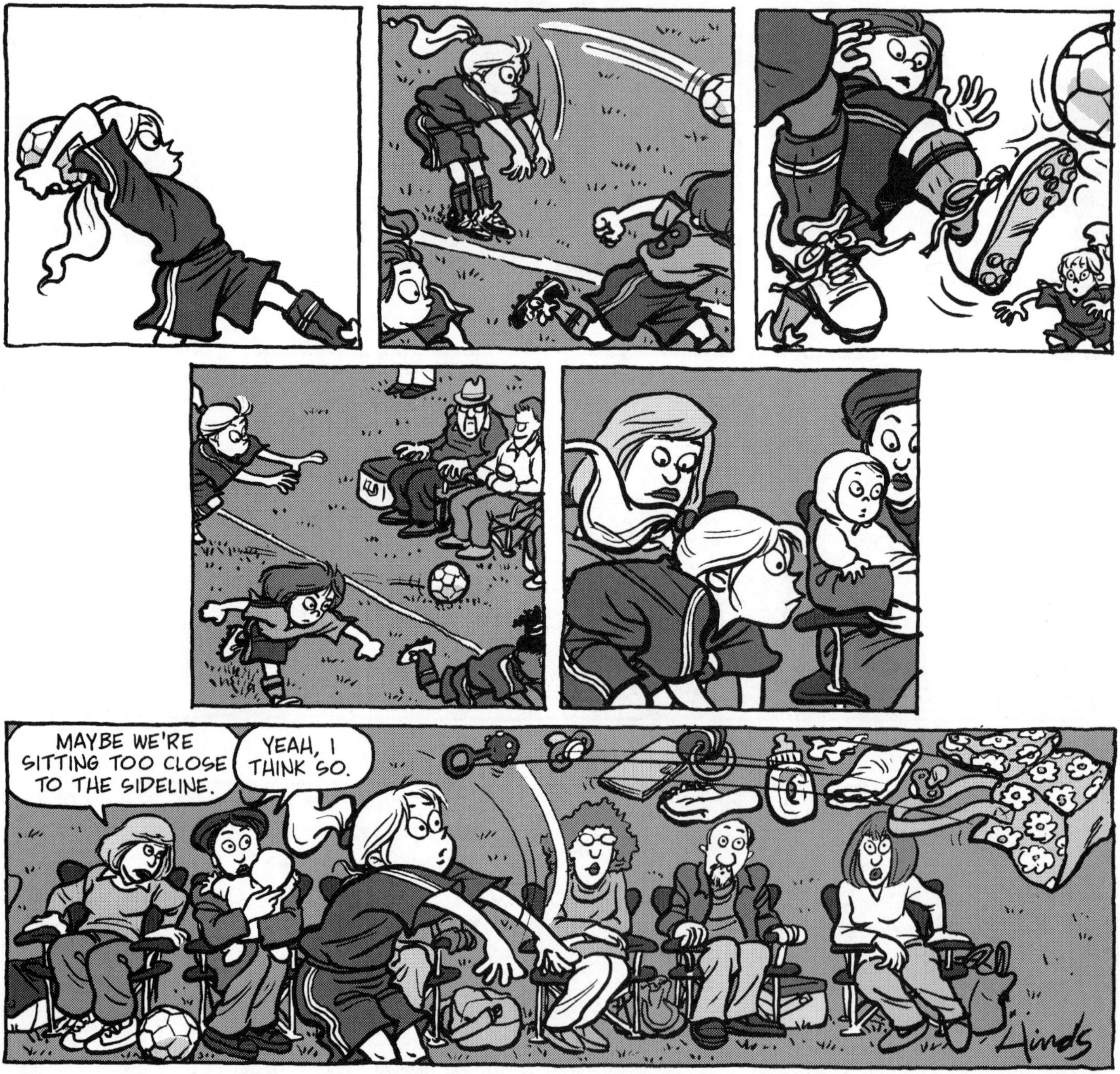
MAYBE WE'RE SITTING TOO CLOSE TO THE SIDELINE.
YEAH, I THINK SO.
Hinds

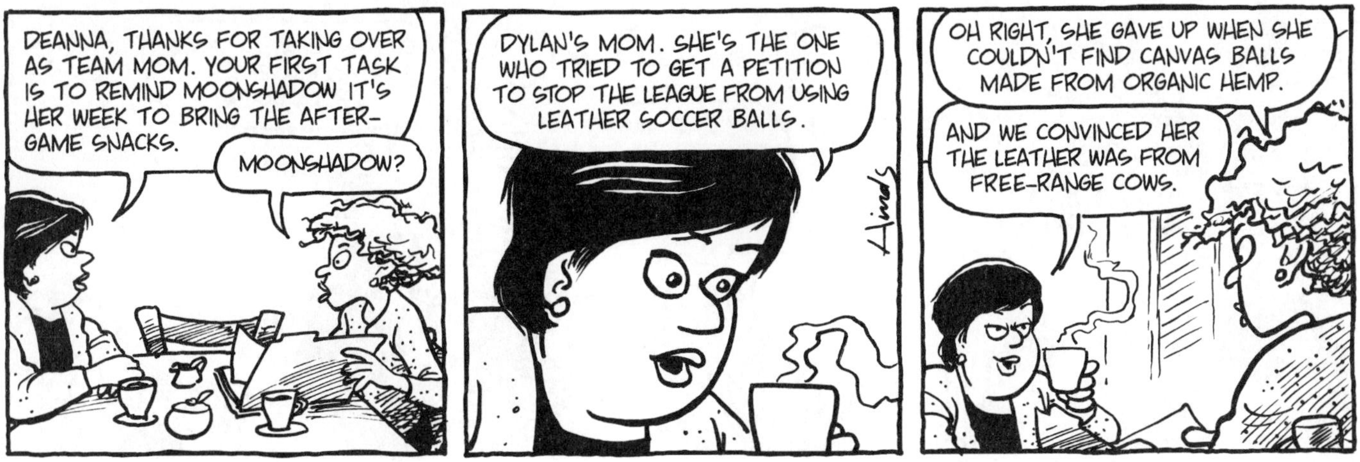
DEANNA, THANKS FOR TAKING OVER AS TEAM MOM. YOUR FIRST TASK IS TO REMIND MOONSHADOW IT'S HER WEEK TO BRING THE AFTER-GAME SNACKS.
MOONSHADOW?
DYLAN'S MOM. SHE'S THE ONE WHO TRIED TO GET A PETITION TO STOP THE LEAGUE FROM USING LEATHER SOCCER BALLS.
Hinds
OH RIGHT, SHE GAVE UP WHEN SHE COULDN'T FIND CANVAS BALLS MADE FROM ORGANIC HEMP.
AND WE CONVINCED HER THE LEATHER WAS FROM FREE-RANGE COWS.

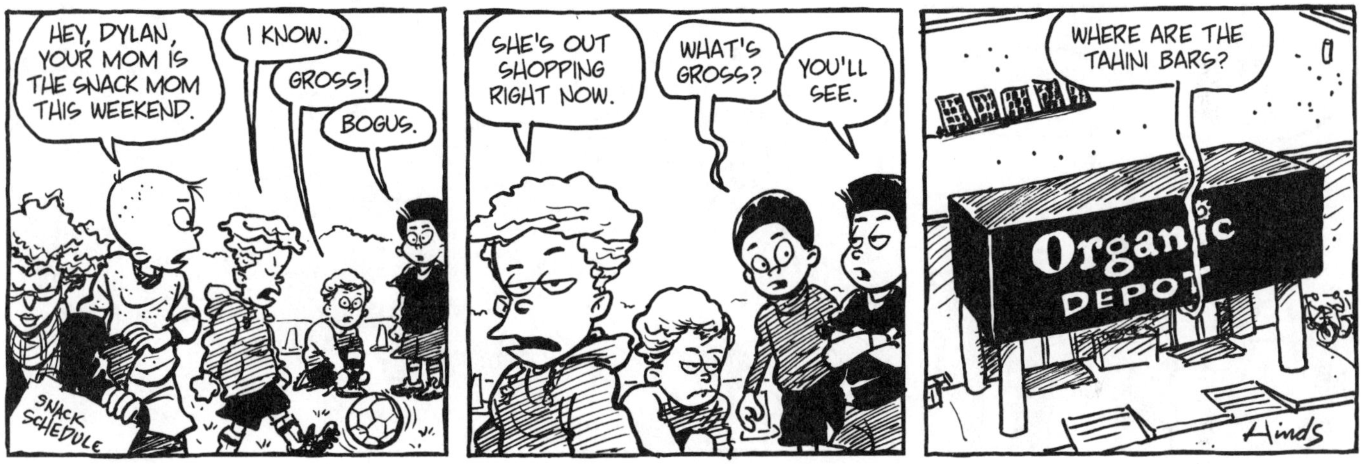
HEY, DYLAN, YOUR MOM IS THE SNACK MOM THIS WEEKEND.
I KNOW.
GROSS!
BOGUS.
SNACK SCHEDULE
SHE'S OUT SHOPPING RIGHT NOW.
WHAT'S GROSS?
YOU'LL SEE.
WHERE ARE THE TAHINI BARS?
Organic DEPOT
Hinds

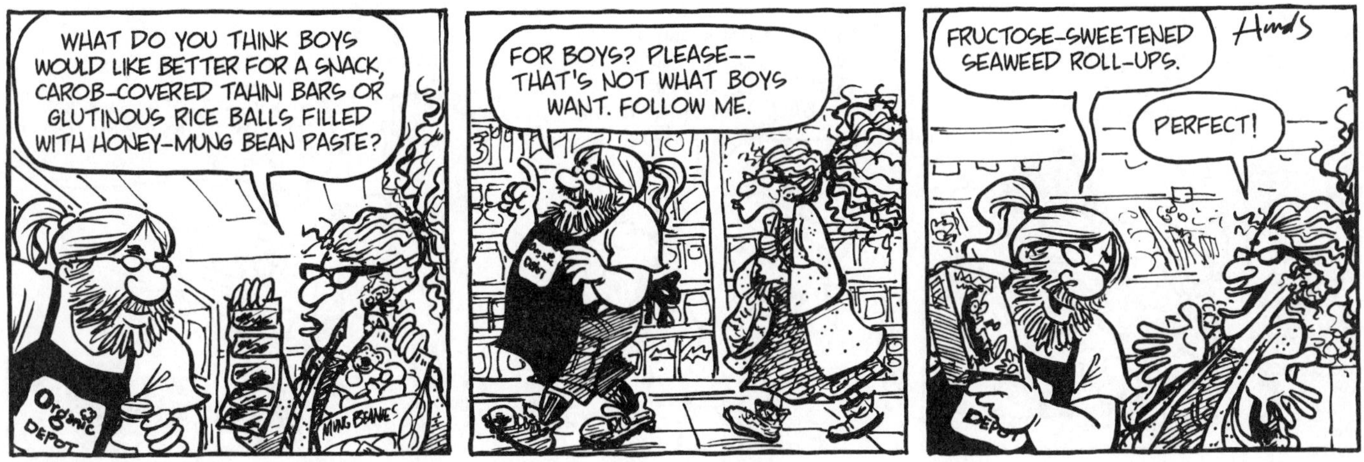
WHAT DO YOU THINK BOYS WOULD LIKE BETTER FOR A SNACK, CAROB-COVERED TAHINI BARS OR GLUTINOUS RICE BALLS FILLED WITH HONEY-MUNG BEAN PASTE?
Organic DEPOT
MUNG BEANS
FOR BOYS? PLEASE-- THAT'S NOT WHAT BOYS WANT. FOLLOW ME.
FRUCTOSE-SWEETENED SEAWEED ROLL-UPS.
Hinds
PERFECT!
DEPOT

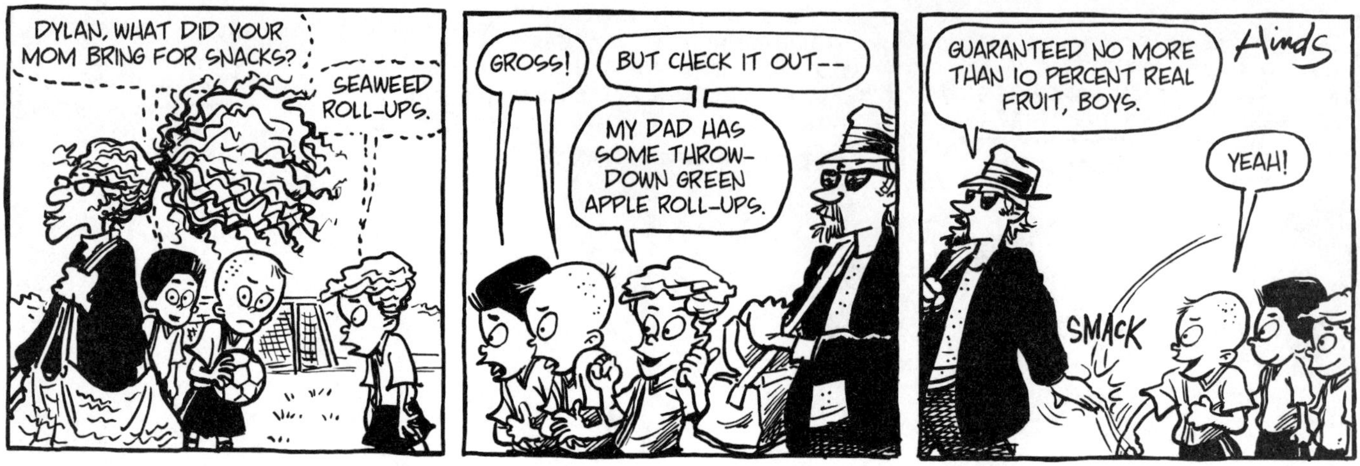
DYLAN, WHAT DID YOUR MOM BRING FOR SNACKS?
SEAWEED ROLL-UPS.
GROSS!
BUT CHECK IT OUT--
MY DAD HAS SOME THROW-DOWN GREEN APPLE ROLL-UPS.
Hinds
GUARANTEED NO MORE THAN 10 PERCENT REAL FRUIT, BOYS.
YEAH!
SMACK

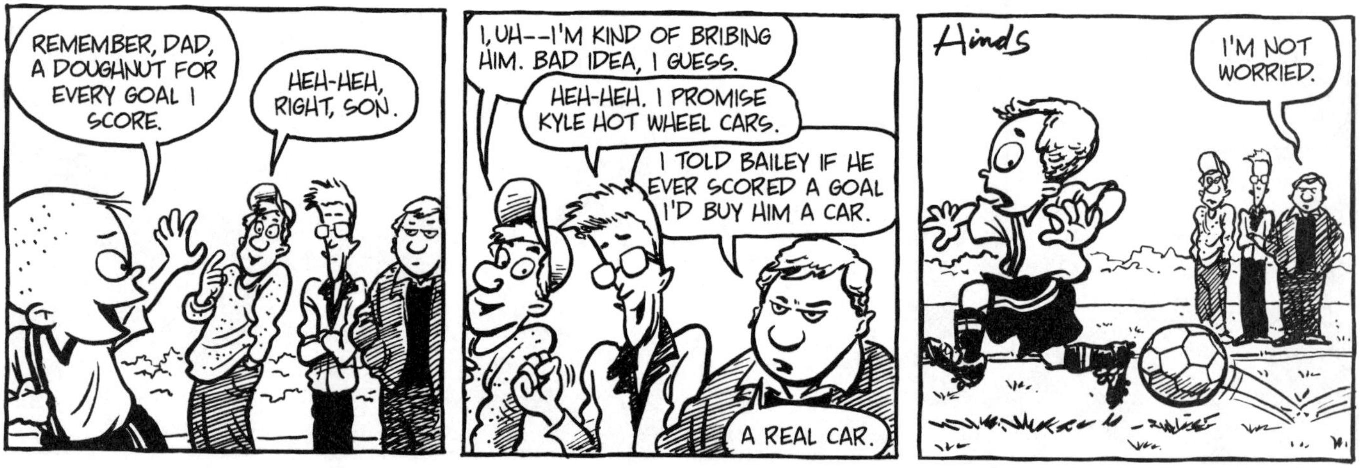
REMEMBER, DAD, A DOUGHNUT FOR EVERY GOAL I SCORE.
HEH-HEH, RIGHT, SON.
I, UH--I'M KIND OF BRIBING HIM. BAD IDEA, I GUESS.
HEH-HEH. I PROMISE KYLE HOT WHEEL CARS.
I TOLD BAILEY IF HE EVER SCORED A GOAL I'D BUY HIM A CAR.
A REAL CAR.
Hinds
I'M NOT WORRIED.

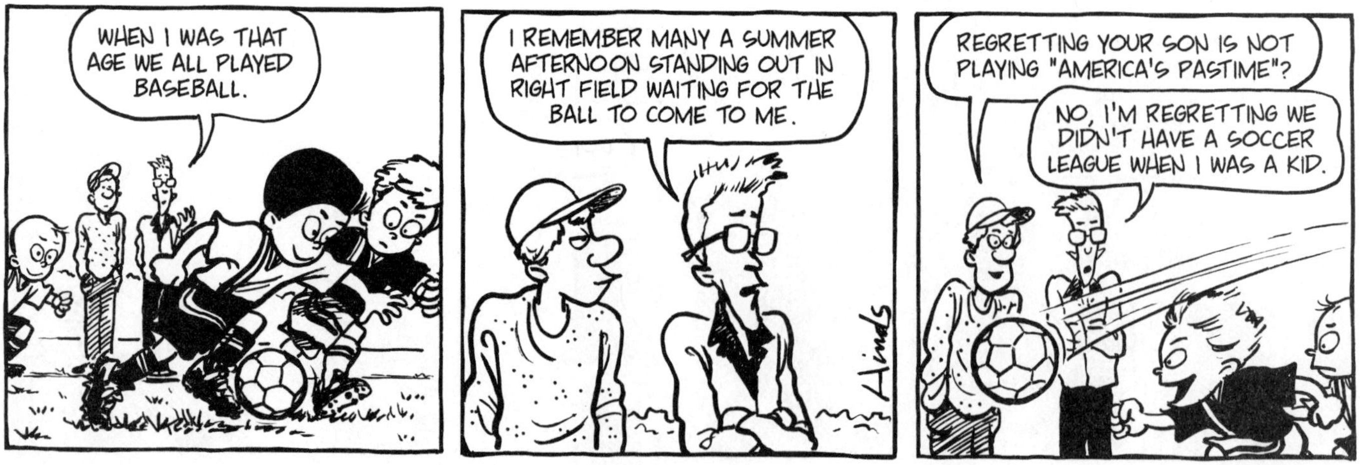
WHEN I WAS THAT AGE WE ALL PLAYED BASEBALL.
I REMEMBER MANY A SUMMER AFTERNOON STANDING OUT IN RIGHT FIELD WAITING FOR THE BALL TO COME TO ME.
Hinds
REGRETTING YOUR SON IS NOT PLAYING "AMERICA'S PASTIME"?
NO, I'M REGRETTING WE DIDN'T HAVE A SOCCER LEAGUE WHEN I WAS A KID.

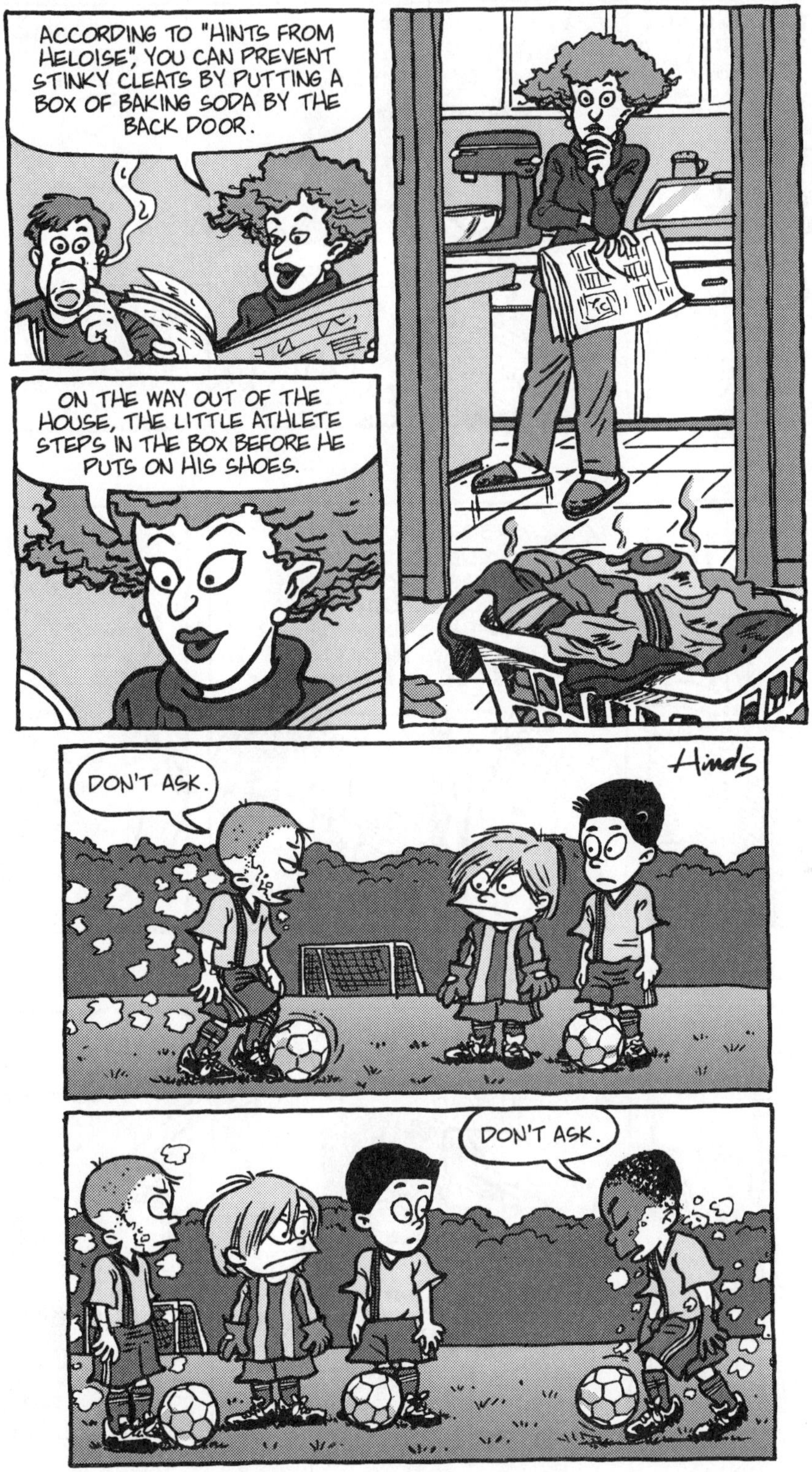
ACCORDING TO "HINTS FROM HELOISE," YOU CAN PREVENT STINKY CLEATS BY PUTTING A BOX OF BAKING SODA BY THE BACK DOOR.
ON THE WAY OUT OF THE HOUSE, THE LITTLE ATHLETE STEPS IN THE BOX BEFORE HE PUTS ON HIS SHOES.
Hinds
DON'T ASK.
DON'T ASK.

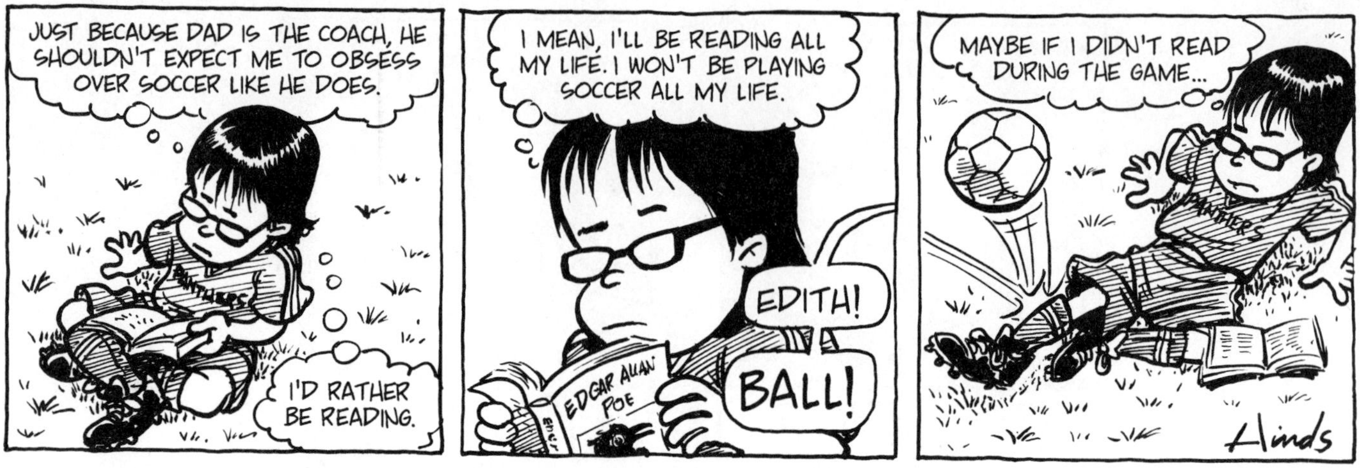
JUST BECAUSE DAD IS THE COACH, HE SHOULDN'T EXPECT ME TO OBSESS OVER SOCCER LIKE HE DOES.
PANTHERS
I'D RATHER BE READING.
I MEAN, I'LL BE READING ALL MY LIFE. I WON'T BE PLAYING SOCCER ALL MY LIFE.
EDITH!
BALL!
EDGAR ALLAN POE
MAYBE IF I DIDN'T READ DURING THE GAME...
PANTHERS
Hinds

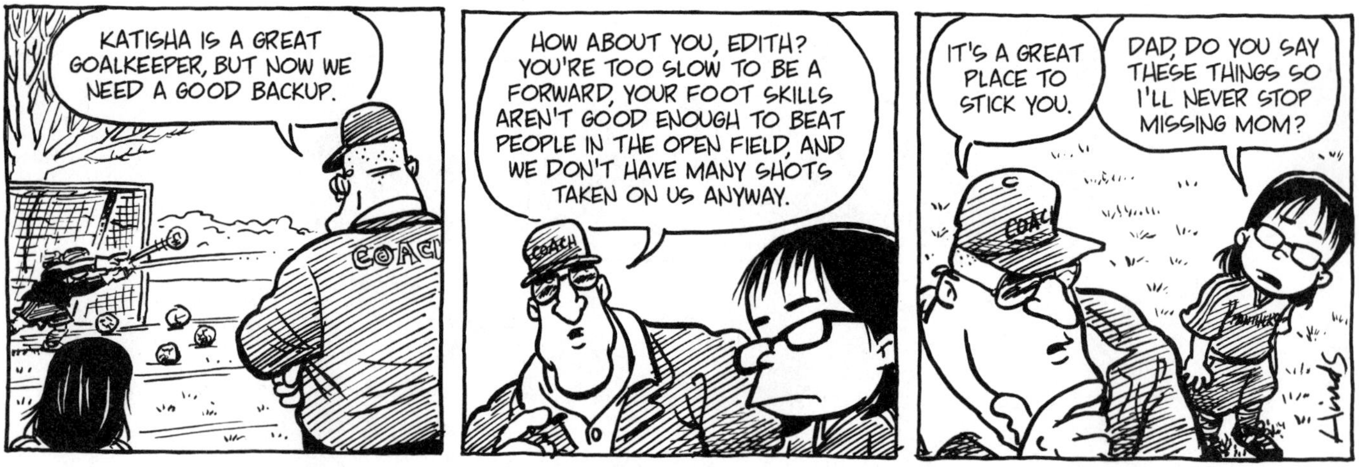
KATISHA IS A GREAT GOALKEEPER, BUT NOW WE NEED A GOOD BACKUP.
COACH
HOW ABOUT YOU, EDITH? YOU'RE TOO SLOW TO BE A FORWARD, YOUR FOOT SKILLS AREN'T GOOD ENOUGH TO BEAT PEOPLE IN THE OPEN FIELD, AND WE DON'T HAVE MANY SHOTS TAKEN ON US ANYWAY.
COACH
IT'S A GREAT PLACE TO STICK YOU.
DAD, DO YOU SAY THESE THINGS SO I'LL NEVER STOP MISSING MOM?
COACH
PANTHERS
Hinds

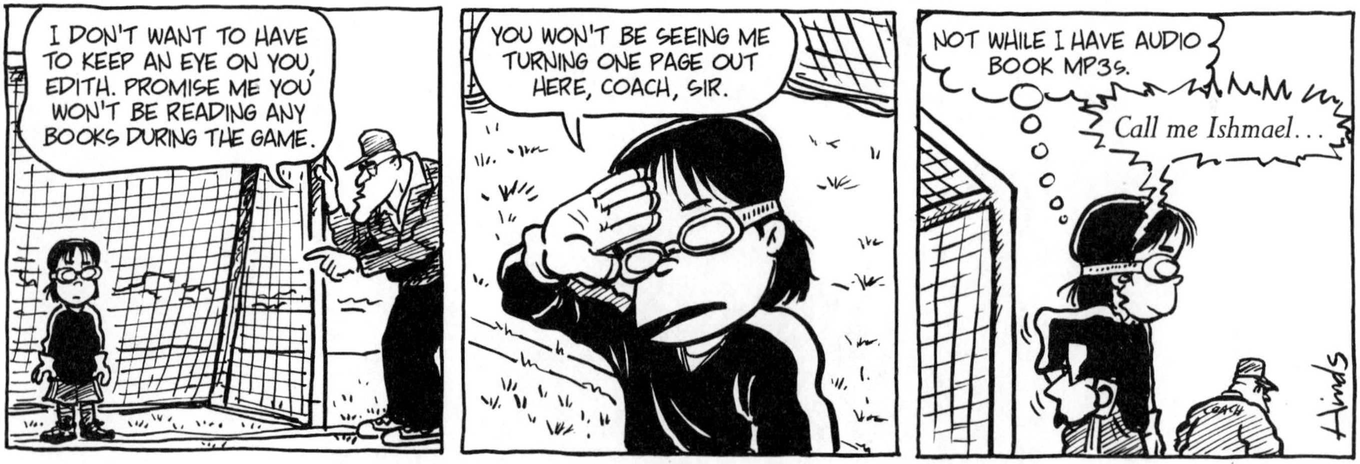
I DON'T WANT TO HAVE TO KEEP AN EYE ON YOU, EDITH. PROMISE ME YOU WON'T BE READING ANY BOOKS DURING THE GAME.
YOU WON'T BE SEEING ME TURNING ONE PAGE OUT HERE, COACH, SIR.
NOT WHILE I HAVE AUDIO BOOK MP3s.
Call me Ishmael...
COACH
Hinds

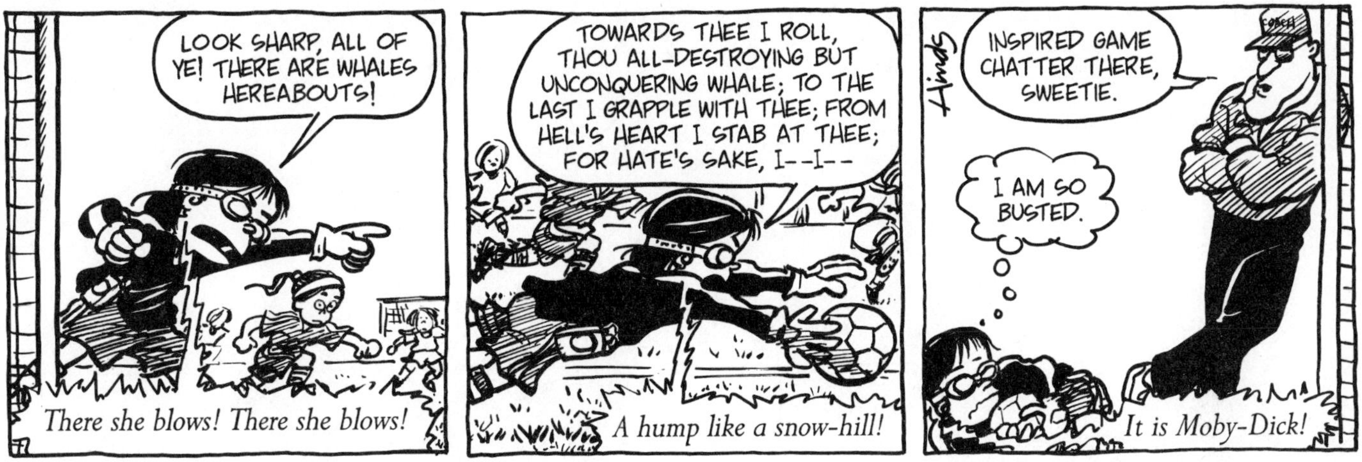
LOOK SHARP, ALL OF YE! THERE ARE WHALES HEREABOUTS!
There she blows! There she blows!
TOWARDS THEE I ROLL, THOU ALL-DESTROYING BUT UNCONQUERING WHALE; TO THE LAST I GRAPPLE WITH THEE; FROM HELL'S HEART I STAB AT THEE; FOR HATE'S SAKE, I--I--
A hump like a snow-hill!
Hinds
INSPIRED GAME CHATTER THERE, SWEETIE.
I AM SO BUSTED.
It is Moby-Dick!

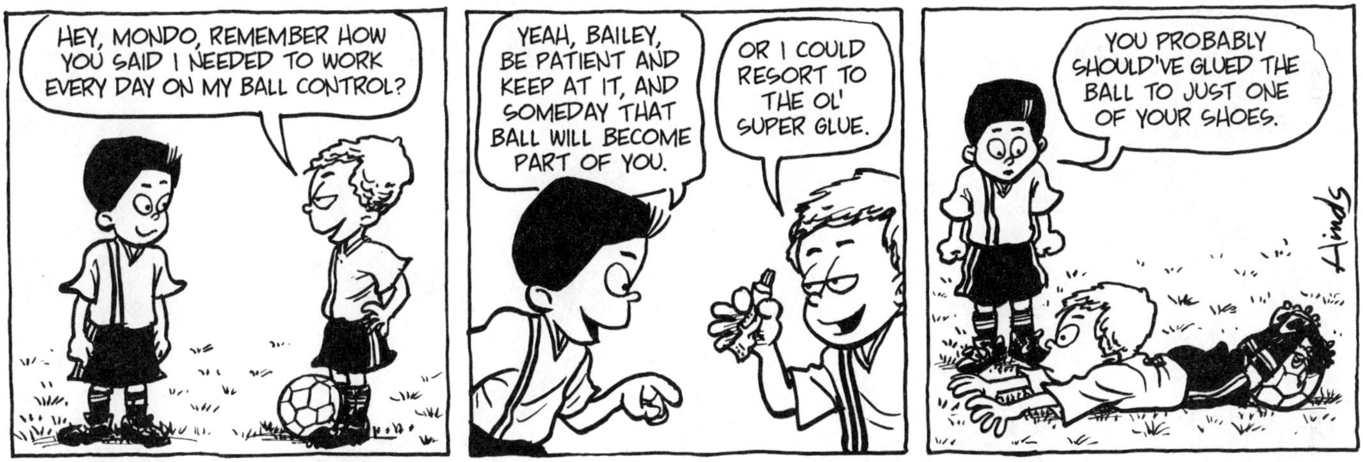
HEY, MONDO, REMEMBER HOW YOU SAID I NEEDED TO WORK EVERY DAY ON MY BALL CONTROL?
YEAH, BAILEY, BE PATIENT AND KEEP AT IT, AND SOMEDAY THAT BALL WILL BECOME PART OF YOU.
OR I COULD RESORT TO THE OL' SUPER GLUE.
YOU PROBABLY SHOULD'VE GLUED THE BALL TO JUST ONE OF YOUR SHOES.
Hinds

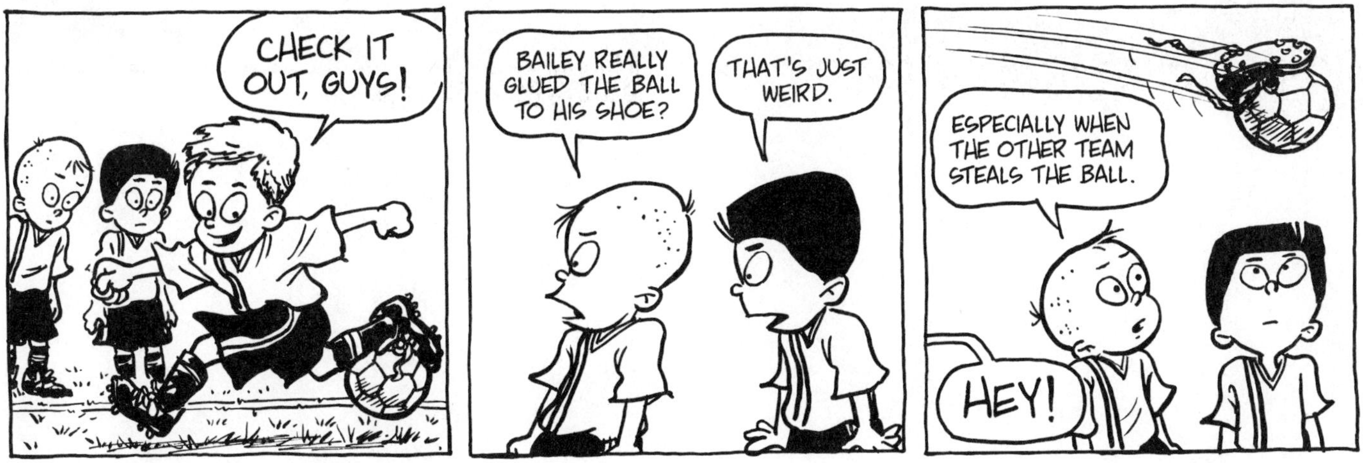
CHECK IT OUT, GUYS!
BAILEY REALLY GLUED THE BALL TO HIS SHOE?
THAT'S JUST WEIRD.
ESPECIALLY WHEN THE OTHER TEAM STEALS THE BALL.
HEY!

ARE YOU LADIES READY FOR ANOTHER OUT-OF-TOWN TOURNAMENT VICTORY?

WE'RE READY TO ROLL, COACH. THE SLEEPING TOWN OF GROVETON IS ABOUT TO BE AWAKENED BY THE ROAR OF THE *PANTHERS!*

OR MAYBE THE *SNORE* OF THE PANTHERS.

Hinds

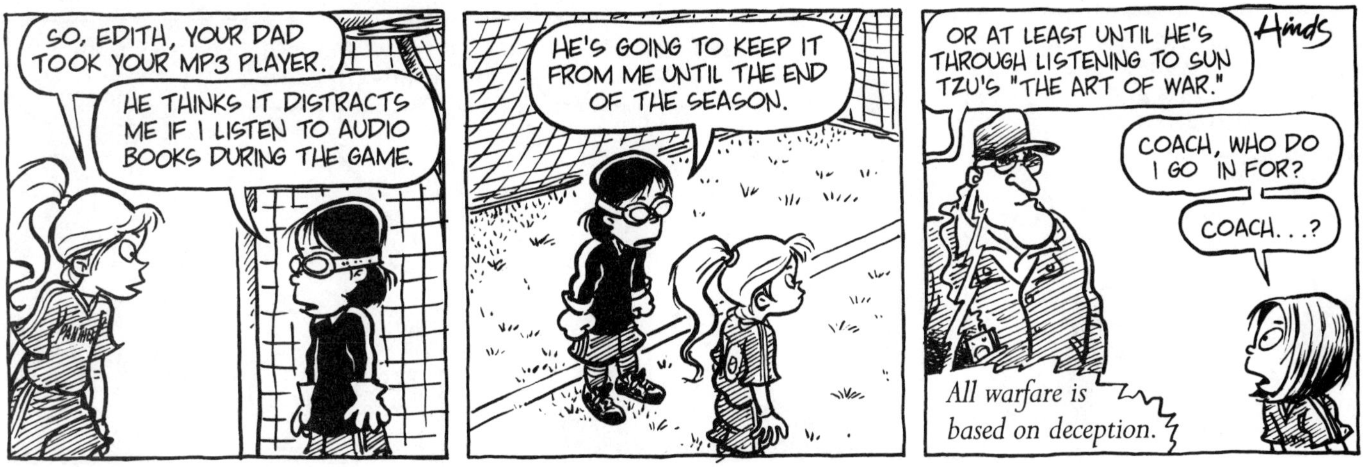
SO, EDITH, YOUR DAD TOOK YOUR MP3 PLAYER.
HE THINKS IT DISTRACTS ME IF I LISTEN TO AUDIO BOOKS DURING THE GAME.
HE'S GOING TO KEEP IT FROM ME UNTIL THE END OF THE SEASON.
OR AT LEAST UNTIL HE'S THROUGH LISTENING TO SUN TZU'S "THE ART OF WAR."
Hinds
All warfare is based on deception.
COACH, WHO DO I GO IN FOR?
COACH...?

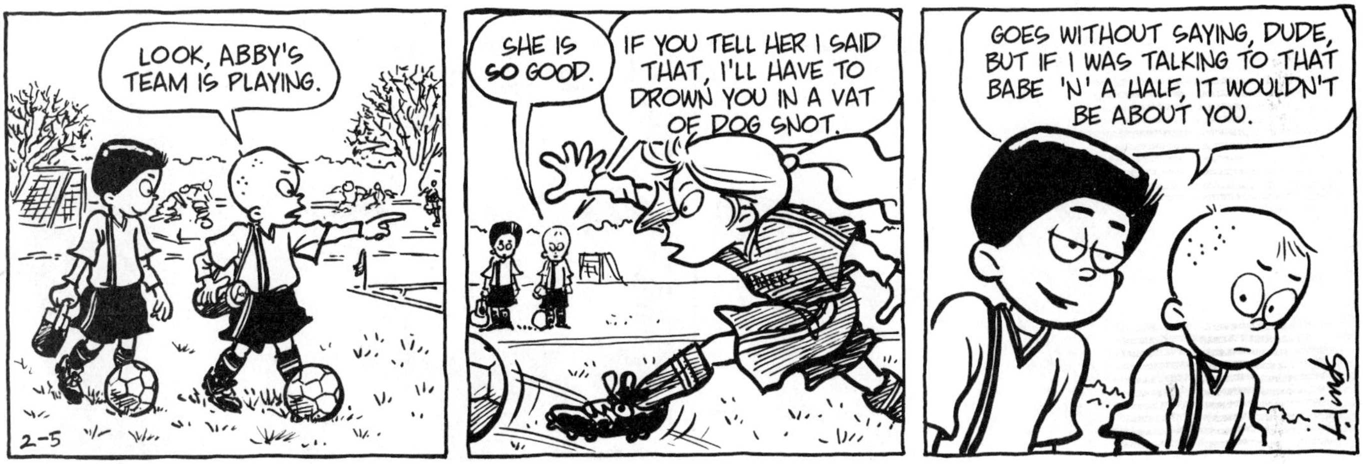
2-5
LOOK, ABBY'S TEAM IS PLAYING.
SHE IS **SO** GOOD.
IF YOU TELL HER I SAID THAT, I'LL HAVE TO DROWN YOU IN A VAT OF DOG SNOT.
GOES WITHOUT SAYING, DUDE, BUT IF I WAS TALKING TO THAT BABE 'N' A HALF, IT WOULDN'T BE ABOUT YOU.
Hinds

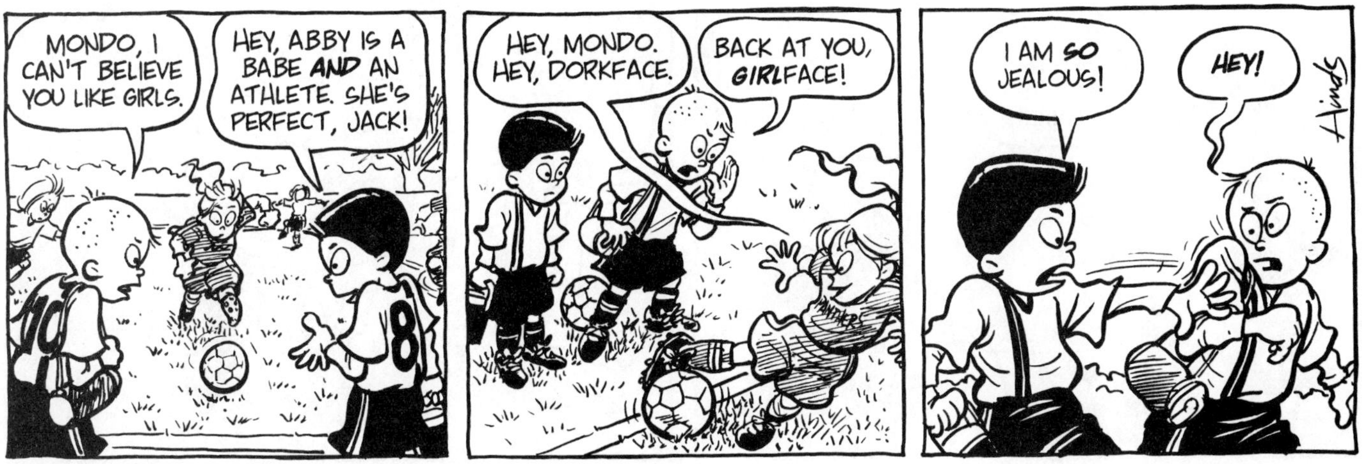
MONDO, I CAN'T BELIEVE YOU LIKE GIRLS.
HEY, ABBY IS A BABE **AND** AN ATHLETE. SHE'S PERFECT, JACK!
HEY, MONDO. HEY, DORKFACE.
BACK AT YOU, **GIRL**FACE!
I AM **SO** JEALOUS!
HEY!
Hinds

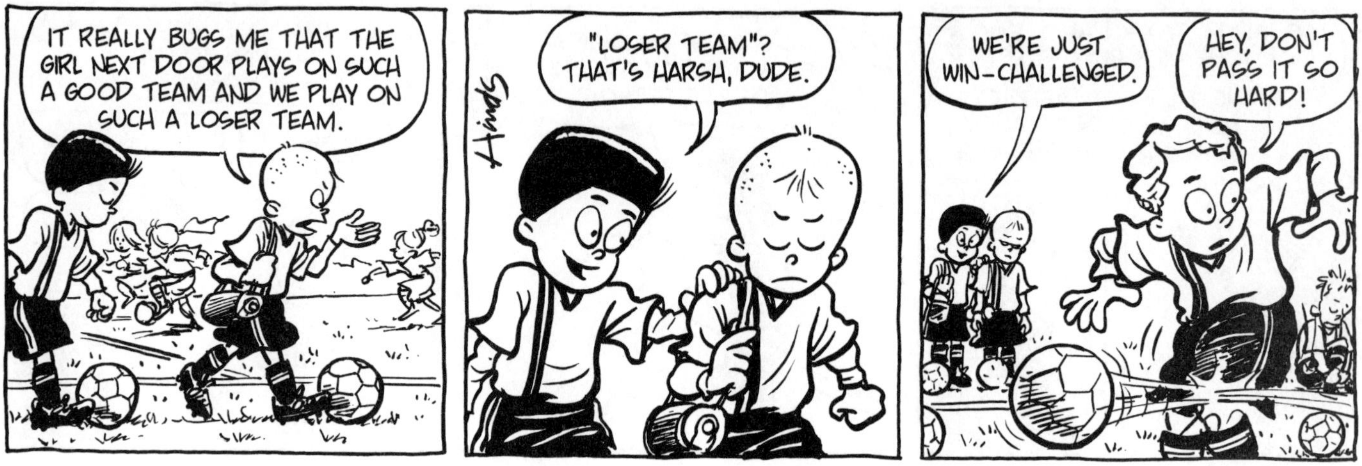
IT REALLY BUGS ME THAT THE GIRL NEXT DOOR PLAYS ON SUCH A GOOD TEAM AND WE PLAY ON SUCH A LOSER TEAM.
"LOSER TEAM"? THAT'S HARSH, DUDE.
WE'RE JUST WIN-CHALLENGED.
HEY, DON'T PASS IT SO HARD!

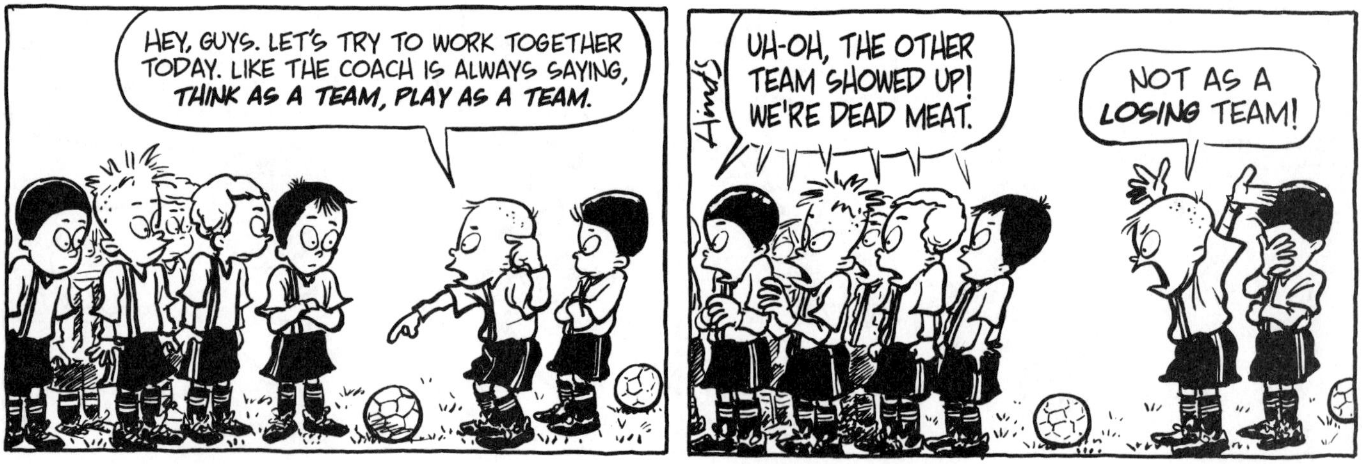
HEY, GUYS. LET'S TRY TO WORK TOGETHER TODAY. LIKE THE COACH IS ALWAYS SAYING, ***THINK AS A TEAM, PLAY AS A TEAM.***
UH-OH, THE OTHER TEAM SHOWED UP! WE'RE DEAD MEAT.
NOT AS A ***LOSING*** TEAM!

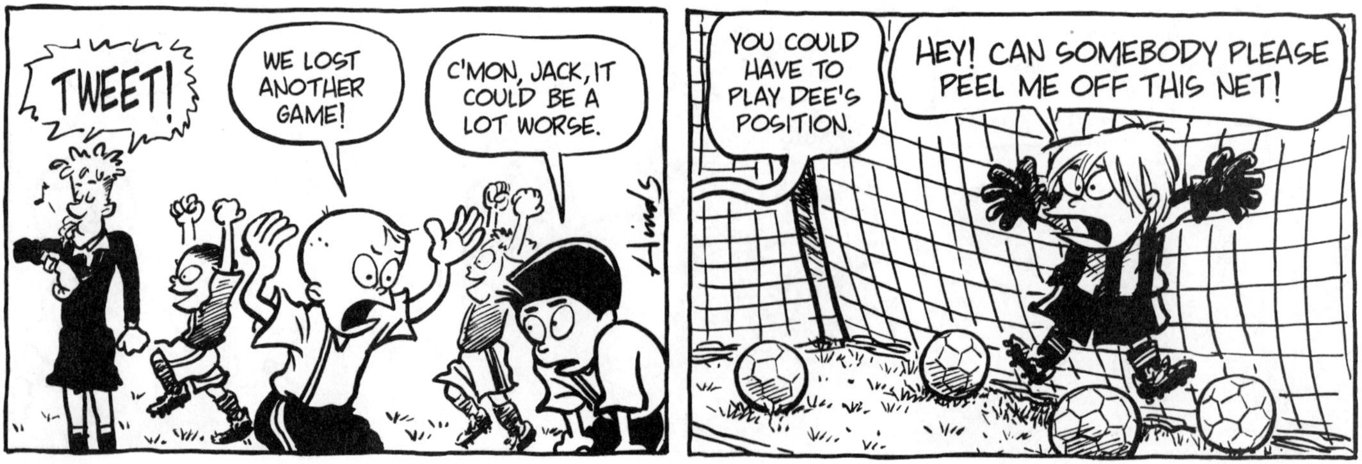
TWEET!
WE LOST ANOTHER GAME!
C'MON, JACK, IT COULD BE A LOT WORSE.
YOU COULD HAVE TO PLAY DEE'S POSITION.
HEY! CAN SOMEBODY PLEASE PEEL ME OFF THIS NET!

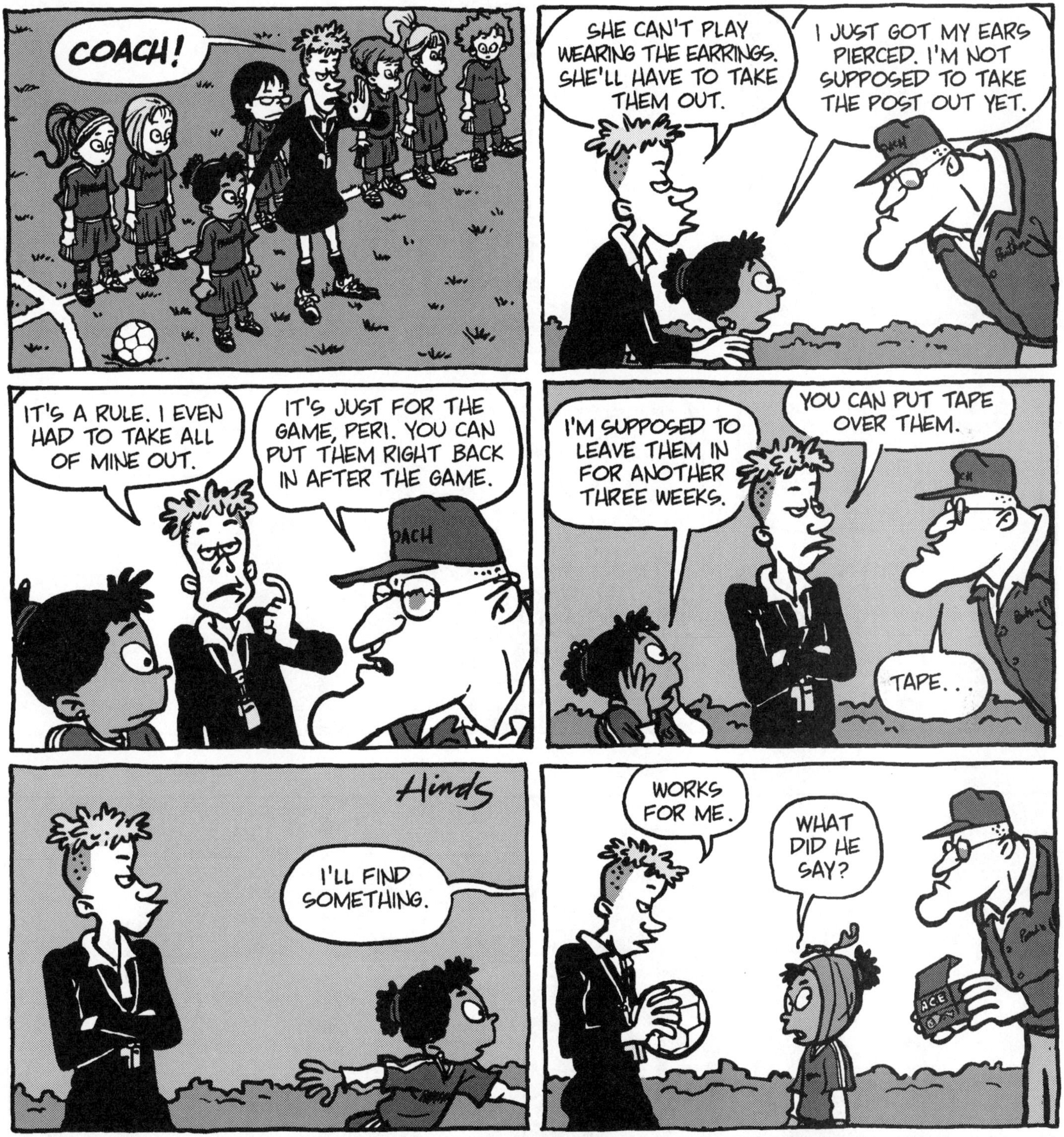
COACH!
SHE CAN'T PLAY WEARING THE EARRINGS. SHE'LL HAVE TO TAKE THEM OUT.
I JUST GOT MY EARS PIERCED. I'M NOT SUPPOSED TO TAKE THE POST OUT YET.
IT'S A RULE. I EVEN HAD TO TAKE ALL OF MINE OUT.
IT'S JUST FOR THE GAME, PERI. YOU CAN PUT THEM RIGHT BACK IN AFTER THE GAME.
I'M SUPPOSED TO LEAVE THEM IN FOR ANOTHER THREE WEEKS.
YOU CAN PUT TAPE OVER THEM.
TAPE...
Hinds
I'LL FIND SOMETHING.
WORKS FOR ME.
WHAT DID HE SAY?
ACE

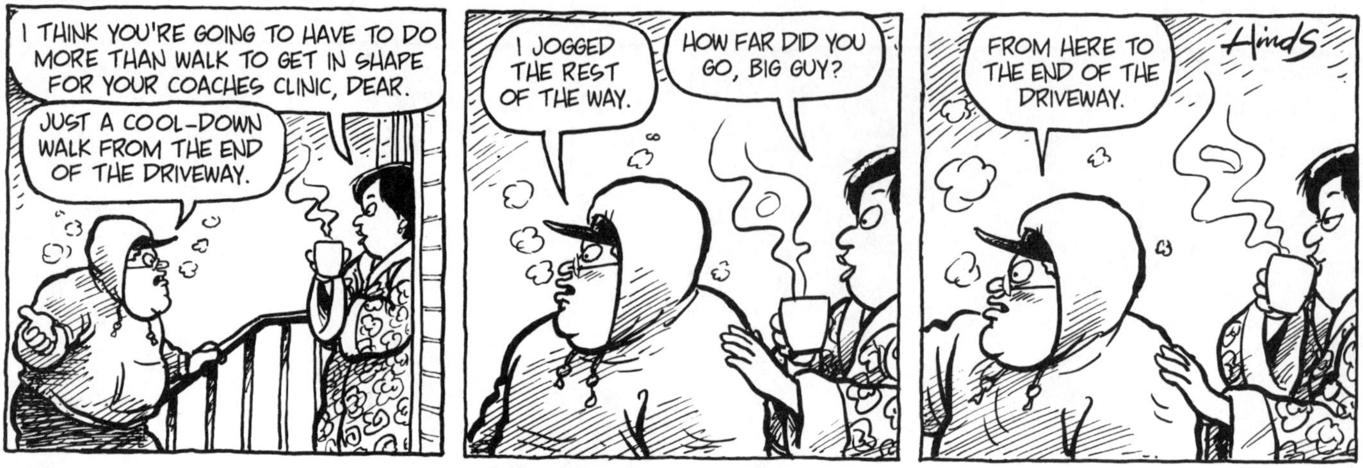
I THINK YOU'RE GOING TO HAVE TO DO MORE THAN WALK TO GET IN SHAPE FOR YOUR COACHES CLINIC, DEAR.
JUST A COOL-DOWN WALK FROM THE END OF THE DRIVEWAY.
I JOGGED THE REST OF THE WAY.
HOW FAR DID YOU GO, BIG GUY?
FROM HERE TO THE END OF THE DRIVEWAY.
Hinds

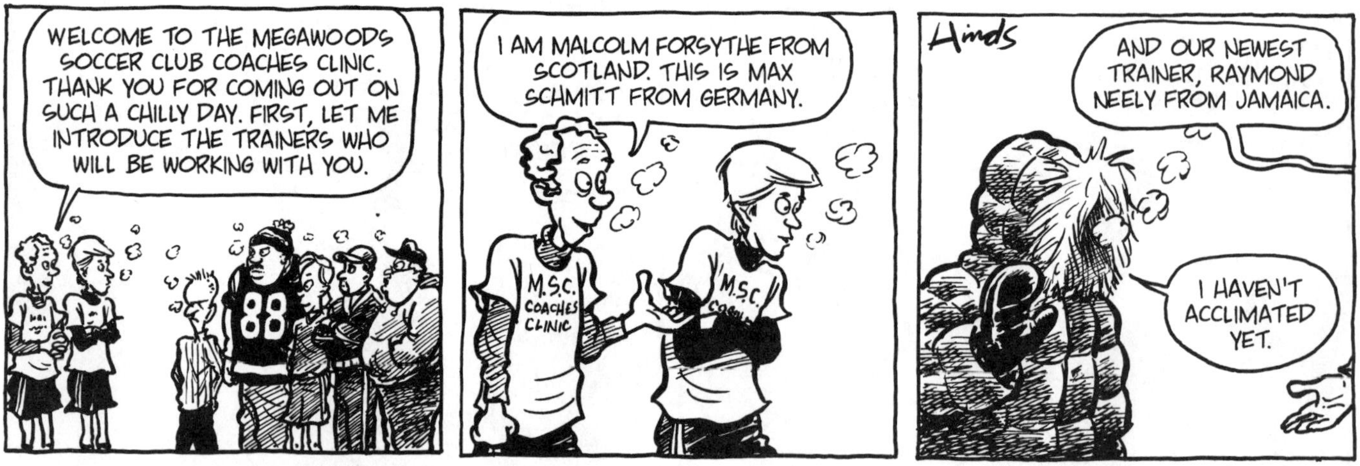
WELCOME TO THE MEGAWOODS SOCCER CLUB COACHES CLINIC. THANK YOU FOR COMING OUT ON SUCH A CHILLY DAY. FIRST, LET ME INTRODUCE THE TRAINERS WHO WILL BE WORKING WITH YOU.
I AM MALCOLM FORSYTHE FROM SCOTLAND. THIS IS MAX SCHMITT FROM GERMANY.
M.S.C. COACHES CLINIC
Hinds
AND OUR NEWEST TRAINER, RAYMOND NEELY FROM JAMAICA.
I HAVEN'T ACCLIMATED YET.

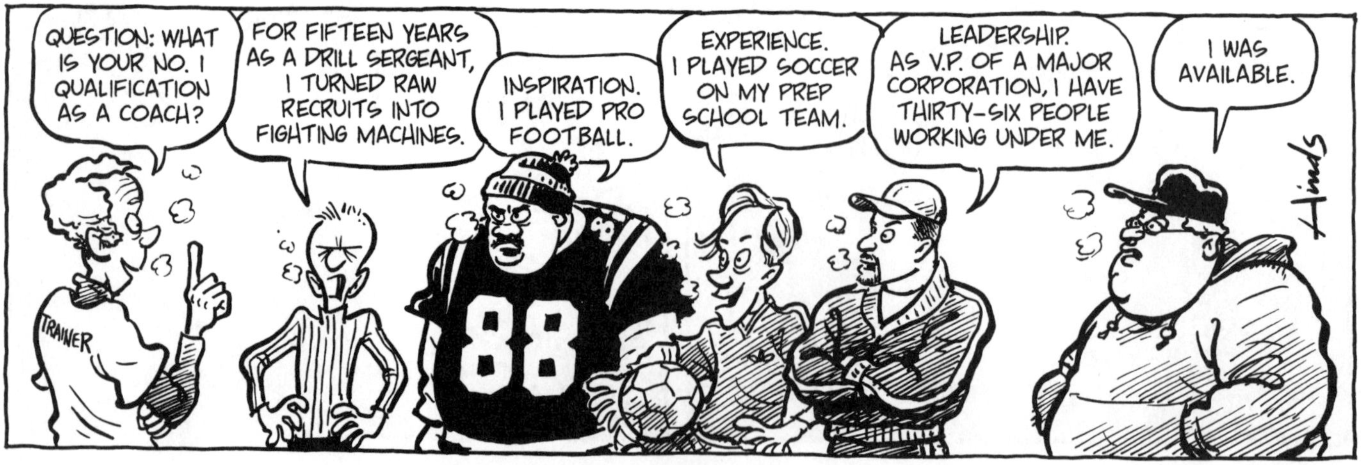
QUESTION: WHAT IS YOUR NO. 1 QUALIFICATION AS A COACH?
FOR FIFTEEN YEARS AS A DRILL SERGEANT, I TURNED RAW RECRUITS INTO FIGHTING MACHINES.
INSPIRATION. I PLAYED PRO FOOTBALL.
EXPERIENCE. I PLAYED SOCCER ON MY PREP SCHOOL TEAM.
LEADERSHIP. AS V.P. OF A MAJOR CORPORATION, I HAVE THIRTY-SIX PEOPLE WORKING UNDER ME.
I WAS AVAILABLE.
TRAINER
88
Hinds

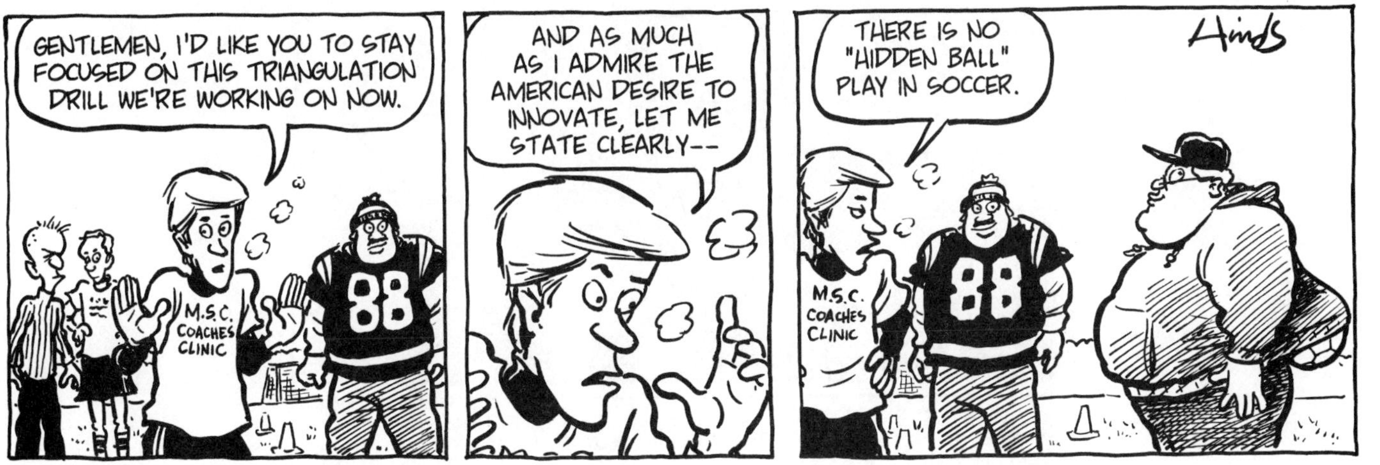
GENTLEMEN, I'D LIKE YOU TO STAY FOCUSED ON THIS TRIANGULATION DRILL WE'RE WORKING ON NOW.
M.S.C. COACHES CLINIC
88
AND AS MUCH AS I ADMIRE THE AMERICAN DESIRE TO INNOVATE, LET ME STATE CLEARLY--
THERE IS NO "HIDDEN BALL" PLAY IN SOCCER.
M.S.C. COACHES CLINIC
88
Hinds

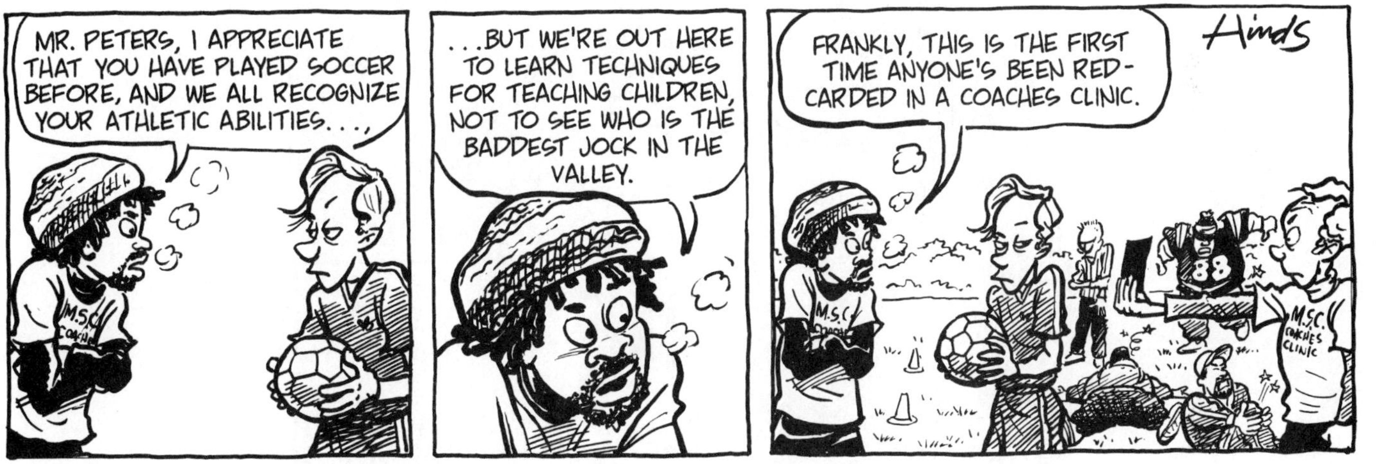
MR. PETERS, I APPRECIATE THAT YOU HAVE PLAYED SOCCER BEFORE, AND WE ALL RECOGNIZE YOUR ATHLETIC ABILITIES...,
...BUT WE'RE OUT HERE TO LEARN TECHNIQUES FOR TEACHING CHILDREN, NOT TO SEE WHO IS THE BADDEST JOCK IN THE VALLEY.
FRANKLY, THIS IS THE FIRST TIME ANYONE'S BEEN RED-CARDED IN A COACHES CLINIC.
Hinds

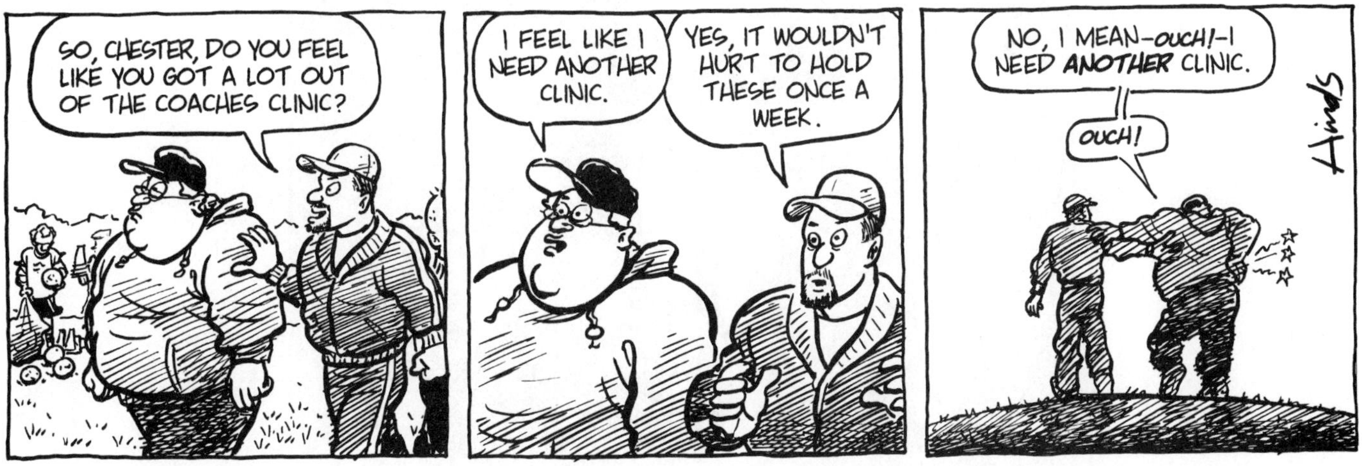
SO, CHESTER, DO YOU FEEL LIKE YOU GOT A LOT OUT OF THE COACHES CLINIC?
I FEEL LIKE I NEED ANOTHER CLINIC.
YES, IT WOULDN'T HURT TO HOLD THESE ONCE A WEEK.
NO, I MEAN--OUCH!--I NEED ANOTHER CLINIC.
OUCH!
Hinds

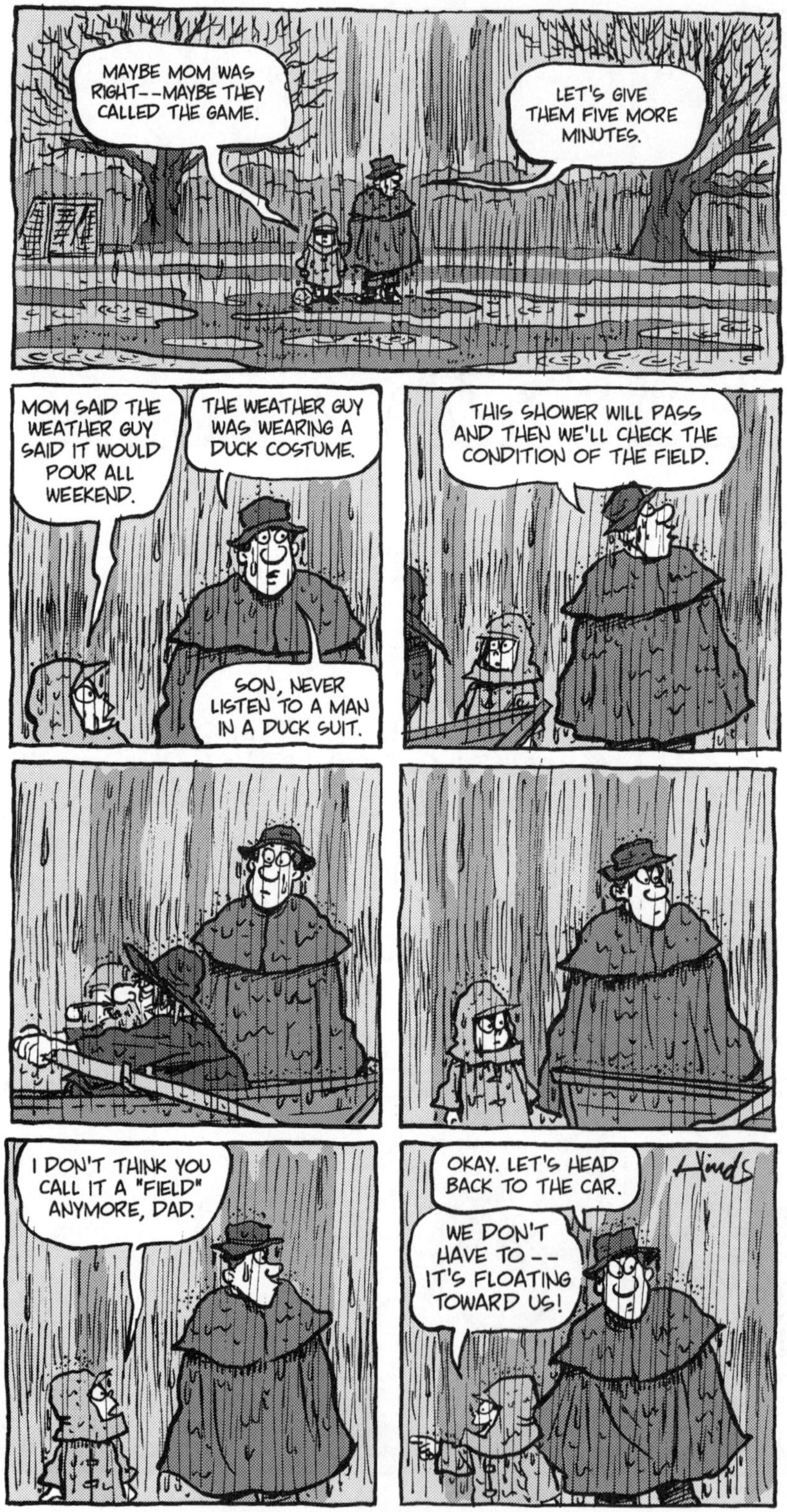
MAYBE MOM WAS RIGHT--MAYBE THEY CALLED THE GAME.
LET'S GIVE THEM FIVE MORE MINUTES.
MOM SAID THE WEATHER GUY SAID IT WOULD POUR ALL WEEKEND.
THE WEATHER GUY WAS WEARING A DUCK COSTUME.
SON, NEVER LISTEN TO A MAN IN A DUCK SUIT.
THIS SHOWER WILL PASS AND THEN WE'LL CHECK THE CONDITION OF THE FIELD.
I DON'T THINK YOU CALL IT A "FIELD" ANYMORE, DAD.
OKAY. LET'S HEAD BACK TO THE CAR.
WE DON'T HAVE TO--IT'S FLOATING TOWARD US!
Hinds

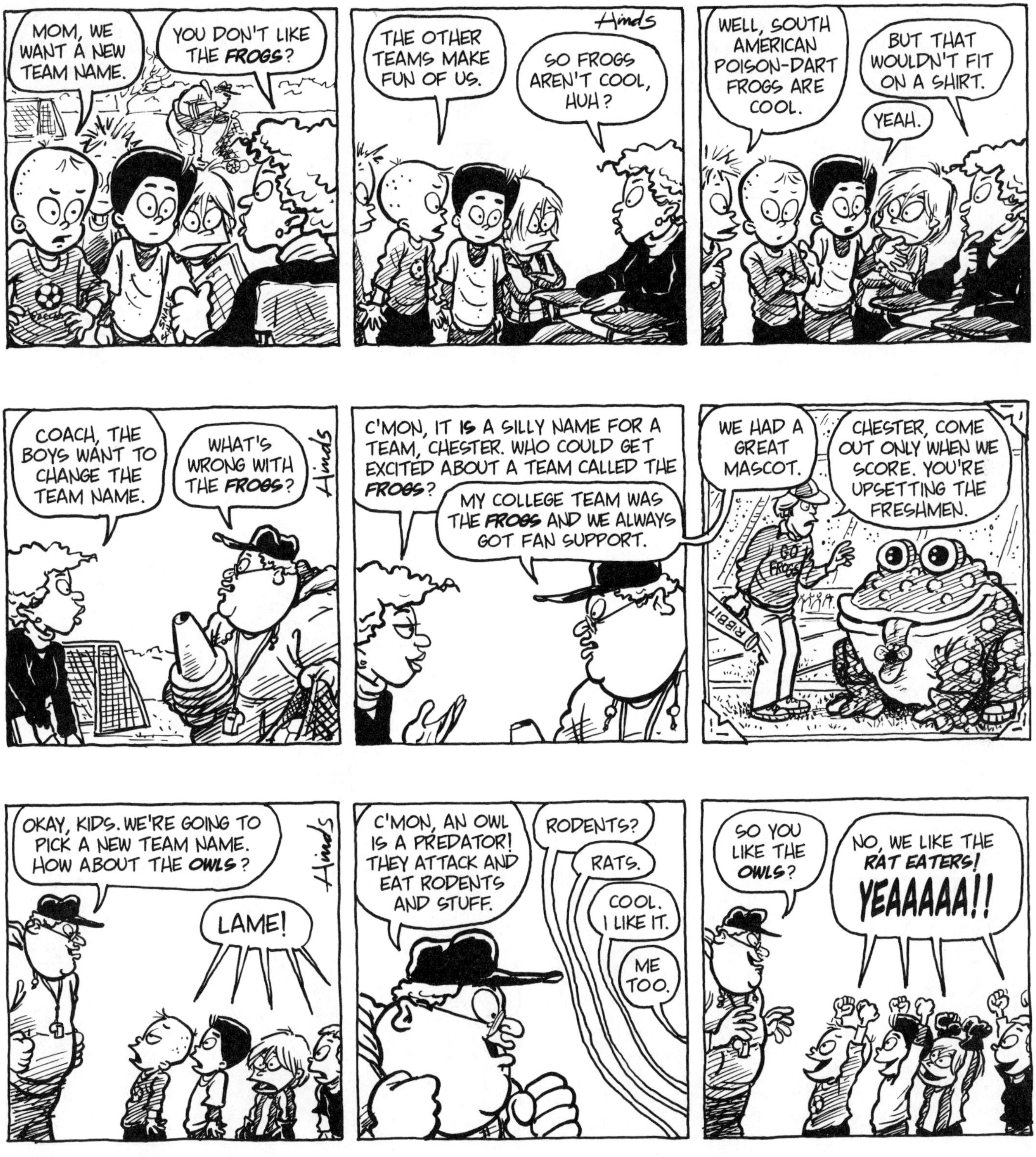

MOM, WE WANT A NEW TEAM NAME.
YOU DON'T LIKE THE FROGS?
Hinds
THE OTHER TEAMS MAKE FUN OF US.
SO FROGS AREN'T COOL, HUH?
WELL, SOUTH AMERICAN POISON-DART FROGS ARE COOL.
BUT THAT WOULDN'T FIT ON A SHIRT.
YEAH.
COACH, THE BOYS WANT TO CHANGE THE TEAM NAME.
WHAT'S WRONG WITH THE FROGS?
Hinds
C'MON, IT IS A SILLY NAME FOR A TEAM, CHESTER. WHO COULD GET EXCITED ABOUT A TEAM CALLED THE FROGS?
MY COLLEGE TEAM WAS THE FROGS AND WE ALWAYS GOT FAN SUPPORT.
WE HAD A GREAT MASCOT.
CHESTER, COME OUT ONLY WHEN WE SCORE. YOU'RE UPSETTING THE FRESHMEN.
GO FROGS
RIBBIT
OKAY, KIDS. WE'RE GOING TO PICK A NEW TEAM NAME. HOW ABOUT THE OWLS?
Hinds
LAME!
C'MON, AN OWL IS A PREDATOR! THEY ATTACK AND EAT RODENTS AND STUFF.
RODENTS?
RATS.
COOL. I LIKE IT.
ME TOO.
SO YOU LIKE THE OWLS?
NO, WE LIKE THE RAT EATERS! YEAAAAA!!

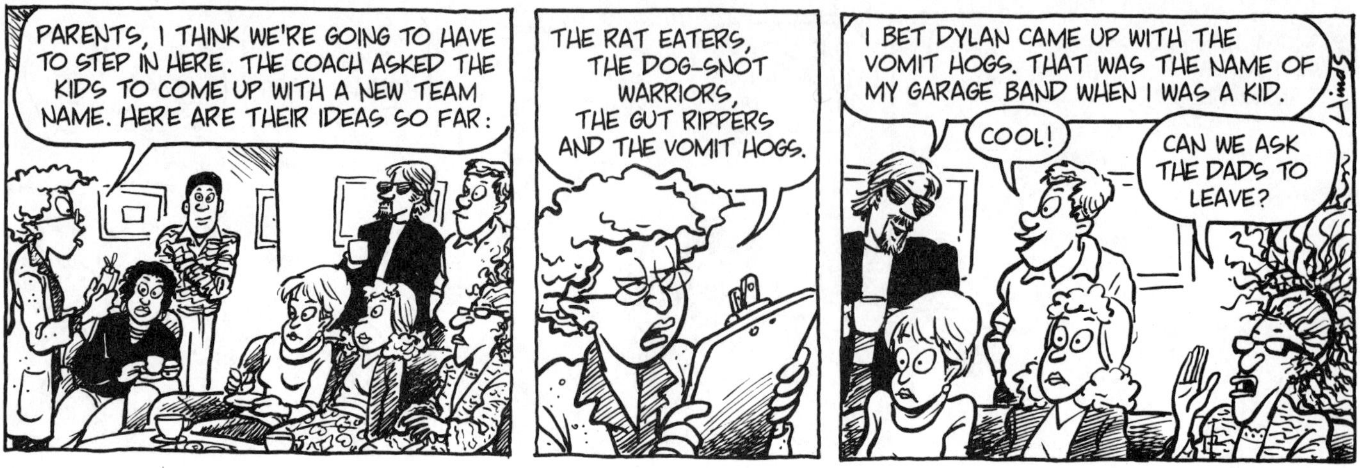
PARENTS, I THINK WE'RE GOING TO HAVE TO STEP IN HERE. THE COACH ASKED THE KIDS TO COME UP WITH A NEW TEAM NAME. HERE ARE THEIR IDEAS SO FAR:
THE RAT EATERS, THE DOG-SNOT WARRIORS, THE GUT RIPPERS AND THE VOMIT HOGS.
I BET DYLAN CAME UP WITH THE VOMIT HOGS. THAT WAS THE NAME OF MY GARAGE BAND WHEN I WAS A KID.
COOL!
CAN WE ASK THE DADS TO LEAVE?
Hinds

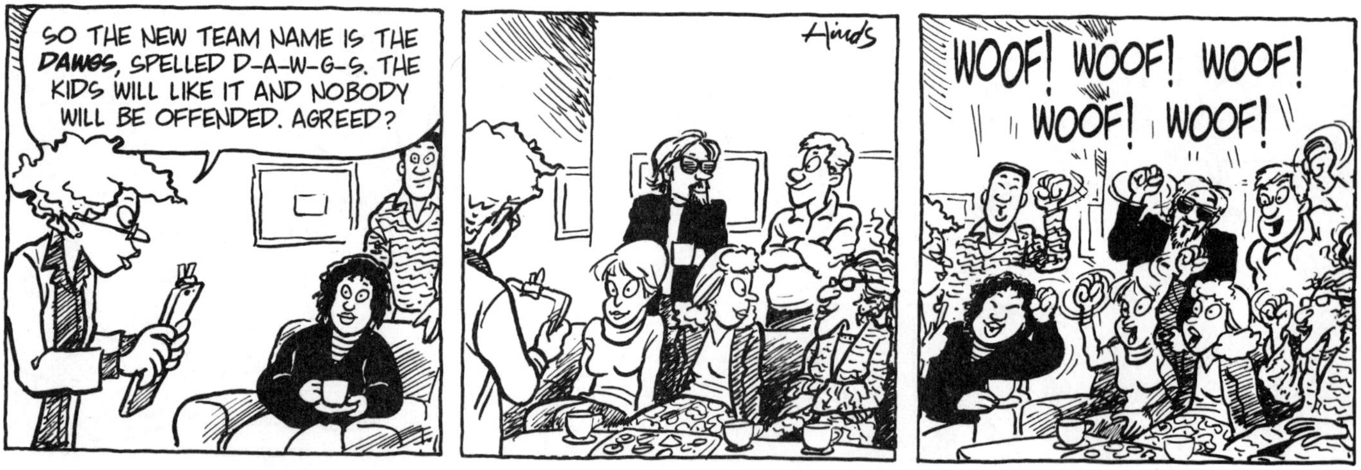
SO THE NEW TEAM NAME IS THE DAWGS, SPELLED D-A-W-G-S. THE KIDS WILL LIKE IT AND NOBODY WILL BE OFFENDED. AGREED?
Hinds
WOOF! WOOF! WOOF! WOOF! WOOF!

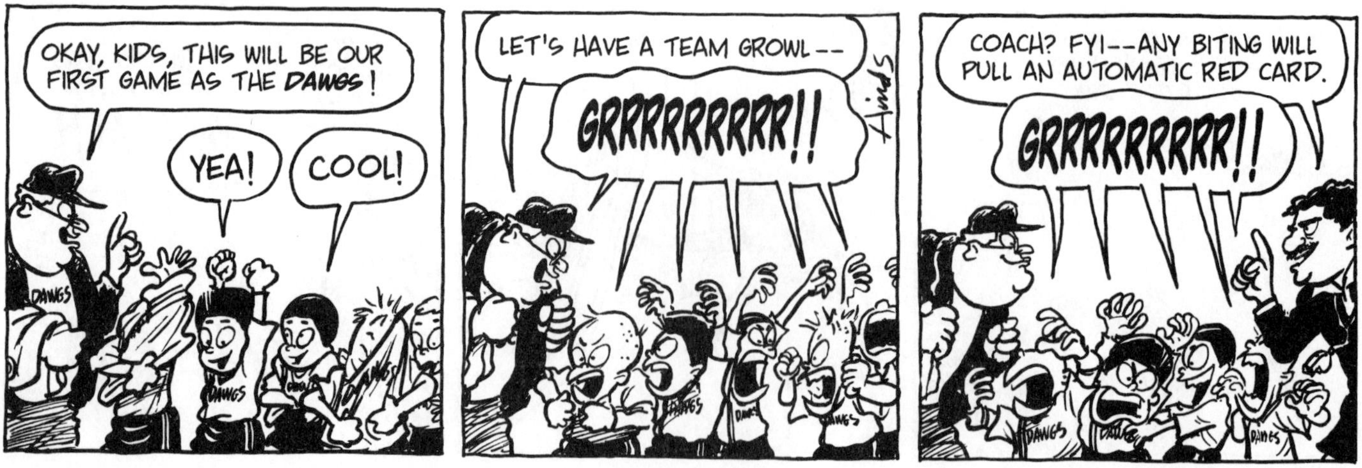
OKAY, KIDS, THIS WILL BE OUR FIRST GAME AS THE DAWGS!
YEA!
COOL!
DAWGS
LET'S HAVE A TEAM GROWL--
GRRRRRRRRR!!
Hinds
COACH? FYI--ANY BITING WILL PULL AN AUTOMATIC RED CARD.
GRRRRRRRRR!!

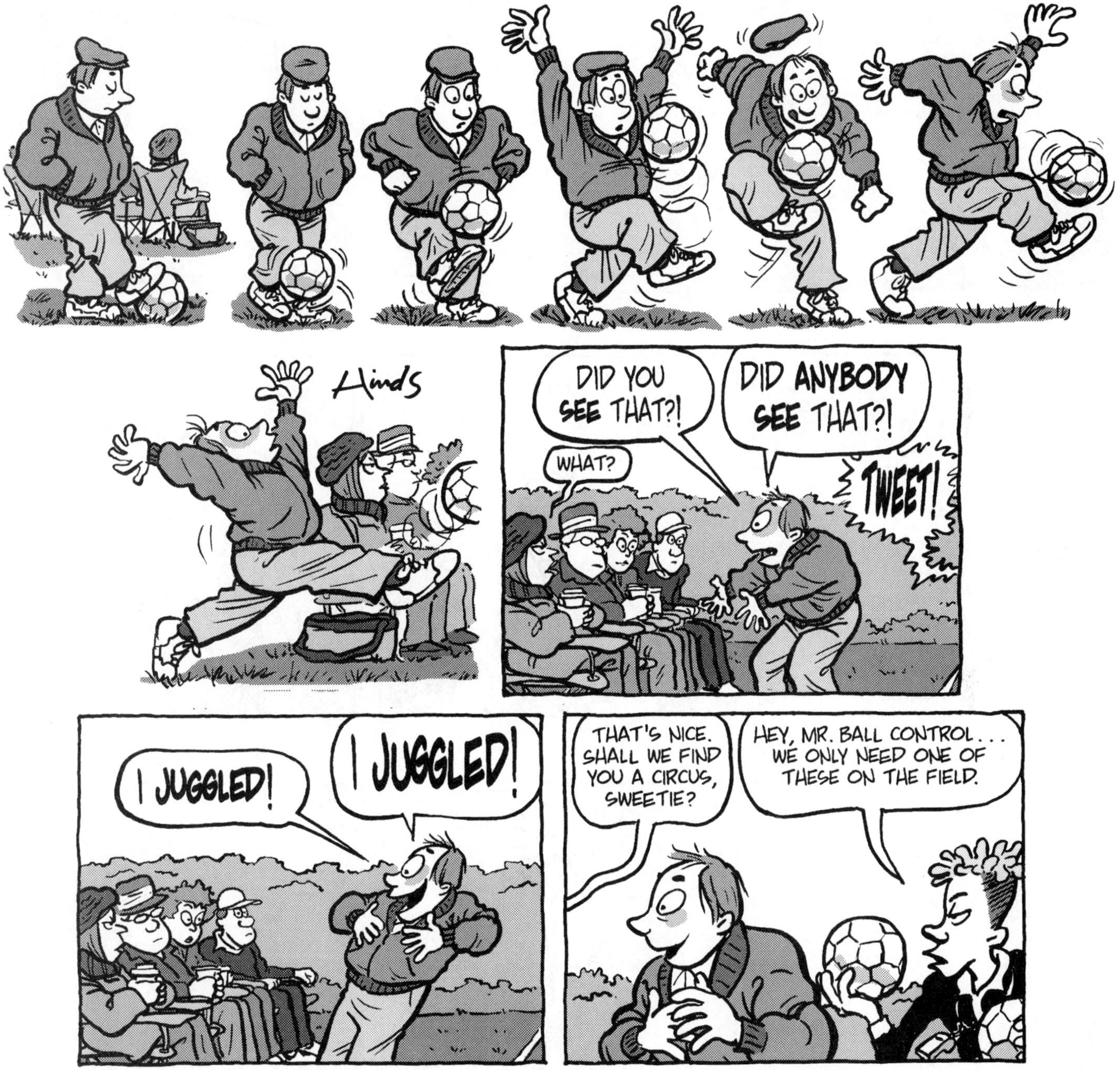
Hinds
DID YOU SEE THAT?!
DID ANYBODY SEE THAT?!
WHAT?
TWEET!
I JUGGLED!
I JUGGLED!
THAT'S NICE. SHALL WE FIND YOU A CIRCUS, SWEETIE?
HEY, MR. BALL CONTROL... WE ONLY NEED ONE OF THESE ON THE FIELD.

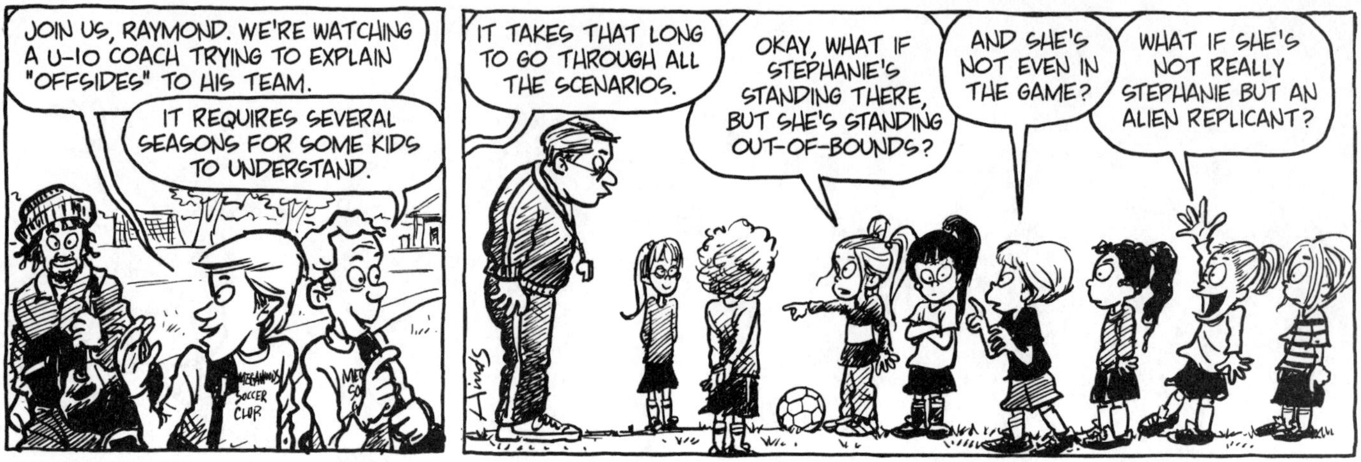
JOIN US, RAYMOND. WE'RE WATCHING A U-10 COACH TRYING TO EXPLAIN "OFFSIDES" TO HIS TEAM.
IT REQUIRES SEVERAL SEASONS FOR SOME KIDS TO UNDERSTAND.
IT TAKES THAT LONG TO GO THROUGH ALL THE SCENARIOS.
OKAY, WHAT IF STEPHANIE'S STANDING THERE, BUT SHE'S STANDING OUT-OF-BOUNDS?
AND SHE'S NOT EVEN IN THE GAME?
WHAT IF SHE'S NOT REALLY STEPHANIE BUT AN ALIEN REPLICANT?
Hinds

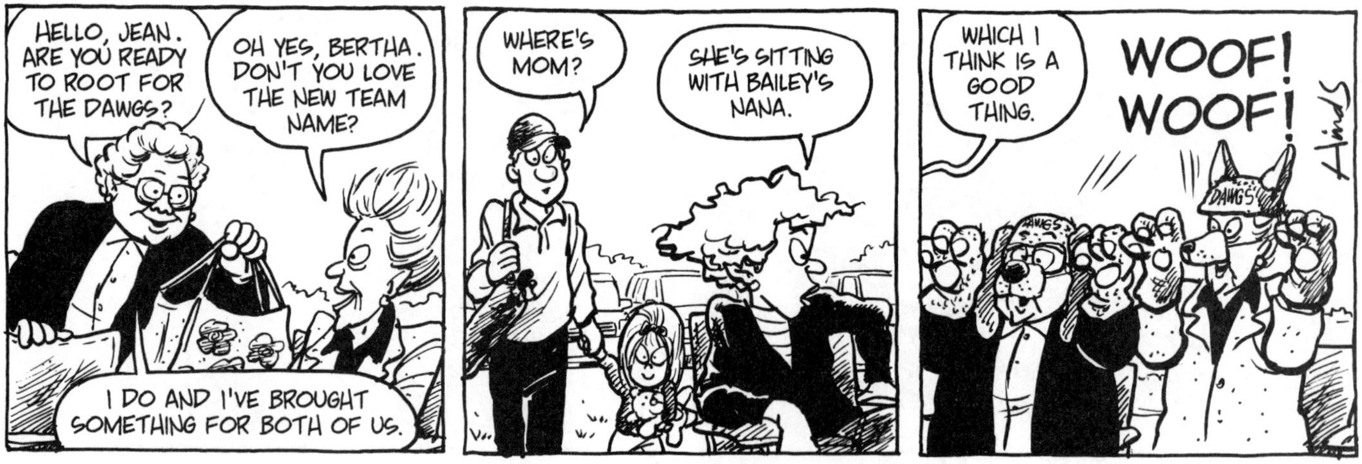
HELLO, JEAN. ARE YOU READY TO ROOT FOR THE DAWGS?
OH YES, BERTHA. DON'T YOU LOVE THE NEW TEAM NAME?
I DO AND I'VE BROUGHT SOMETHING FOR BOTH OF US.
WHERE'S MOM?
SHE'S SITTING WITH BAILEY'S NANA.
WHICH I THINK IS A GOOD THING.
WOOF! WOOF!
DAWGS
Hinds

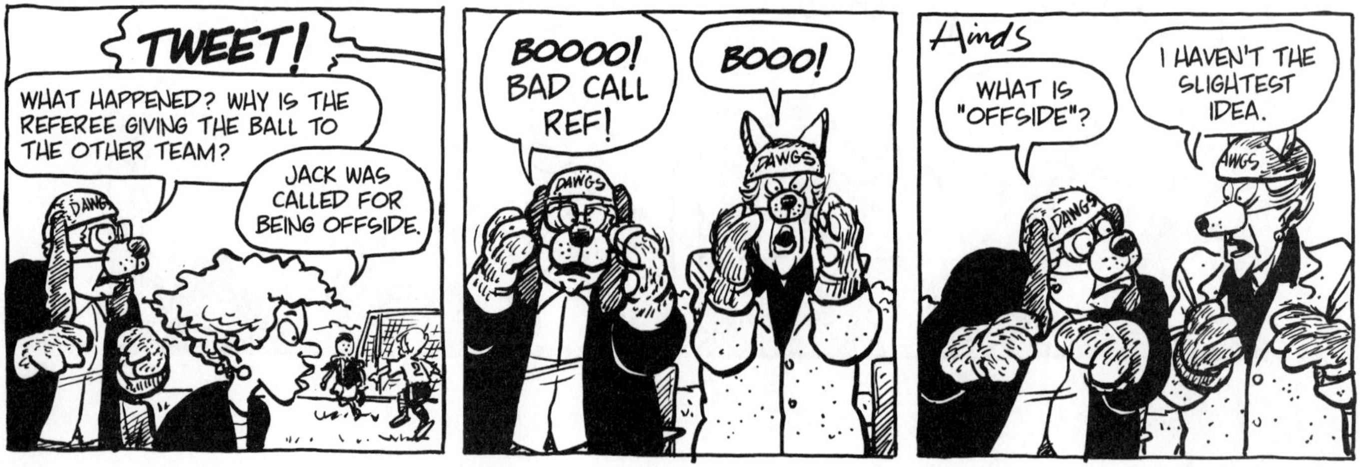
TWEET!
WHAT HAPPENED? WHY IS THE REFEREE GIVING THE BALL TO THE OTHER TEAM?
JACK WAS CALLED FOR BEING OFFSIDE.
BOOOOO! BAD CALL REF!
BOOO!
DAWGS
Hinds
WHAT IS "OFFSIDE"?
I HAVEN'T THE SLIGHTEST IDEA.

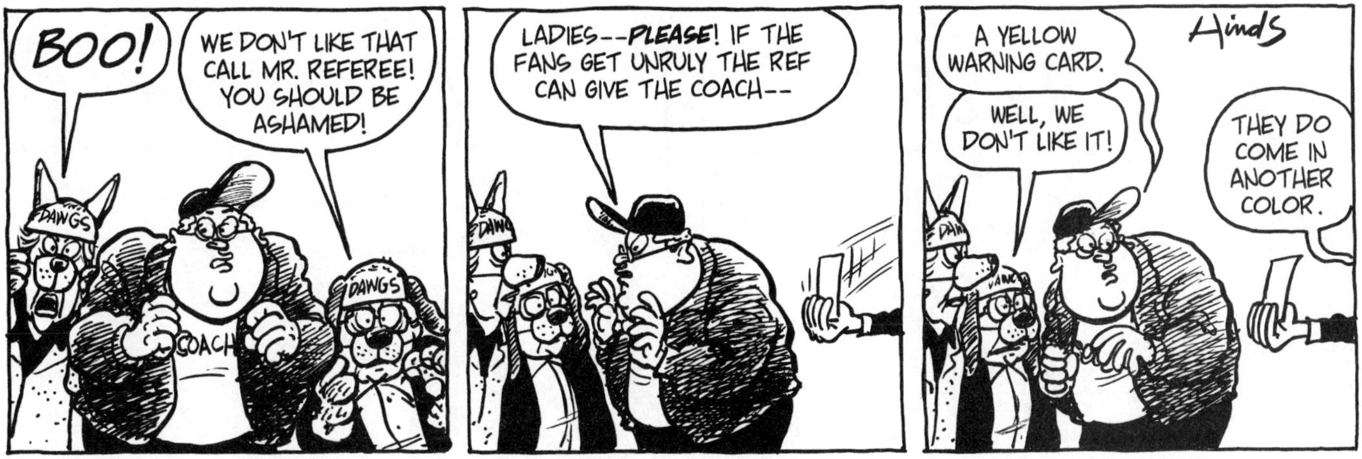
BOO!
WE DON'T LIKE THAT CALL MR. REFEREE! YOU SHOULD BE ASHAMED!
LADIES--PLEASE! IF THE FANS GET UNRULY THE REF CAN GIVE THE COACH--
A YELLOW WARNING CARD.
WELL, WE DON'T LIKE IT!
THEY DO COME IN ANOTHER COLOR.
Hinds

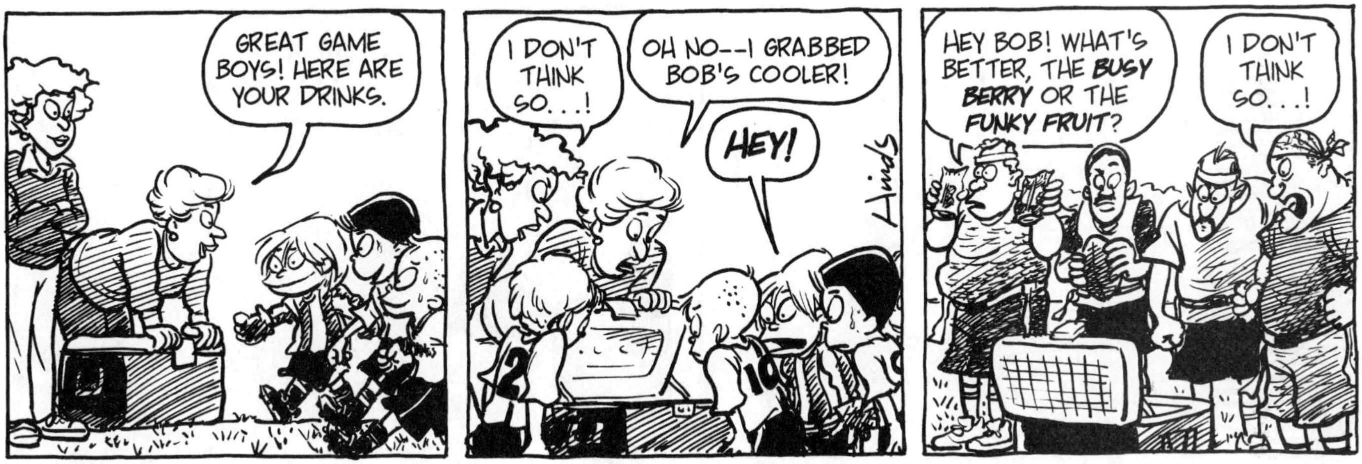
GREAT GAME BOYS! HERE ARE YOUR DRINKS.
I DON'T THINK SO...!
OH NO--I GRABBED BOB'S COOLER!
HEY!
Hinds
HEY BOB! WHAT'S BETTER, THE BUSY BERRY OR THE FUNKY FRUIT?
I DON'T THINK SO...!

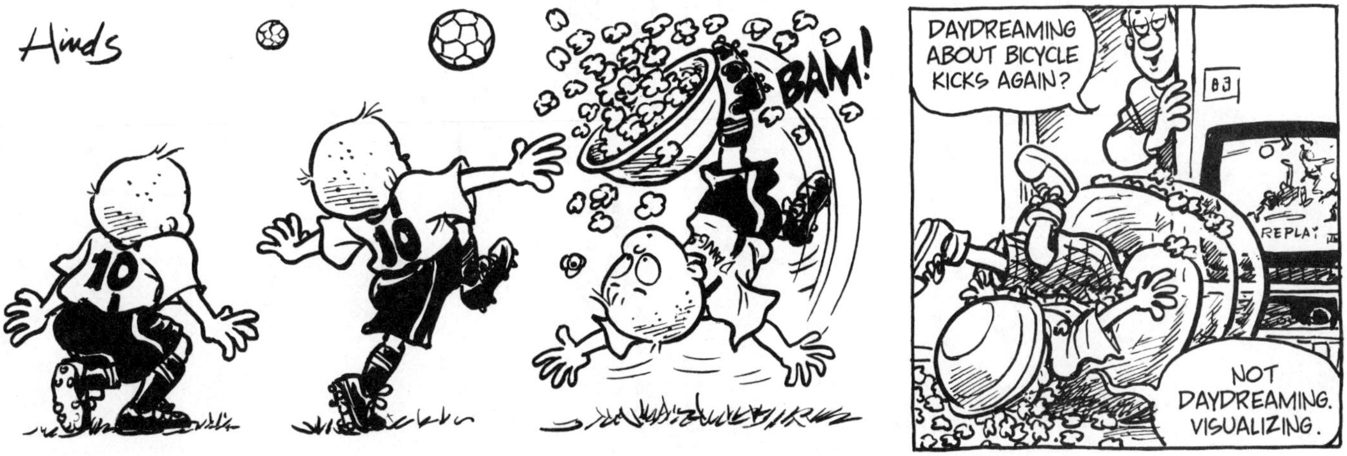
Hinds
BAM!
DAYDREAMING ABOUT BICYCLE KICKS AGAIN?
REPLAY
NOT DAYDREAMING. VISUALIZING.

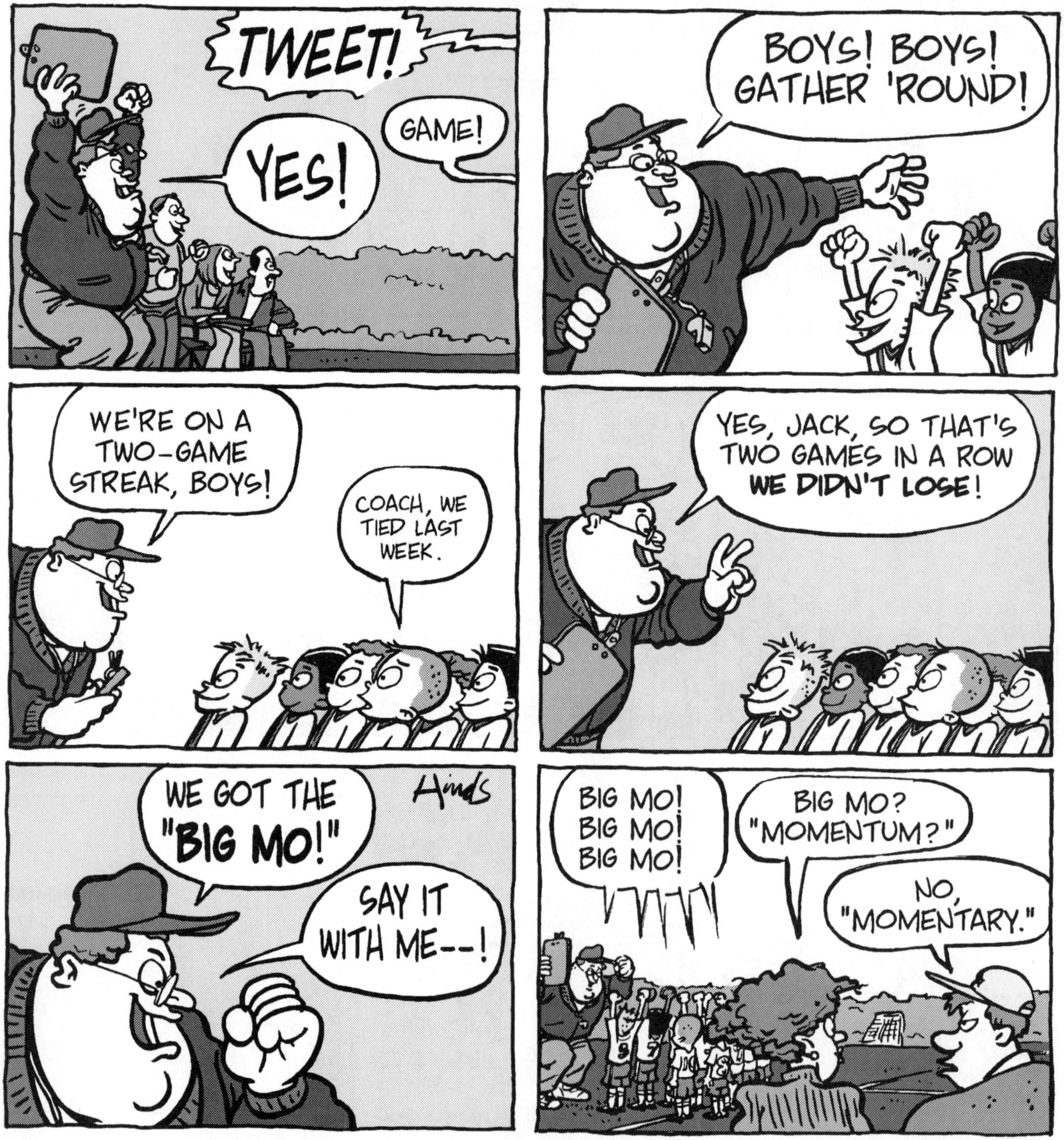
TWEET!
YES!
GAME!
BOYS! BOYS! GATHER 'ROUND!
WE'RE ON A TWO-GAME STREAK, BOYS!
COACH, WE TIED LAST WEEK.
YES, JACK, SO THAT'S TWO GAMES IN A ROW **WE DIDN'T LOSE**!
WE GOT THE "**BIG MO**!"
Hinds
SAY IT WITH ME--!
BIG MO! BIG MO! BIG MO!
BIG MO? "MOMENTUM?"
NO, "MOMENTARY."

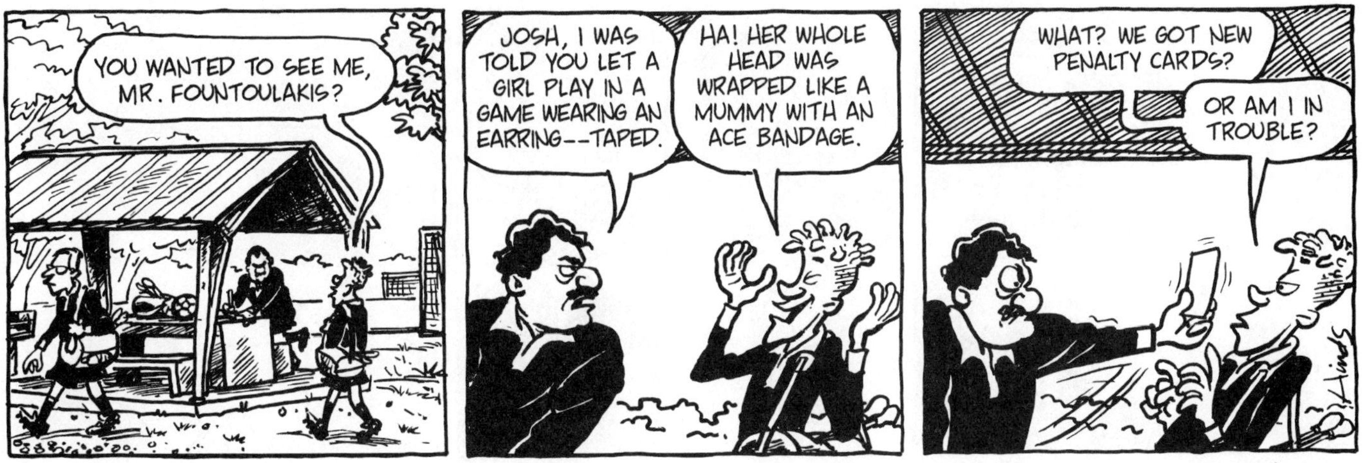
YOU WANTED TO SEE ME, MR. FOUNTOULAKIS?
JOSH, I WAS TOLD YOU LET A GIRL PLAY IN A GAME WEARING AN EARRING--TAPED.
HA! HER WHOLE HEAD WAS WRAPPED LIKE A MUMMY WITH AN ACE BANDAGE.
WHAT? WE GOT NEW PENALTY CARDS?
OR AM I IN TROUBLE?
Hinds

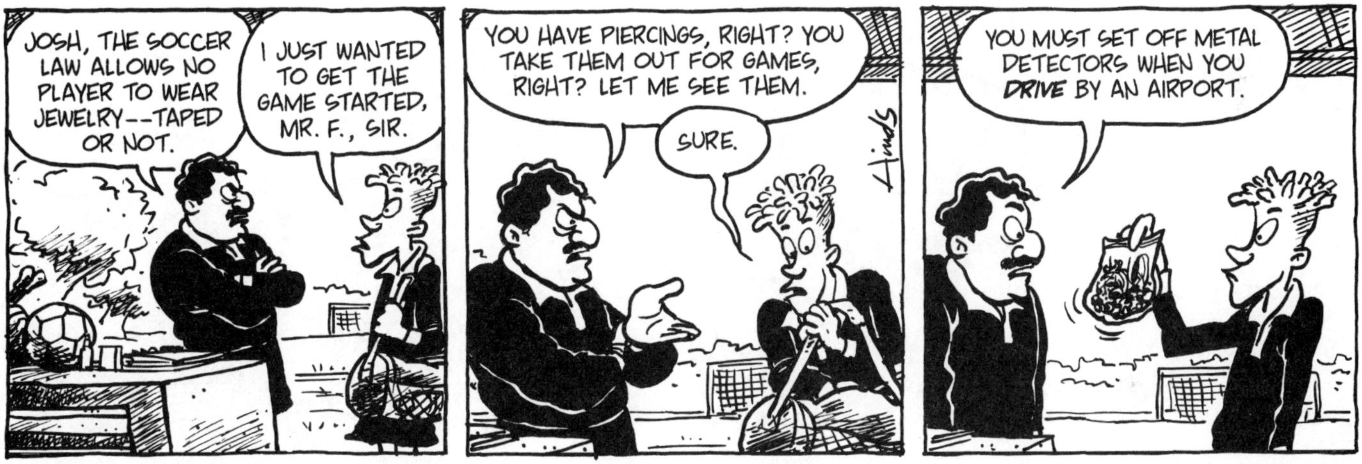
JOSH, THE SOCCER LAW ALLOWS NO PLAYER TO WEAR JEWELRY--TAPED OR NOT.
I JUST WANTED TO GET THE GAME STARTED, MR. F., SIR.
YOU HAVE PIERCINGS, RIGHT? YOU TAKE THEM OUT FOR GAMES, RIGHT? LET ME SEE THEM.
SURE.
Hinds
YOU MUST SET OFF METAL DETECTORS WHEN YOU DRIVE BY AN AIRPORT.

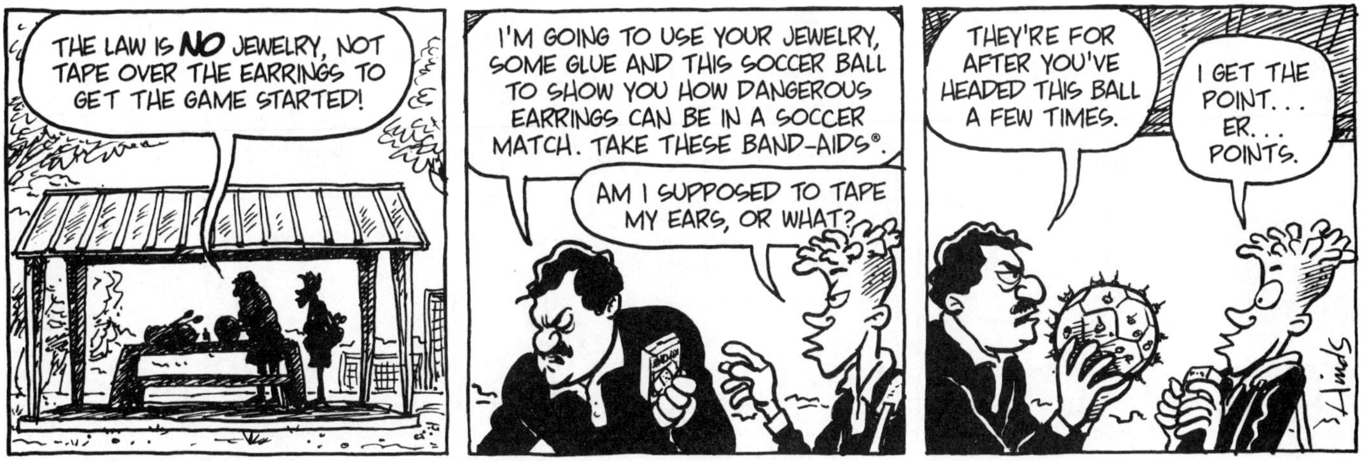
THE LAW IS NO JEWELRY, NOT TAPE OVER THE EARRINGS TO GET THE GAME STARTED!
I'M GOING TO USE YOUR JEWELRY, SOME GLUE AND THIS SOCCER BALL TO SHOW YOU HOW DANGEROUS EARRINGS CAN BE IN A SOCCER MATCH. TAKE THESE BAND-AIDS®.
AM I SUPPOSED TO TAPE MY EARS, OR WHAT?
THEY'RE FOR AFTER YOU'VE HEADED THIS BALL A FEW TIMES.
I GET THE POINT... ER... POINTS.
Hinds

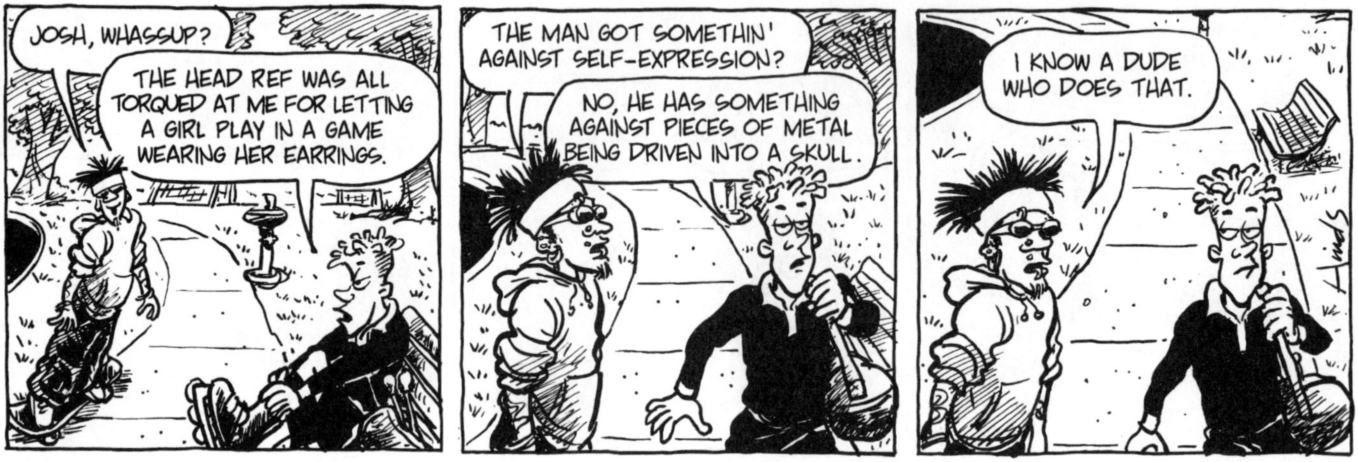
JOSH, WHASSUP?
THE HEAD REF WAS ALL TORQUED AT ME FOR LETTING A GIRL PLAY IN A GAME WEARING HER EARRINGS.
THE MAN GOT SOMETHIN' AGAINST SELF-EXPRESSION?
NO, HE HAS SOMETHING AGAINST PIECES OF METAL BEING DRIVEN INTO A SKULL.
I KNOW A DUDE WHO DOES THAT.
Hinds

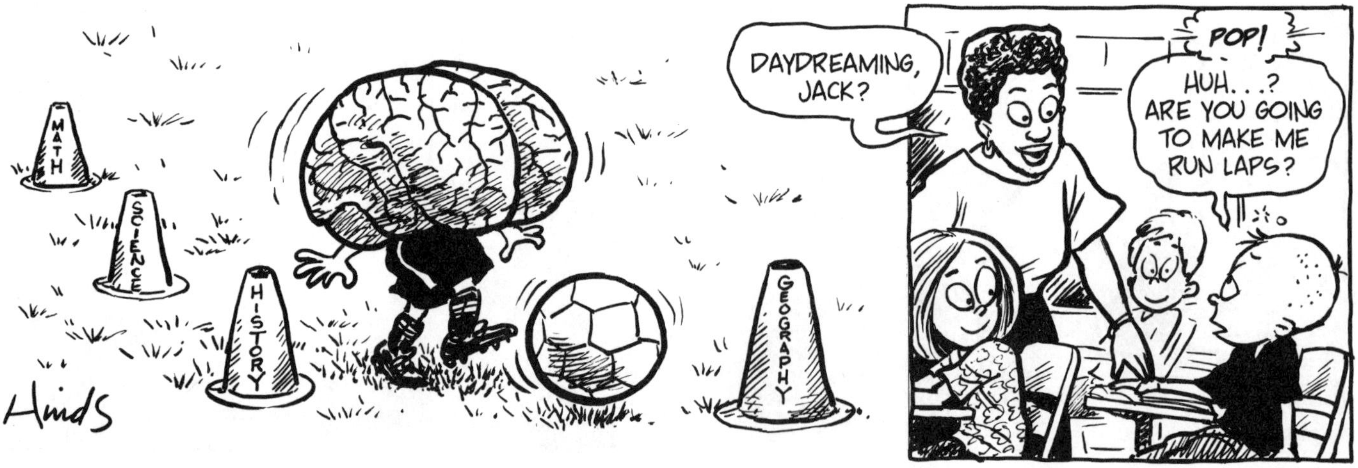
MATH
SCIENCE
HISTORY
GEOGRAPHY
Hinds
DAYDREAMING, JACK?
POP!
HUH. . .? ARE YOU GOING TO MAKE ME RUN LAPS?

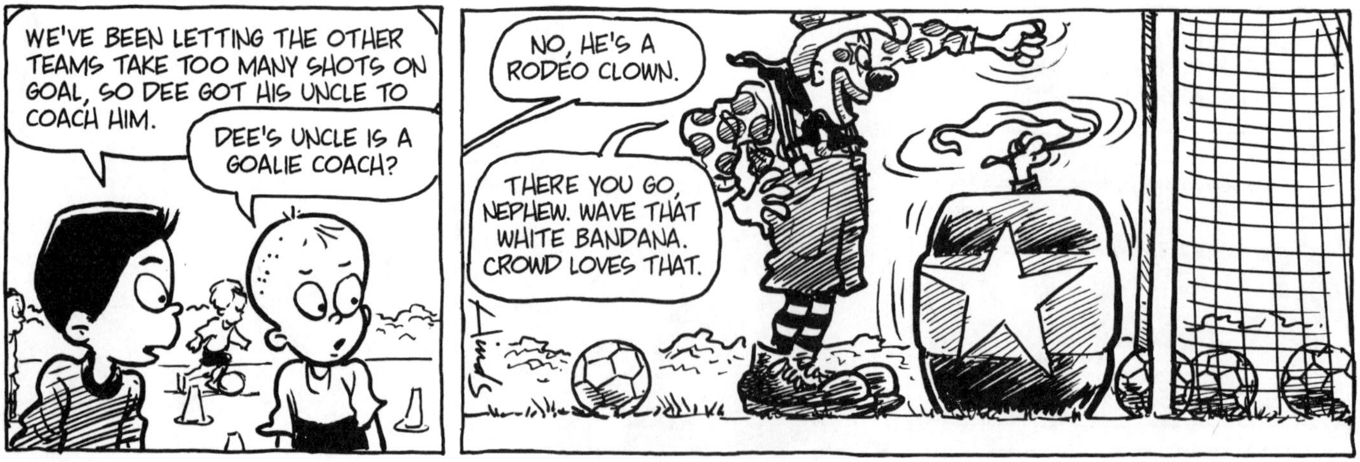
WE'VE BEEN LETTING THE OTHER TEAMS TAKE TOO MANY SHOTS ON GOAL, SO DEE GOT HIS UNCLE TO COACH HIM.
DEE'S UNCLE IS A GOALIE COACH?
NO, HE'S A RODEO CLOWN.
THERE YOU GO, NEPHEW. WAVE THAT WHITE BANDANA. CROWD LOVES THAT.
Hinds

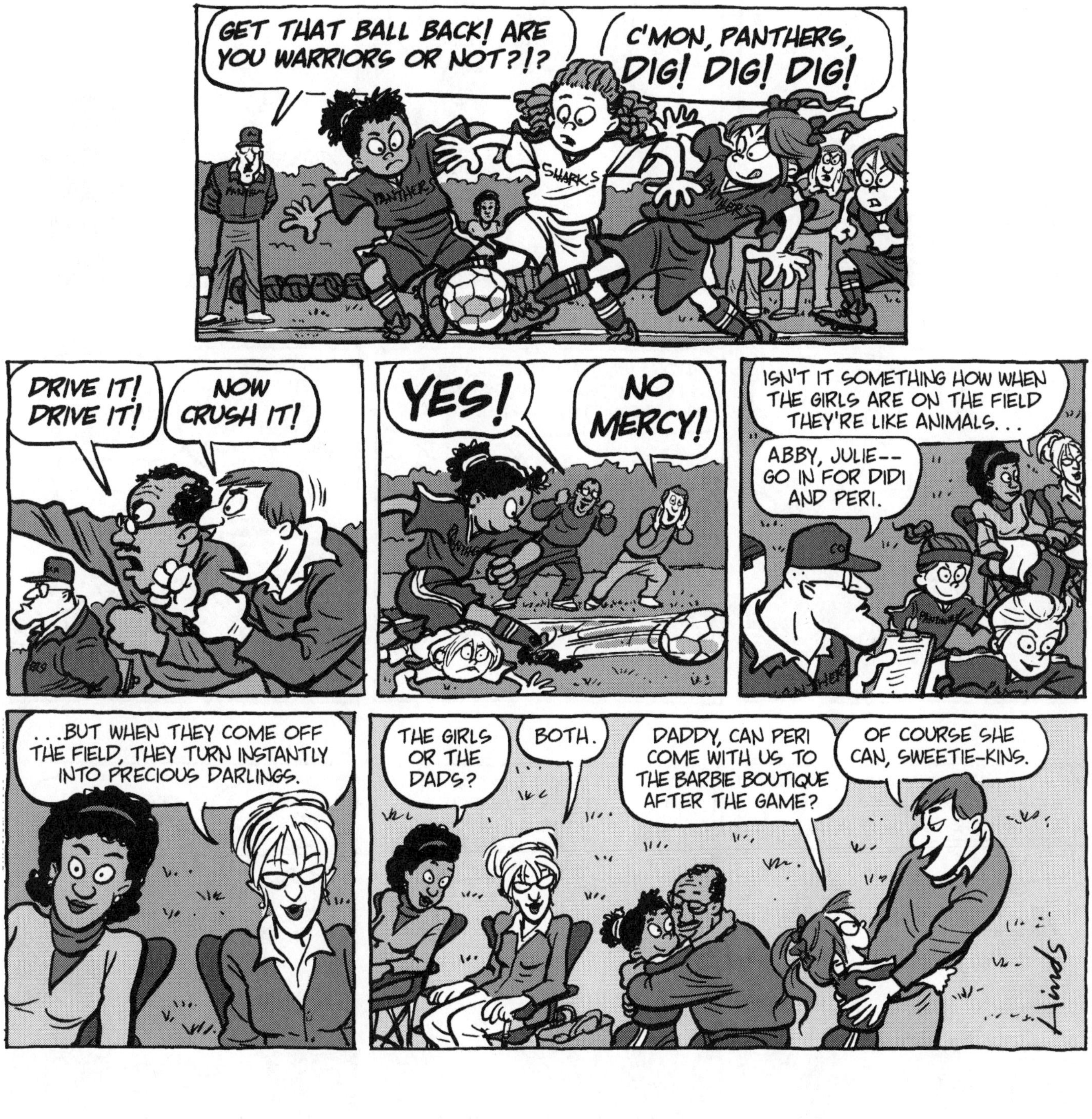
GET THAT BALL BACK! ARE YOU WARRIORS OR NOT?!?
C'MON, PANTHERS, DIG! DIG! DIG!
SHARKS
PANTHERS
DRIVE IT! DRIVE IT!
NOW CRUSH IT!
YES!
NO MERCY!
ISN'T IT SOMETHING HOW WHEN THE GIRLS ARE ON THE FIELD THEY'RE LIKE ANIMALS...
ABBY, JULIE-- GO IN FOR DIDI AND PERI.
...BUT WHEN THEY COME OFF THE FIELD, THEY TURN INSTANTLY INTO PRECIOUS DARLINGS.
THE GIRLS OR THE DADS?
BOTH.
DADDY, CAN PERI COME WITH US TO THE BARBIE BOUTIQUE AFTER THE GAME?
OF COURSE SHE CAN, SWEETIE-KINS.
Hinds

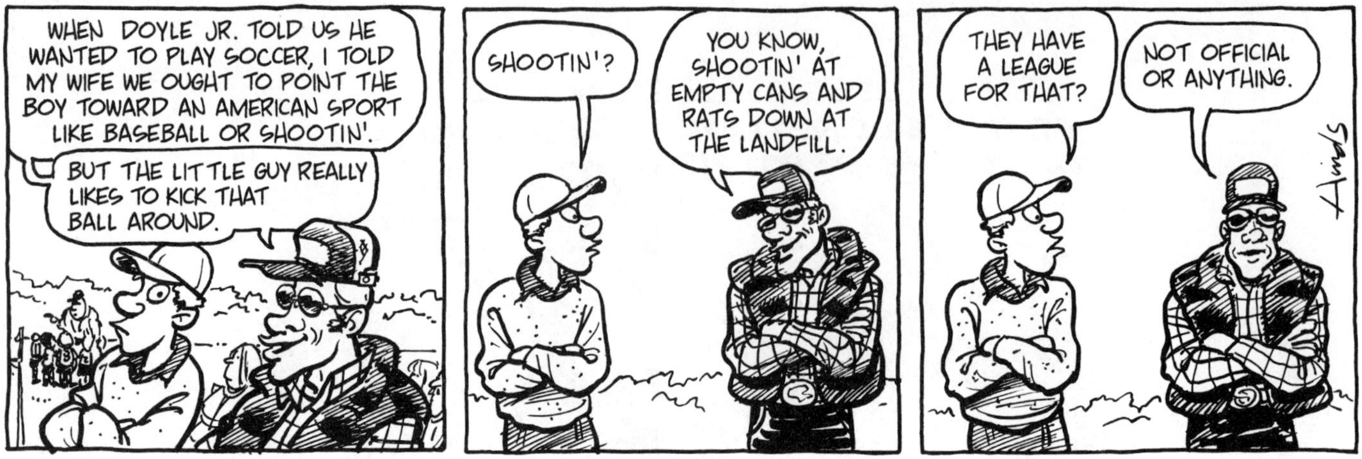
WHEN DOYLE JR. TOLD US HE WANTED TO PLAY SOCCER, I TOLD MY WIFE WE OUGHT TO POINT THE BOY TOWARD AN AMERICAN SPORT LIKE BASEBALL OR SHOOTIN'.
BUT THE LITTLE GUY REALLY LIKES TO KICK THAT BALL AROUND.
SHOOTIN'?
YOU KNOW, SHOOTIN' AT EMPTY CANS AND RATS DOWN AT THE LANDFILL.
THEY HAVE A LEAGUE FOR THAT?
NOT OFFICIAL OR ANYTHING.

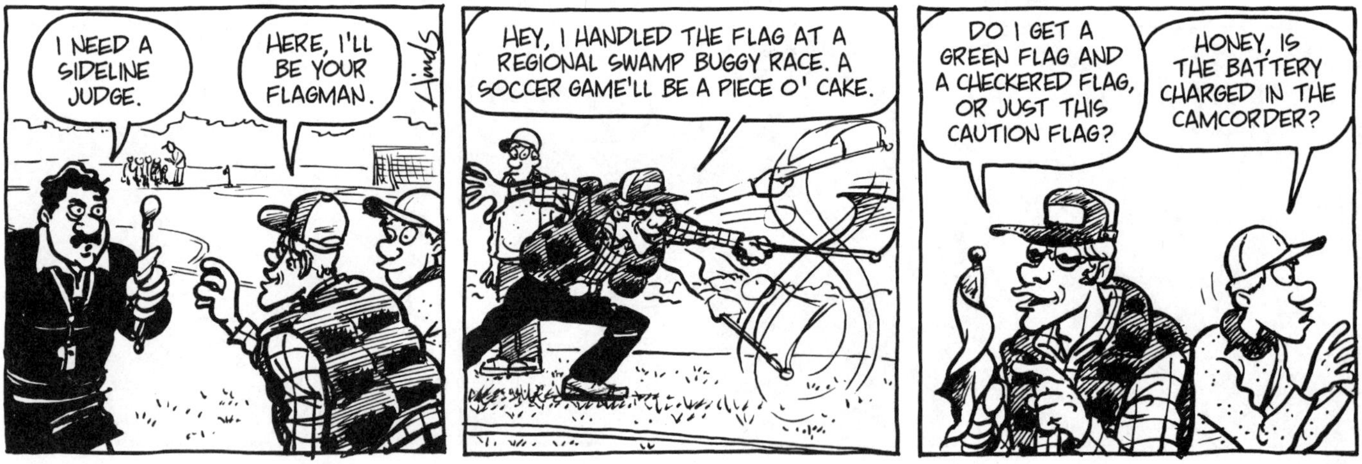
I NEED A SIDELINE JUDGE.
HERE, I'LL BE YOUR FLAGMAN.
HEY, I HANDLED THE FLAG AT A REGIONAL SWAMP BUGGY RACE. A SOCCER GAME'LL BE A PIECE O' CAKE.
DO I GET A GREEN FLAG AND A CHECKERED FLAG, OR JUST THIS CAUTION FLAG?
HONEY, IS THE BATTERY CHARGED IN THE CAMCORDER?

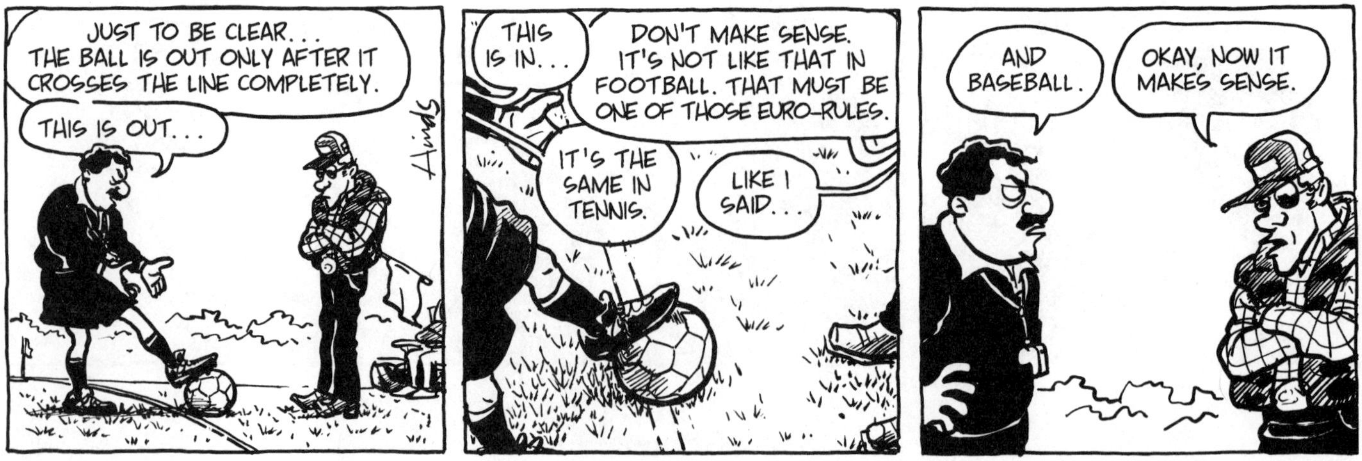
JUST TO BE CLEAR... THE BALL IS OUT ONLY AFTER IT CROSSES THE LINE COMPLETELY.
THIS IS OUT...
THIS IS IN...
DON'T MAKE SENSE. IT'S NOT LIKE THAT IN FOOTBALL. THAT MUST BE ONE OF THOSE EURO-RULES.
IT'S THE SAME IN TENNIS.
LIKE I SAID...
AND BASEBALL.
OKAY, NOW IT MAKES SENSE.

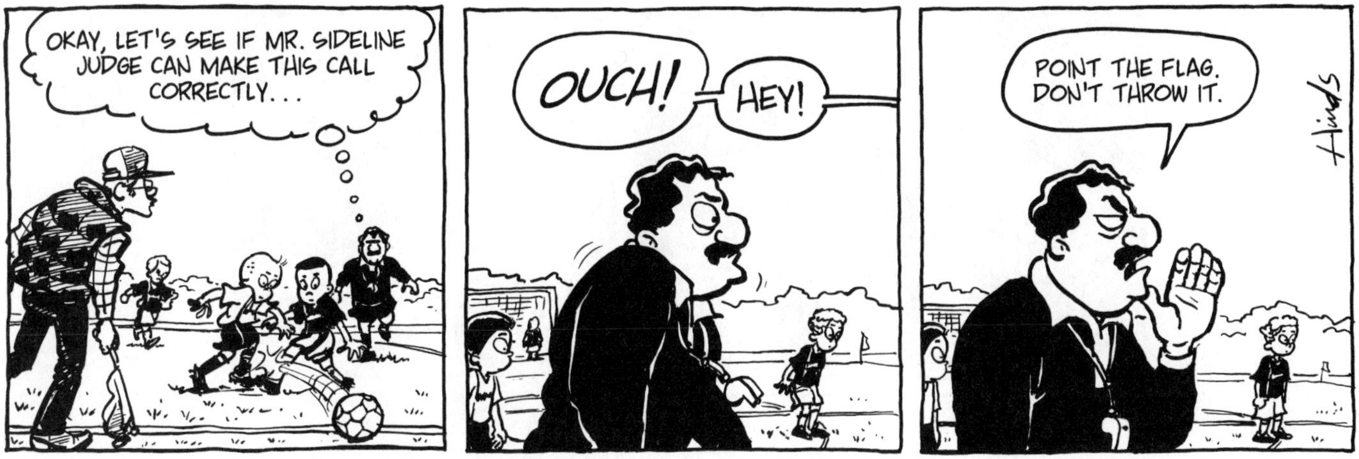
OKAY, LET'S SEE IF MR. SIDELINE JUDGE CAN MAKE THIS CALL CORRECTLY...
OUCH!
HEY!
POINT THE FLAG. DON'T THROW IT.
Hinds

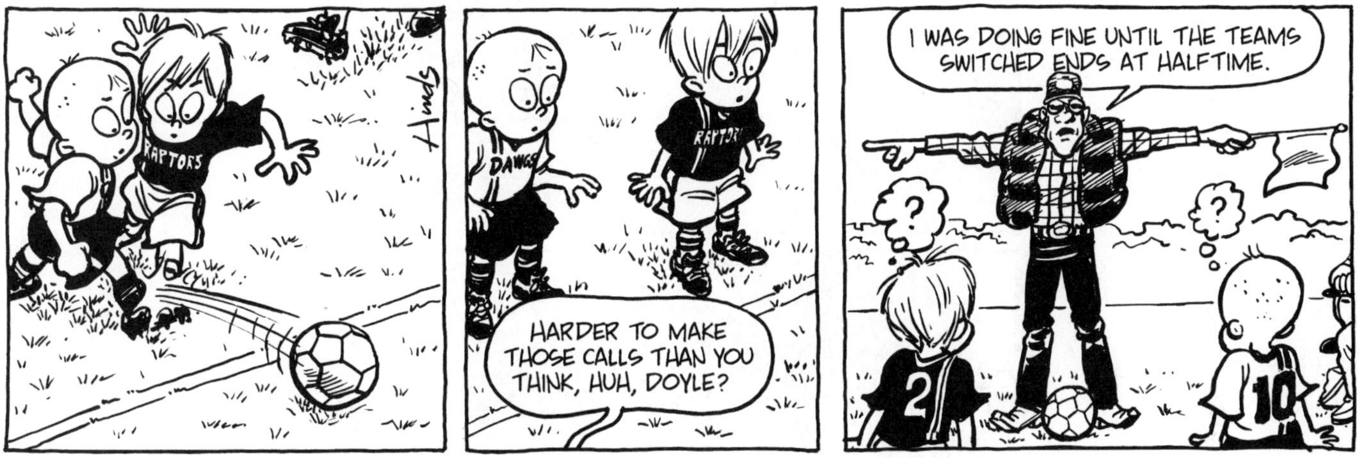
RAPTORS
Hinds
DAWGS
HARDER TO MAKE THOSE CALLS THAN YOU THINK, HUH, DOYLE?
I WAS DOING FINE UNTIL THE TEAMS SWITCHED ENDS AT HALFTIME.
?
?
2
10

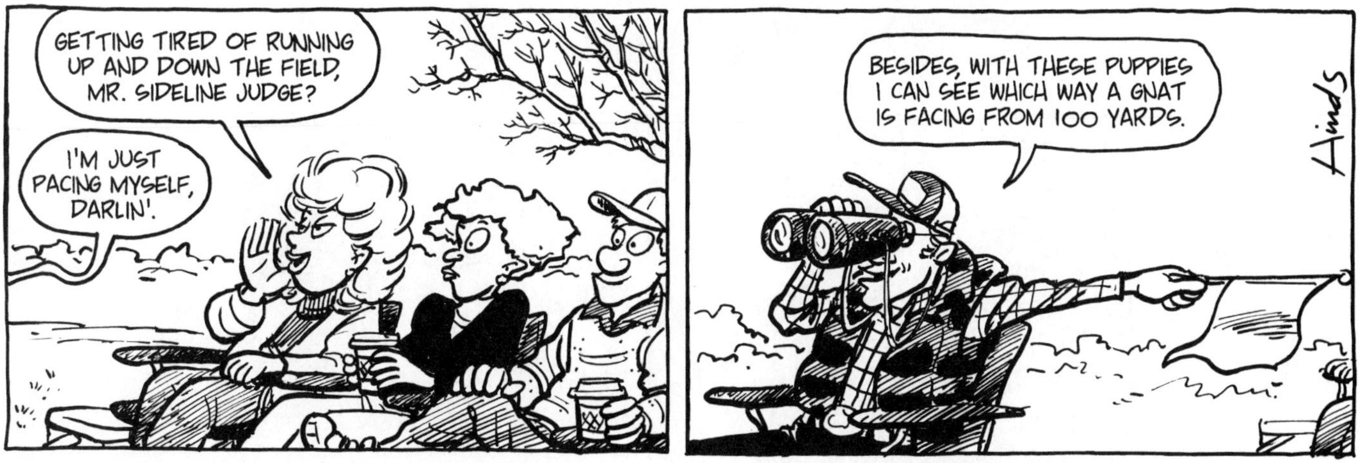
GETTING TIRED OF RUNNING UP AND DOWN THE FIELD, MR. SIDELINE JUDGE?
I'M JUST PACING MYSELF, DARLIN'.
BESIDES, WITH THESE PUPPIES I CAN SEE WHICH WAY A GNAT IS FACING FROM 100 YARDS.
Hinds

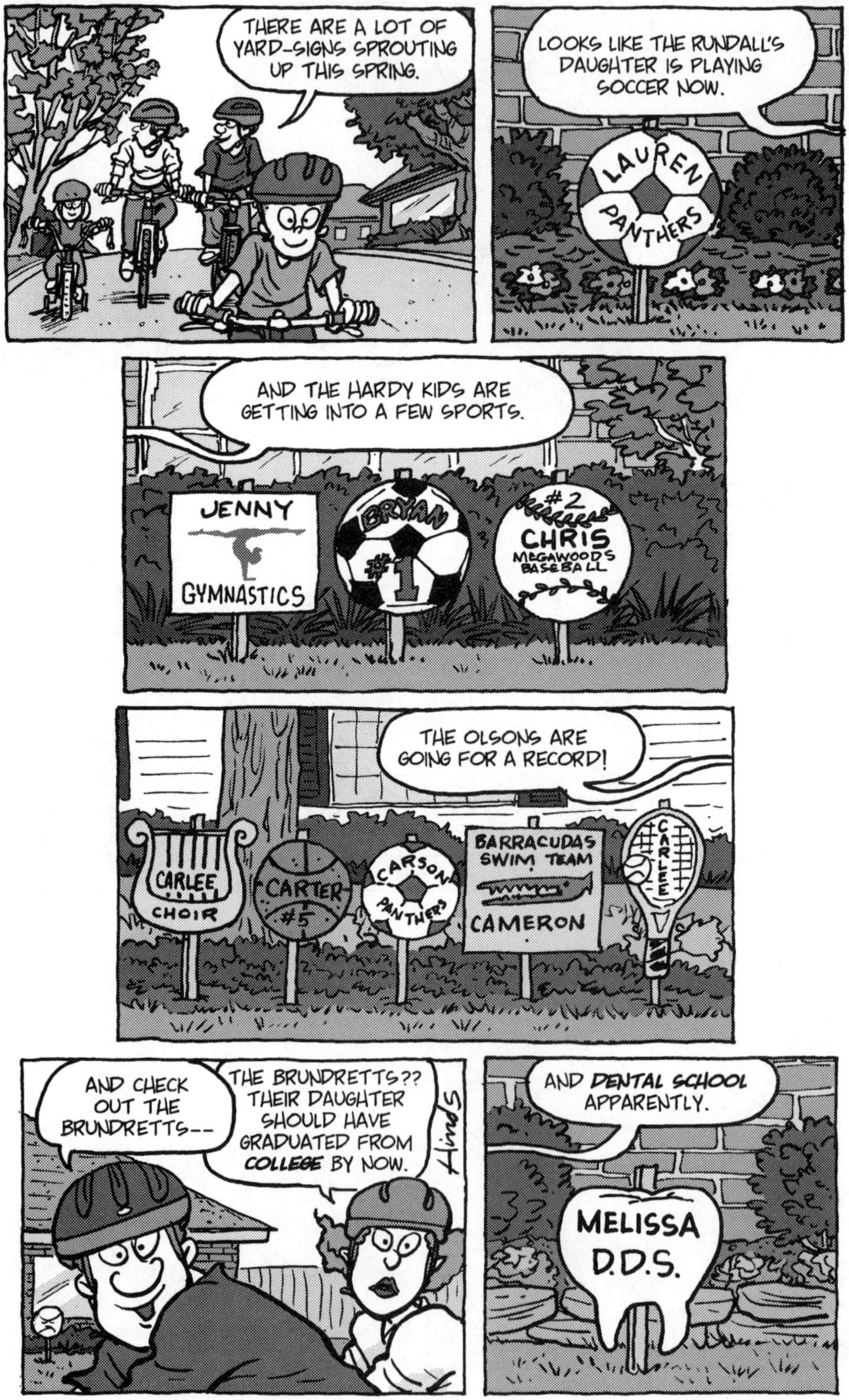
THERE ARE A LOT OF YARD-SIGNS SPROUTING UP THIS SPRING.
LOOKS LIKE THE RUNDALL'S DAUGHTER IS PLAYING SOCCER NOW.
LAUREN PANTHERS
AND THE HARDY KIDS ARE GETTING INTO A FEW SPORTS.
JENNY GYMNASTICS
BRYAN #1
#2 CHRIS MEGAWOODS BASEBALL
THE OLSONS ARE GOING FOR A RECORD!
CARLEE CHOIR
CARTER #5
CARSON PANTHERS
BARRACUDAS SWIM TEAM CAMERON
CARLEE
AND CHECK OUT THE BRUNDRETTS--
THE BRUNDRETTS?? THEIR DAUGHTER SHOULD HAVE GRADUATED FROM COLLEGE BY NOW.
Hinds
AND DENTAL SCHOOL APPARENTLY.
MELISSA D.D.S.

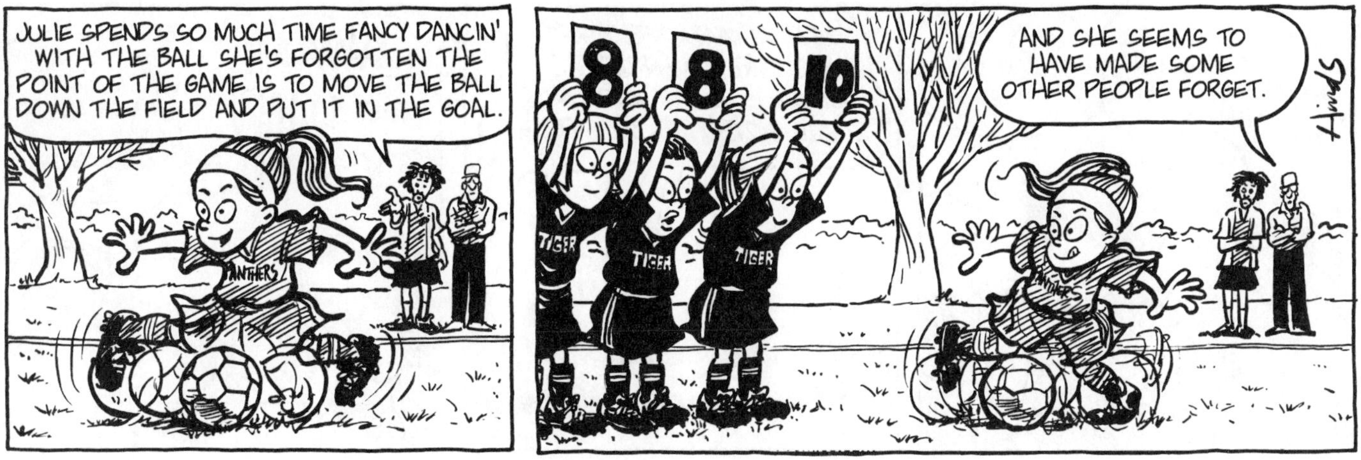
JULIE SPENDS SO MUCH TIME FANCY DANCIN' WITH THE BALL SHE'S FORGOTTEN THE POINT OF THE GAME IS TO MOVE THE BALL DOWN THE FIELD AND PUT IT IN THE GOAL.
8
8
10
AND SHE SEEMS TO HAVE MADE SOME OTHER PEOPLE FORGET.
Hinds

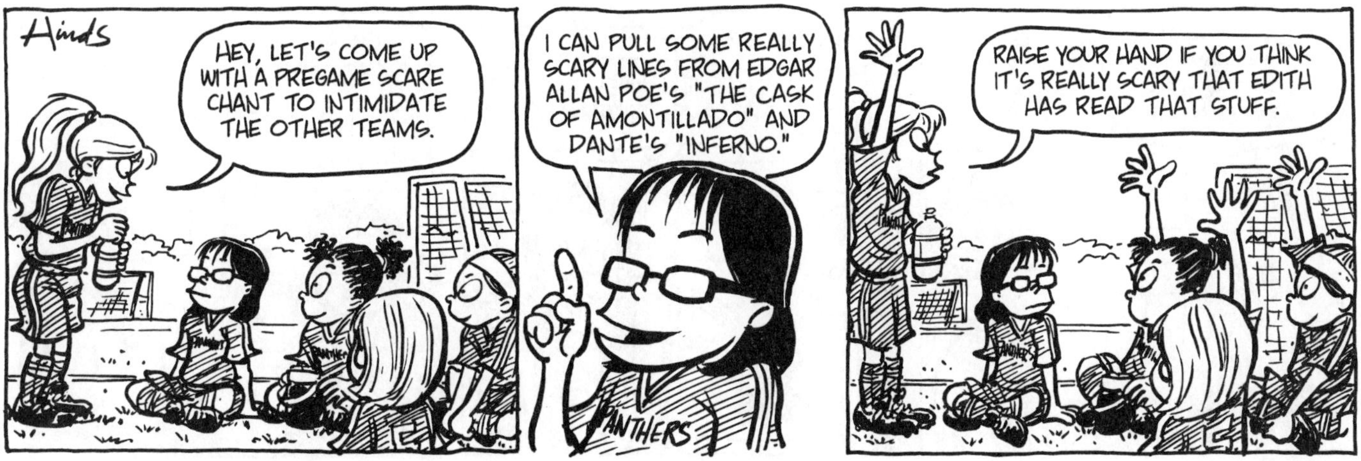
Hinds
HEY, LET'S COME UP WITH A PREGAME SCARE CHANT TO INTIMIDATE THE OTHER TEAMS.
I CAN PULL SOME REALLY SCARY LINES FROM EDGAR ALLAN POE'S "THE CASK OF AMONTILLADO" AND DANTE'S "INFERNO."
RAISE YOUR HAND IF YOU THINK IT'S REALLY SCARY THAT EDITH HAS READ THAT STUFF.

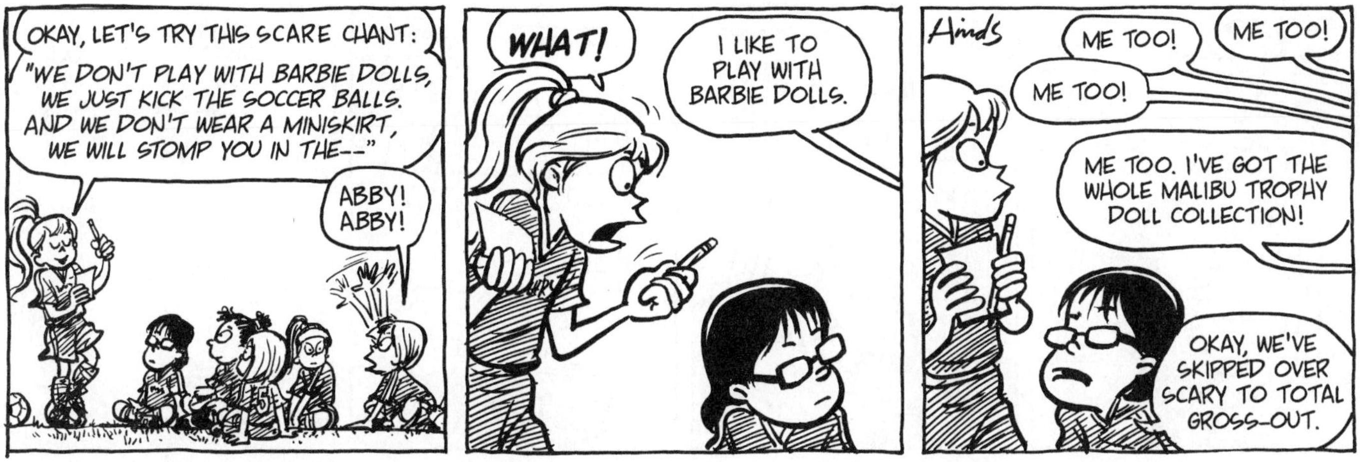
OKAY, LET'S TRY THIS SCARE CHANT:
"WE DON'T PLAY WITH BARBIE DOLLS, WE JUST KICK THE SOCCER BALLS. AND WE DON'T WEAR A MINISKIRT, WE WILL STOMP YOU IN THE--"
ABBY! ABBY!
WHAT!
I LIKE TO PLAY WITH BARBIE DOLLS.
Hinds
ME TOO!
ME TOO!
ME TOO!
ME TOO. I'VE GOT THE WHOLE MALIBU TROPHY DOLL COLLECTION!
OKAY, WE'VE SKIPPED OVER SCARY TO TOTAL GROSS-OUT.

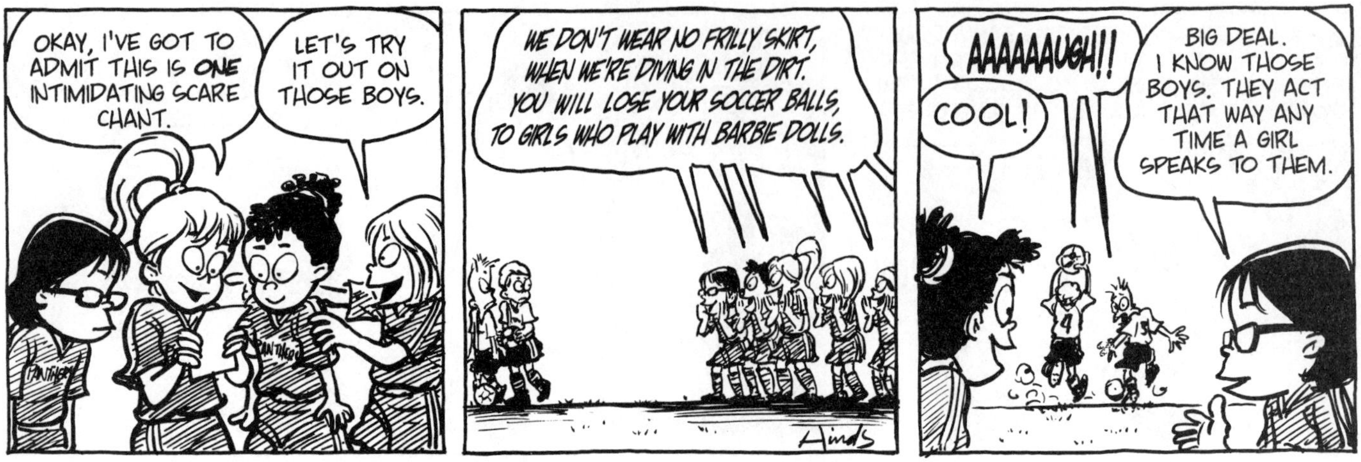
OKAY, I'VE GOT TO ADMIT THIS IS ONE INTIMIDATING SCARE CHANT.
LET'S TRY IT OUT ON THOSE BOYS.
WE DON'T WEAR NO FRILLY SKIRT, WHEN WE'RE DIVING IN THE DIRT. YOU WILL LOSE YOUR SOCCER BALLS, TO GIRLS WHO PLAY WITH BARBIE DOLLS.
Hinds
AAAAAAUGH!!
COOL!
BIG DEAL. I KNOW THOSE BOYS. THEY ACT THAT WAY ANY TIME A GIRL SPEAKS TO THEM.

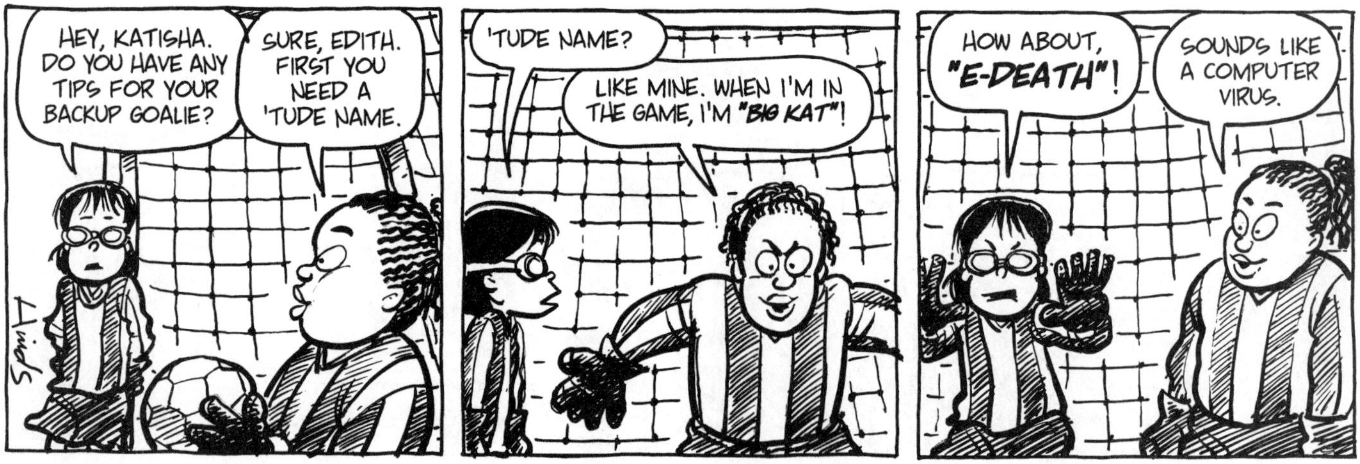
HEY, KATISHA. DO YOU HAVE ANY TIPS FOR YOUR BACKUP GOALIE?
SURE, EDITH. FIRST YOU NEED A 'TUDE NAME.
Hinds
'TUDE NAME?
LIKE MINE. WHEN I'M IN THE GAME, I'M "BIG KAT"!
HOW ABOUT, "E-DEATH"!
SOUNDS LIKE A COMPUTER VIRUS.

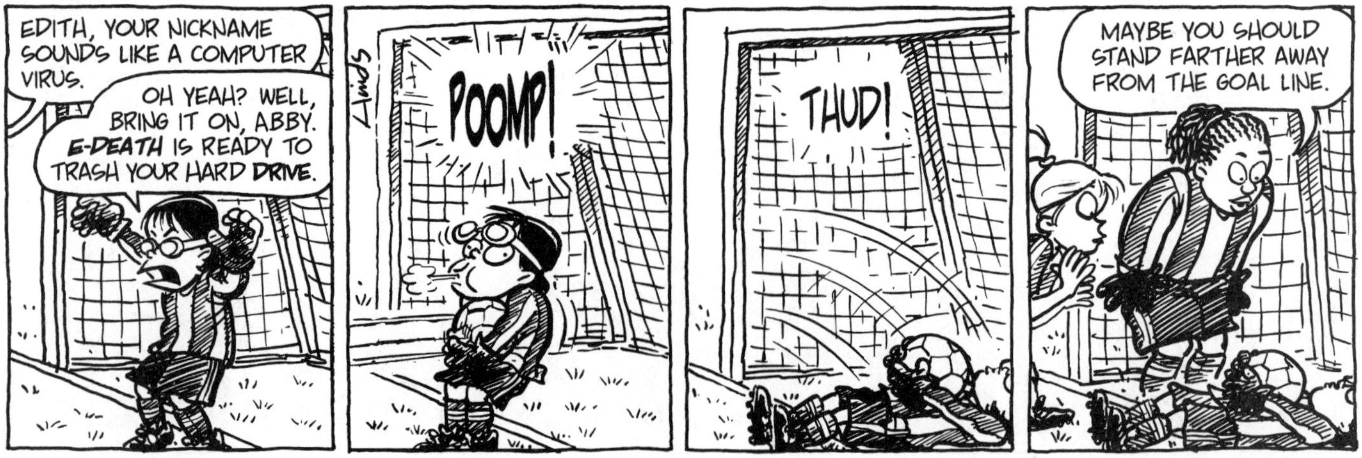
EDITH, YOUR NICKNAME SOUNDS LIKE A COMPUTER VIRUS.
OH YEAH? WELL, BRING IT ON, ABBY. E-DEATH IS READY TO TRASH YOUR HARD DRIVE.
Hinds
POOMP!
THUD!
MAYBE YOU SHOULD STAND FARTHER AWAY FROM THE GOAL LINE.

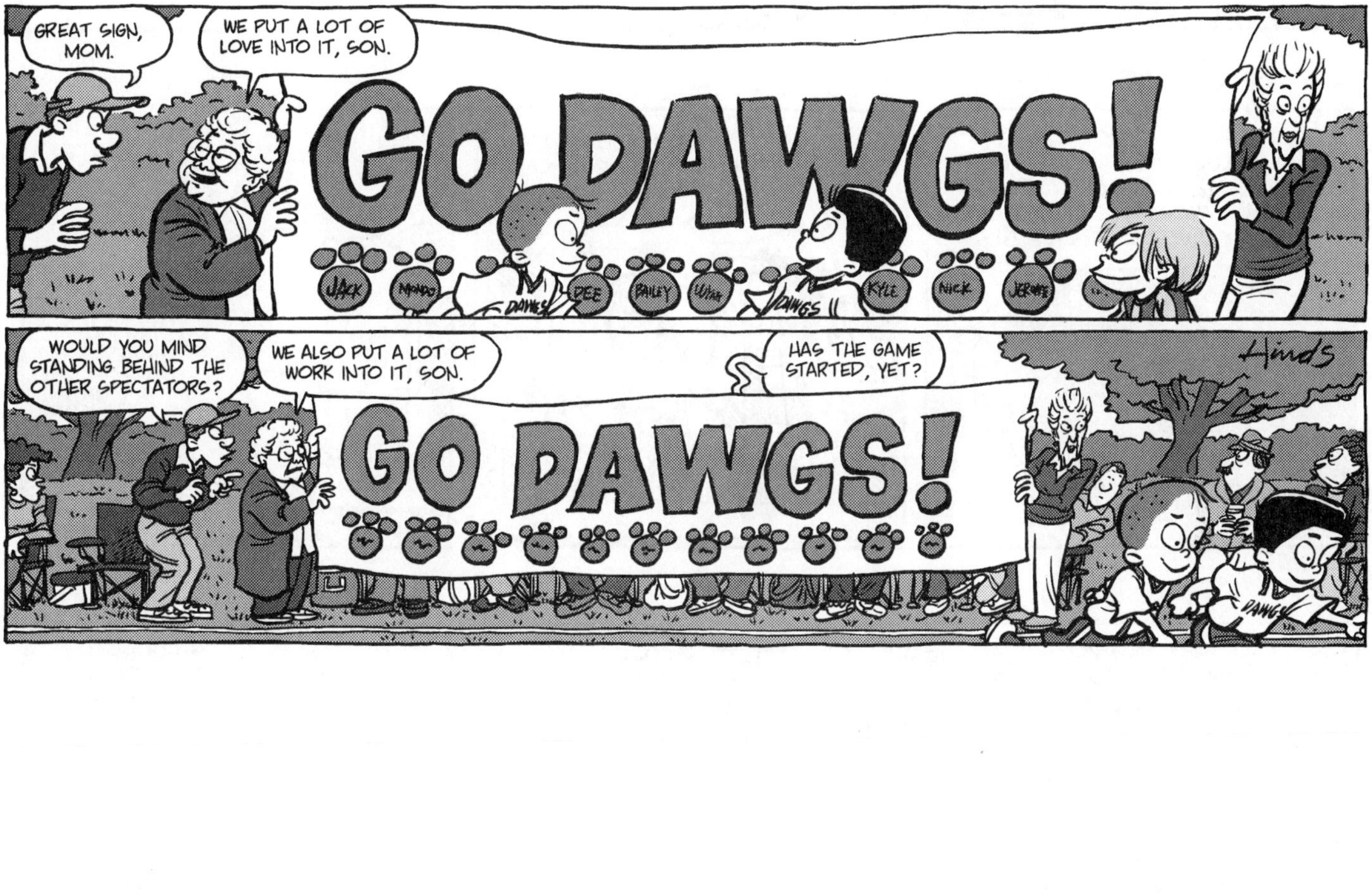
GREAT SIGN, MOM.
WE PUT A LOT OF LOVE INTO IT, SON.
GO DAWGS!
JACK
DEE
BAILEY
KYLE
NICK
JEROME
WOULD YOU MIND STANDING BEHIND THE OTHER SPECTATORS?
WE ALSO PUT A LOT OF WORK INTO IT, SON.
HAS THE GAME STARTED, YET?
GO DAWGS!
Hinds

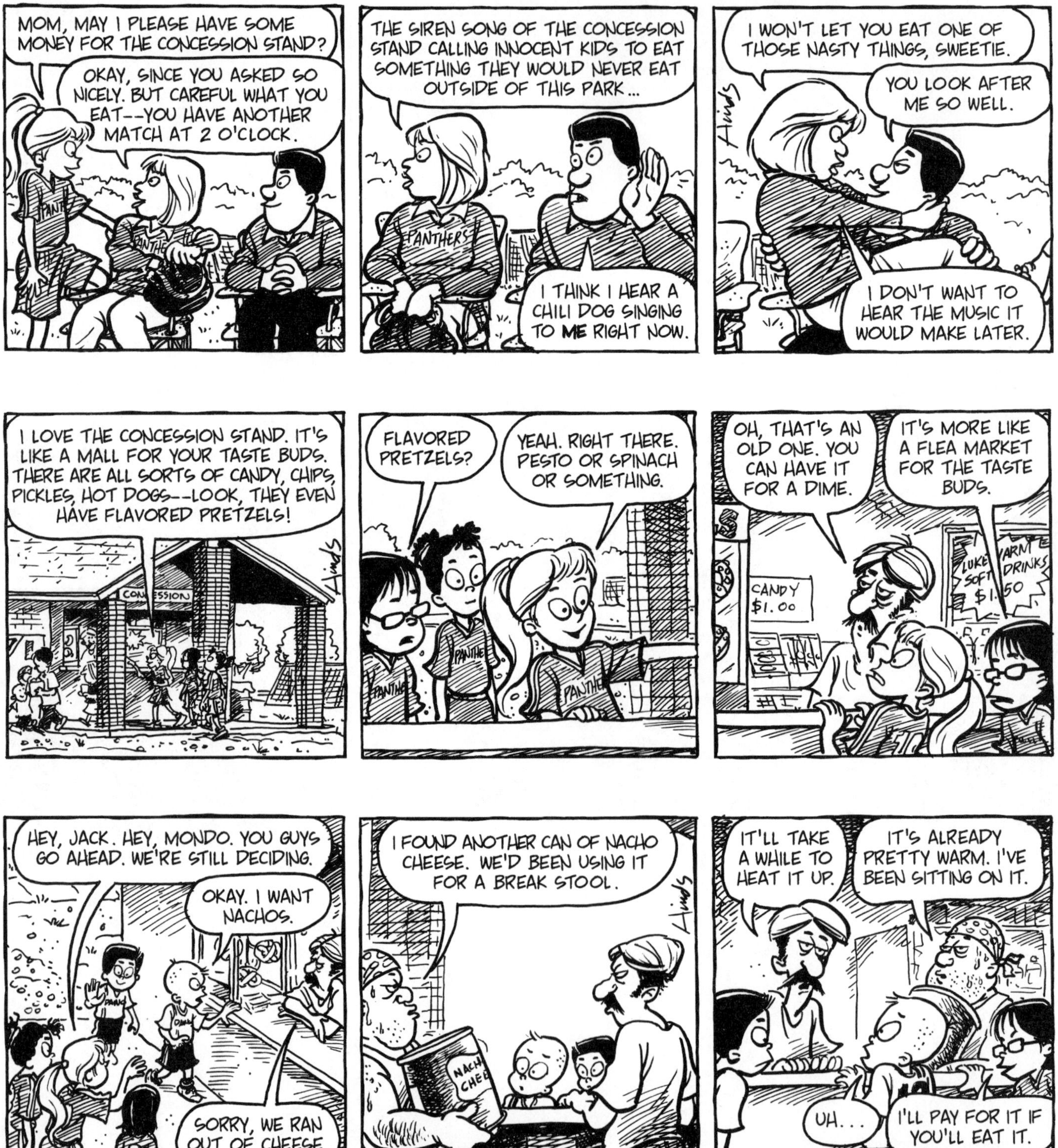
MOM, MAY I PLEASE HAVE SOME MONEY FOR THE CONCESSION STAND?
OKAY, SINCE YOU ASKED SO NICELY. BUT CAREFUL WHAT YOU EAT--YOU HAVE ANOTHER MATCH AT 2 O'CLOCK.
PANTHERS
THE SIREN SONG OF THE CONCESSION STAND CALLING INNOCENT KIDS TO EAT SOMETHING THEY WOULD NEVER EAT OUTSIDE OF THIS PARK...
I THINK I HEAR A CHILI DOG SINGING TO **ME** RIGHT NOW.
I WON'T LET YOU EAT ONE OF THOSE NASTY THINGS, SWEETIE.
YOU LOOK AFTER ME SO WELL.
I DON'T WANT TO HEAR THE MUSIC IT WOULD MAKE LATER.
I LOVE THE CONCESSION STAND. IT'S LIKE A MALL FOR YOUR TASTE BUDS. THERE ARE ALL SORTS OF CANDY, CHIPS, PICKLES, HOT DOGS--LOOK, THEY EVEN HAVE FLAVORED PRETZELS!
CONCESSION
FLAVORED PRETZELS?
YEAH. RIGHT THERE. PESTO OR SPINACH OR SOMETHING.
OH, THAT'S AN OLD ONE. YOU CAN HAVE IT FOR A DIME.
IT'S MORE LIKE A FLEA MARKET FOR THE TASTE BUDS.
CANDY $1.00
LUKEWARM SOFT DRINKS $1.50
HEY, JACK. HEY, MONDO. YOU GUYS GO AHEAD. WE'RE STILL DECIDING.
OKAY. I WANT NACHOS.
SORRY, WE RAN OUT OF CHEESE.
I FOUND ANOTHER CAN OF NACHO CHEESE. WE'D BEEN USING IT FOR A BREAK STOOL.
IT'LL TAKE A WHILE TO HEAT IT UP.
IT'S ALREADY PRETTY WARM. I'VE BEEN SITTING ON IT.
UH...
I'LL PAY FOR IT IF YOU'LL EAT IT.

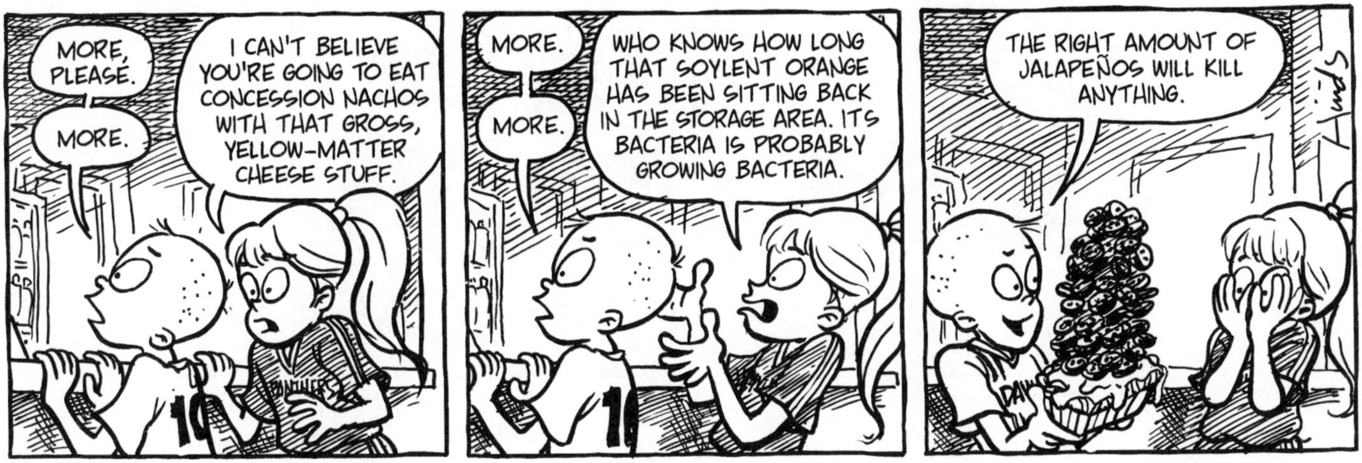
MORE, PLEASE.
MORE.
I CAN'T BELIEVE YOU'RE GOING TO EAT CONCESSION NACHOS WITH THAT GROSS, YELLOW-MATTER CHEESE STUFF.
MORE.
MORE.
WHO KNOWS HOW LONG THAT SOYLENT ORANGE HAS BEEN SITTING BACK IN THE STORAGE AREA. ITS BACTERIA IS PROBABLY GROWING BACTERIA.
THE RIGHT AMOUNT OF JALAPEÑOS WILL KILL ANYTHING.

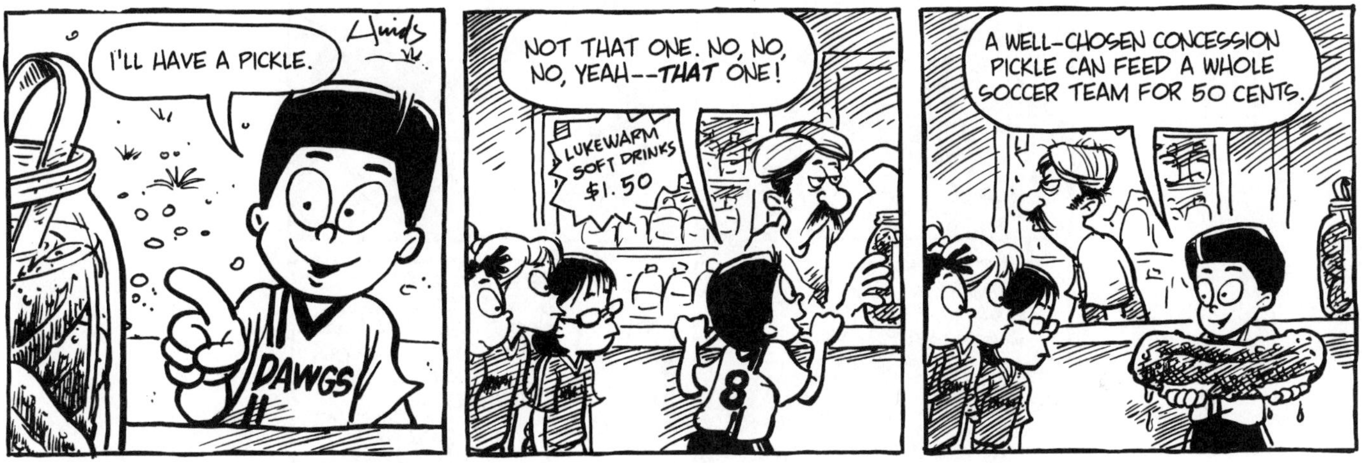
I'LL HAVE A PICKLE.
DAWGS
NOT THAT ONE. NO, NO, NO, YEAH--THAT ONE!
LUKEWARM SOFT DRINKS $1.50
A WELL-CHOSEN CONCESSION PICKLE CAN FEED A WHOLE SOCCER TEAM FOR 50 CENTS.

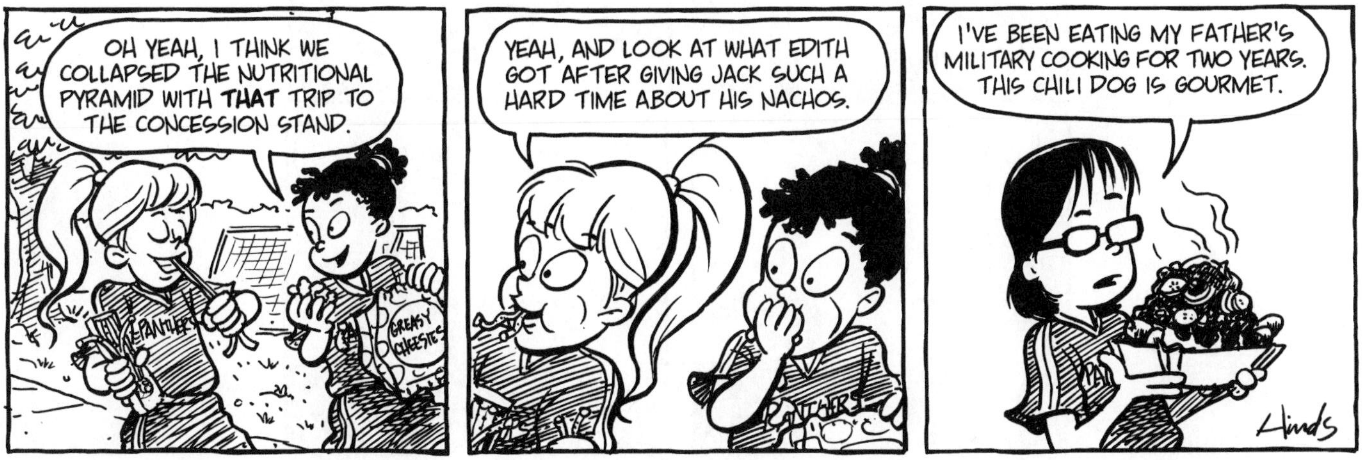
OH YEAH, I THINK WE COLLAPSED THE NUTRITIONAL PYRAMID WITH THAT TRIP TO THE CONCESSION STAND.
GREASY CHEESIES
YEAH, AND LOOK AT WHAT EDITH GOT AFTER GIVING JACK SUCH A HARD TIME ABOUT HIS NACHOS.
I'VE BEEN EATING MY FATHER'S MILITARY COOKING FOR TWO YEARS. THIS CHILI DOG IS GOURMET.

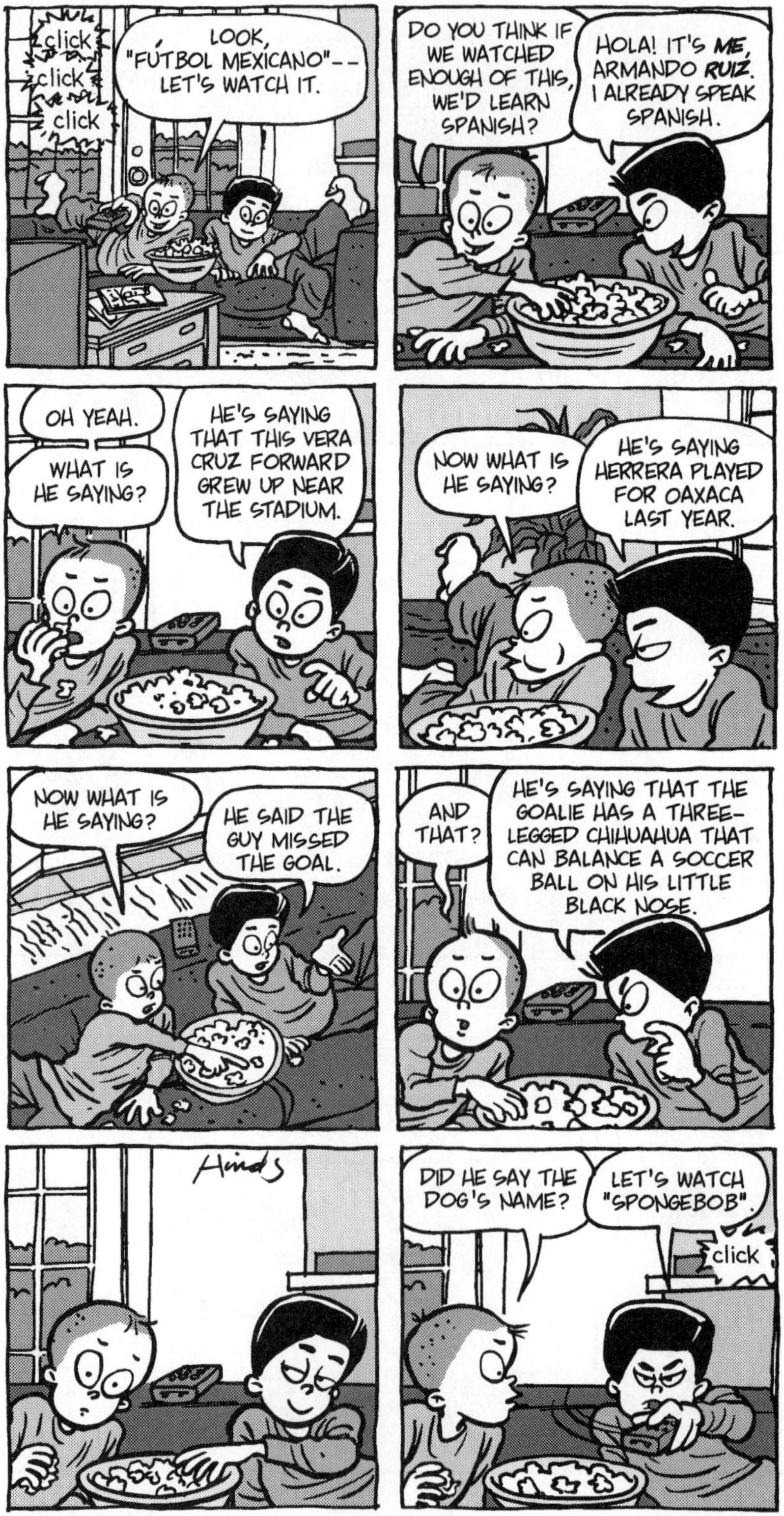
click
click
click
LOOK, "FÚTBOL MEXICANO"-- LET'S WATCH IT.
DO YOU THINK IF WE WATCHED ENOUGH OF THIS, WE'D LEARN SPANISH?
HOLA! IT'S ME, ARMANDO RUIZ. I ALREADY SPEAK SPANISH.
OH YEAH.
WHAT IS HE SAYING?
HE'S SAYING THAT THIS VERA CRUZ FORWARD GREW UP NEAR THE STADIUM.
NOW WHAT IS HE SAYING?
HE'S SAYING HERRERA PLAYED FOR OAXACA LAST YEAR.
NOW WHAT IS HE SAYING?
HE SAID THE GUY MISSED THE GOAL.
AND THAT?
HE'S SAYING THAT THE GOALIE HAS A THREE-LEGGED CHIHUAHUA THAT CAN BALANCE A SOCCER BALL ON HIS LITTLE BLACK NOSE.
Hinds
DID HE SAY THE DOG'S NAME?
LET'S WATCH "SPONGEBOB".
click

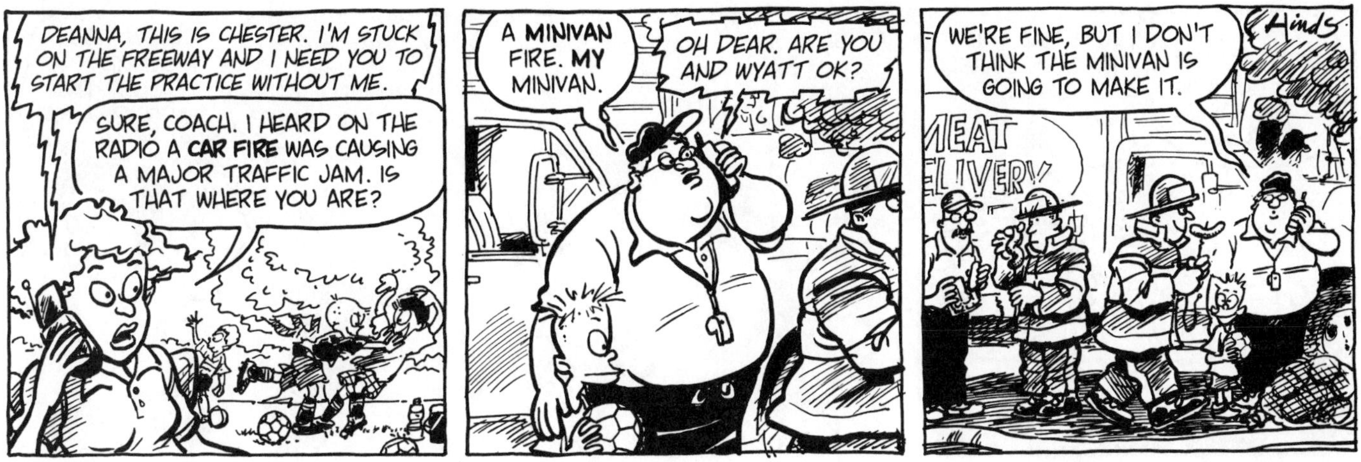
DEANNA, THIS IS CHESTER. I'M STUCK ON THE FREEWAY AND I NEED YOU TO START THE PRACTICE WITHOUT ME.
SURE, COACH. I HEARD ON THE RADIO A **CAR FIRE** WAS CAUSING A MAJOR TRAFFIC JAM. IS THAT WHERE YOU ARE?
A **MINIVAN** FIRE. **MY** MINIVAN.
OH DEAR. ARE YOU AND WYATT OK?
Hinds
WE'RE FINE, BUT I DON'T THINK THE MINIVAN IS GOING TO MAKE IT.
MEAT DELIVERY

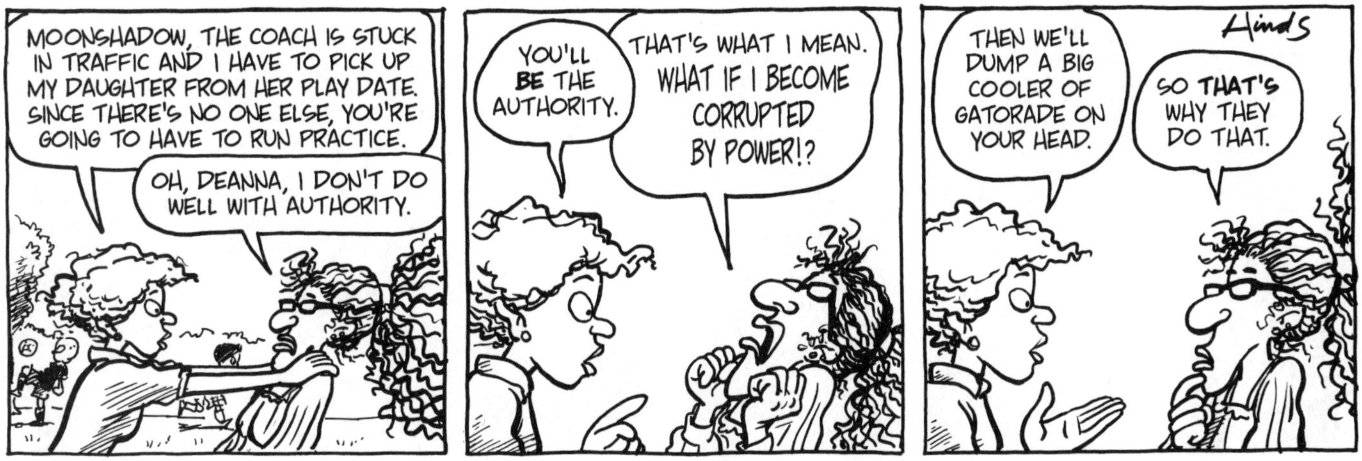
MOONSHADOW, THE COACH IS STUCK IN TRAFFIC AND I HAVE TO PICK UP MY DAUGHTER FROM HER PLAY DATE. SINCE THERE'S NO ONE ELSE, YOU'RE GOING TO HAVE TO RUN PRACTICE.
OH, DEANNA, I DON'T DO WELL WITH AUTHORITY.
YOU'LL **BE** THE AUTHORITY.
THAT'S WHAT I MEAN. WHAT IF I BECOME CORRUPTED BY POWER!?
Hinds
THEN WE'LL DUMP A BIG COOLER OF GATORADE ON YOUR HEAD.
SO **THAT'S** WHY THEY DO THAT.

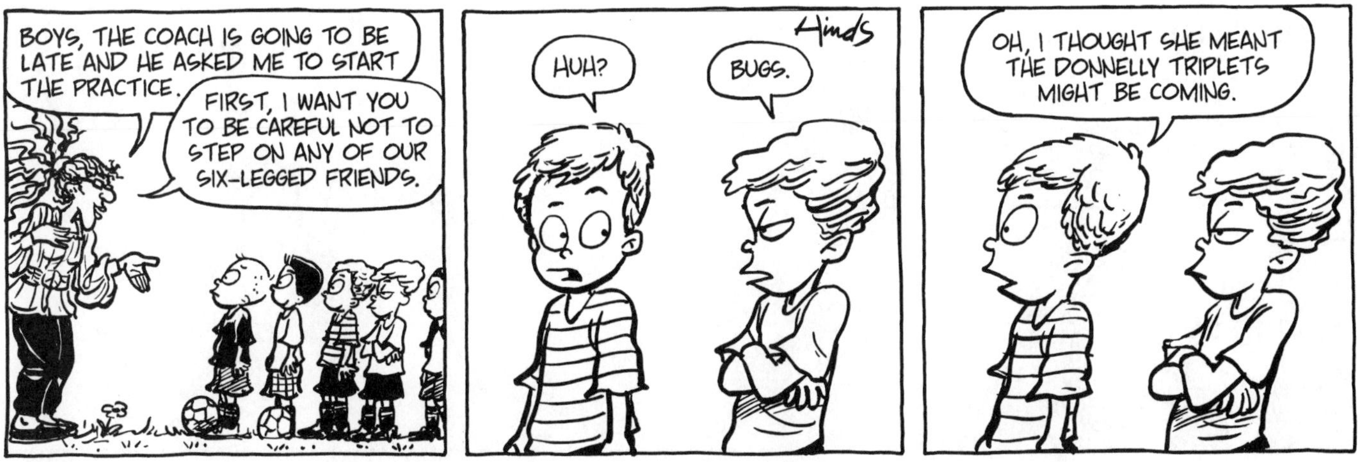
BOYS, THE COACH IS GOING TO BE LATE AND HE ASKED ME TO START THE PRACTICE.
FIRST, I WANT YOU TO BE CAREFUL NOT TO STEP ON ANY OF OUR SIX-LEGGED FRIENDS.
Hinds
HUH?
BUGS.
OH, I THOUGHT SHE MEANT THE DONNELLY TRIPLETS MIGHT BE COMING.

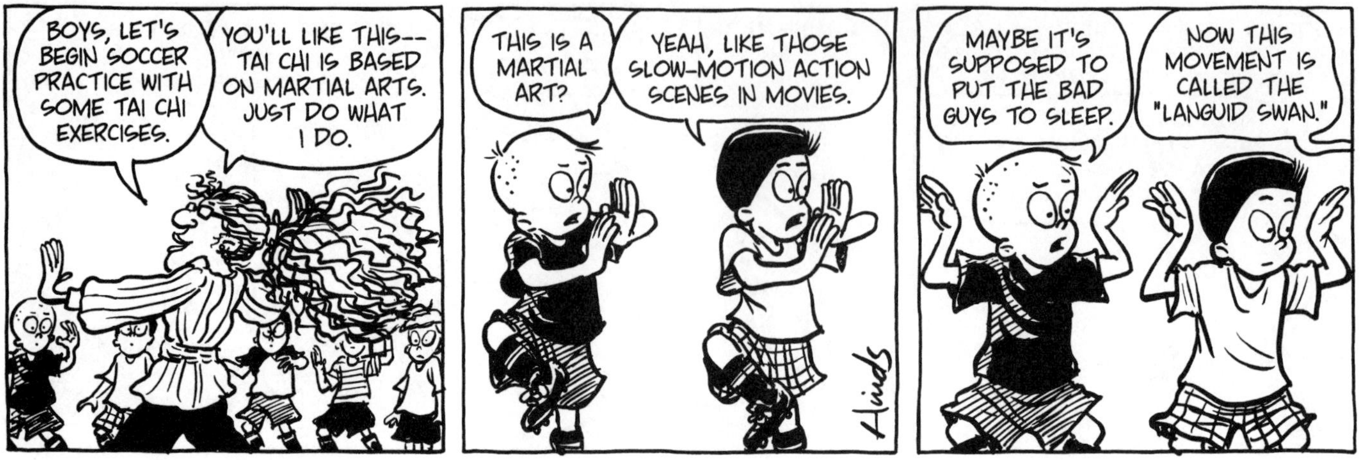
BOYS, LET'S BEGIN SOCCER PRACTICE WITH SOME TAI CHI EXERCISES.
YOU'LL LIKE THIS-- TAI CHI IS BASED ON MARTIAL ARTS. JUST DO WHAT I DO.
THIS IS A MARTIAL ART?
YEAH, LIKE THOSE SLOW-MOTION ACTION SCENES IN MOVIES.
Hinds
MAYBE IT'S SUPPOSED TO PUT THE BAD GUYS TO SLEEP.
NOW THIS MOVEMENT IS CALLED THE "LANGUID SWAN."

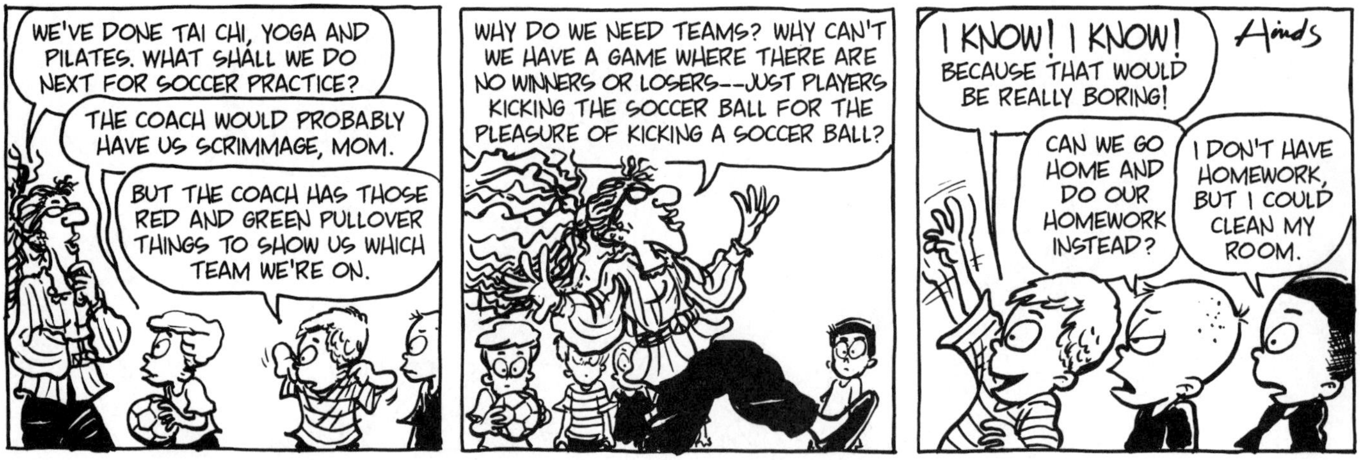
WE'VE DONE TAI CHI, YOGA AND PILATES. WHAT SHALL WE DO NEXT FOR SOCCER PRACTICE?
THE COACH WOULD PROBABLY HAVE US SCRIMMAGE, MOM.
BUT THE COACH HAS THOSE RED AND GREEN PULLOVER THINGS TO SHOW US WHICH TEAM WE'RE ON.
WHY DO WE NEED TEAMS? WHY CAN'T WE HAVE A GAME WHERE THERE ARE NO WINNERS OR LOSERS--JUST PLAYERS KICKING THE SOCCER BALL FOR THE PLEASURE OF KICKING A SOCCER BALL?
Hinds
I KNOW! I KNOW! BECAUSE THAT WOULD BE REALLY BORING!
CAN WE GO HOME AND DO OUR HOMEWORK INSTEAD?
I DON'T HAVE HOMEWORK, BUT I COULD CLEAN MY ROOM.

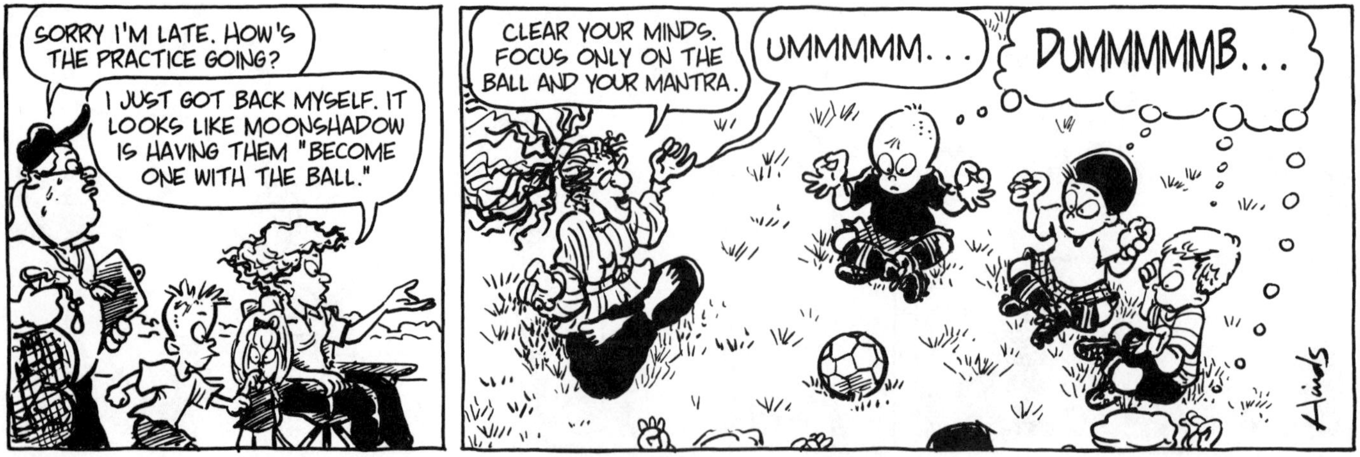
SORRY I'M LATE. HOW'S THE PRACTICE GOING?
I JUST GOT BACK MYSELF. IT LOOKS LIKE MOONSHADOW IS HAVING THEM "BECOME ONE WITH THE BALL."
CLEAR YOUR MINDS. FOCUS ONLY ON THE BALL AND YOUR MANTRA.
UMMMMM. . .
DUMMMMMB. . .
Hinds

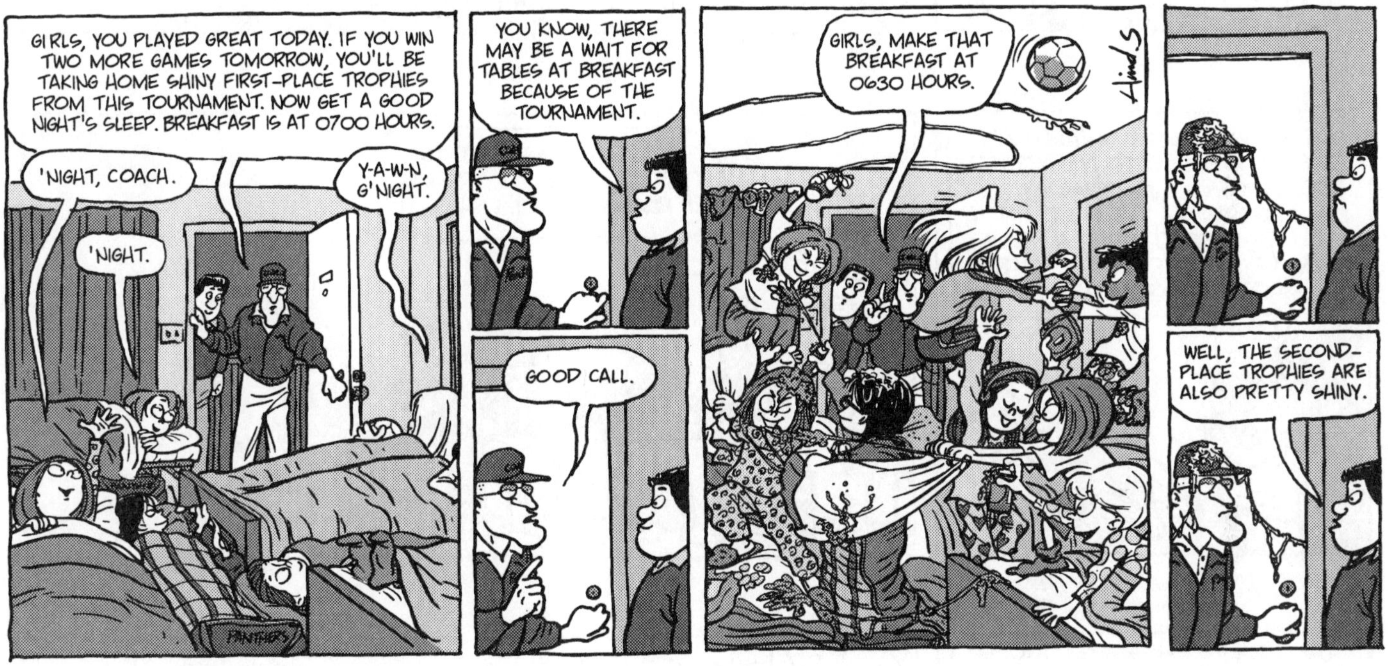
GIRLS, YOU PLAYED GREAT TODAY. IF YOU WIN TWO MORE GAMES TOMORROW, YOU'LL BE TAKING HOME SHINY FIRST-PLACE TROPHIES FROM THIS TOURNAMENT. NOW GET A GOOD NIGHT'S SLEEP. BREAKFAST IS AT 0700 HOURS.
'NIGHT, COACH.
Y-A-W-N, G'NIGHT.
'NIGHT.
PANTHERS
YOU KNOW, THERE MAY BE A WAIT FOR TABLES AT BREAKFAST BECAUSE OF THE TOURNAMENT.
GOOD CALL.
GIRLS, MAKE THAT BREAKFAST AT 0630 HOURS.
WELL, THE SECOND-PLACE TROPHIES ARE ALSO PRETTY SHINY.

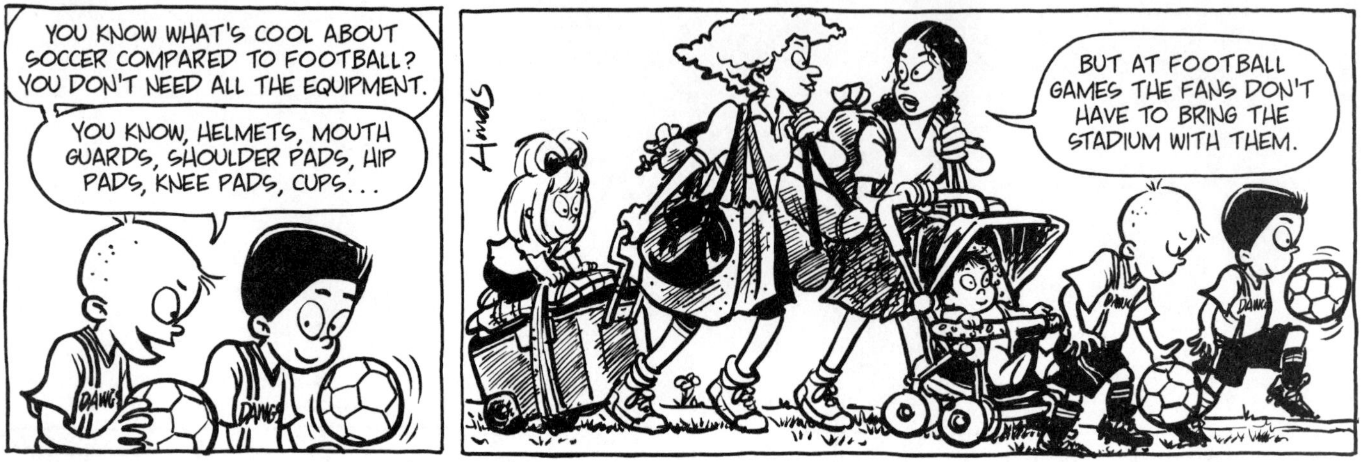
YOU KNOW WHAT'S COOL ABOUT SOCCER COMPARED TO FOOTBALL? YOU DON'T NEED ALL THE EQUIPMENT.
YOU KNOW, HELMETS, MOUTH GUARDS, SHOULDER PADS, HIP PADS, KNEE PADS, CUPS...
BUT AT FOOTBALL GAMES THE FANS DON'T HAVE TO BRING THE STADIUM WITH THEM.
Hinds

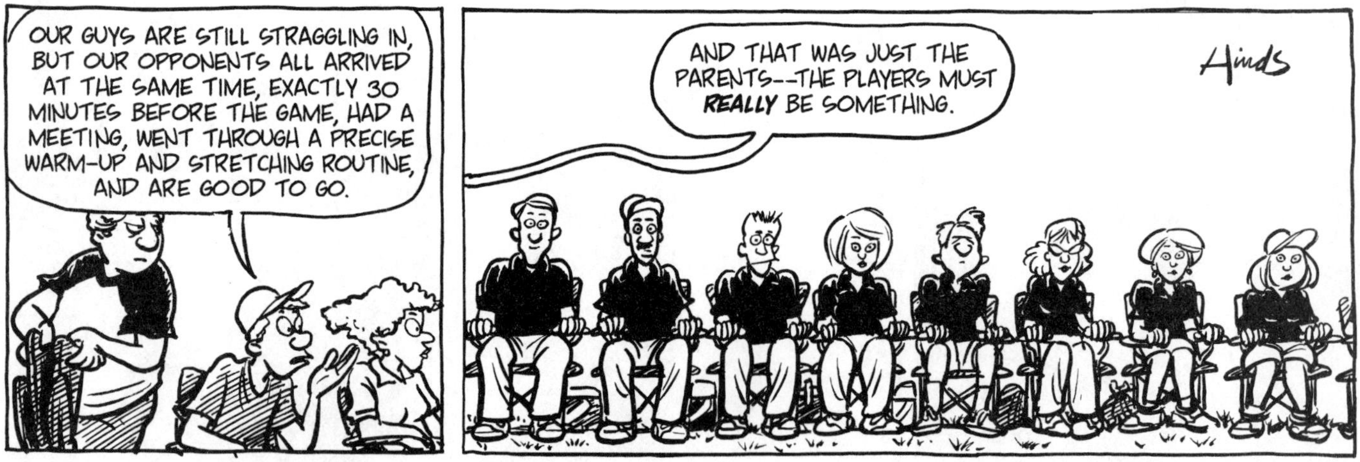
OUR GUYS ARE STILL STRAGGLING IN, BUT OUR OPPONENTS ALL ARRIVED AT THE SAME TIME, EXACTLY 30 MINUTES BEFORE THE GAME, HAD A MEETING, WENT THROUGH A PRECISE WARM-UP AND STRETCHING ROUTINE, AND ARE GOOD TO GO.
AND THAT WAS JUST THE PARENTS--THE PLAYERS MUST **REALLY** BE SOMETHING.
Hinds

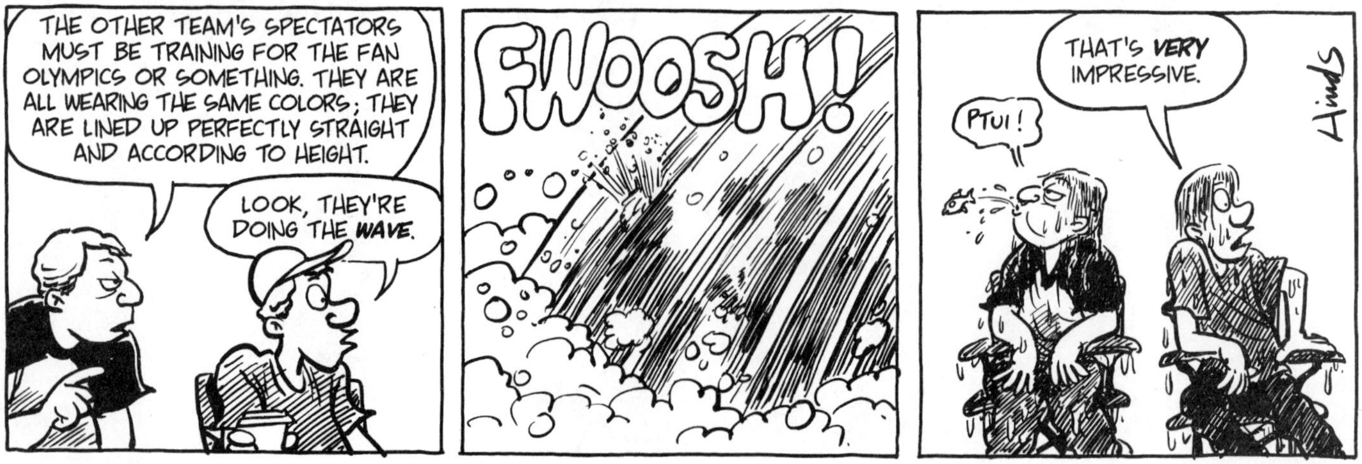
THE OTHER TEAM'S SPECTATORS MUST BE TRAINING FOR THE FAN OLYMPICS OR SOMETHING. THEY ARE ALL WEARING THE SAME COLORS; THEY ARE LINED UP PERFECTLY STRAIGHT AND ACCORDING TO HEIGHT.
LOOK, THEY'RE DOING THE **WAVE**.
FWOOSH!
PTUI!
THAT'S **VERY** IMPRESSIVE.
Hinds

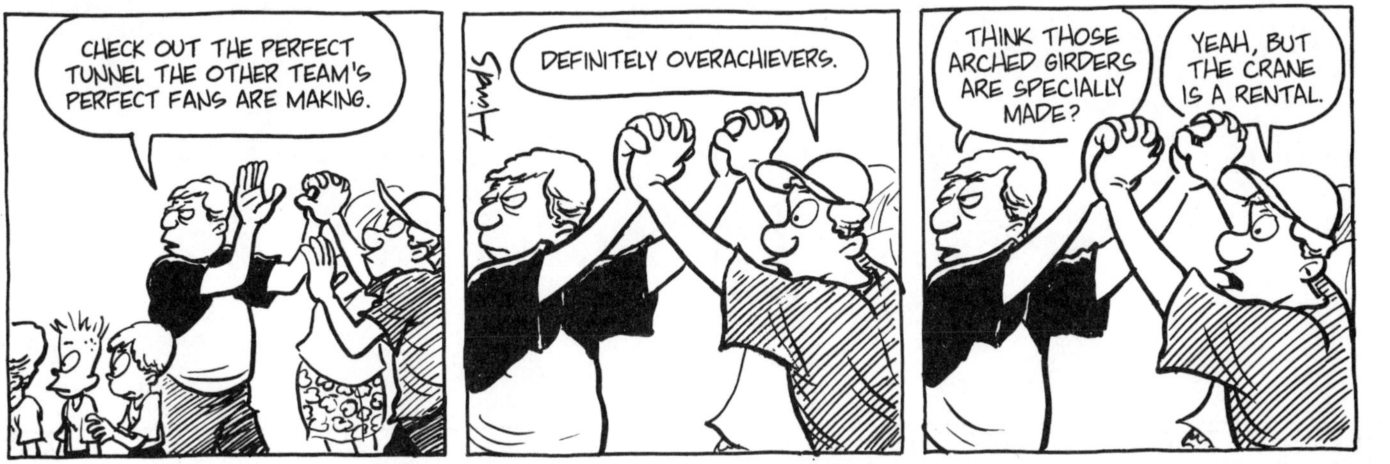
CHECK OUT THE PERFECT TUNNEL THE OTHER TEAM'S PERFECT FANS ARE MAKING.
Hinds
DEFINITELY OVERACHIEVERS.
THINK THOSE ARCHED GIRDERS ARE SPECIALLY MADE?
YEAH, BUT THE CRANE IS A RENTAL.

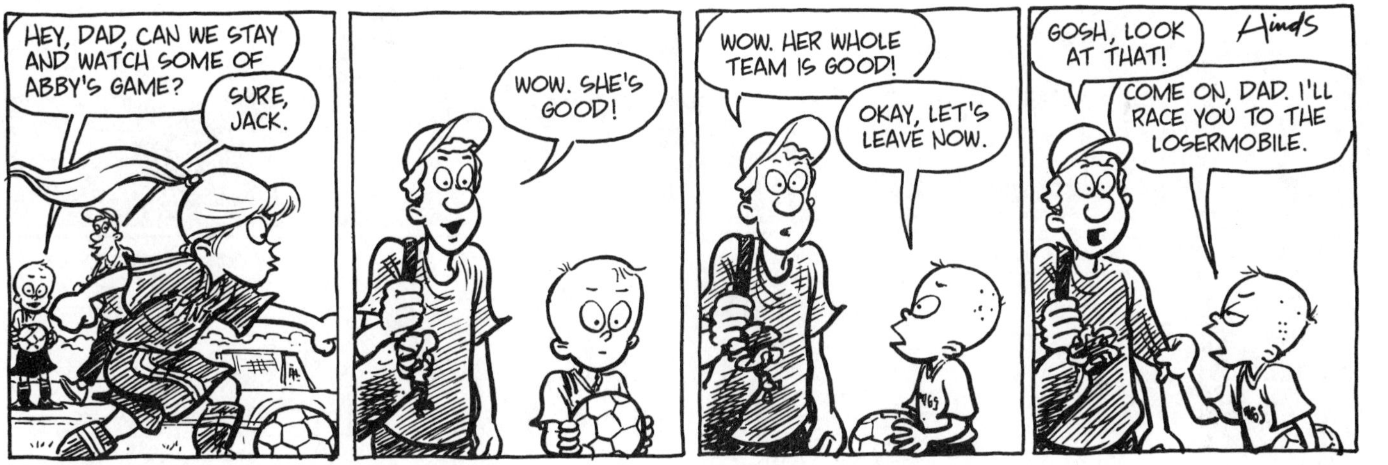
HEY, DAD, CAN WE STAY AND WATCH SOME OF ABBY'S GAME?
SURE, JACK.
WOW. SHE'S GOOD!
WOW. HER WHOLE TEAM IS GOOD!
OKAY, LET'S LEAVE NOW.
GOSH, LOOK AT THAT!
Hinds
COME ON, DAD. I'LL RACE YOU TO THE LOSERMOBILE.

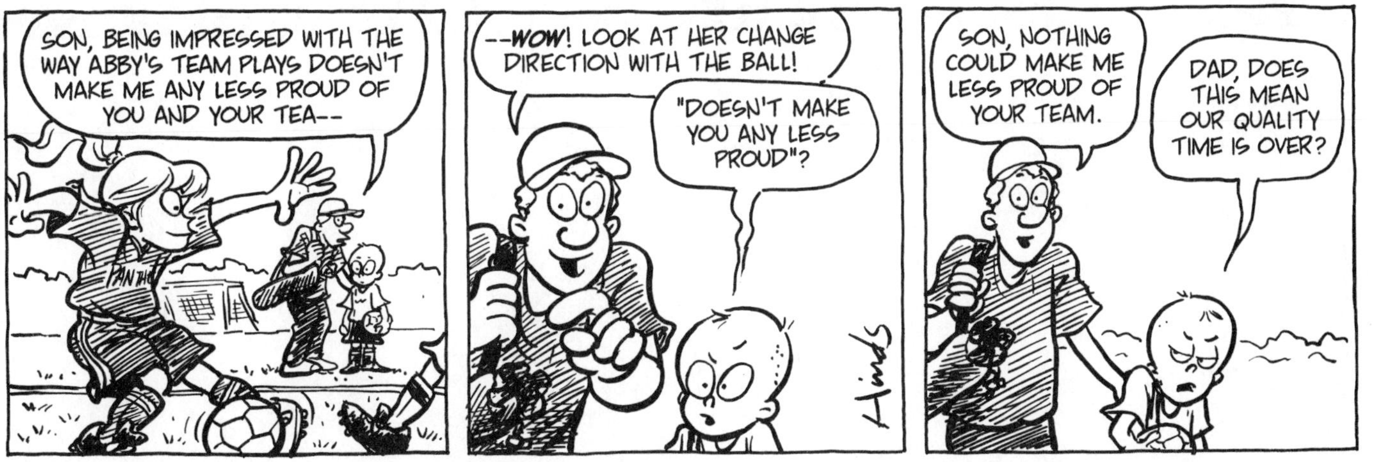
SON, BEING IMPRESSED WITH THE WAY ABBY'S TEAM PLAYS DOESN'T MAKE ME ANY LESS PROUD OF YOU AND YOUR TEA--
--***WOW***! LOOK AT HER CHANGE DIRECTION WITH THE BALL!
"DOESN'T MAKE YOU ANY LESS PROUD"?
Hinds
SON, NOTHING COULD MAKE ME LESS PROUD OF YOUR TEAM.
DAD, DOES THIS MEAN OUR QUALITY TIME IS OVER?

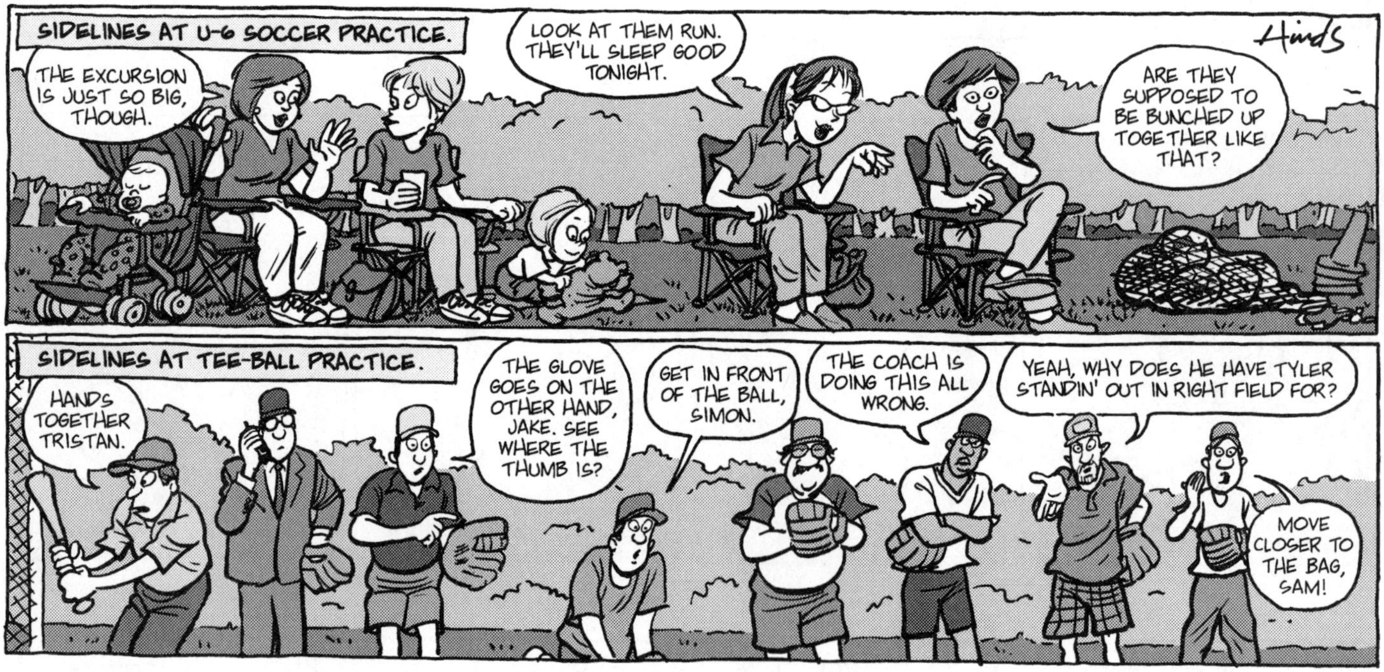
SIDELINES AT U-6 SOCCER PRACTICE.
THE EXCURSION IS JUST SO BIG, THOUGH.
LOOK AT THEM RUN. THEY'LL SLEEP GOOD TONIGHT.
ARE THEY SUPPOSED TO BE BUNCHED UP TOGETHER LIKE THAT?
Hinds
SIDELINES AT TEE-BALL PRACTICE.
HANDS TOGETHER TRISTAN.
THE GLOVE GOES ON THE OTHER HAND, JAKE. SEE WHERE THE THUMB IS?
GET IN FRONT OF THE BALL, SIMON.
THE COACH IS DOING THIS ALL WRONG.
YEAH, WHY DOES HE HAVE TYLER STANDIN' OUT IN RIGHT FIELD FOR?
MOVE CLOSER TO THE BAG, SAM!

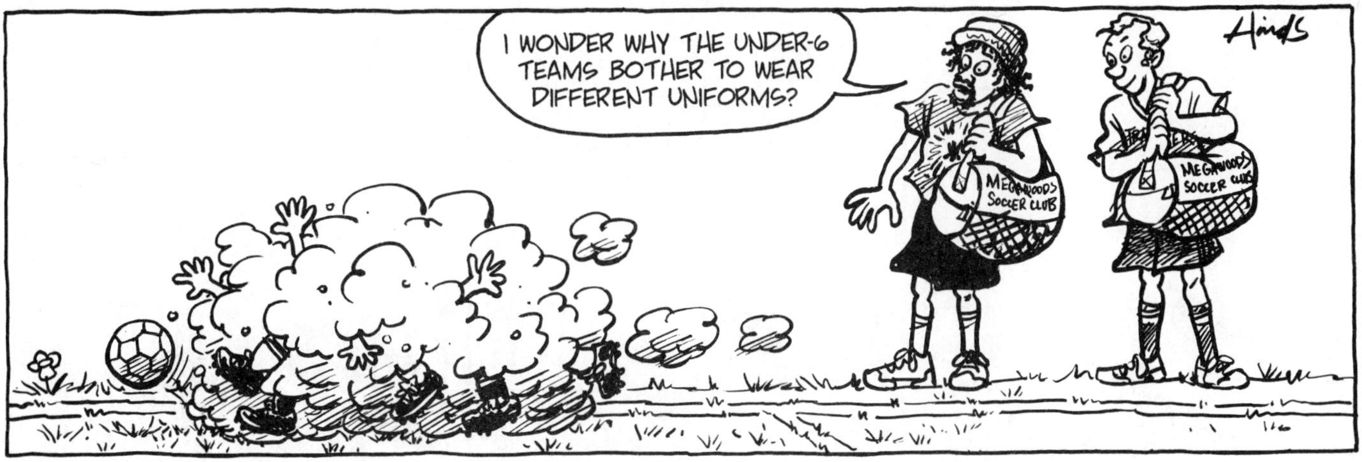
Hinds
I WONDER WHY THE UNDER-6 TEAMS BOTHER TO WEAR DIFFERENT UNIFORMS?
MEGAWOODS SOCCER CLUB

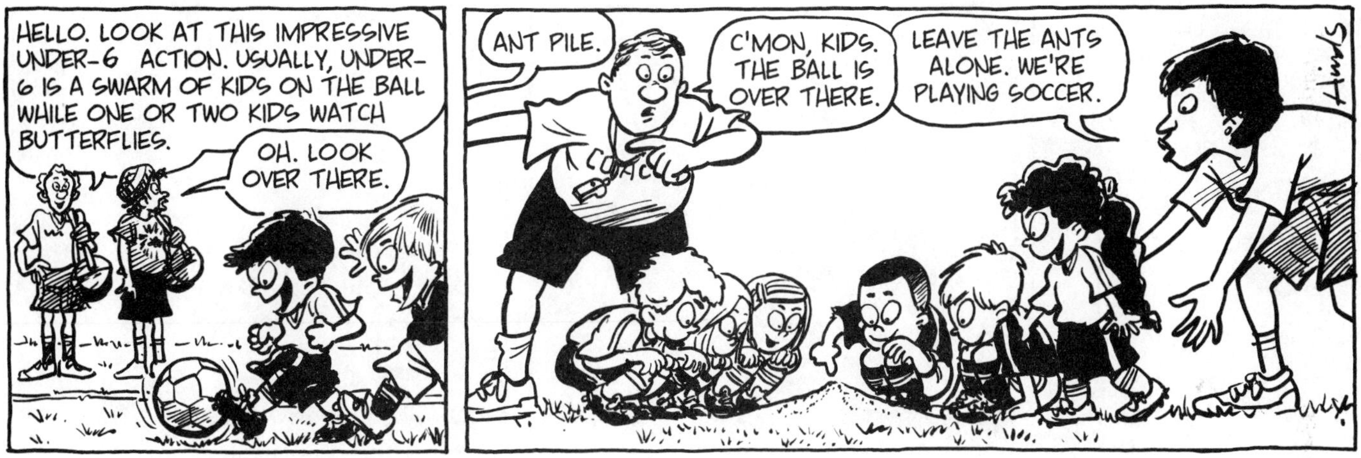
HELLO. LOOK AT THIS IMPRESSIVE UNDER-6 ACTION. USUALLY, UNDER-6 IS A SWARM OF KIDS ON THE BALL WHILE ONE OR TWO KIDS WATCH BUTTERFLIES.
OH. LOOK OVER THERE.
ANT PILE.
C'MON, KIDS. THE BALL IS OVER THERE.
LEAVE THE ANTS ALONE. WE'RE PLAYING SOCCER.
Hinds

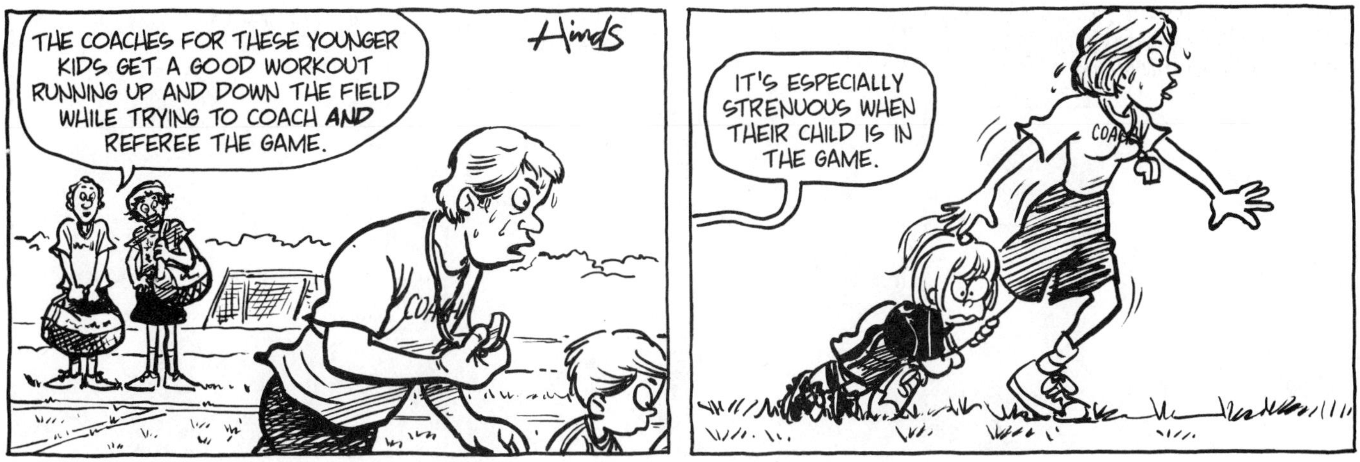
Hinds
THE COACHES FOR THESE YOUNGER KIDS GET A GOOD WORKOUT RUNNING UP AND DOWN THE FIELD WHILE TRYING TO COACH **AND** REFEREE THE GAME.
IT'S ESPECIALLY STRENUOUS WHEN THEIR CHILD IS IN THE GAME.

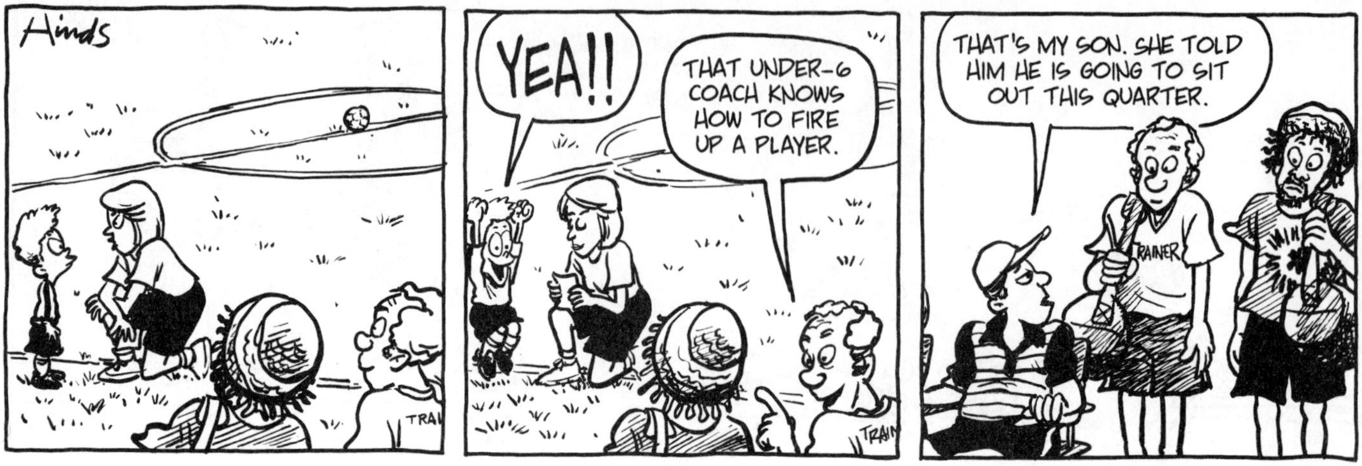
Hinds
YEA!!
THAT UNDER-6 COACH KNOWS HOW TO FIRE UP A PLAYER.
THAT'S MY SON. SHE TOLD HIM HE IS GOING TO SIT OUT THIS QUARTER.
TRAINER

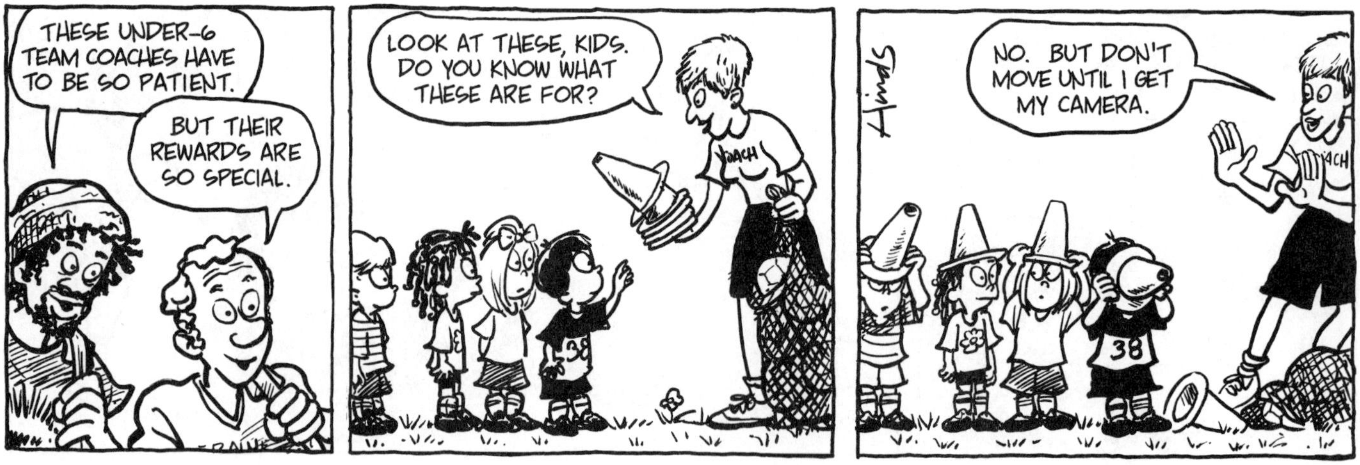
THESE UNDER-6 TEAM COACHES HAVE TO BE SO PATIENT.
BUT THEIR REWARDS ARE SO SPECIAL.
LOOK AT THESE, KIDS. DO YOU KNOW WHAT THESE ARE FOR?
COACH
Hinds
NO. BUT DON'T MOVE UNTIL I GET MY CAMERA.

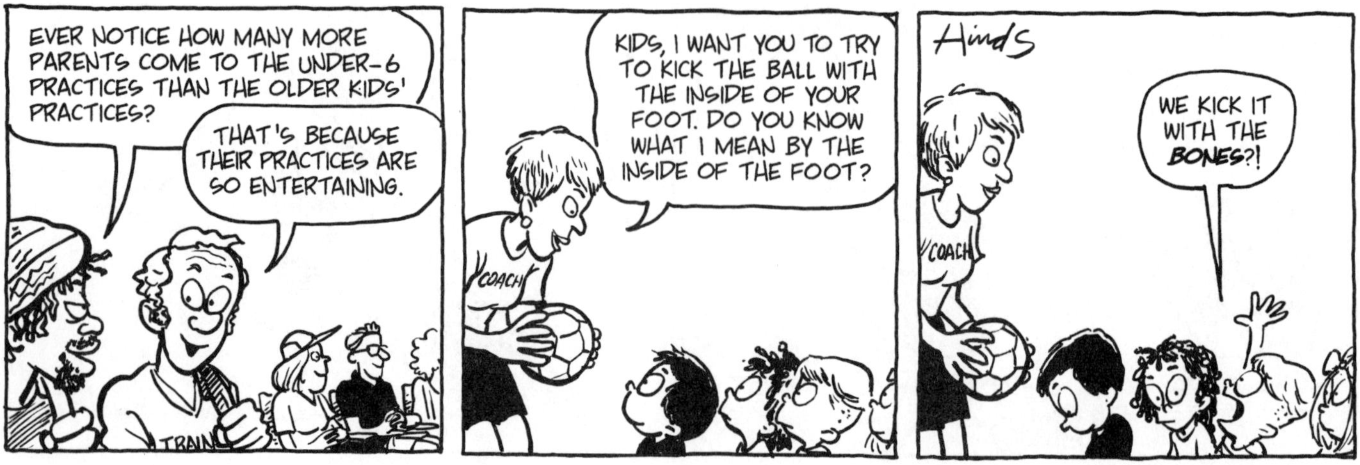
EVER NOTICE HOW MANY MORE PARENTS COME TO THE UNDER-6 PRACTICES THAN THE OLDER KIDS' PRACTICES?
THAT'S BECAUSE THEIR PRACTICES ARE SO ENTERTAINING.
KIDS, I WANT YOU TO TRY TO KICK THE BALL WITH THE INSIDE OF YOUR FOOT. DO YOU KNOW WHAT I MEAN BY THE INSIDE OF THE FOOT?
COACH
Hinds
WE KICK IT WITH THE *BONES*?!

Silent Sunday at Megawoods Park Soccer Fields. A day when the fans and coaches voluntarily remain silent on the sidelines during the soccer matches.

The benefits are many.

A songbird sings its song uninterrupted.

Players are able to concentrate. Many play their best game.

Referees easily control the game, undistracted by sideline critique.

And parents get a rigorous isometric workout.

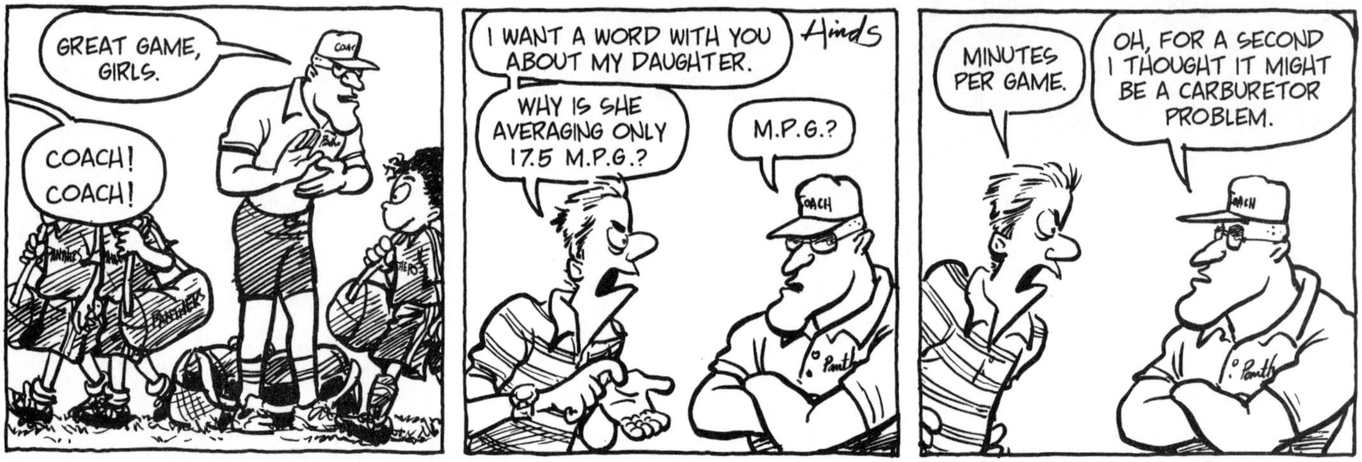
GREAT GAME, GIRLS.
COACH! COACH!
I WANT A WORD WITH YOU ABOUT MY DAUGHTER.
WHY IS SHE AVERAGING ONLY 17.5 M.P.G.?
M.P.G.?
MINUTES PER GAME.
OH, FOR A SECOND I THOUGHT IT MIGHT BE A CARBURETOR PROBLEM.
Hinds

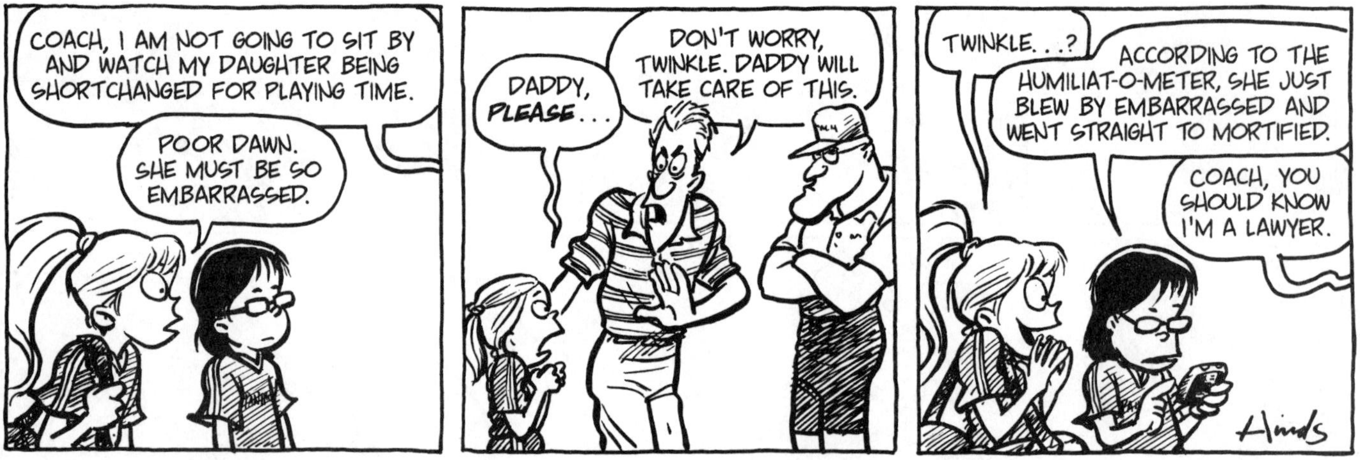
COACH, I AM NOT GOING TO SIT BY AND WATCH MY DAUGHTER BEING SHORTCHANGED FOR PLAYING TIME.
POOR DAWN. SHE MUST BE SO EMBARRASSED.
DADDY, PLEASE...
DON'T WORRY, TWINKLE. DADDY WILL TAKE CARE OF THIS.
TWINKLE...?
ACCORDING TO THE HUMILIAT-O-METER, SHE JUST BLEW BY EMBARRASSED AND WENT STRAIGHT TO MORTIFIED.
COACH, YOU SHOULD KNOW I'M A LAWYER.
Hinds

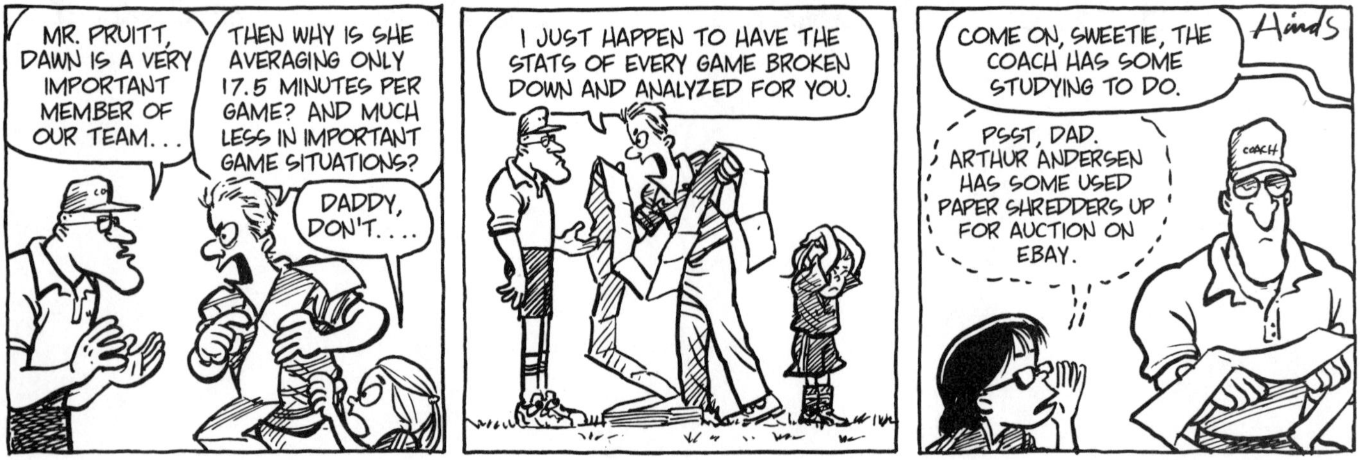
MR. PRUITT, DAWN IS A VERY IMPORTANT MEMBER OF OUR TEAM...
THEN WHY IS SHE AVERAGING ONLY 17.5 MINUTES PER GAME? AND MUCH LESS IN IMPORTANT GAME SITUATIONS?
DADDY, DON'T....
I JUST HAPPEN TO HAVE THE STATS OF EVERY GAME BROKEN DOWN AND ANALYZED FOR YOU.
COME ON, SWEETIE, THE COACH HAS SOME STUDYING TO DO.
PSST, DAD. ARTHUR ANDERSEN HAS SOME USED PAPER SHREDDERS UP FOR AUCTION ON EBAY.
Hinds

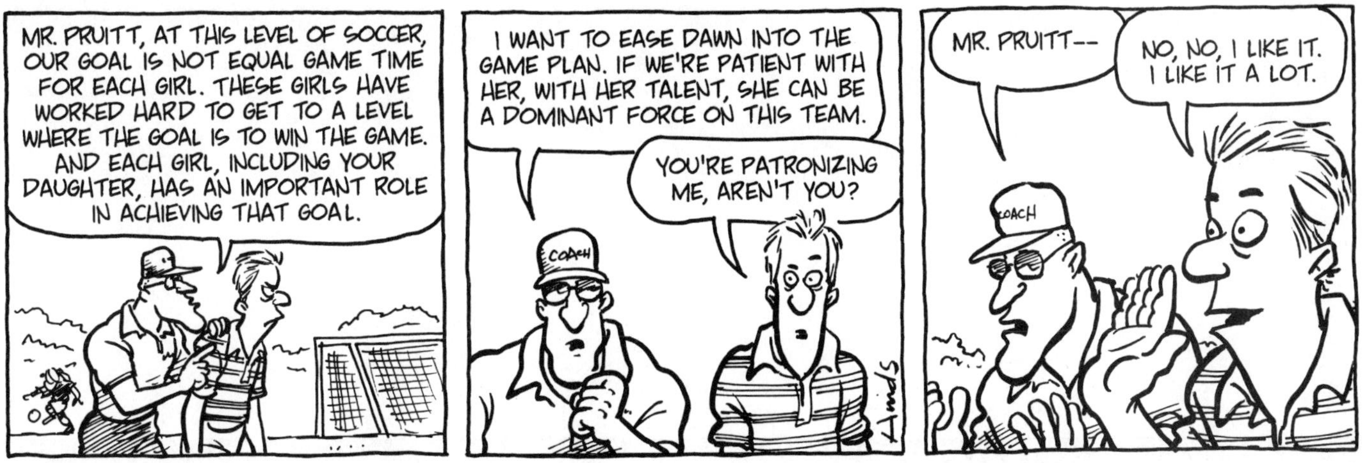
MR. PRUITT, AT THIS LEVEL OF SOCCER, OUR GOAL IS NOT EQUAL GAME TIME FOR EACH GIRL. THESE GIRLS HAVE WORKED HARD TO GET TO A LEVEL WHERE THE GOAL IS TO WIN THE GAME. AND EACH GIRL, INCLUDING YOUR DAUGHTER, HAS AN IMPORTANT ROLE IN ACHIEVING THAT GOAL.
I WANT TO EASE DAWN INTO THE GAME PLAN. IF WE'RE PATIENT WITH HER, WITH HER TALENT, SHE CAN BE A DOMINANT FORCE ON THIS TEAM.
YOU'RE PATRONIZING ME, AREN'T YOU?
COACH
MR. PRUITT--
NO, NO, I LIKE IT. I LIKE IT A LOT.

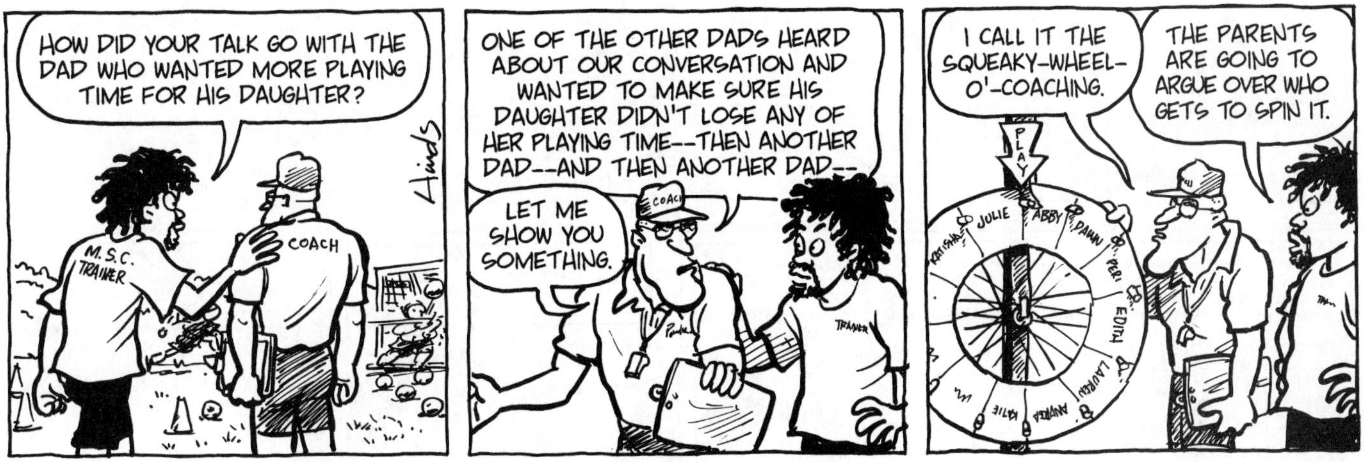
HOW DID YOUR TALK GO WITH THE DAD WHO WANTED MORE PLAYING TIME FOR HIS DAUGHTER?
M.S.C. TRAINER
COACH
ONE OF THE OTHER DADS HEARD ABOUT OUR CONVERSATION AND WANTED TO MAKE SURE HIS DAUGHTER DIDN'T LOSE ANY OF HER PLAYING TIME--THEN ANOTHER DAD--AND THEN ANOTHER DAD--
LET ME SHOW YOU SOMETHING.
TRAINER
I CALL IT THE SQUEAKY-WHEEL-O'-COACHING.
THE PARENTS ARE GOING TO ARGUE OVER WHO GETS TO SPIN IT.
PLAY
JULIE
ABBY
DAWN
PERI
EDITH
LAUREN
ANDREA
KATIE

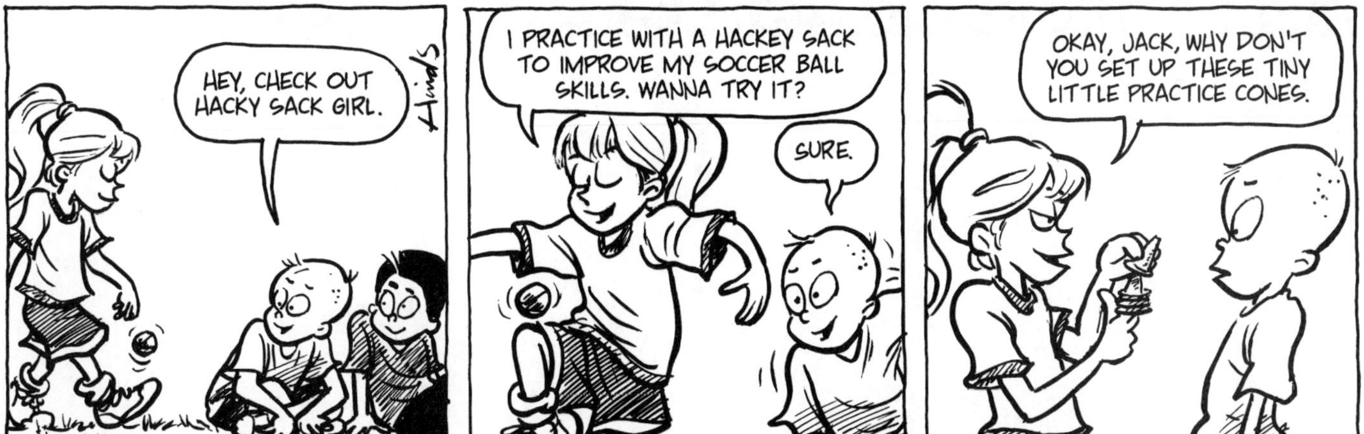
HEY, CHECK OUT HACKY SACK GIRL.
I PRACTICE WITH A HACKEY SACK TO IMPROVE MY SOCCER BALL SKILLS. WANNA TRY IT?
SURE.
OKAY, JACK, WHY DON'T YOU SET UP THESE TINY LITTLE PRACTICE CONES.

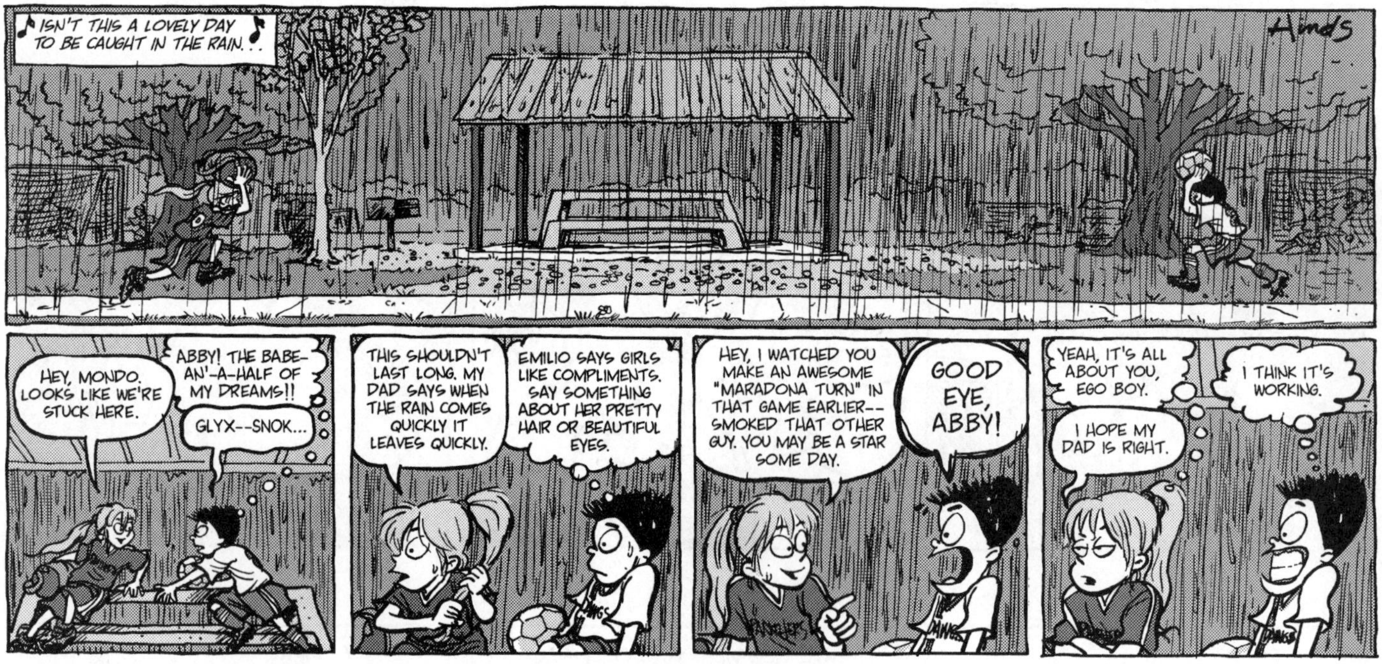
ISN'T THIS A LOVELY DAY TO BE CAUGHT IN THE RAIN. . .
Hinds
HEY, MONDO. LOOKS LIKE WE'RE STUCK HERE.
ABBY! THE BABE-AN'-A-HALF OF MY DREAMS!!
GLYX--SNOK...
THIS SHOULDN'T LAST LONG. MY DAD SAYS WHEN THE RAIN COMES QUICKLY IT LEAVES QUICKLY.
EMILIO SAYS GIRLS LIKE COMPLIMENTS. SAY SOMETHING ABOUT HER PRETTY HAIR OR BEAUTIFUL EYES.
HEY, I WATCHED YOU MAKE AN AWESOME "MARADONA TURN" IN THAT GAME EARLIER--SMOKED THAT OTHER GUY. YOU MAY BE A STAR SOME DAY.
GOOD EYE, ABBY!
YEAH, IT'S ALL ABOUT YOU, EGO BOY.
I HOPE MY DAD IS RIGHT.
I THINK IT'S WORKING.

Panel 1: BOYS, DEE IS OUR STARTING GOALIE, BUT THERE MAY BE GAMES WHEN HE IS UNABLE TO PLAY.

COACH, WHY WOULDN'T DEE BE ABLE TO PLAY?

Panel 2: YOU KNOW--HE MIGHT HAVE GOTTEN HIS NOSE SMASHED BY A SOCCER BALL.

OR HIS FINGERS GOT BROKEN WHEN SOMEBODY KICKED AT THE BALL WHILE HE WAS HOLDING IT.

Panel 3: OR HIS EYE MIGHT POP OUT WHEN HE DIVES FOR A BALL AND HE HITS THE GOALPOST.

OR I MIGHT BE HOME HIDING IN MY CLOSET.

Panel 4: BOYS, IF FOR ANY REASON DEE CAN'T PLAY, ONE OF YOU WILL HAVE TO JUMP INTO THE GOALKEEPER POSITION.

Panel 5: SO TODAY WE'RE GOING TO WORK ON--YES, BAILEY, WHAT IS IT?

COACH, REMEMBER THAT NOTE FROM MY MOM?

Panel 6: YES. OKAY, BAILEY PLAYS KEEPER ONLY IF NOBODY ELSE ON THE TEAM SHOWS UP.

AND THE OTHER TEAM DOESN'T SHOW UP.

RIGHT.

Panel 7: WHEN YOU'RE GOALIE, YOU HAVE THREE OPTIONS TO DISTRIBUTE THE BALL TO YOUR TEAM. REMEMBER--**ROLL** TO **CONTROL**, **THROW** IF YOU **KNOW**, **KICK** IF IT'S **THICK**.

5-1

Panel 8: IF THE AREA IS CLEAR, **ROLL** THE BALL TO YOUR PLAYER BECAUSE THAT'S EASY TO **CONTROL**. IF THERE ARE OPPONENTS NEARBY AND YOU **KNOW** YOU CAN **THROW** IT SAFELY TO YOUR PLAYER DOWNFIELD, DO THAT. AND IF THE AREA IS **THICK** WITH BAD GUYS, THEN **KICK** THE BALL TO MOVE IT TO THE OTHER END OF THE FIELD.

ANY QUESTIONS?

THICK?

Panel 9: WELL, IT RHYMED WITH KICK.

HOW ABOUT, KICK IF IT'S SICK?

OR, PUNT IF YOU'RE A RUNT?

I KNOW! BOOT IT OR TOOT IT.

LET'S NOT LOSE OUR FOCUS, BOYS.

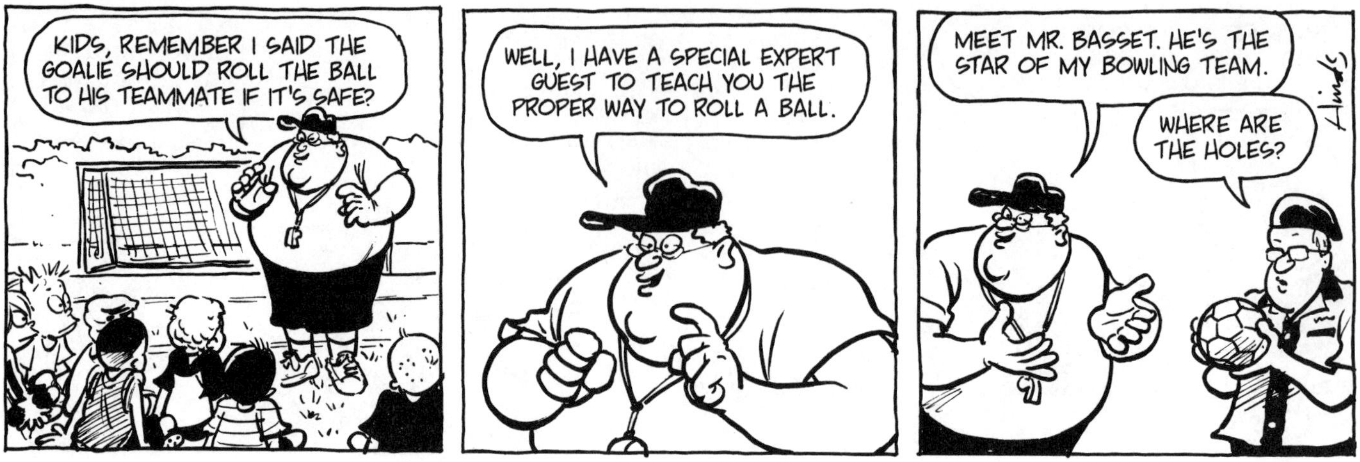
KIDS, REMEMBER I SAID THE GOALIE SHOULD ROLL THE BALL TO HIS TEAMMATE IF IT'S SAFE?
WELL, I HAVE A SPECIAL EXPERT GUEST TO TEACH YOU THE PROPER WAY TO ROLL A BALL.
MEET MR. BASSET. HE'S THE STAR OF MY BOWLING TEAM.
WHERE ARE THE HOLES?
Hinds

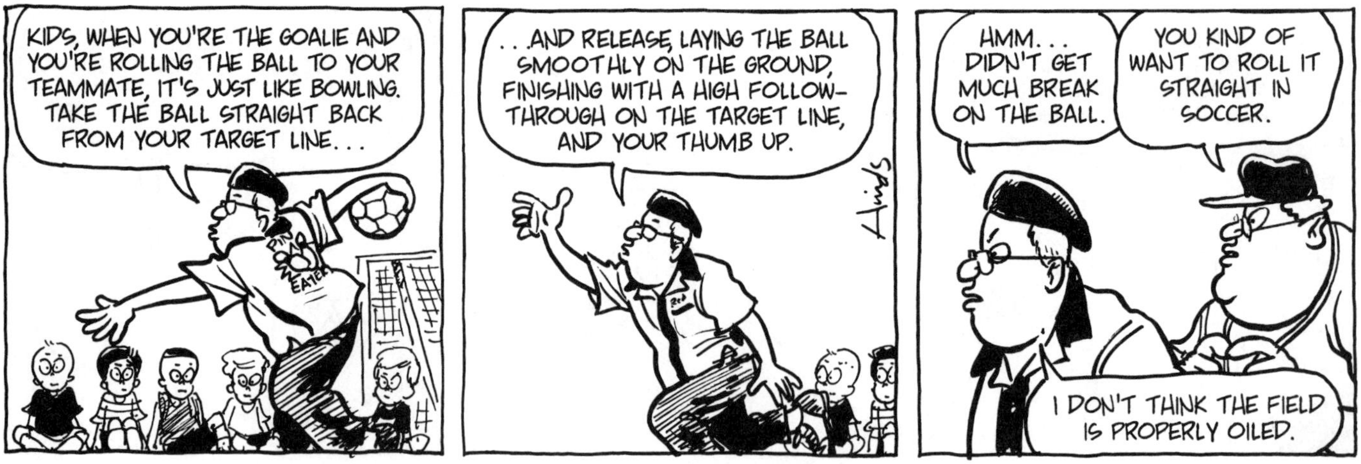
KIDS, WHEN YOU'RE THE GOALIE AND YOU'RE ROLLING THE BALL TO YOUR TEAMMATE, IT'S JUST LIKE BOWLING. TAKE THE BALL STRAIGHT BACK FROM YOUR TARGET LINE...
...AND RELEASE, LAYING THE BALL SMOOTHLY ON THE GROUND, FINISHING WITH A HIGH FOLLOW-THROUGH ON THE TARGET LINE, AND YOUR THUMB UP.
Hinds
HMM... DIDN'T GET MUCH BREAK ON THE BALL.
YOU KIND OF WANT TO ROLL IT STRAIGHT IN SOCCER.
I DON'T THINK THE FIELD IS PROPERLY OILED.

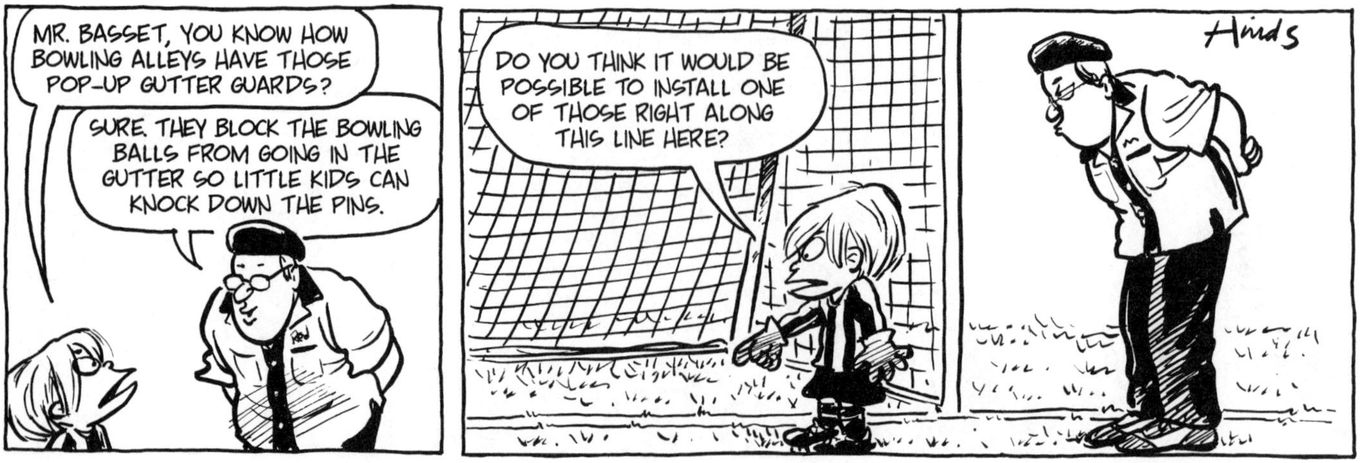
MR. BASSET, YOU KNOW HOW BOWLING ALLEYS HAVE THOSE POP-UP GUTTER GUARDS?
SURE. THEY BLOCK THE BOWLING BALLS FROM GOING IN THE GUTTER SO LITTLE KIDS CAN KNOCK DOWN THE PINS.
DO YOU THINK IT WOULD BE POSSIBLE TO INSTALL ONE OF THOSE RIGHT ALONG THIS LINE HERE?
Hinds

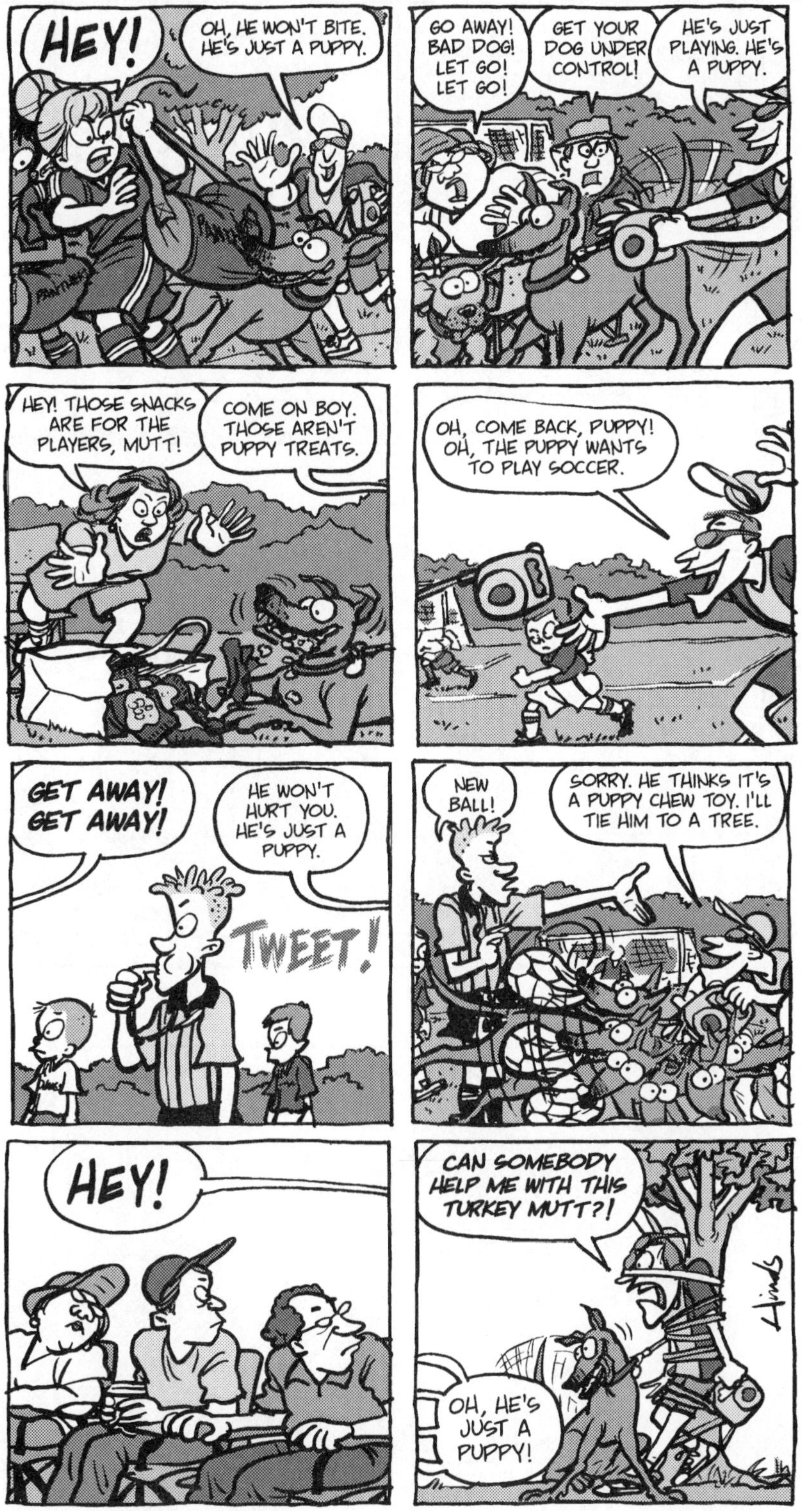
HEY!
OH, HE WON'T BITE. HE'S JUST A PUPPY.
GO AWAY! BAD DOG! LET GO! LET GO!
GET YOUR DOG UNDER CONTROL!
HE'S JUST PLAYING. HE'S A PUPPY.
HEY! THOSE SNACKS ARE FOR THE PLAYERS, MUTT!
COME ON BOY. THOSE AREN'T PUPPY TREATS.
OH, COME BACK, PUPPY! OH, THE PUPPY WANTS TO PLAY SOCCER.
GET AWAY! GET AWAY!
HE WON'T HURT YOU. HE'S JUST A PUPPY.
TWEET!
NEW BALL!
SORRY. HE THINKS IT'S A PUPPY CHEW TOY. I'LL TIE HIM TO A TREE.
HEY!
CAN SOMEBODY HELP ME WITH THIS TURKEY MUTT?!
OH, HE'S JUST A PUPPY!
Hinds

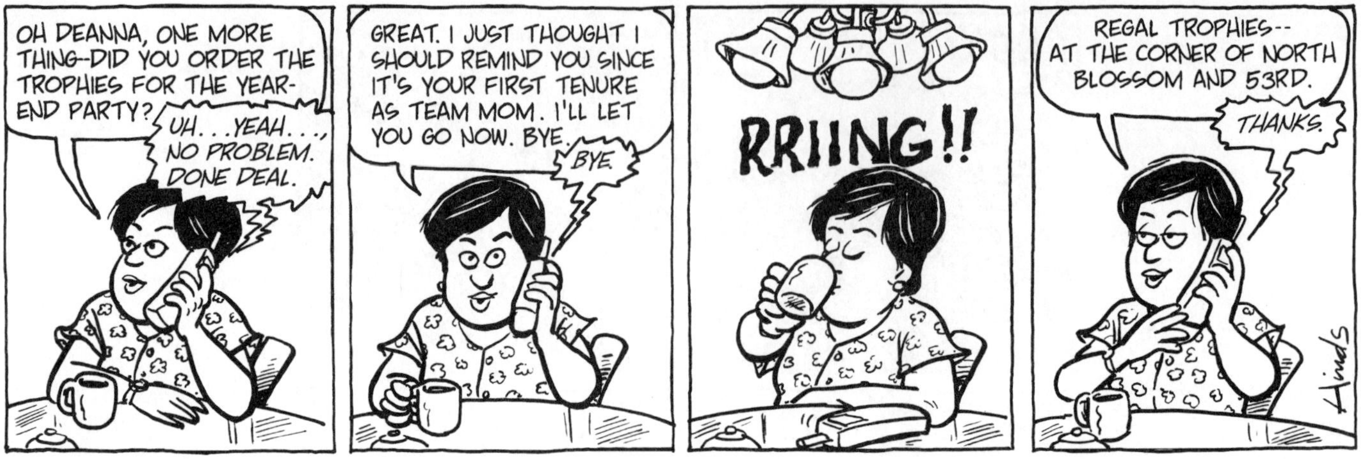
OH DEANNA, ONE MORE THING--DID YOU ORDER THE TROPHIES FOR THE YEAR-END PARTY?
UH...YEAH..., NO PROBLEM. DONE DEAL.
GREAT. I JUST THOUGHT I SHOULD REMIND YOU SINCE IT'S YOUR FIRST TENURE AS TEAM MOM. I'LL LET YOU GO NOW. BYE.
BYE.
RRIING!!
REGAL TROPHIES-- AT THE CORNER OF NORTH BLOSSOM AND 53RD.
THANKS.
Hinds

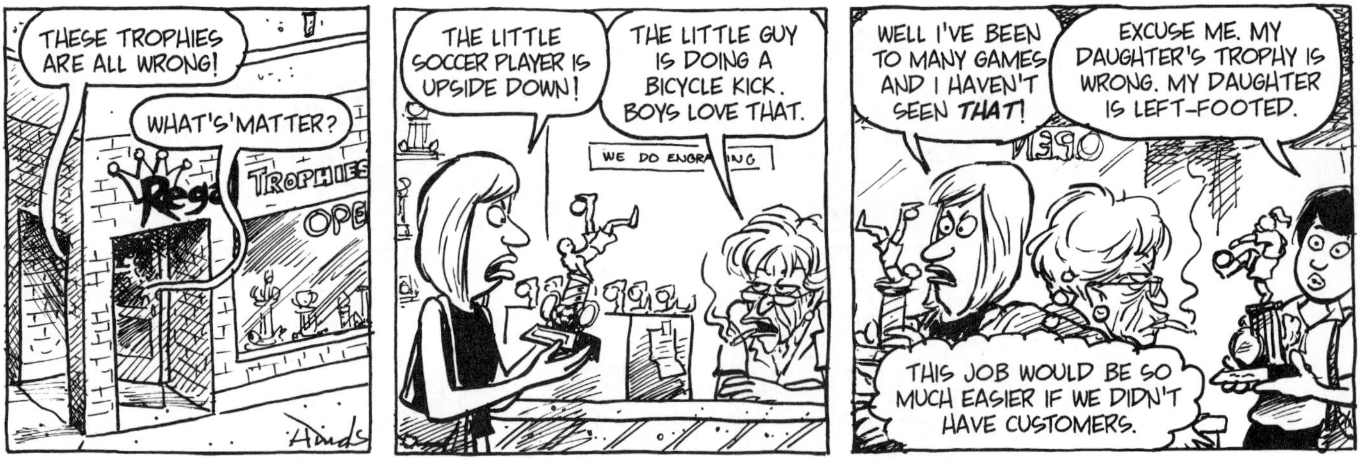
THESE TROPHIES ARE ALL WRONG!
WHAT'S'MATTER?
TROPHIES
Hinds
THE LITTLE SOCCER PLAYER IS UPSIDE DOWN!
THE LITTLE GUY IS DOING A BICYCLE KICK. BOYS LOVE THAT.
WELL I'VE BEEN TO MANY GAMES AND I HAVEN'T SEEN THAT!
EXCUSE ME. MY DAUGHTER'S TROPHY IS WRONG. MY DAUGHTER IS LEFT-FOOTED.
THIS JOB WOULD BE SO MUCH EASIER IF WE DIDN'T HAVE CUSTOMERS.

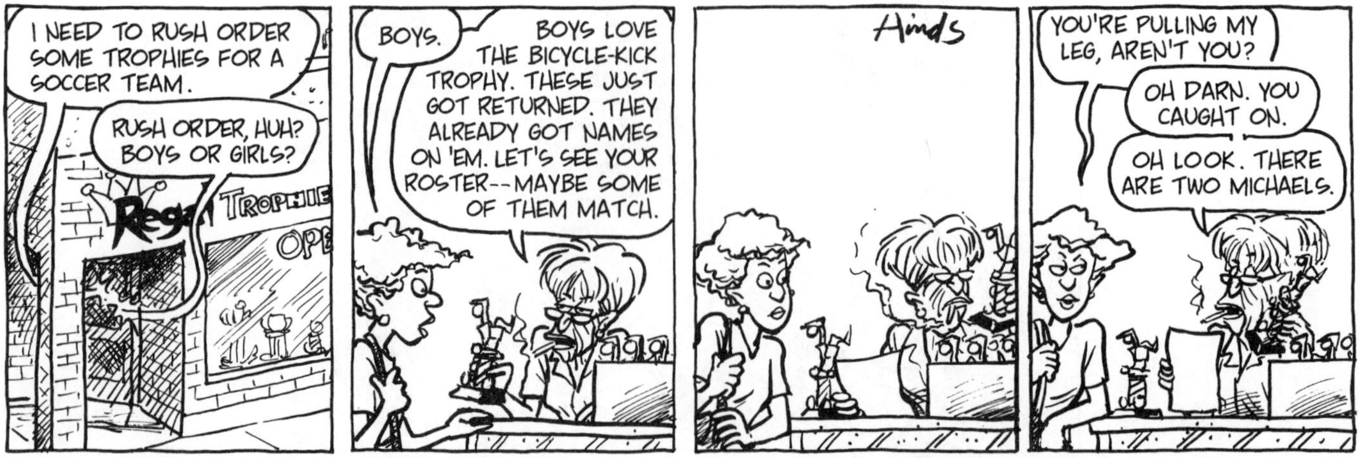
I NEED TO RUSH ORDER SOME TROPHIES FOR A SOCCER TEAM.
RUSH ORDER, HUH? BOYS OR GIRLS?
BOYS.
BOYS LOVE THE BICYCLE-KICK TROPHY. THESE JUST GOT RETURNED. THEY ALREADY GOT NAMES ON 'EM. LET'S SEE YOUR ROSTER--MAYBE SOME OF THEM MATCH.
Hinds
YOU'RE PULLING MY LEG, AREN'T YOU?
OH DARN. YOU CAUGHT ON.
OH LOOK. THERE ARE TWO MICHAELS.

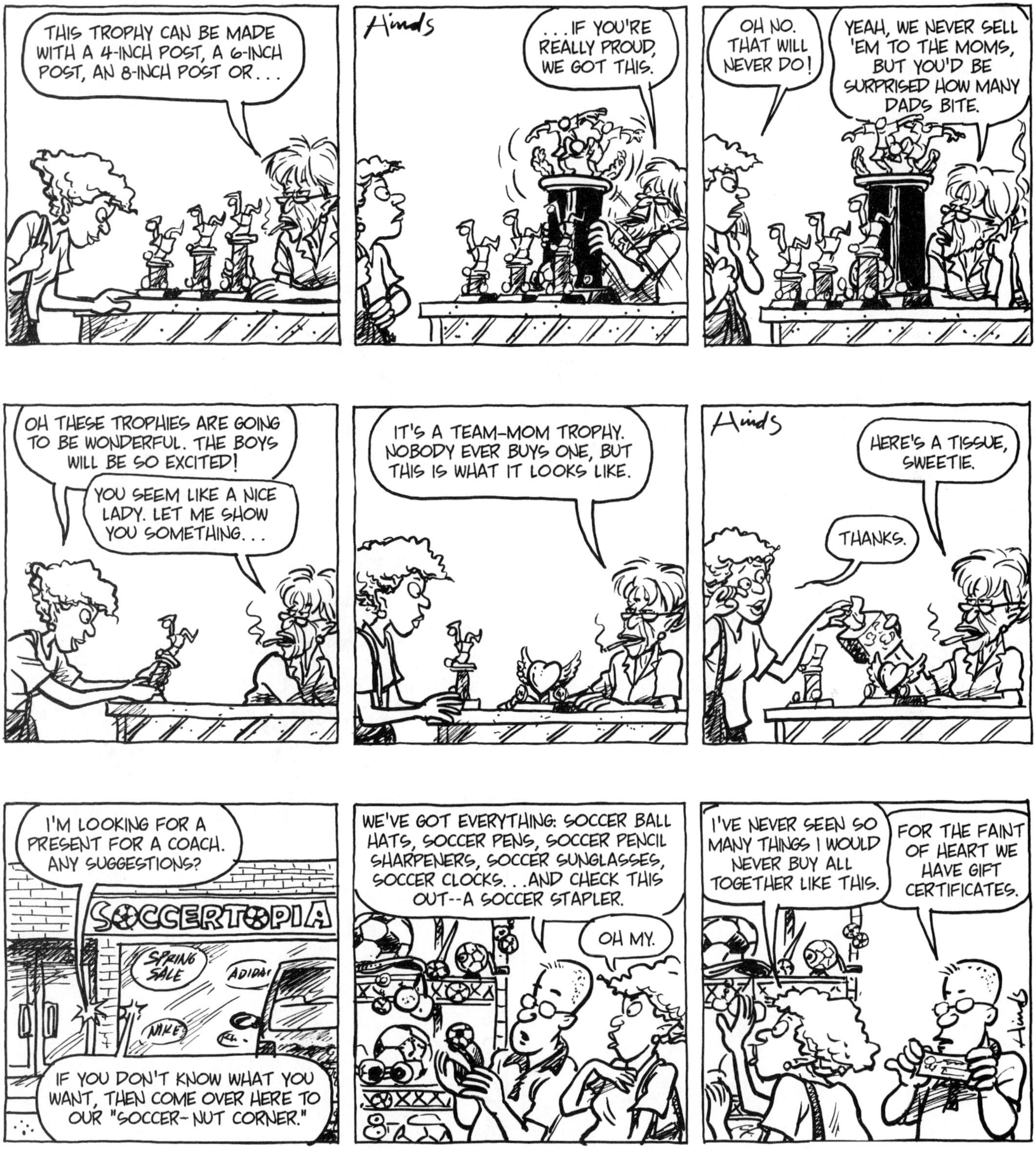
THIS TROPHY CAN BE MADE WITH A 4-INCH POST, A 6-INCH POST, AN 8-INCH POST OR . . .
Hinds
. . . IF YOU'RE REALLY PROUD, WE GOT THIS.
OH NO. THAT WILL NEVER DO!
YEAH, WE NEVER SELL 'EM TO THE MOMS, BUT YOU'D BE SURPRISED HOW MANY DADS BITE.
OH THESE TROPHIES ARE GOING TO BE WONDERFUL. THE BOYS WILL BE SO EXCITED!
YOU SEEM LIKE A NICE LADY. LET ME SHOW YOU SOMETHING . . .
IT'S A TEAM-MOM TROPHY. NOBODY EVER BUYS ONE, BUT THIS IS WHAT IT LOOKS LIKE.
Hinds
HERE'S A TISSUE, SWEETIE.
THANKS.
I'M LOOKING FOR A PRESENT FOR A COACH. ANY SUGGESTIONS?
SOCCERTOPIA
SPRING SALE
NIKE
IF YOU DON'T KNOW WHAT YOU WANT, THEN COME OVER HERE TO OUR "SOCCER-NUT CORNER."
WE'VE GOT EVERYTHING: SOCCER BALL HATS, SOCCER PENS, SOCCER PENCIL SHARPENERS, SOCCER SUNGLASSES, SOCCER CLOCKS . . . AND CHECK THIS OUT--A SOCCER STAPLER.
OH MY.
I'VE NEVER SEEN SO MANY THINGS I WOULD NEVER BUY ALL TOGETHER LIKE THIS.
FOR THE FAINT OF HEART WE HAVE GIFT CERTIFICATES.
Hinds

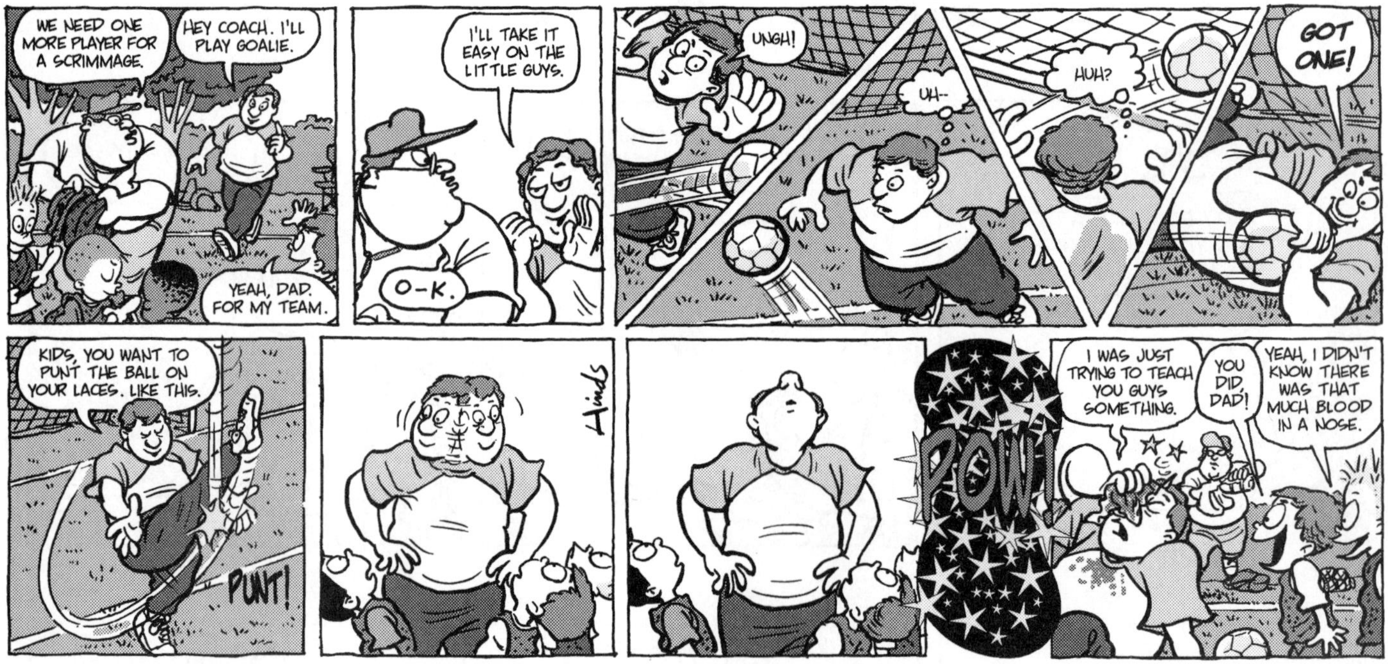
WE NEED ONE MORE PLAYER FOR A SCRIMMAGE.
HEY COACH. I'LL PLAY GOALIE.
YEAH, DAD. FOR MY TEAM.
I'LL TAKE IT EASY ON THE LITTLE GUYS.
O-K.
UNGH!
UH--
HUH?
GOT ONE!
KIDS, YOU WANT TO PUNT THE BALL ON YOUR LACES. LIKE THIS.
PUNT!
Hinds
POW!
I WAS JUST TRYING TO TEACH YOU GUYS SOMETHING.
YOU DID, DAD!
YEAH, I DIDN'T KNOW THERE WAS THAT MUCH BLOOD IN A NOSE.

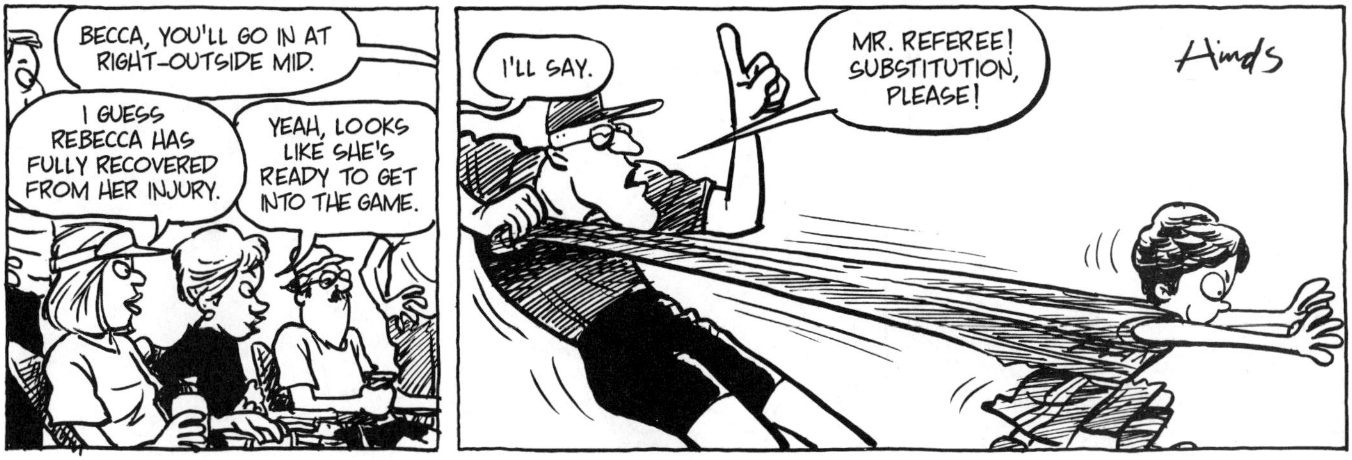
BECCA, YOU'LL GO IN AT RIGHT-OUTSIDE MID.
I GUESS REBECCA HAS FULLY RECOVERED FROM HER INJURY.
YEAH, LOOKS LIKE SHE'S READY TO GET INTO THE GAME.
I'LL SAY.
MR. REFEREE! SUBSTITUTION, PLEASE!
Hinds

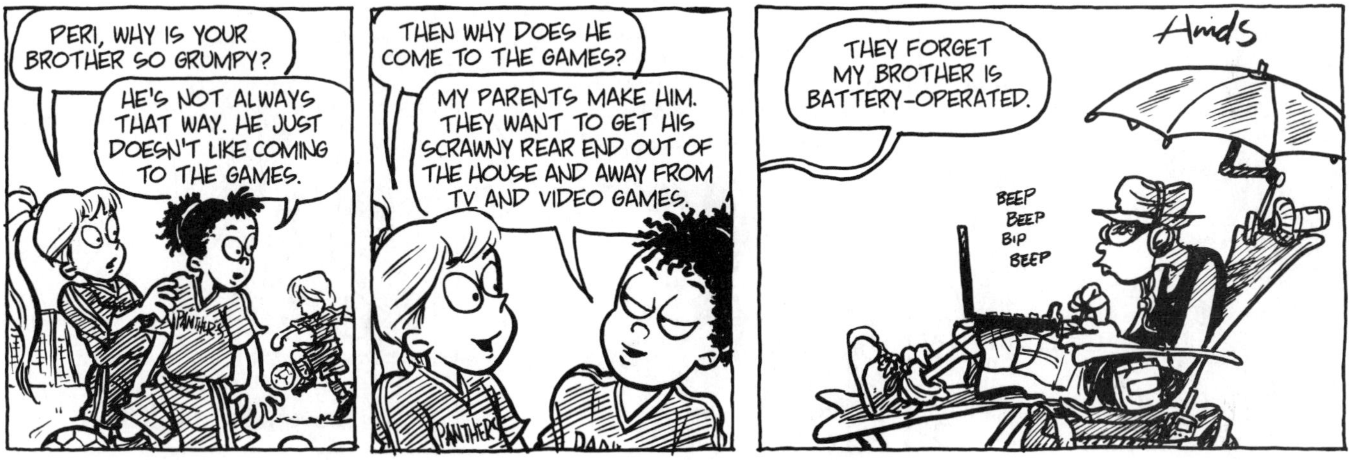
PERI, WHY IS YOUR BROTHER SO GRUMPY?
HE'S NOT ALWAYS THAT WAY. HE JUST DOESN'T LIKE COMING TO THE GAMES.
THEN WHY DOES HE COME TO THE GAMES?
MY PARENTS MAKE HIM. THEY WANT TO GET HIS SCRAWNY REAR END OUT OF THE HOUSE AND AWAY FROM TV AND VIDEO GAMES.
THEY FORGET MY BROTHER IS BATTERY-OPERATED.
BEEP BEEP BIP BEEP
Hinds

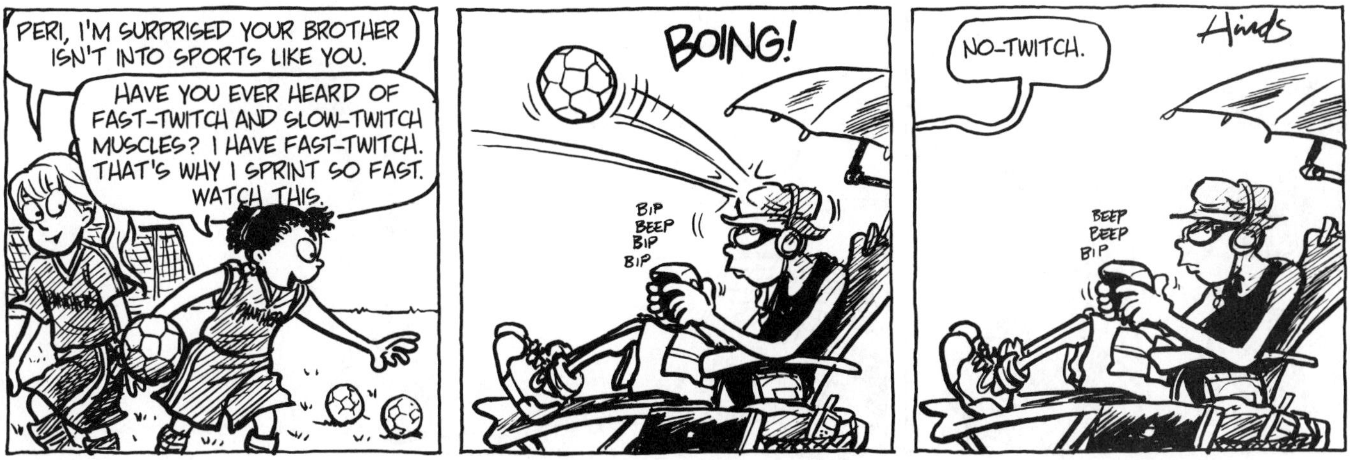
PERI, I'M SURPRISED YOUR BROTHER ISN'T INTO SPORTS LIKE YOU.
HAVE YOU EVER HEARD OF FAST-TWITCH AND SLOW-TWITCH MUSCLES? I HAVE FAST-TWITCH. THAT'S WHY I SPRINT SO FAST. WATCH THIS.
BOING!
BIP BEEP BIP BIP
NO-TWITCH.
BEEP BEEP BIP
Hinds

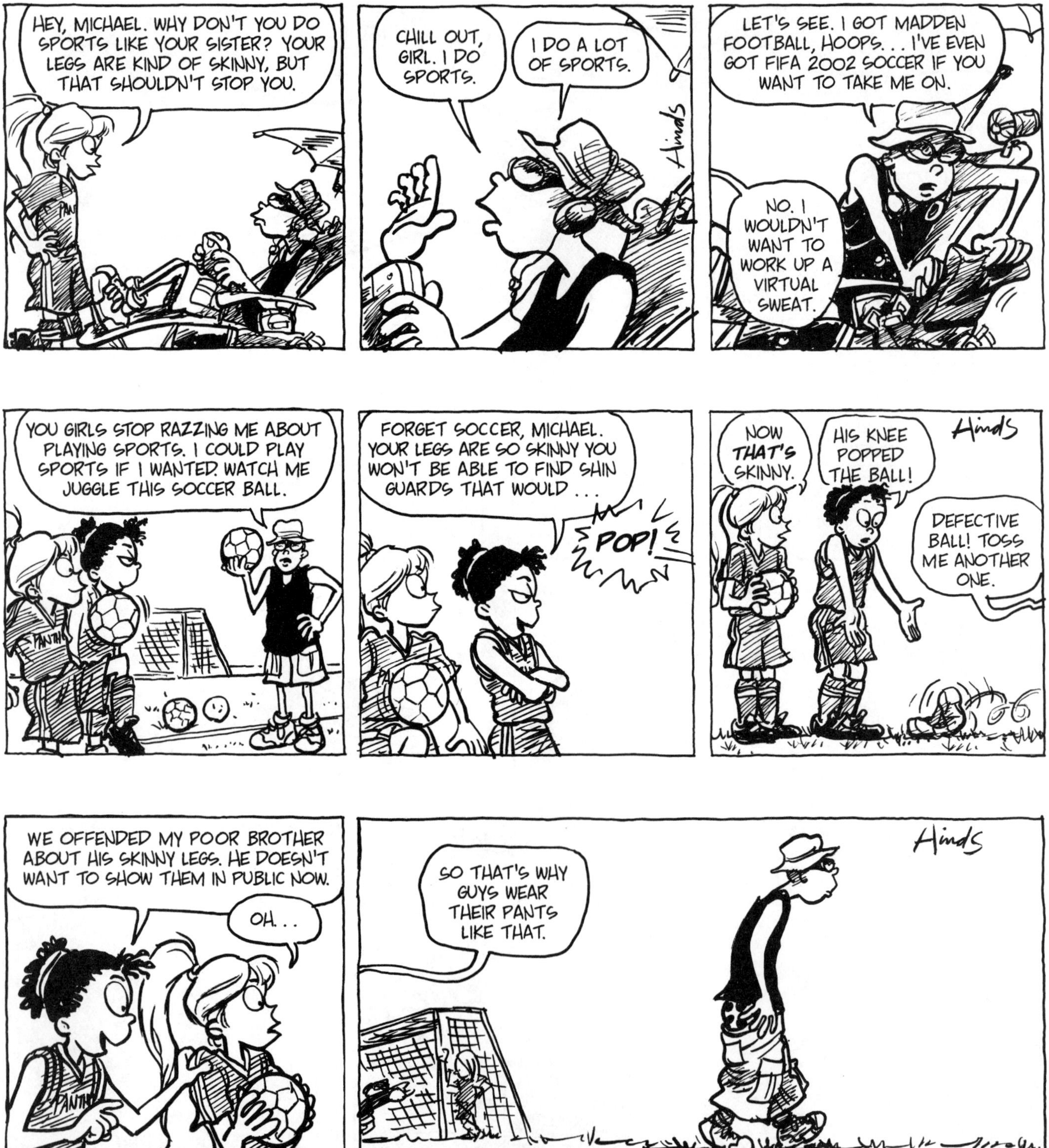
HEY, MICHAEL. WHY DON'T YOU DO SPORTS LIKE YOUR SISTER? YOUR LEGS ARE KIND OF SKINNY, BUT THAT SHOULDN'T STOP YOU.
CHILL OUT, GIRL. I DO SPORTS.
I DO A LOT OF SPORTS.
Hinds
LET'S SEE. I GOT MADDEN FOOTBALL, HOOPS... I'VE EVEN GOT FIFA 2002 SOCCER IF YOU WANT TO TAKE ME ON.
NO. I WOULDN'T WANT TO WORK UP A VIRTUAL SWEAT.
YOU GIRLS STOP RAZZING ME ABOUT PLAYING SPORTS. I COULD PLAY SPORTS IF I WANTED. WATCH ME JUGGLE THIS SOCCER BALL.
FORGET SOCCER, MICHAEL. YOUR LEGS ARE SO SKINNY YOU WON'T BE ABLE TO FIND SHIN GUARDS THAT WOULD . . .
POP!
Hinds
NOW THAT'S SKINNY.
HIS KNEE POPPED THE BALL!
DEFECTIVE BALL! TOSS ME ANOTHER ONE.
WE OFFENDED MY POOR BROTHER ABOUT HIS SKINNY LEGS. HE DOESN'T WANT TO SHOW THEM IN PUBLIC NOW.
OH. . .
Hinds
SO THAT'S WHY GUYS WEAR THEIR PANTS LIKE THAT.

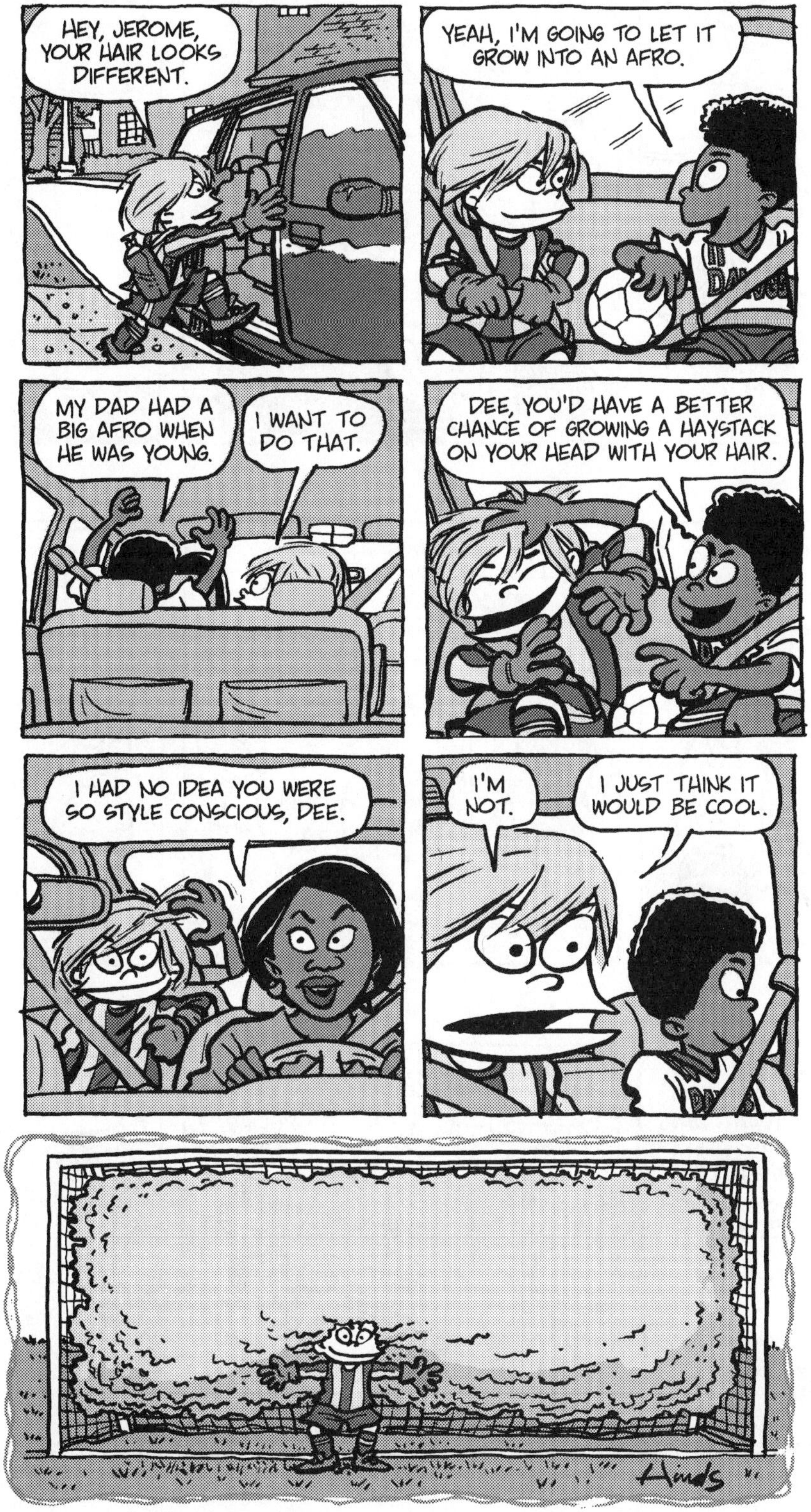
HEY, JEROME, YOUR HAIR LOOKS DIFFERENT.
YEAH, I'M GOING TO LET IT GROW INTO AN AFRO.
MY DAD HAD A BIG AFRO WHEN HE WAS YOUNG.
I WANT TO DO THAT.
DEE, YOU'D HAVE A BETTER CHANCE OF GROWING A HAYSTACK ON YOUR HEAD WITH YOUR HAIR.
I HAD NO IDEA YOU WERE SO STYLE CONSCIOUS, DEE.
I'M NOT.
I JUST THINK IT WOULD BE COOL.
Hinds

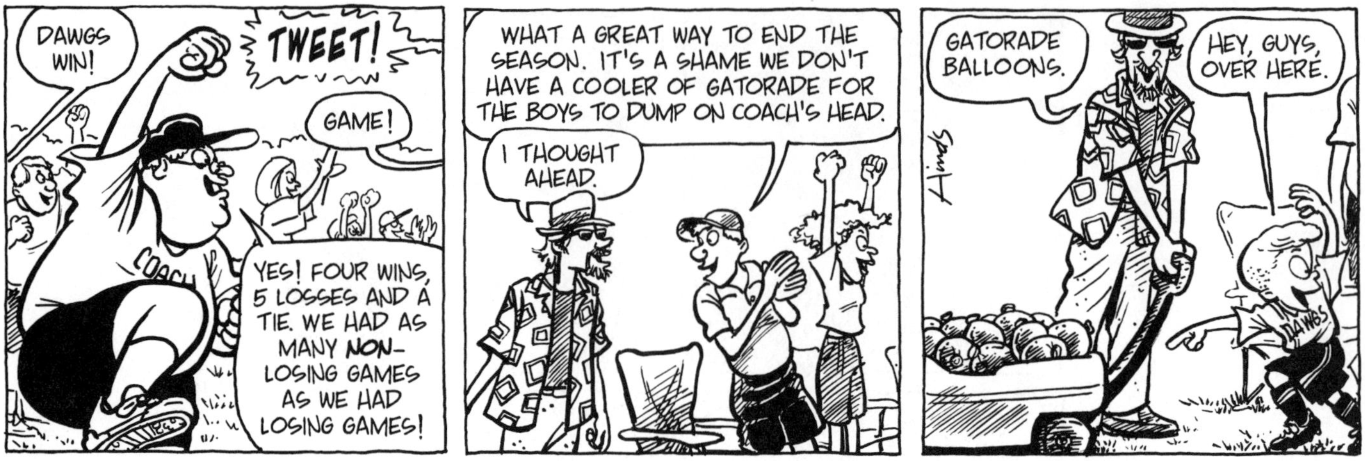
DAWGS WIN!
TWEET!
GAME!
YES! FOUR WINS, 5 LOSSES AND A TIE. WE HAD AS MANY **NON**-LOSING GAMES AS WE HAD LOSING GAMES!
COACH
WHAT A GREAT WAY TO END THE SEASON. IT'S A SHAME WE DON'T HAVE A COOLER OF GATORADE FOR THE BOYS TO DUMP ON COACH'S HEAD.
I THOUGHT AHEAD.
GATORADE BALLOONS.
HEY, GUYS, OVER HERE.
Hinds
DAWGS

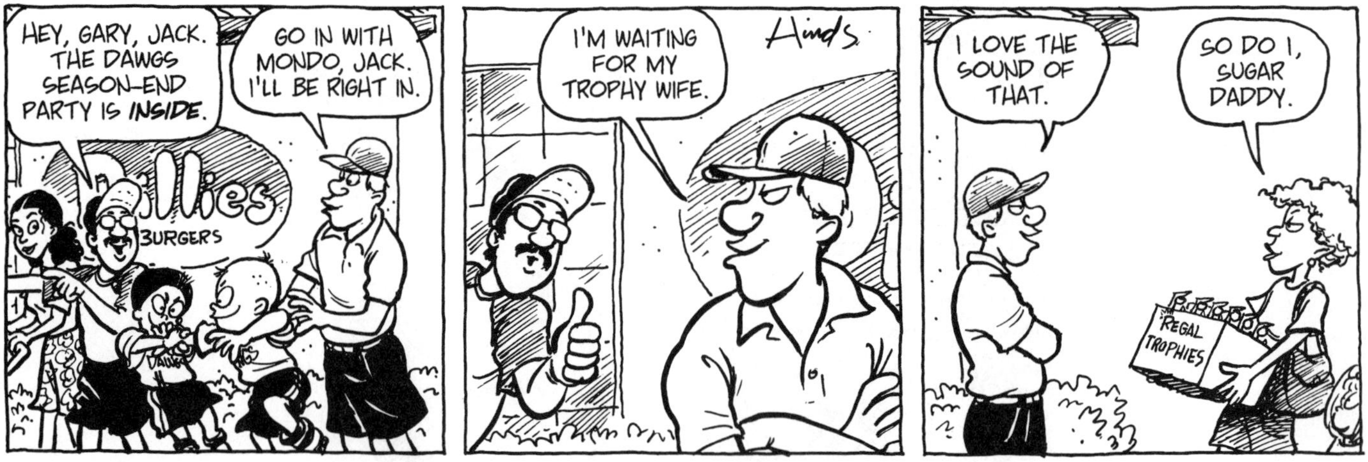
HEY, GARY, JACK. THE DAWGS SEASON-END PARTY IS ***INSIDE***.
GO IN WITH MONDO, JACK. I'LL BE RIGHT IN.
Dillies BURGERS
I'M WAITING FOR MY TROPHY WIFE.
Hinds
I LOVE THE SOUND OF THAT.
SO DO I, SUGAR DADDY.
REGAL TROPHIES

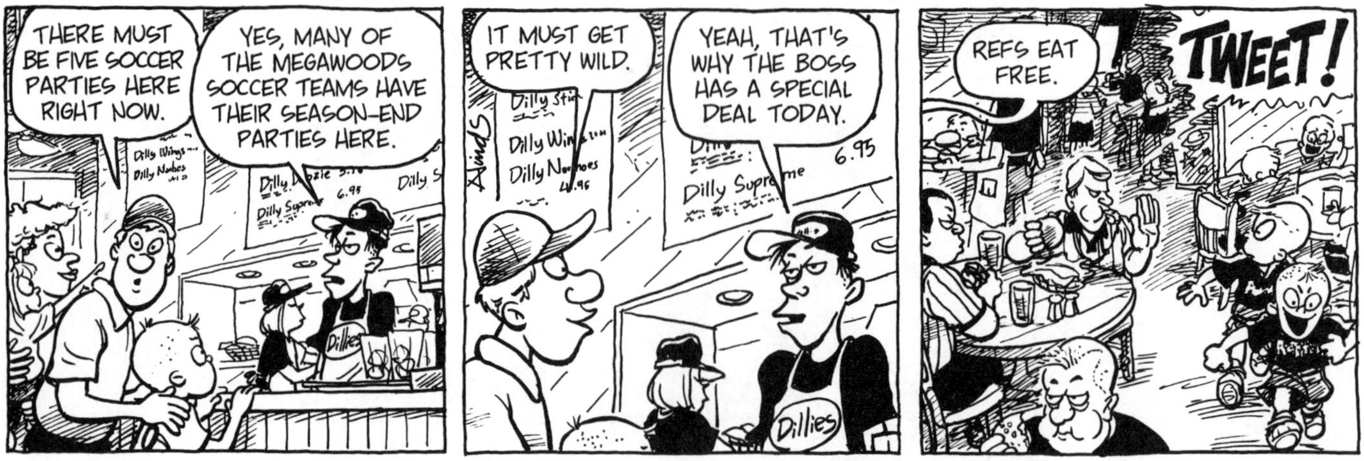
THERE MUST BE FIVE SOCCER PARTIES HERE RIGHT NOW.
YES, MANY OF THE MEGAWOODS SOCCER TEAMS HAVE THEIR SEASON-END PARTIES HERE.
IT MUST GET PRETTY WILD.
YEAH, THAT'S WHY THE BOSS HAS A SPECIAL DEAL TODAY.
Dilly Supreme 6.95
Hinds
REFS EAT FREE.
TWEET!
Dillies

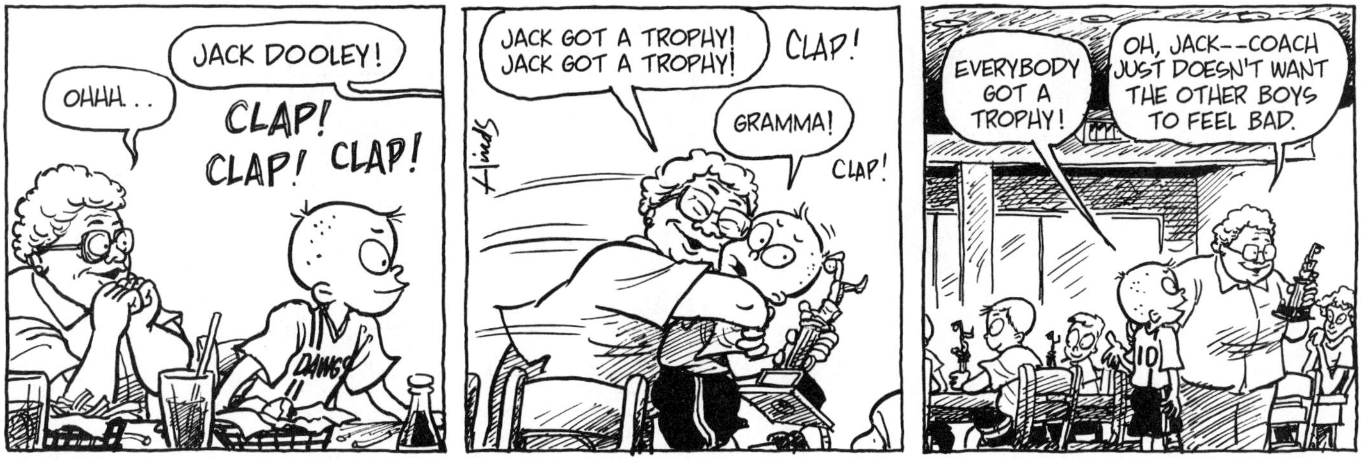
OHHH. . .
JACK DOOLEY!
CLAP! CLAP! CLAP!
JACK GOT A TROPHY! JACK GOT A TROPHY!
CLAP!
GRAMMA!
CLAP!
EVERYBODY GOT A TROPHY!
OH, JACK--COACH JUST DOESN'T WANT THE OTHER BOYS TO FEEL BAD.

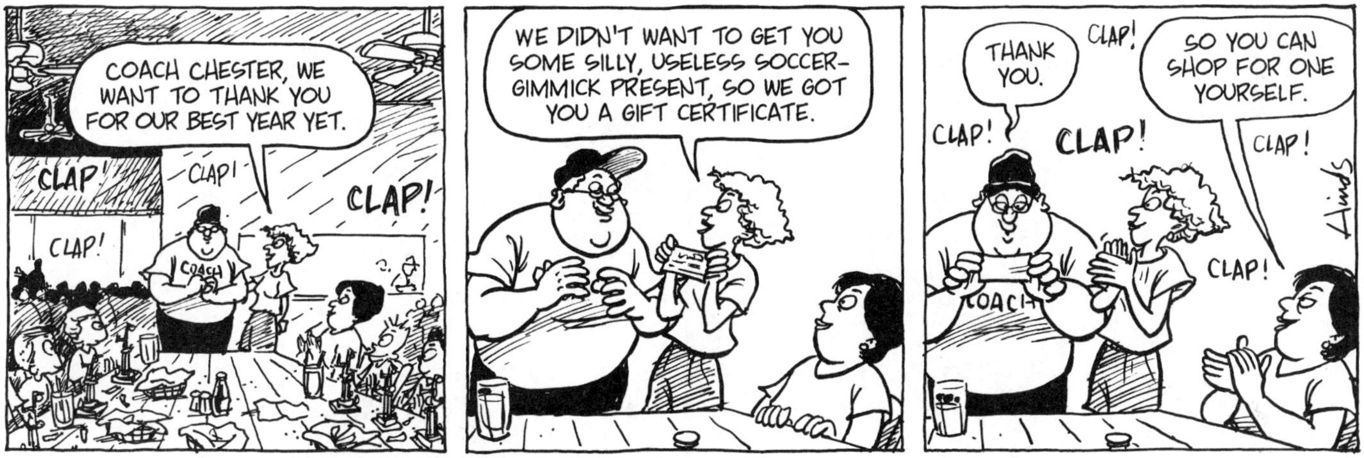
COACH CHESTER, WE WANT TO THANK YOU FOR OUR BEST YEAR YET.
CLAP!
CLAP!
CLAP!
CLAP!
WE DIDN'T WANT TO GET YOU SOME SILLY, USELESS SOCCER-GIMMICK PRESENT, SO WE GOT YOU A GIFT CERTIFICATE.
THANK YOU.
CLAP!
SO YOU CAN SHOP FOR ONE YOURSELF.
CLAP!
CLAP!
CLAP!
CLAP!

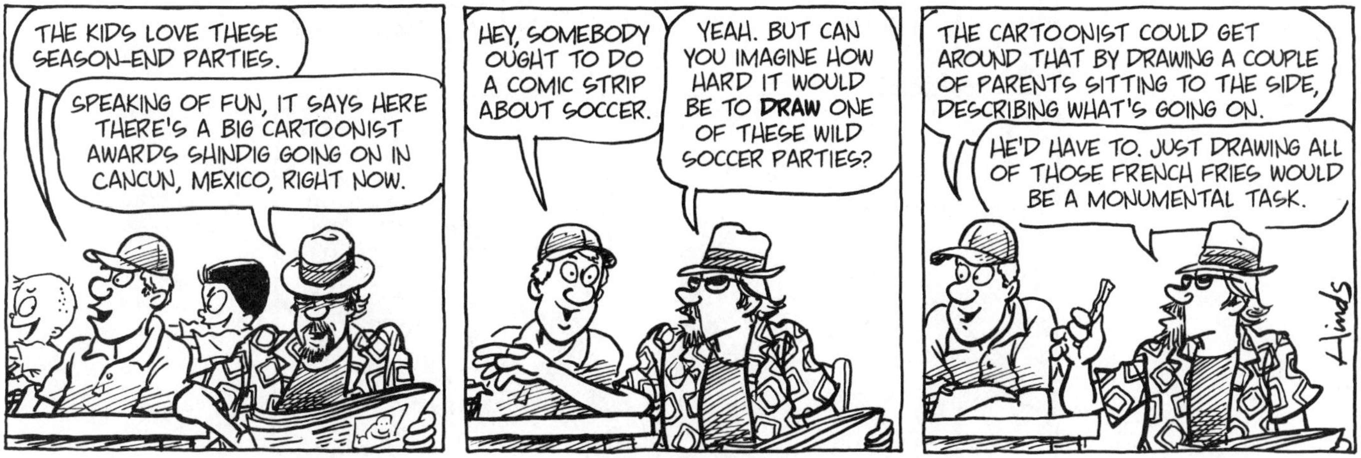
THE KIDS LOVE THESE SEASON-END PARTIES.
SPEAKING OF FUN, IT SAYS HERE THERE'S A BIG CARTOONIST AWARDS SHINDIG GOING ON IN CANCUN, MEXICO, RIGHT NOW.
HEY, SOMEBODY OUGHT TO DO A COMIC STRIP ABOUT SOCCER.
YEAH. BUT CAN YOU IMAGINE HOW HARD IT WOULD BE TO DRAW ONE OF THESE WILD SOCCER PARTIES?
THE CARTOONIST COULD GET AROUND THAT BY DRAWING A COUPLE OF PARENTS SITTING TO THE SIDE, DESCRIBING WHAT'S GOING ON.
HE'D HAVE TO. JUST DRAWING ALL OF THOSE FRENCH FRIES WOULD BE A MONUMENTAL TASK.

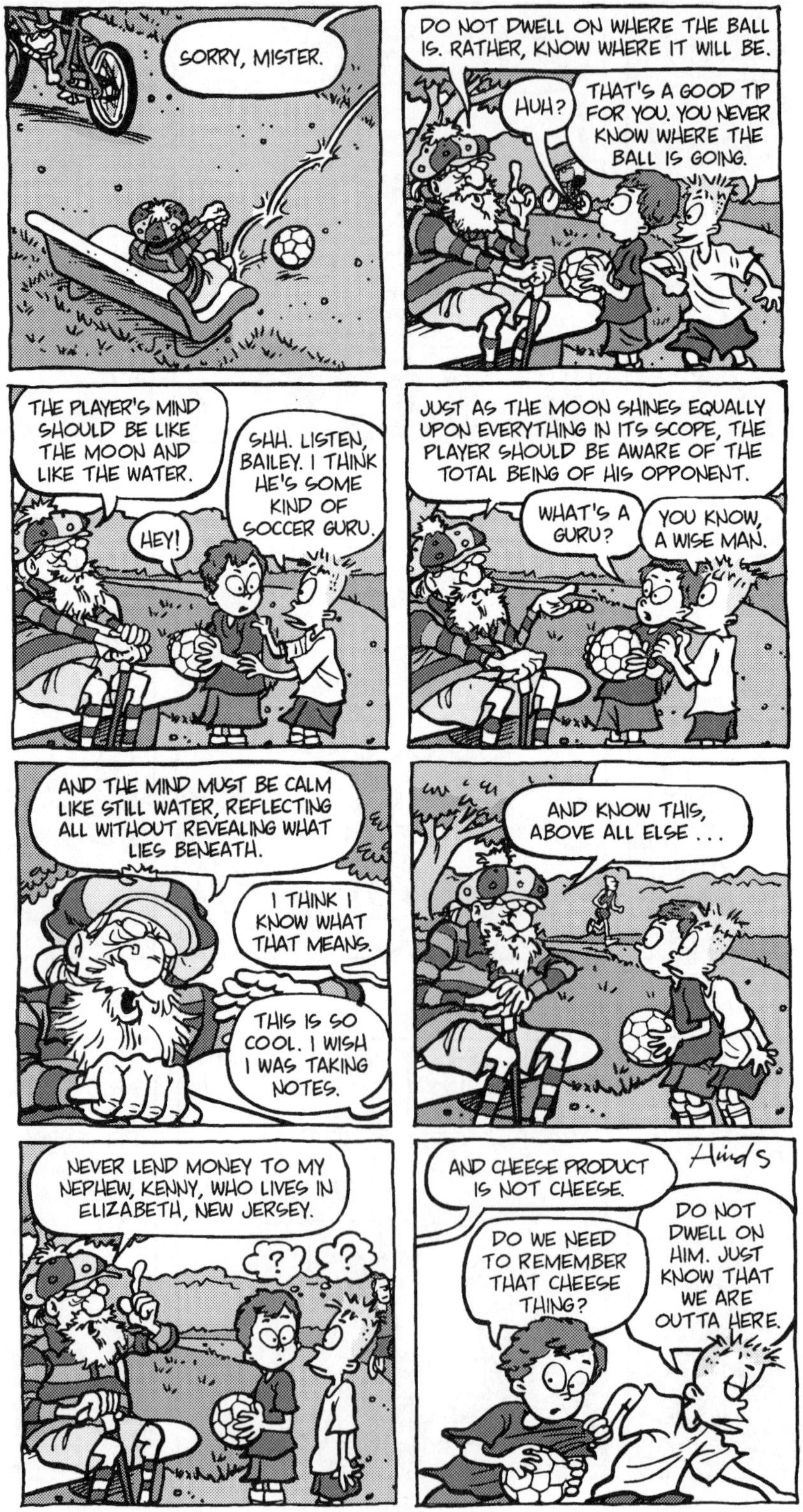
SORRY, MISTER.
DO NOT DWELL ON WHERE THE BALL IS. RATHER, KNOW WHERE IT WILL BE.
HUH?
THAT'S A GOOD TIP FOR YOU. YOU NEVER KNOW WHERE THE BALL IS GOING.
THE PLAYER'S MIND SHOULD BE LIKE THE MOON AND LIKE THE WATER.
HEY!
SHH. LISTEN, BAILEY. I THINK HE'S SOME KIND OF SOCCER GURU.
JUST AS THE MOON SHINES EQUALLY UPON EVERYTHING IN ITS SCOPE, THE PLAYER SHOULD BE AWARE OF THE TOTAL BEING OF HIS OPPONENT.
WHAT'S A GURU?
YOU KNOW, A WISE MAN.
AND THE MIND MUST BE CALM LIKE STILL WATER, REFLECTING ALL WITHOUT REVEALING WHAT LIES BENEATH.
I THINK I KNOW WHAT THAT MEANS.
THIS IS SO COOL. I WISH I WAS TAKING NOTES.
AND KNOW THIS, ABOVE ALL ELSE . . .
NEVER LEND MONEY TO MY NEPHEW, KENNY, WHO LIVES IN ELIZABETH, NEW JERSEY.
?
?
Hinds
AND CHEESE PRODUCT IS NOT CHEESE.
DO WE NEED TO REMEMBER THAT CHEESE THING?
DO NOT DWELL ON HIM. JUST KNOW THAT WE ARE OUTTA HERE.

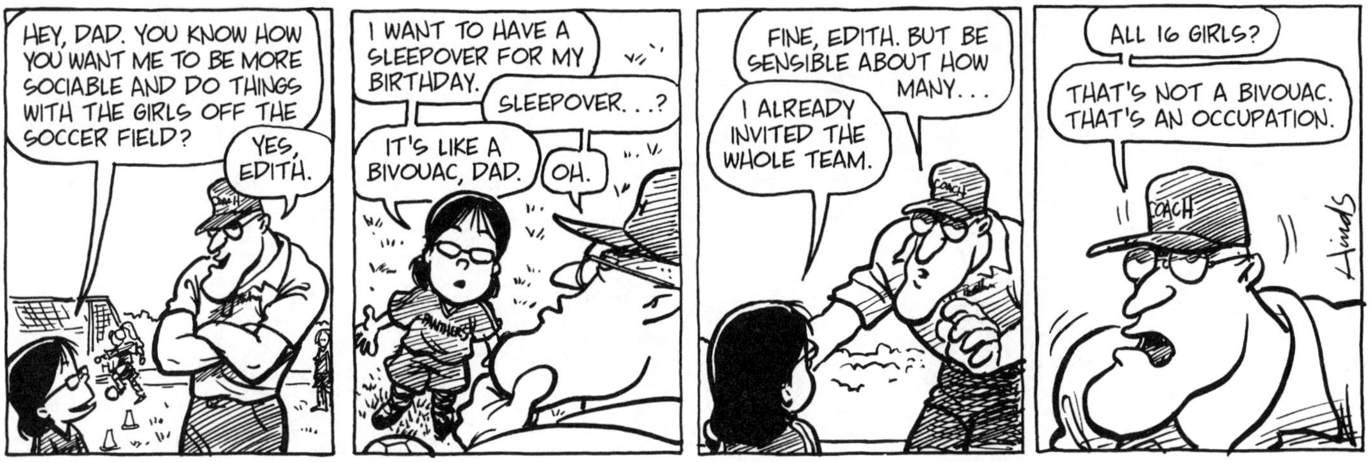
HEY, DAD. YOU KNOW HOW YOU WANT ME TO BE MORE SOCIABLE AND DO THINGS WITH THE GIRLS OFF THE SOCCER FIELD?
YES, EDITH.
I WANT TO HAVE A SLEEPOVER FOR MY BIRTHDAY.
SLEEPOVER...?
IT'S LIKE A BIVOUAC, DAD.
OH.
FINE, EDITH. BUT BE SENSIBLE ABOUT HOW MANY...
I ALREADY INVITED THE WHOLE TEAM.
ALL 16 GIRLS?
THAT'S NOT A BIVOUAC. THAT'S AN OCCUPATION.
Hinds

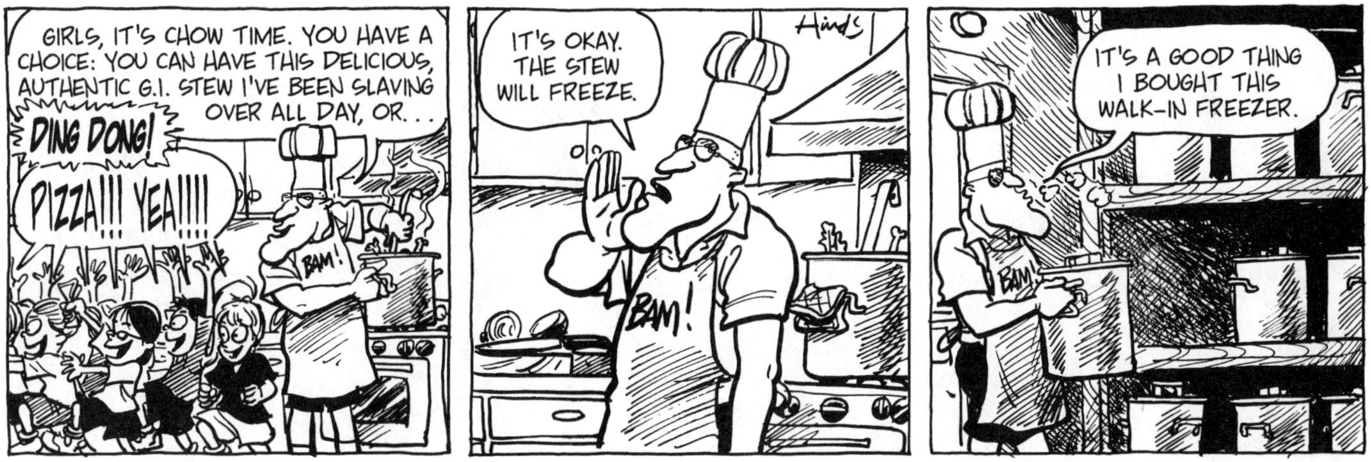
GIRLS, IT'S CHOW TIME. YOU HAVE A CHOICE: YOU CAN HAVE THIS DELICIOUS, AUTHENTIC G.I. STEW I'VE BEEN SLAVING OVER ALL DAY, OR...
DING DONG!
PIZZA!!! YEA!!!!
BAM!
IT'S OKAY. THE STEW WILL FREEZE.
Hinds
IT'S A GOOD THING I BOUGHT THIS WALK-IN FREEZER.

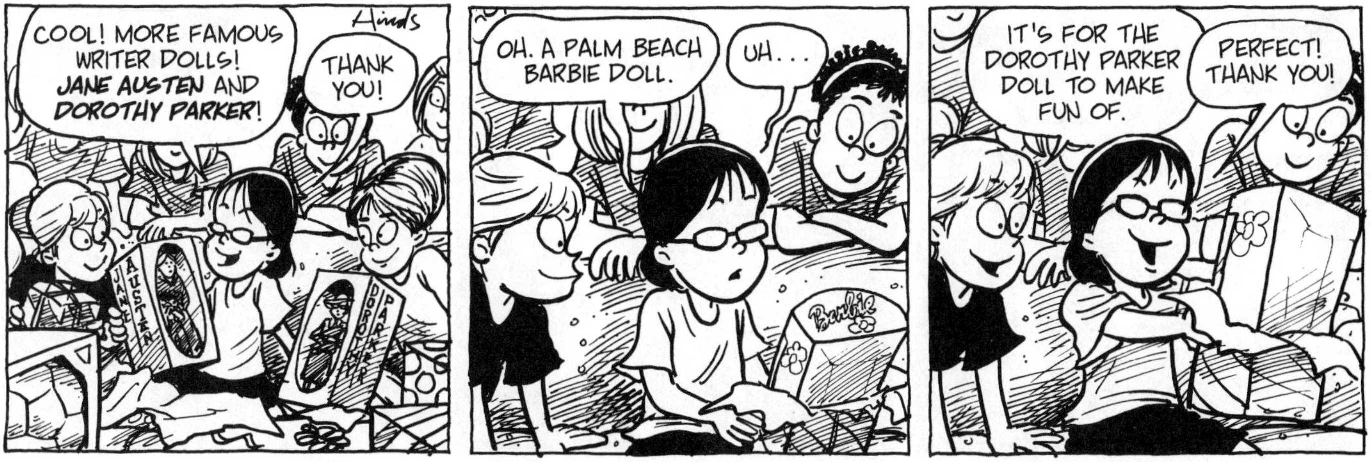
COOL! MORE FAMOUS WRITER DOLLS! JANE AUSTEN AND DOROTHY PARKER!
THANK YOU!
Hinds
JANE AUSTEN
DOROTHY PARKER
OH. A PALM BEACH BARBIE DOLL.
UH...
Barbie
IT'S FOR THE DOROTHY PARKER DOLL TO MAKE FUN OF.
PERFECT! THANK YOU!

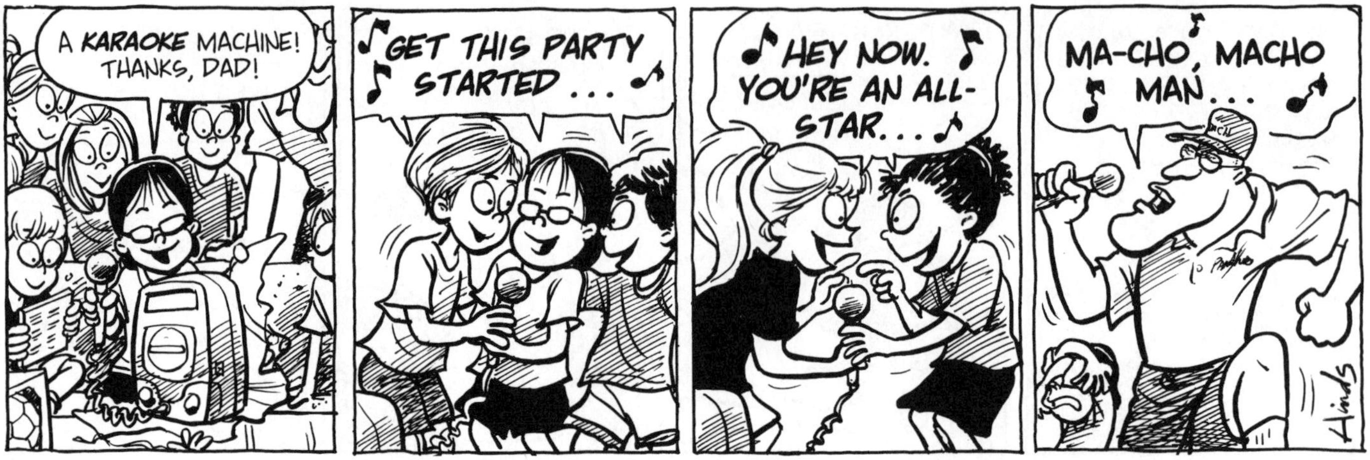
A KARAOKE MACHINE! THANKS, DAD!
GET THIS PARTY STARTED . . .
HEY NOW. YOU'RE AN ALL-STAR. . .
MA-CHO, MACHO MAN . . .
Hinds

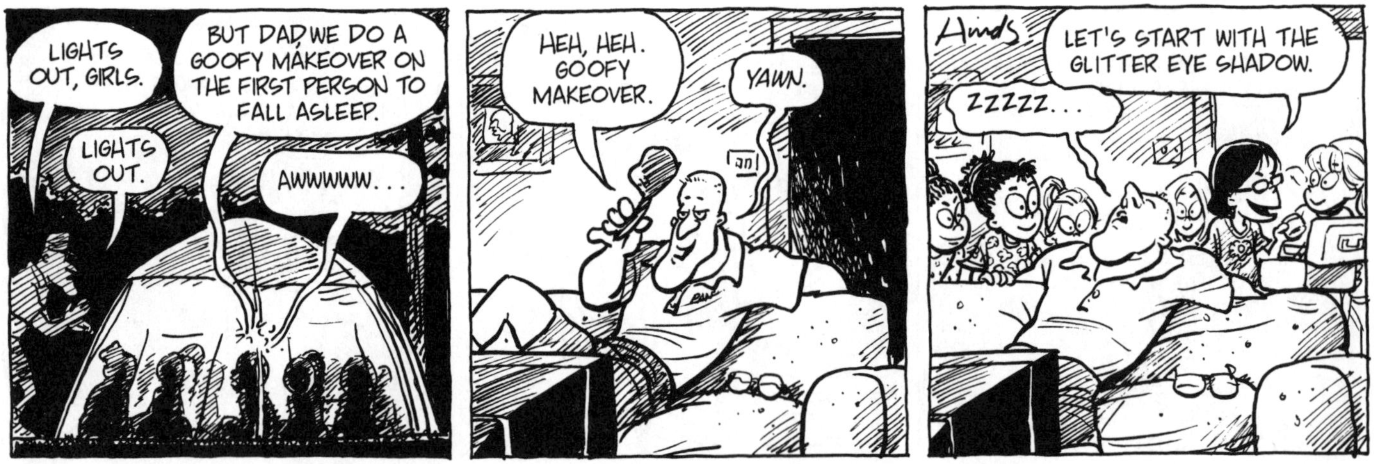
LIGHTS OUT, GIRLS.
LIGHTS OUT.
BUT DAD, WE DO A GOOFY MAKEOVER ON THE FIRST PERSON TO FALL ASLEEP.
AWWWWW. . .
HEH, HEH. GOOFY MAKEOVER.
YAWN.
Hinds
LET'S START WITH THE GLITTER EYE SHADOW.
ZZZZZ. . .

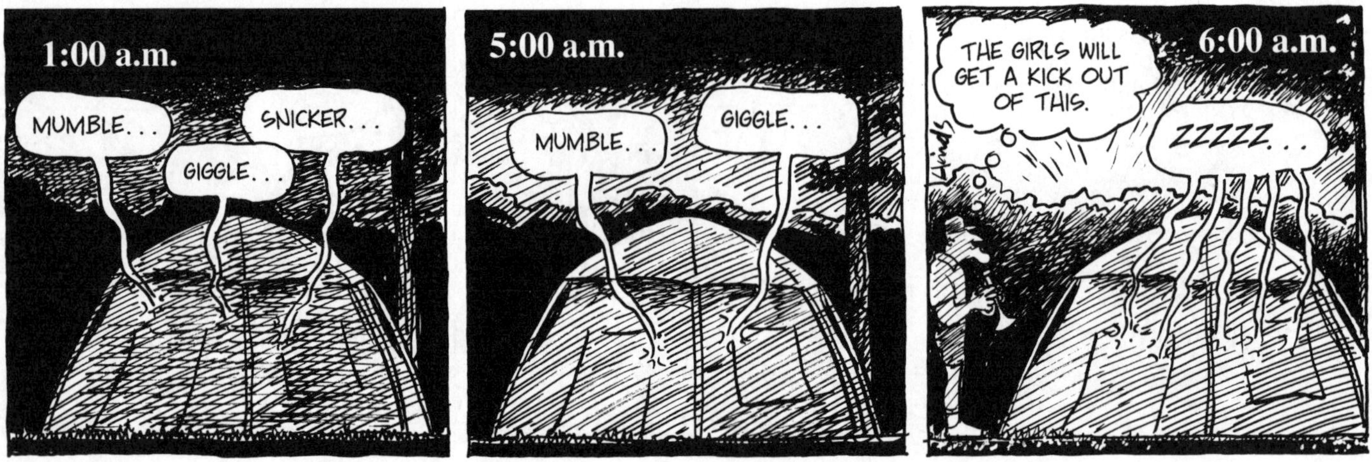
1:00 a.m.
MUMBLE. . .
GIGGLE. . .
SNICKER. . .
5:00 a.m.
MUMBLE. . .
GIGGLE. . .
THE GIRLS WILL GET A KICK OUT OF THIS.
6:00 a.m.
ZZZZZ. . .
Hinds

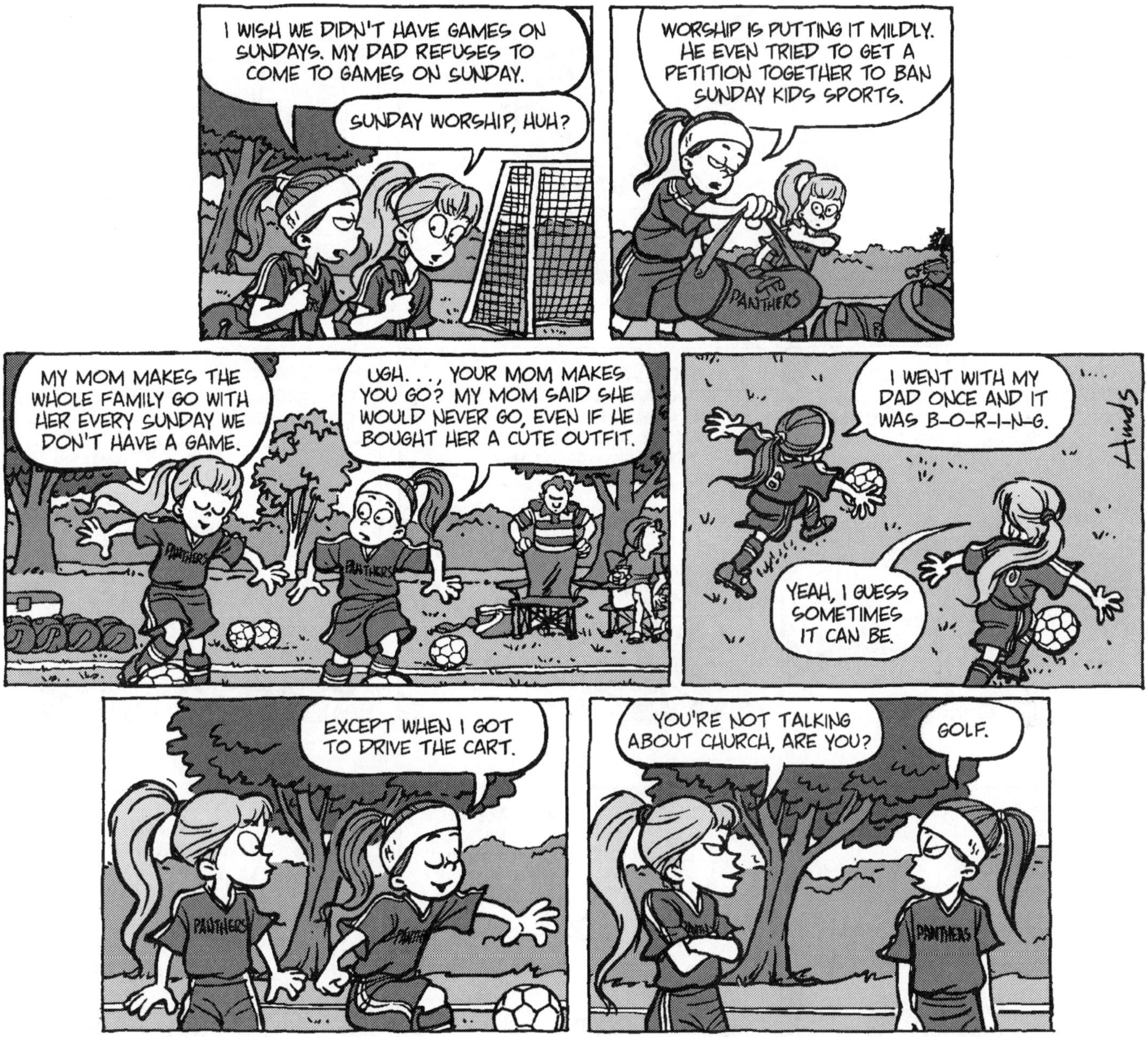
I WISH WE DIDN'T HAVE GAMES ON SUNDAYS. MY DAD REFUSES TO COME TO GAMES ON SUNDAY.
SUNDAY WORSHIP, HUH?
WORSHIP IS PUTTING IT MILDLY. HE EVEN TRIED TO GET A PETITION TOGETHER TO BAN SUNDAY KIDS SPORTS.
PANTHERS
MY MOM MAKES THE WHOLE FAMILY GO WITH HER EVERY SUNDAY WE DON'T HAVE A GAME.
UGH. . . , YOUR MOM MAKES YOU GO? MY MOM SAID SHE WOULD NEVER GO, EVEN IF HE BOUGHT HER A CUTE OUTFIT.
I WENT WITH MY DAD ONCE AND IT WAS B–O–R–I–N–G.
YEAH, I GUESS SOMETIMES IT CAN BE.
Hinds
EXCEPT WHEN I GOT TO DRIVE THE CART.
YOU'RE NOT TALKING ABOUT CHURCH, ARE YOU?
GOLF.

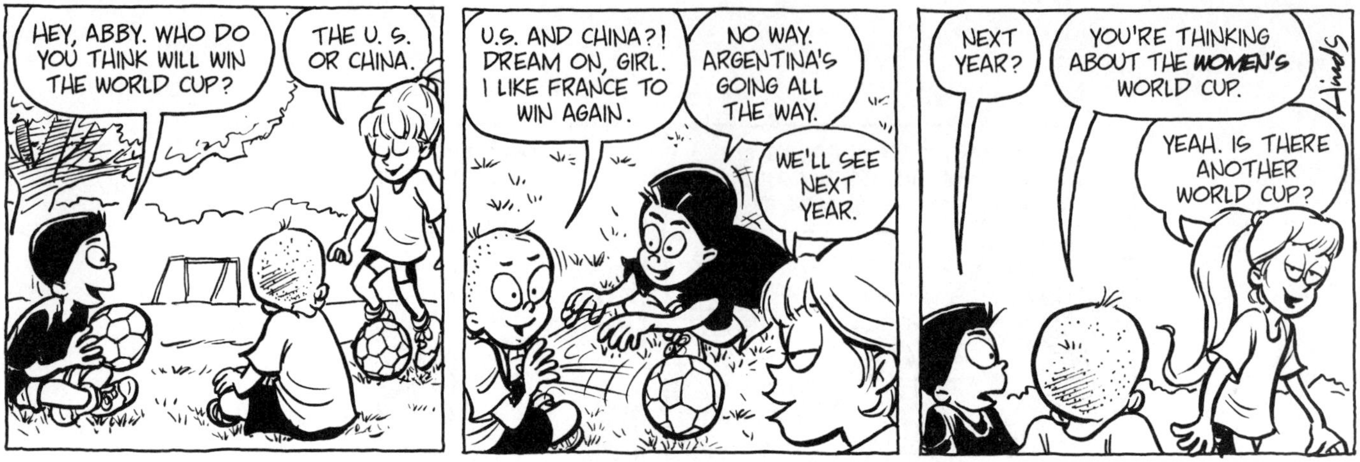
HEY, ABBY. WHO DO YOU THINK WILL WIN THE WORLD CUP?
THE U. S. OR CHINA.
U.S. AND CHINA?! DREAM ON, GIRL. I LIKE FRANCE TO WIN AGAIN.
NO WAY. ARGENTINA'S GOING ALL THE WAY.
WE'LL SEE NEXT YEAR.
NEXT YEAR?
YOU'RE THINKING ABOUT THE **WOMEN'S** WORLD CUP.
YEAH. IS THERE ANOTHER WORLD CUP?
Hinds

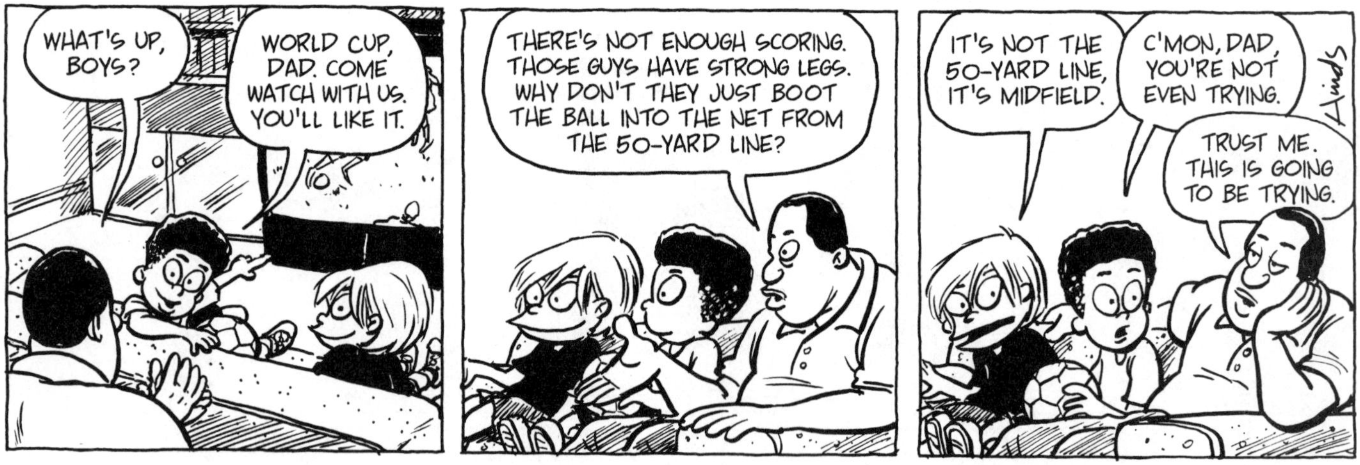
WHAT'S UP, BOYS?
WORLD CUP, DAD. COME WATCH WITH US. YOU'LL LIKE IT.
THERE'S NOT ENOUGH SCORING. THOSE GUYS HAVE STRONG LEGS. WHY DON'T THEY JUST BOOT THE BALL INTO THE NET FROM THE 50-YARD LINE?
IT'S NOT THE 50-YARD LINE, IT'S MIDFIELD.
C'MON, DAD, YOU'RE NOT EVEN TRYING.
TRUST ME. THIS IS GOING TO BE TRYING.
Hinds

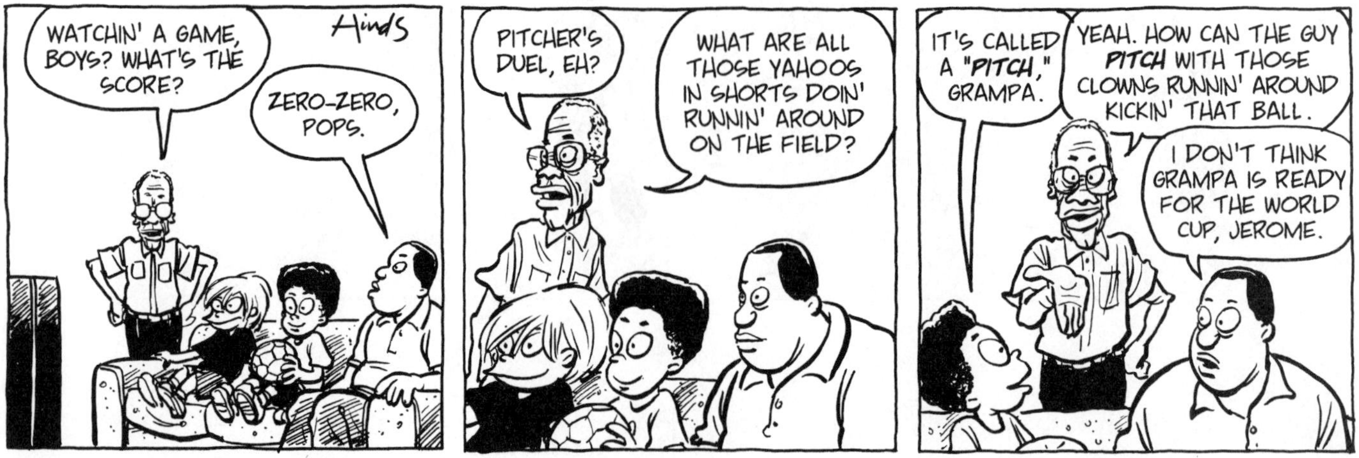
WATCHIN' A GAME, BOYS? WHAT'S THE SCORE?
Hinds
ZERO-ZERO, POPS.
PITCHER'S DUEL, EH?
WHAT ARE ALL THOSE YAHOOS IN SHORTS DOIN' RUNNIN' AROUND ON THE FIELD?
IT'S CALLED A "**PITCH**," GRAMPA.
YEAH. HOW CAN THE GUY **PITCH** WITH THOSE CLOWNS RUNNIN' AROUND KICKIN' THAT BALL.
I DON'T THINK GRAMPA IS READY FOR THE WORLD CUP, JEROME.

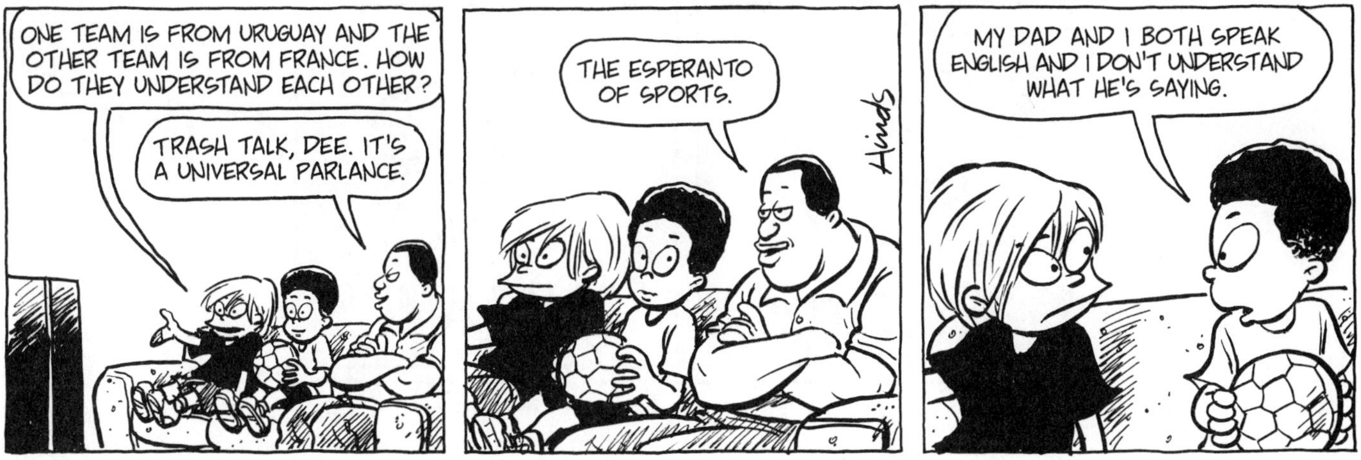
ONE TEAM IS FROM URUGUAY AND THE OTHER TEAM IS FROM FRANCE. HOW DO THEY UNDERSTAND EACH OTHER?
TRASH TALK, DEE. IT'S A UNIVERSAL PARLANCE.
THE ESPERANTO OF SPORTS.
Hinds
MY DAD AND I BOTH SPEAK ENGLISH AND I DON'T UNDERSTAND WHAT HE'S SAYING.

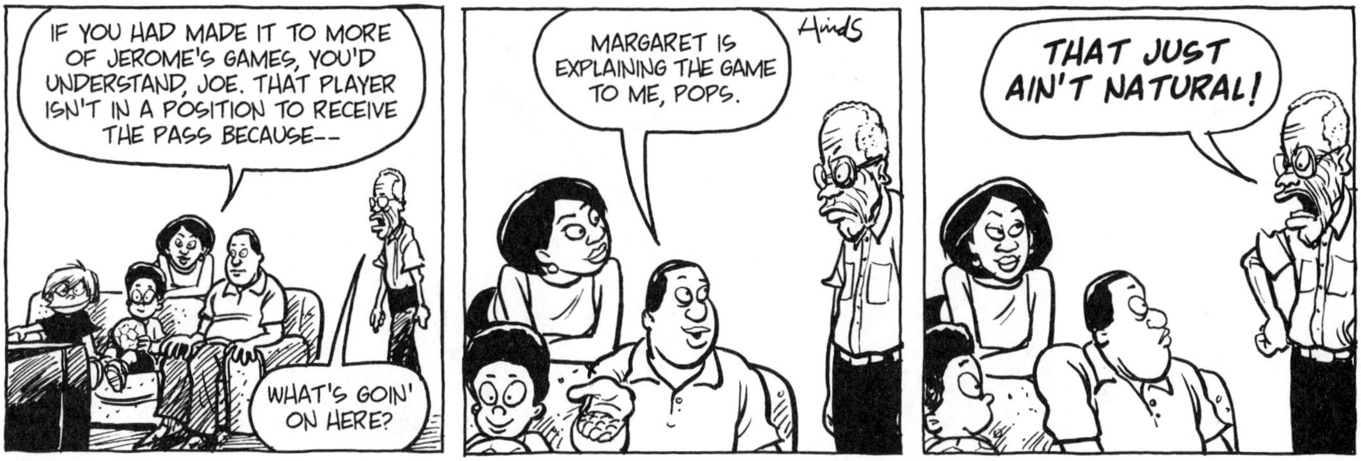
IF YOU HAD MADE IT TO MORE OF JEROME'S GAMES, YOU'D UNDERSTAND, JOE. THAT PLAYER ISN'T IN A POSITION TO RECEIVE THE PASS BECAUSE--
WHAT'S GOIN' ON HERE?
Hinds
MARGARET IS EXPLAINING THE GAME TO ME, POPS.
THAT JUST AIN'T NATURAL!

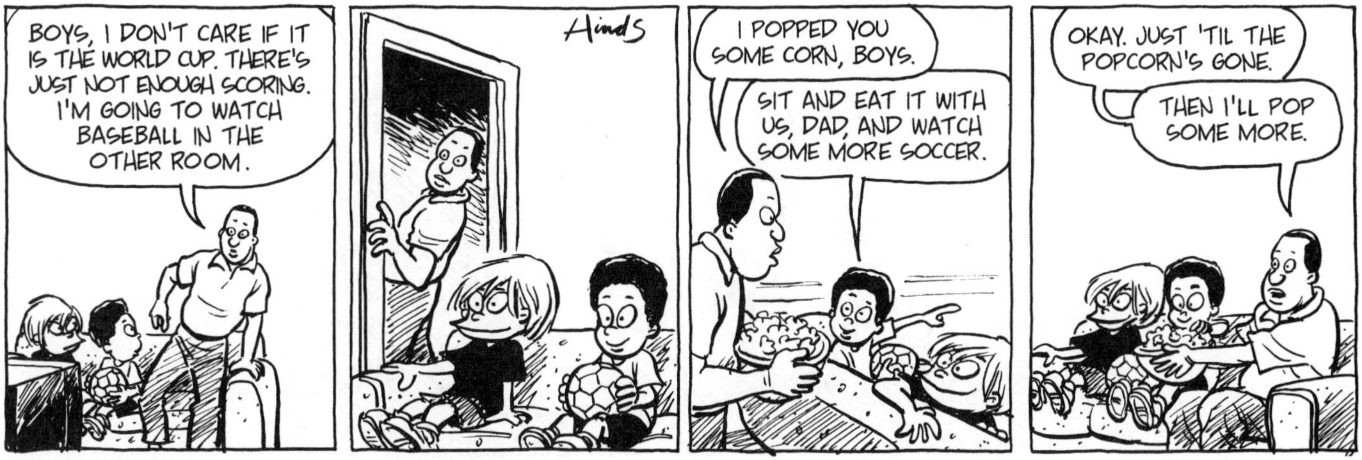
BOYS, I DON'T CARE IF IT IS THE WORLD CUP. THERE'S JUST NOT ENOUGH SCORING. I'M GOING TO WATCH BASEBALL IN THE OTHER ROOM.
Hinds
I POPPED YOU SOME CORN, BOYS.
SIT AND EAT IT WITH US, DAD, AND WATCH SOME MORE SOCCER.
OKAY. JUST 'TIL THE POPCORN'S GONE.
THEN I'LL POP SOME MORE.

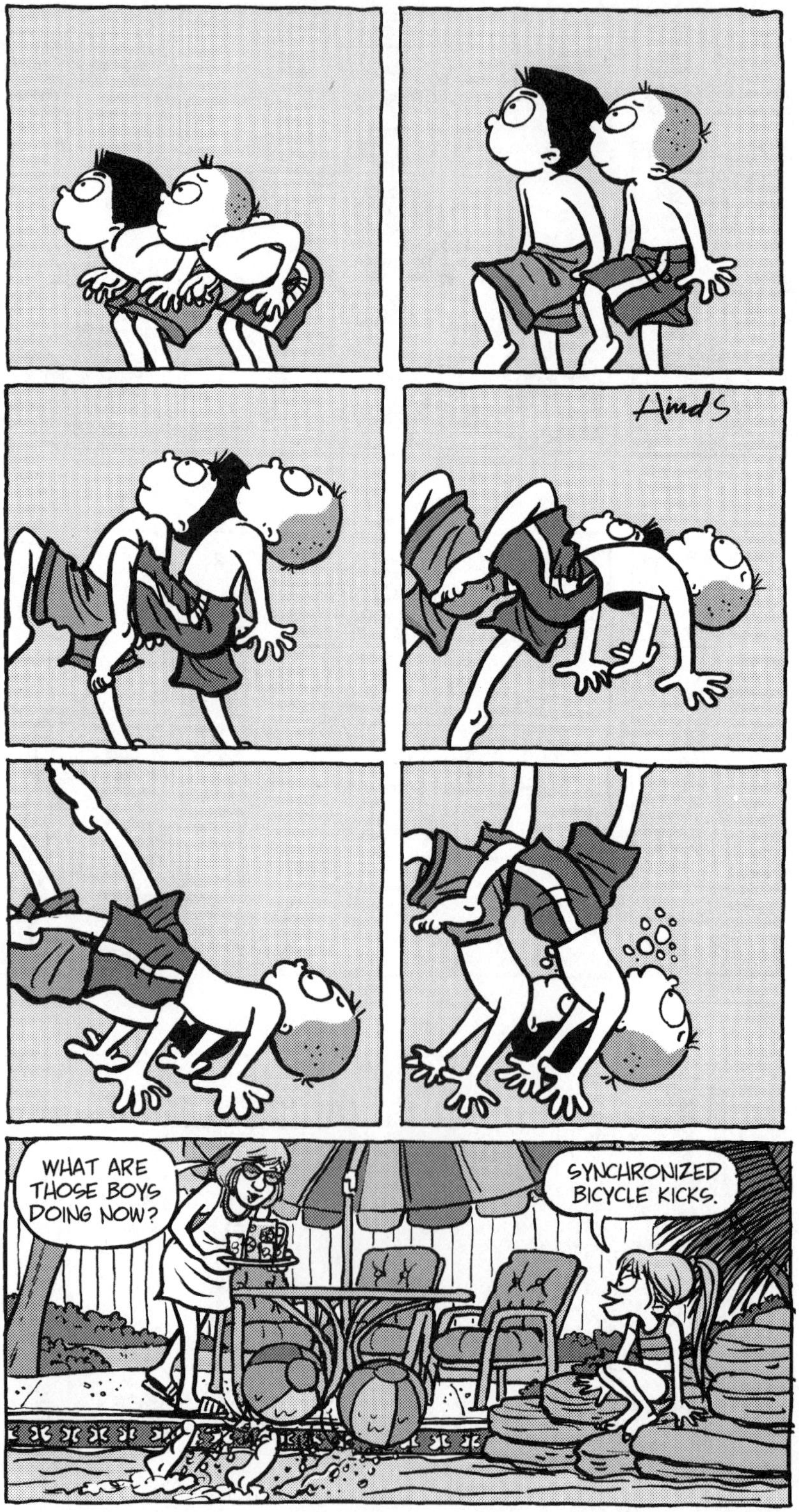
Hinds
WHAT ARE THOSE BOYS DOING NOW?
SYNCHRONIZED BICYCLE KICKS.

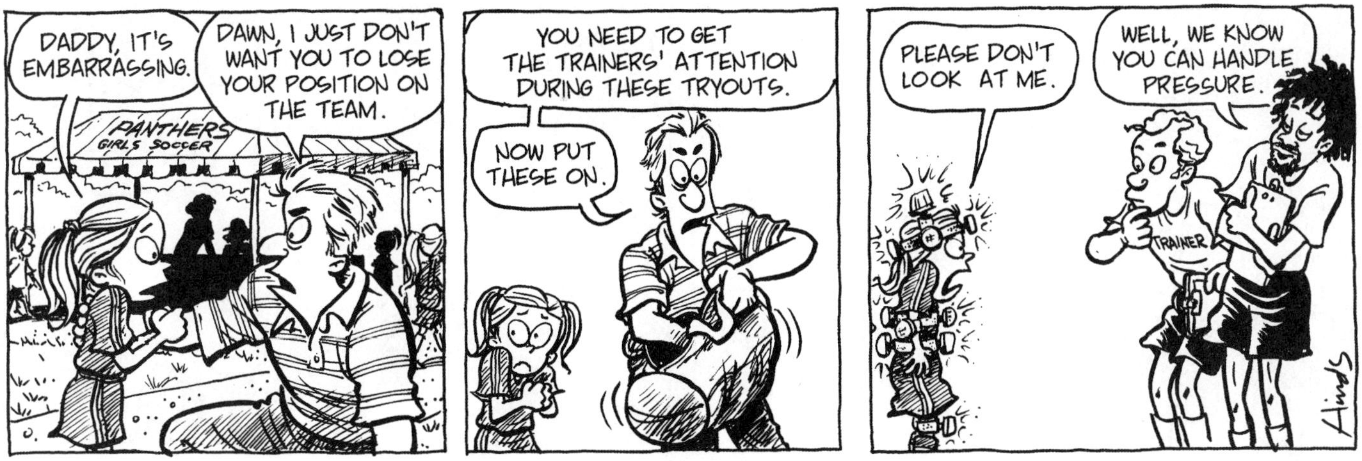
DADDY, IT'S EMBARRASSING.
DAWN, I JUST DON'T WANT YOU TO LOSE YOUR POSITION ON THE TEAM.
PANTHERS
GIRLS SOCCER
YOU NEED TO GET THE TRAINERS' ATTENTION DURING THESE TRYOUTS.
NOW PUT THESE ON.
PLEASE DON'T LOOK AT ME.
WELL, WE KNOW YOU CAN HANDLE PRESSURE.
TRAINER
Hinds

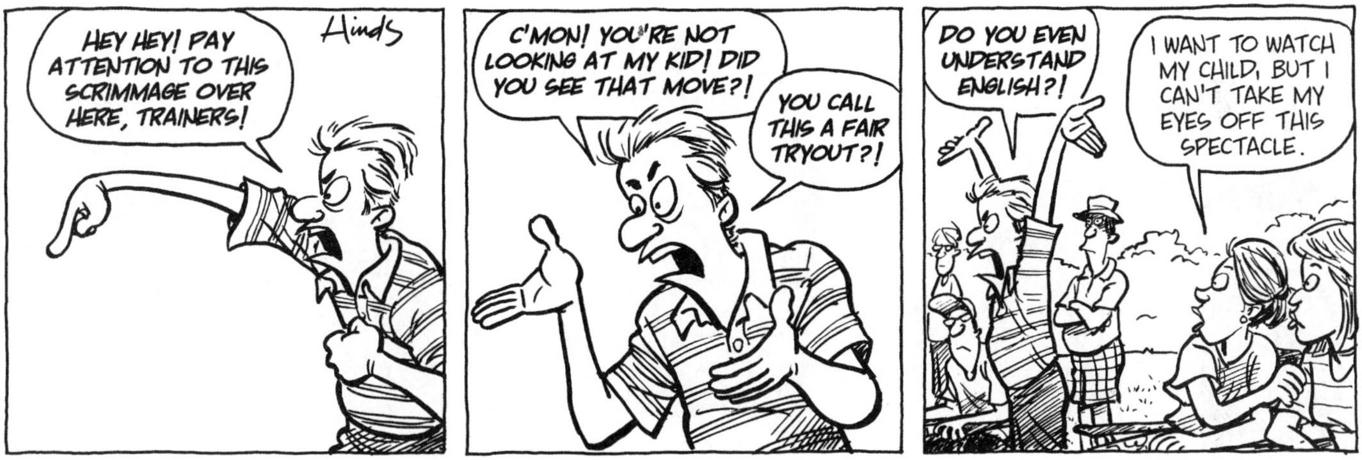
HEY HEY! PAY ATTENTION TO THIS SCRIMMAGE OVER HERE, TRAINERS!
Hinds
C'MON! YOU'RE NOT LOOKING AT MY KID! DID YOU SEE THAT MOVE?!
YOU CALL THIS A FAIR TRYOUT?!
DO YOU EVEN UNDERSTAND ENGLISH?!
I WANT TO WATCH MY CHILD, BUT I CAN'T TAKE MY EYES OFF THIS SPECTACLE.

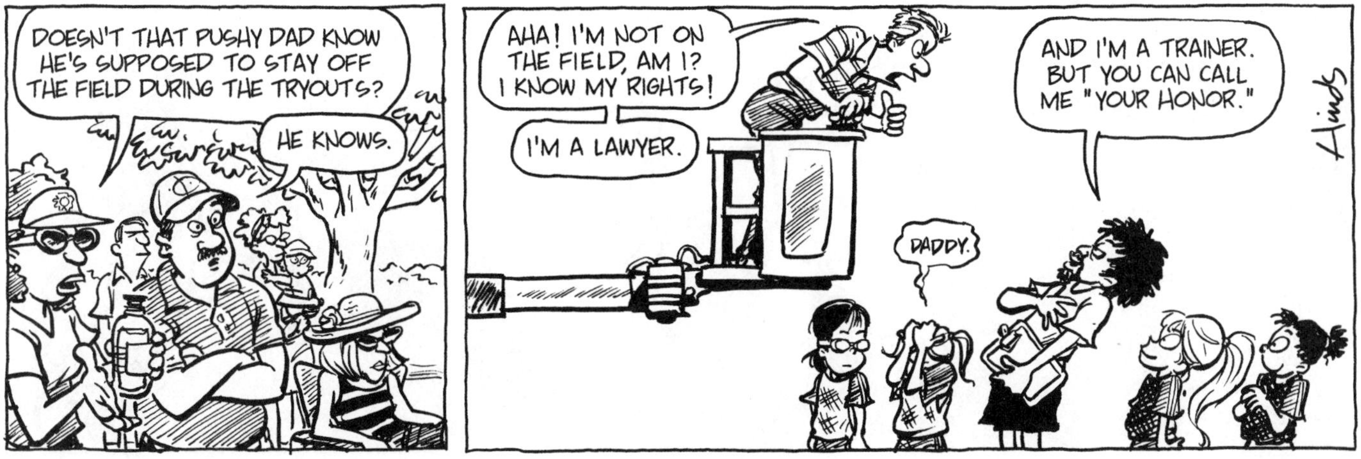
DOESN'T THAT PUSHY DAD KNOW HE'S SUPPOSED TO STAY OFF THE FIELD DURING THE TRYOUTS?
HE KNOWS.
AHA! I'M NOT ON THE FIELD, AM I? I KNOW MY RIGHTS!
I'M A LAWYER.
AND I'M A TRAINER. BUT YOU CAN CALL ME "YOUR HONOR."
DADDY.
Hinds

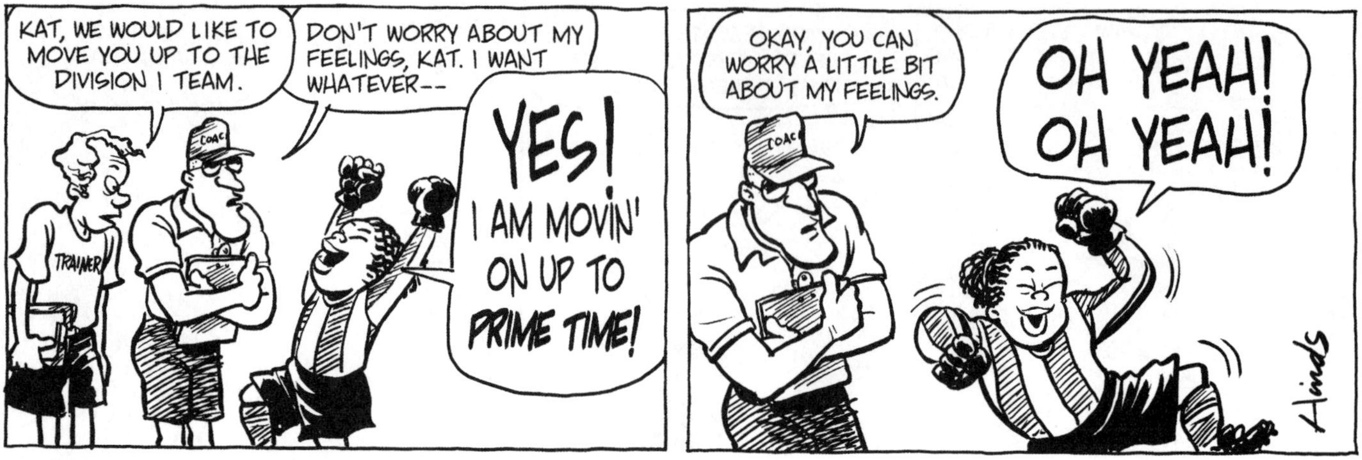
KAT, WE WOULD LIKE TO MOVE YOU UP TO THE DIVISION I TEAM.
DON'T WORRY ABOUT MY FEELINGS, KAT. I WANT WHATEVER--
YES! I AM MOVIN' ON UP TO PRIME TIME!
OKAY, YOU CAN WORRY A LITTLE BIT ABOUT MY FEELINGS.
OH YEAH! OH YEAH!
Hinds

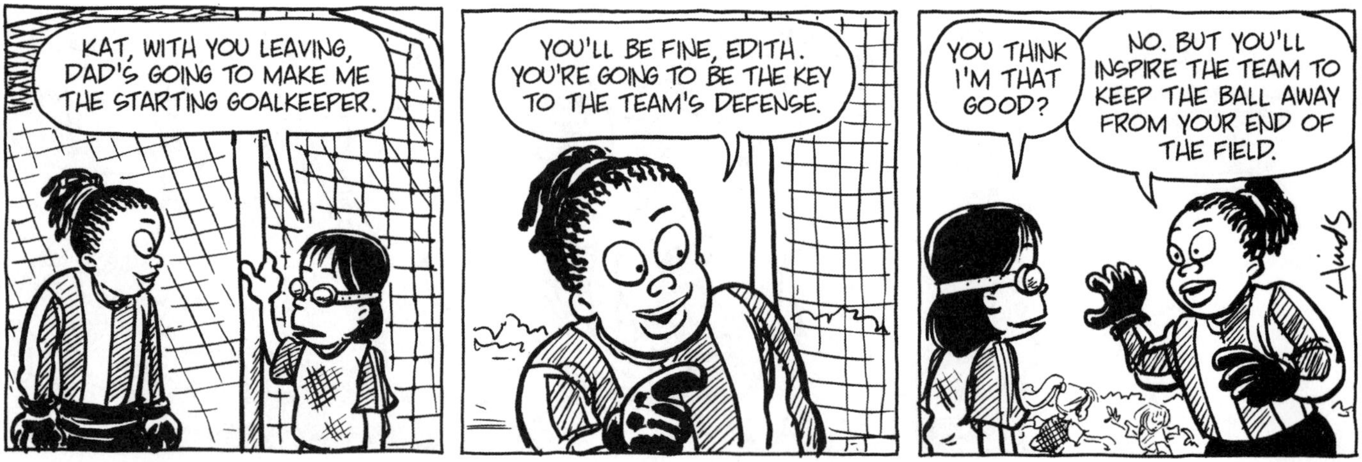
KAT, WITH YOU LEAVING, DAD'S GOING TO MAKE ME THE STARTING GOALKEEPER.
YOU'LL BE FINE, EDITH. YOU'RE GOING TO BE THE KEY TO THE TEAM'S DEFENSE.
YOU THINK I'M THAT GOOD?
NO. BUT YOU'LL INSPIRE THE TEAM TO KEEP THE BALL AWAY FROM YOUR END OF THE FIELD.
Hinds

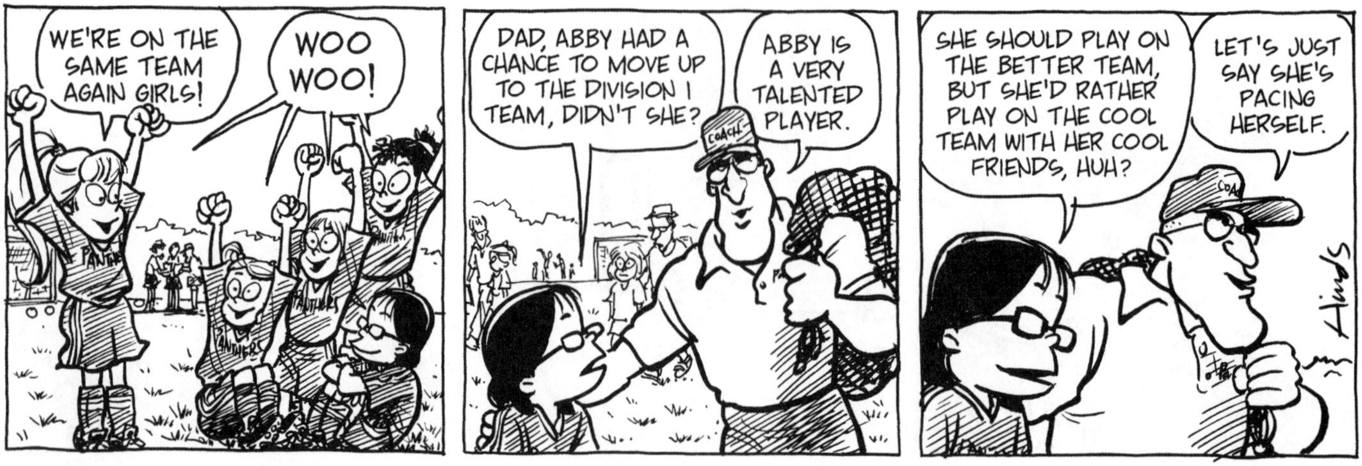
WE'RE ON THE SAME TEAM AGAIN GIRLS!
WOO WOO!
DAD, ABBY HAD A CHANCE TO MOVE UP TO THE DIVISION I TEAM, DIDN'T SHE?
ABBY IS A VERY TALENTED PLAYER.
SHE SHOULD PLAY ON THE BETTER TEAM, BUT SHE'D RATHER PLAY ON THE COOL TEAM WITH HER COOL FRIENDS, HUH?
LET'S JUST SAY SHE'S PACING HERSELF.
Hinds

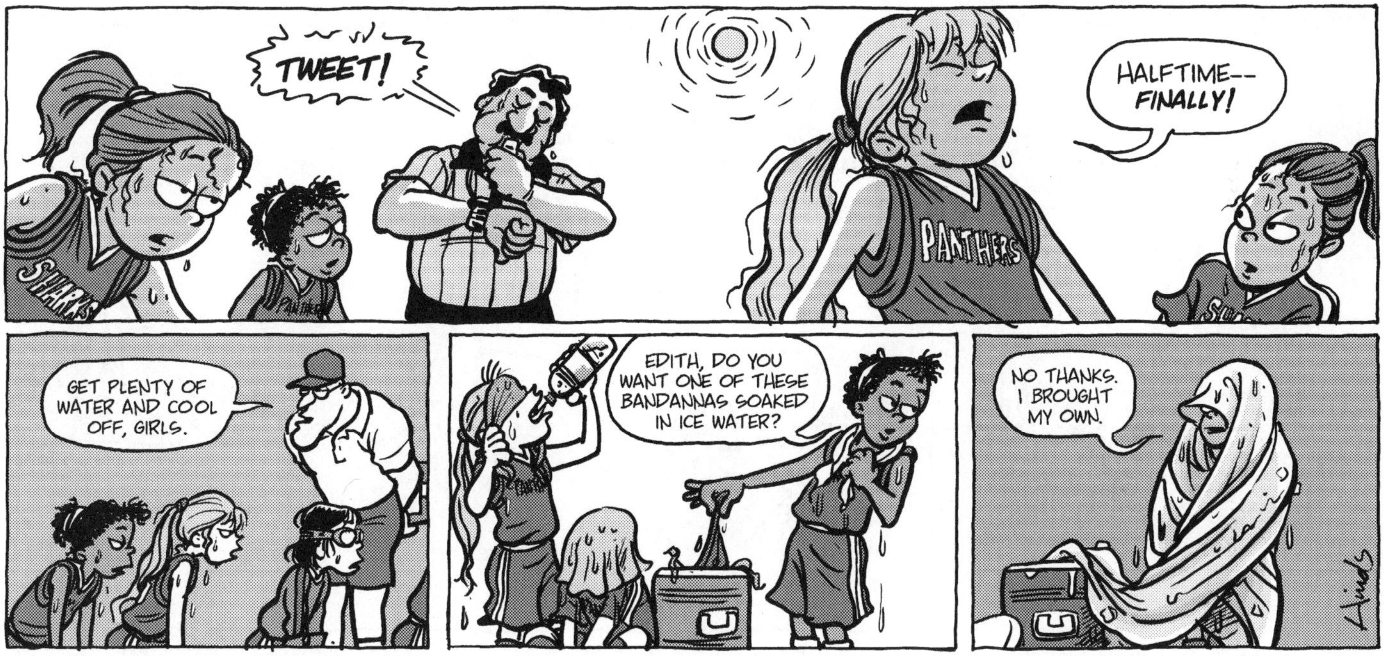
TWEET!
HALFTIME--
FINALLY!
SHARKS
PANTHERS
GET PLENTY OF WATER AND COOL OFF, GIRLS.
EDITH, DO YOU WANT ONE OF THESE BANDANNAS SOAKED IN ICE WATER?
NO THANKS. I BROUGHT MY OWN.
Hinds

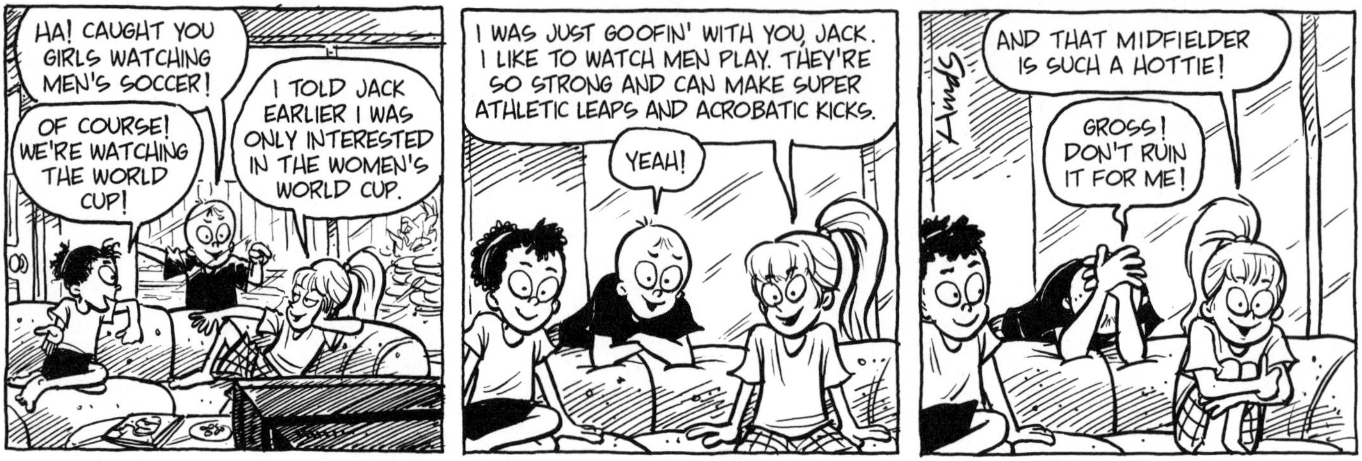
HA! CAUGHT YOU GIRLS WATCHING MEN'S SOCCER!
OF COURSE! WE'RE WATCHING THE WORLD CUP!
I TOLD JACK EARLIER I WAS ONLY INTERESTED IN THE WOMEN'S WORLD CUP.
I WAS JUST GOOFIN' WITH YOU, JACK. I LIKE TO WATCH MEN PLAY. THEY'RE SO STRONG AND CAN MAKE SUPER ATHLETIC LEAPS AND ACROBATIC KICKS.
YEAH!
Hinds
AND THAT MIDFIELDER IS SUCH A HOTTIE!
GROSS! DON'T RUIN IT FOR ME!

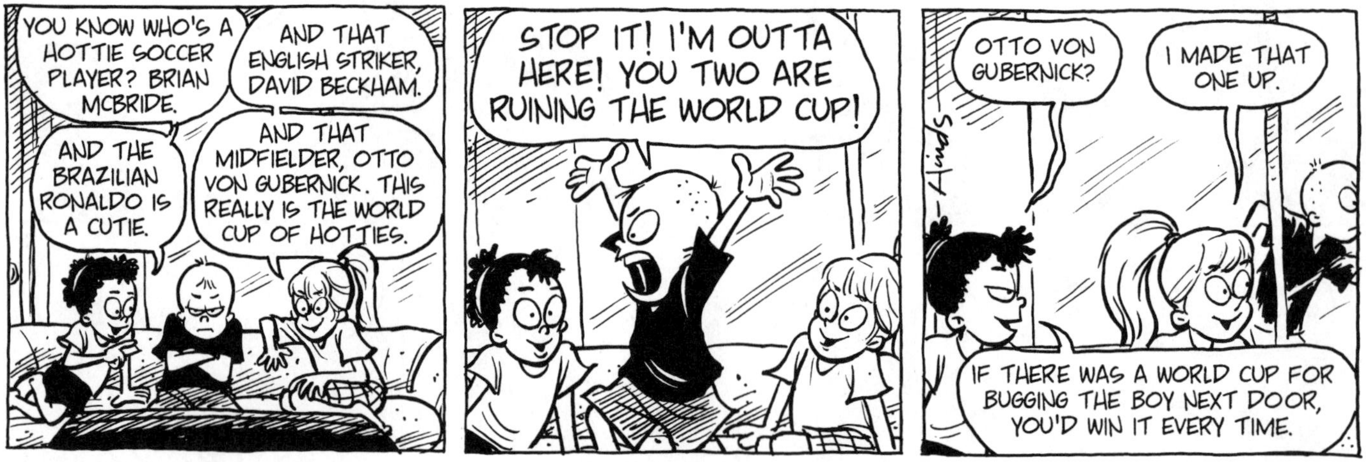
YOU KNOW WHO'S A HOTTIE SOCCER PLAYER? BRIAN MCBRIDE.
AND THAT ENGLISH STRIKER, DAVID BECKHAM.
AND THE BRAZILIAN RONALDO IS A CUTIE.
AND THAT MIDFIELDER, OTTO VON GUBERNICK. THIS REALLY IS THE WORLD CUP OF HOTTIES.
STOP IT! I'M OUTTA HERE! YOU TWO ARE RUINING THE WORLD CUP!
Hinds
OTTO VON GUBERNICK?
I MADE THAT ONE UP.
IF THERE WAS A WORLD CUP FOR BUGGING THE BOY NEXT DOOR, YOU'D WIN IT EVERY TIME.

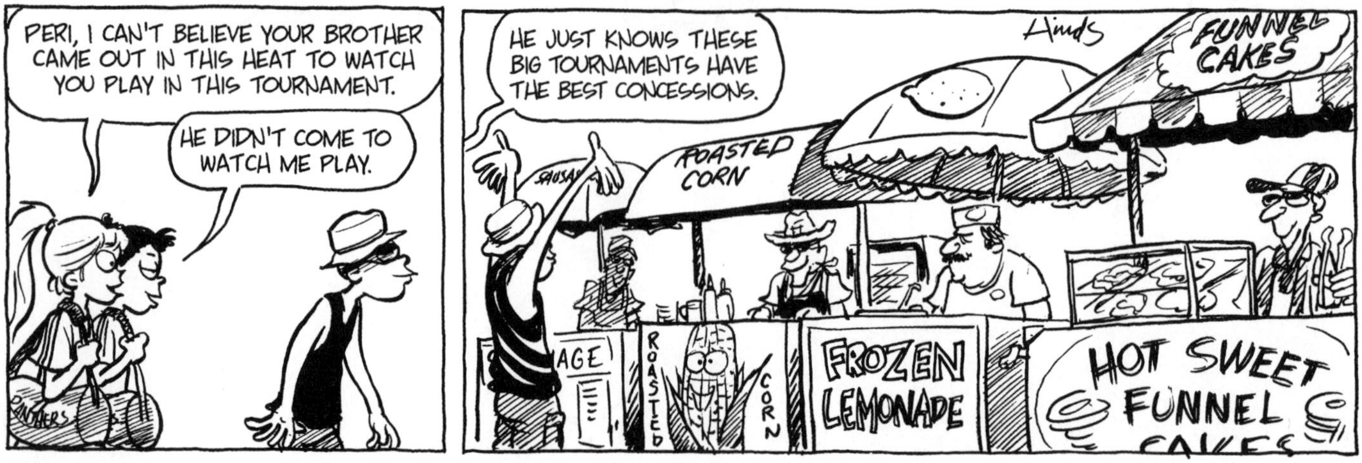
PERI, I CAN'T BELIEVE YOUR BROTHER CAME OUT IN THIS HEAT TO WATCH YOU PLAY IN THIS TOURNAMENT.
HE DIDN'T COME TO WATCH ME PLAY.
HE JUST KNOWS THESE BIG TOURNAMENTS HAVE THE BEST CONCESSIONS.
Hinds
FUNNEL CAKES
ROASTED CORN
ROASTED CORN
FROZEN LEMONADE
HOT SWEET FUNNEL

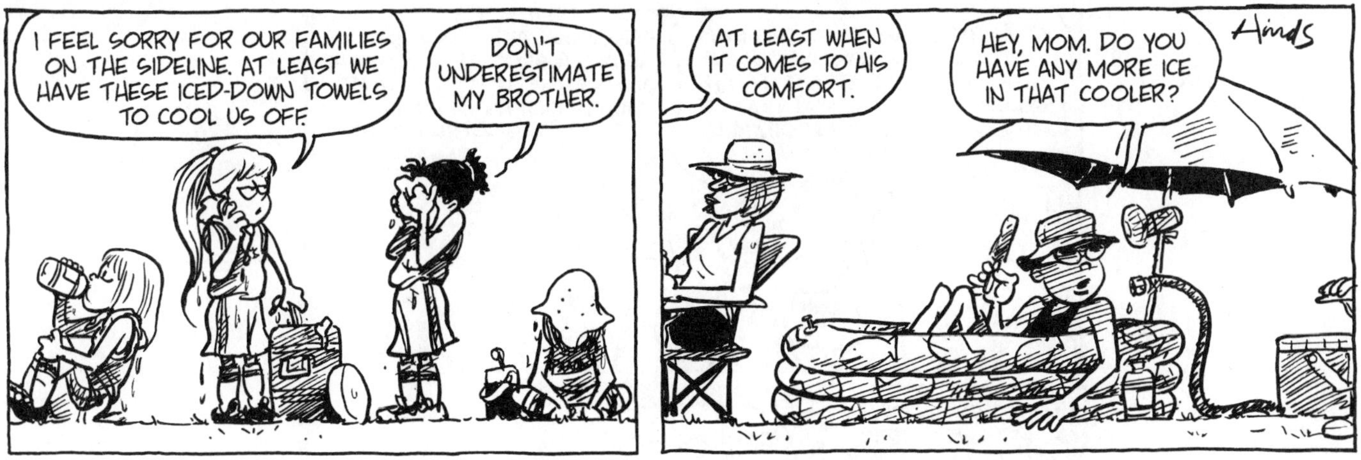
I FEEL SORRY FOR OUR FAMILIES ON THE SIDELINE. AT LEAST WE HAVE THESE ICED-DOWN TOWELS TO COOL US OFF.
DON'T UNDERESTIMATE MY BROTHER.
AT LEAST WHEN IT COMES TO HIS COMFORT.
HEY, MOM. DO YOU HAVE ANY MORE ICE IN THAT COOLER?
Hinds

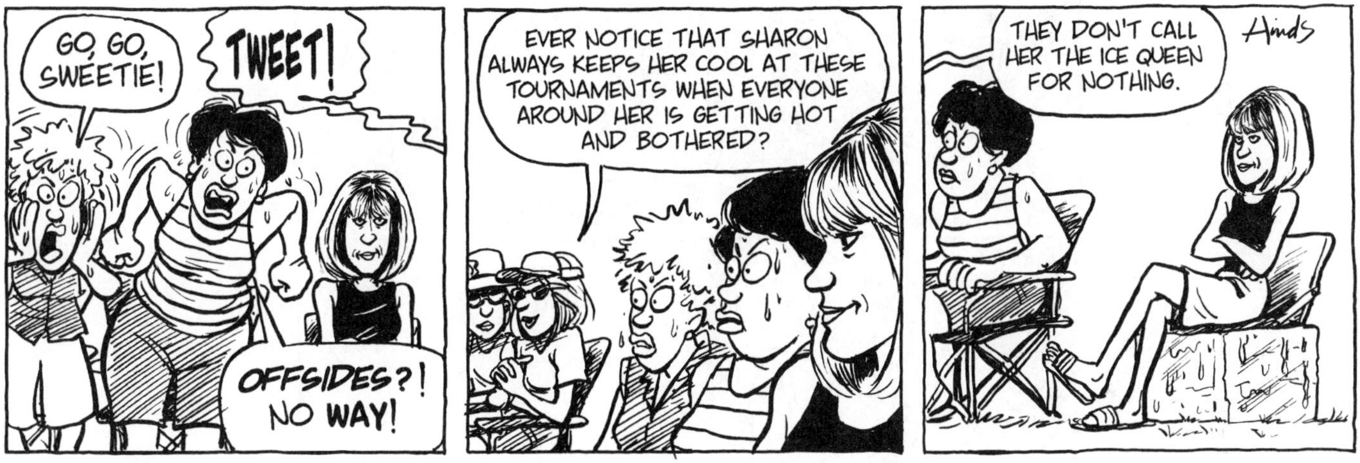
GO, GO, SWEETIE!
TWEET!
OFFSIDES?! NO WAY!
EVER NOTICE THAT SHARON ALWAYS KEEPS HER COOL AT THESE TOURNAMENTS WHEN EVERYONE AROUND HER IS GETTING HOT AND BOTHERED?
THEY DON'T CALL HER THE ICE QUEEN FOR NOTHING.
Hinds

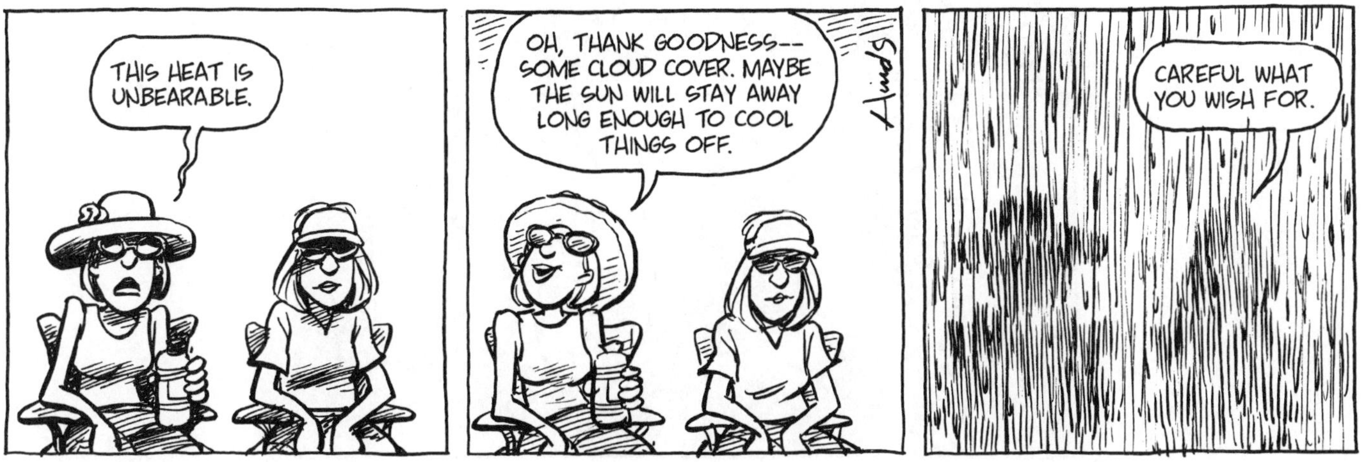
THIS HEAT IS UNBEARABLE.
OH, THANK GOODNESS-- SOME CLOUD COVER. MAYBE THE SUN WILL STAY AWAY LONG ENOUGH TO COOL THINGS OFF.
Hinds
CAREFUL WHAT YOU WISH FOR.

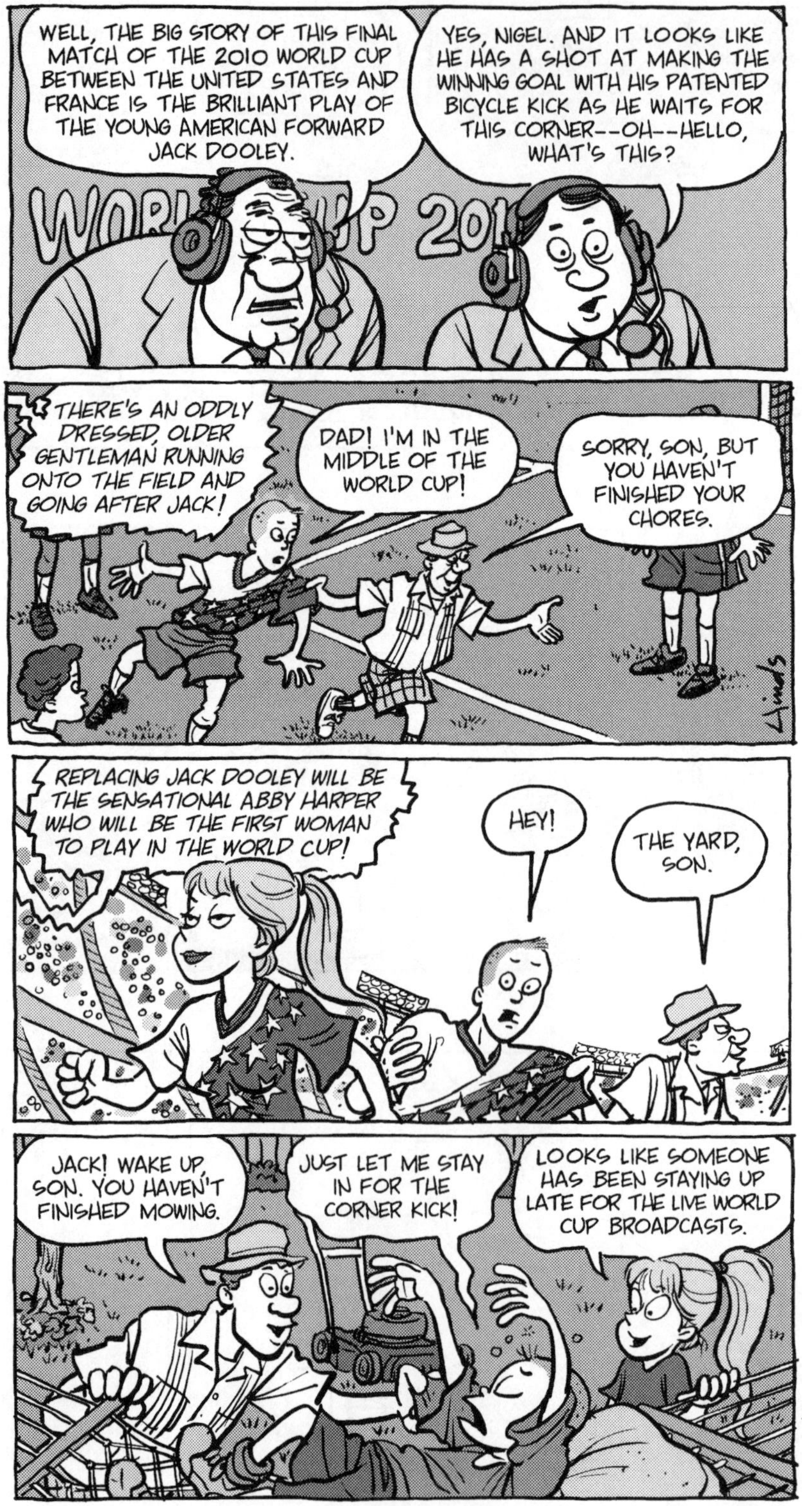
WELL, THE BIG STORY OF THIS FINAL MATCH OF THE 2010 WORLD CUP BETWEEN THE UNITED STATES AND FRANCE IS THE BRILLIANT PLAY OF THE YOUNG AMERICAN FORWARD JACK DOOLEY.
YES, NIGEL. AND IT LOOKS LIKE HE HAS A SHOT AT MAKING THE WINNING GOAL WITH HIS PATENTED BICYCLE KICK AS HE WAITS FOR THIS CORNER--OH--HELLO, WHAT'S THIS?
THERE'S AN ODDLY DRESSED, OLDER GENTLEMAN RUNNING ONTO THE FIELD AND GOING AFTER JACK!
DAD! I'M IN THE MIDDLE OF THE WORLD CUP!
SORRY, SON, BUT YOU HAVEN'T FINISHED YOUR CHORES.
REPLACING JACK DOOLEY WILL BE THE SENSATIONAL ABBY HARPER WHO WILL BE THE FIRST WOMAN TO PLAY IN THE WORLD CUP!
HEY!
THE YARD, SON.
JACK! WAKE UP, SON. YOU HAVEN'T FINISHED MOWING.
JUST LET ME STAY IN FOR THE CORNER KICK!
LOOKS LIKE SOMEONE HAS BEEN STAYING UP LATE FOR THE LIVE WORLD CUP BROADCASTS.

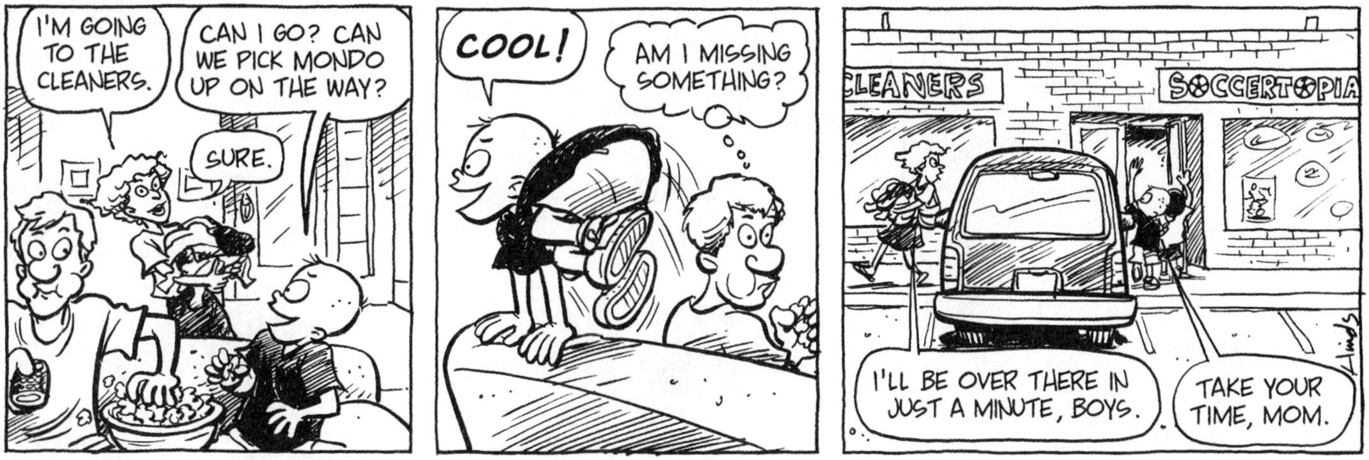
I'M GOING TO THE CLEANERS.
CAN I GO? CAN WE PICK MONDO UP ON THE WAY?
SURE.
COOL!
AM I MISSING SOMETHING?
CLEANERS
SOCCERTOPIA
I'LL BE OVER THERE IN JUST A MINUTE, BOYS.
TAKE YOUR TIME, MOM.

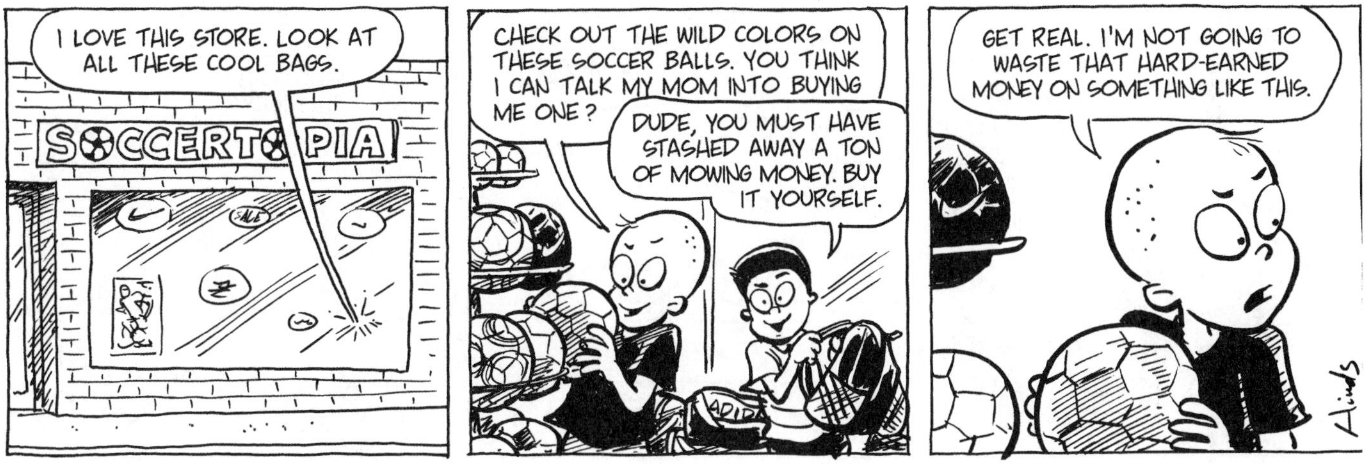
I LOVE THIS STORE. LOOK AT ALL THESE COOL BAGS.
SOCCERTOPIA
CHECK OUT THE WILD COLORS ON THESE SOCCER BALLS. YOU THINK I CAN TALK MY MOM INTO BUYING ME ONE?
DUDE, YOU MUST HAVE STASHED AWAY A TON OF MOWING MONEY. BUY IT YOURSELF.
GET REAL. I'M NOT GOING TO WASTE THAT HARD-EARNED MONEY ON SOMETHING LIKE THIS.

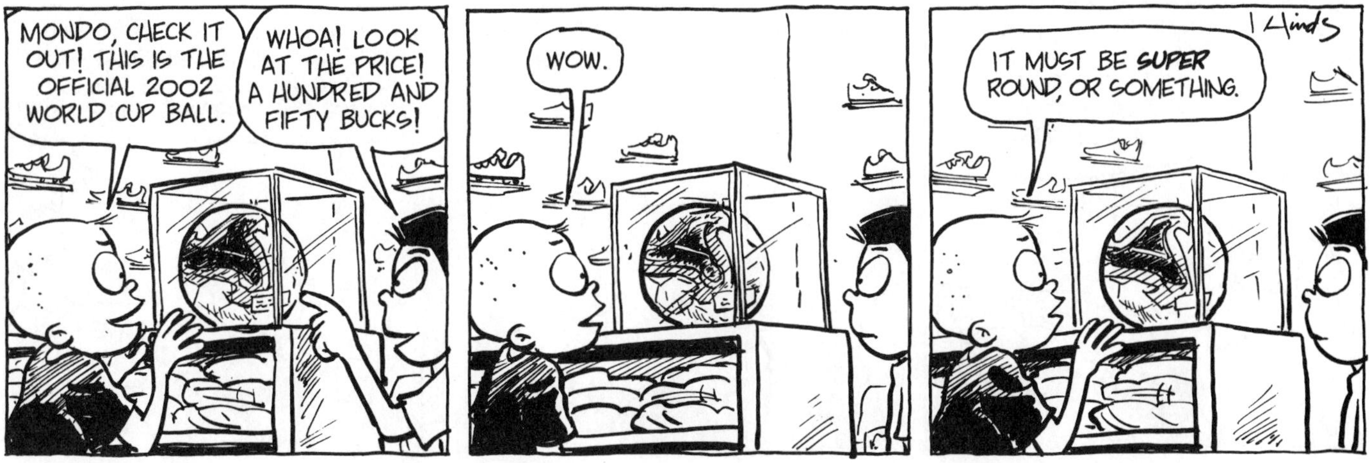
MONDO, CHECK IT OUT! THIS IS THE OFFICIAL 2002 WORLD CUP BALL.
WHOA! LOOK AT THE PRICE! A HUNDRED AND FIFTY BUCKS!
WOW.
IT MUST BE SUPER ROUND, OR SOMETHING.

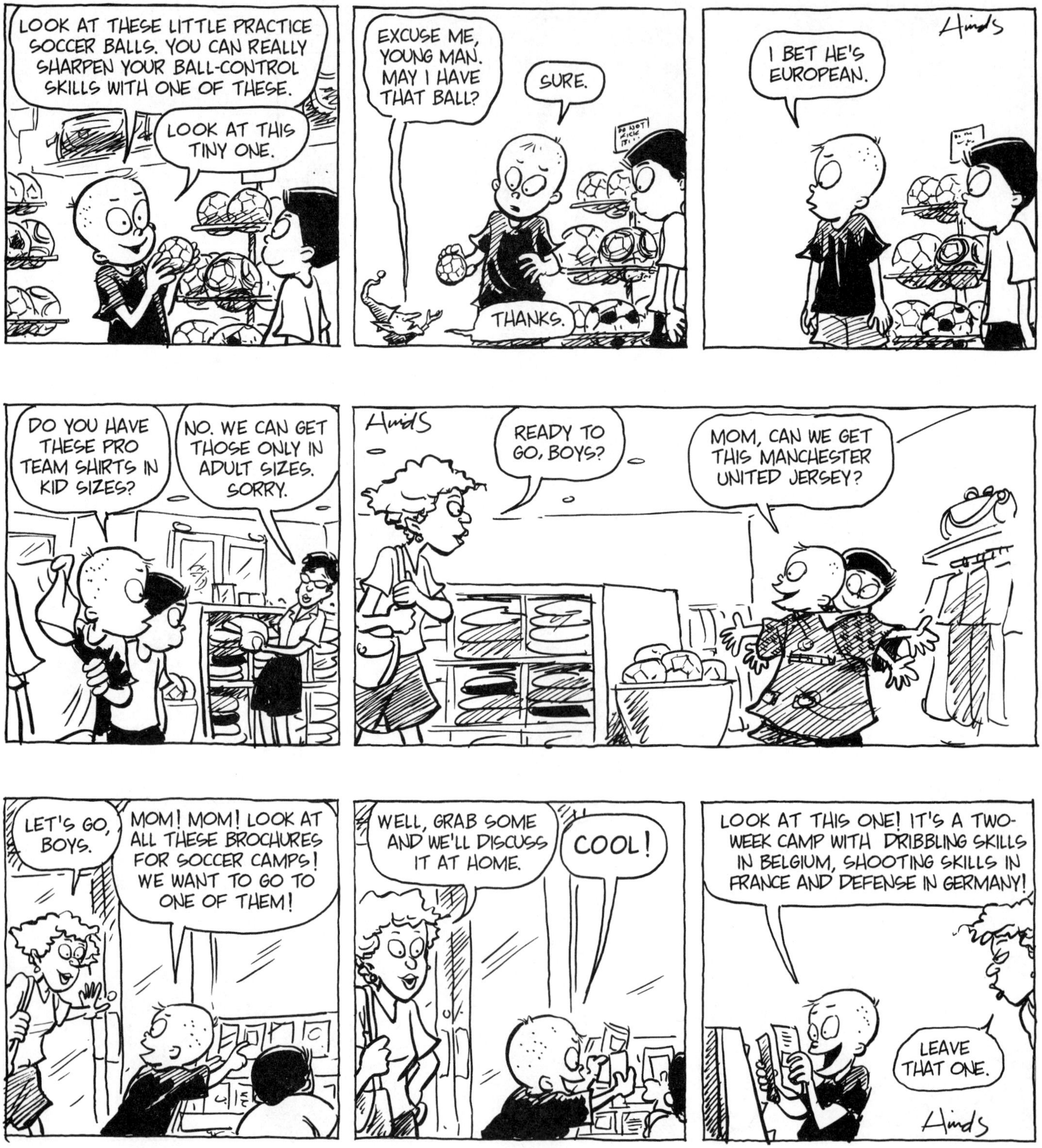
LOOK AT THESE LITTLE PRACTICE SOCCER BALLS. YOU CAN REALLY SHARPEN YOUR BALL-CONTROL SKILLS WITH ONE OF THESE.
LOOK AT THIS TINY ONE.
EXCUSE ME, YOUNG MAN. MAY I HAVE THAT BALL?
SURE.
THANKS.
Hinds
I BET HE'S EUROPEAN.
DO YOU HAVE THESE PRO TEAM SHIRTS IN KID SIZES?
NO. WE CAN GET THOSE ONLY IN ADULT SIZES. SORRY.
Hinds
READY TO GO, BOYS?
MOM, CAN WE GET THIS MANCHESTER UNITED JERSEY?
LET'S GO, BOYS.
MOM! MOM! LOOK AT ALL THESE BROCHURES FOR SOCCER CAMPS! WE WANT TO GO TO ONE OF THEM!
WELL, GRAB SOME AND WE'LL DISCUSS IT AT HOME.
COOL!
LOOK AT THIS ONE! IT'S A TWO-WEEK CAMP WITH DRIBBLING SKILLS IN BELGIUM, SHOOTING SKILLS IN FRANCE AND DEFENSE IN GERMANY!
LEAVE THAT ONE.
Hinds

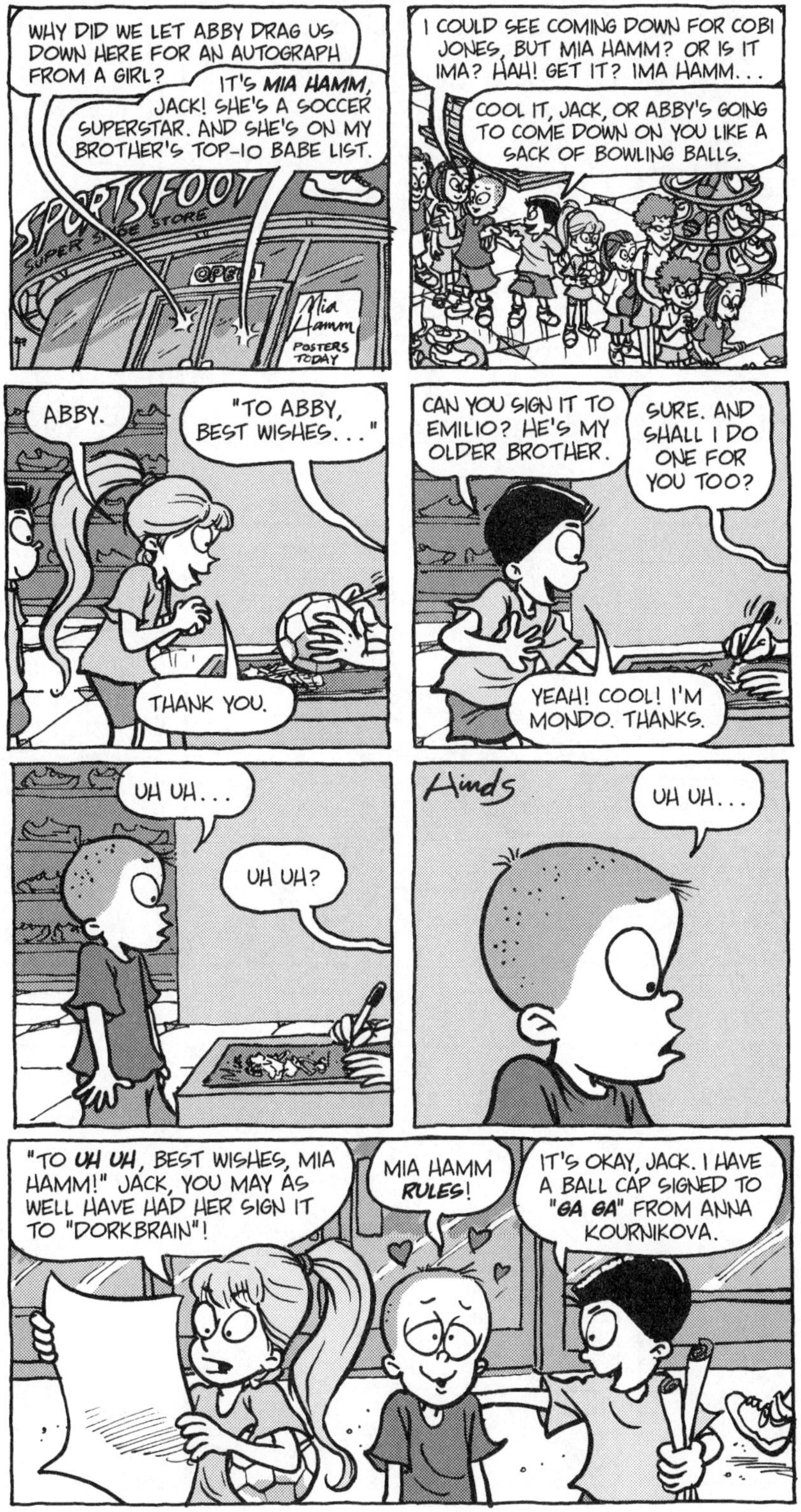
WHY DID WE LET ABBY DRAG US DOWN HERE FOR AN AUTOGRAPH FROM A GIRL?
IT'S **MIA HAMM**, JACK! SHE'S A SOCCER SUPERSTAR. AND SHE'S ON MY BROTHER'S TOP-10 BABE LIST.
SPORTSFOOT
SUPER SHOE STORE
OPEN
Mia Hamm
POSTERS TODAY
I COULD SEE COMING DOWN FOR COBI JONES, BUT MIA HAMM? OR IS IT IMA? HAH! GET IT? IMA HAMM...
COOL IT, JACK, OR ABBY'S GOING TO COME DOWN ON YOU LIKE A SACK OF BOWLING BALLS.
ABBY.
"TO ABBY, BEST WISHES..."
THANK YOU.
CAN YOU SIGN IT TO EMILIO? HE'S MY OLDER BROTHER.
SURE. AND SHALL I DO ONE FOR YOU TOO?
YEAH! COOL! I'M MONDO. THANKS.
UH UH...
UH UH?
Hinds
UH UH...
"TO **UH UH**, BEST WISHES, MIA HAMM!" JACK, YOU MAY AS WELL HAVE HAD HER SIGN IT TO "DORKBRAIN"!
MIA HAMM **RULES**!
IT'S OKAY, JACK. I HAVE A BALL CAP SIGNED TO "**GA GA**" FROM ANNA KOURNIKOVA.

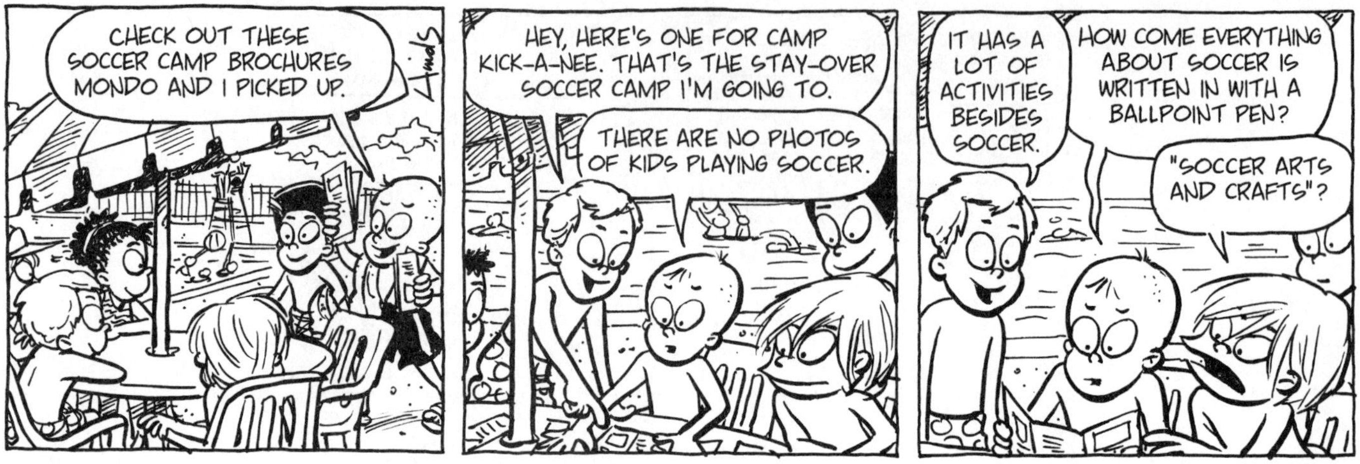
CHECK OUT THESE SOCCER CAMP BROCHURES MONDO AND I PICKED UP.
HEY, HERE'S ONE FOR CAMP KICK-A-NEE. THAT'S THE STAY-OVER SOCCER CAMP I'M GOING TO.
THERE ARE NO PHOTOS OF KIDS PLAYING SOCCER.
IT HAS A LOT OF ACTIVITIES BESIDES SOCCER.
HOW COME EVERYTHING ABOUT SOCCER IS WRITTEN IN WITH A BALLPOINT PEN?
"SOCCER ARTS AND CRAFTS"?

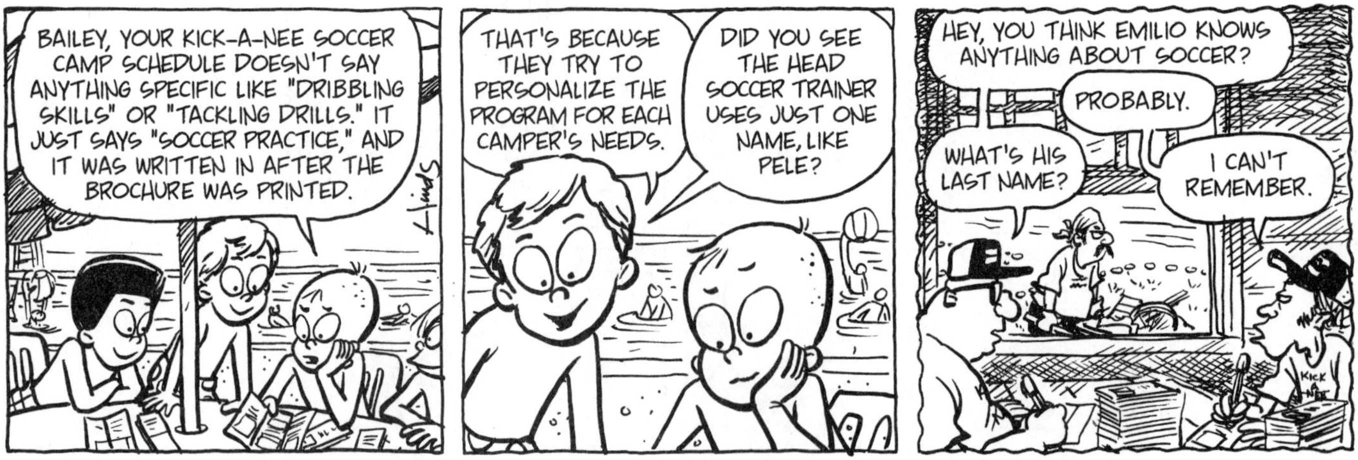
BAILEY, YOUR KICK-A-NEE SOCCER CAMP SCHEDULE DOESN'T SAY ANYTHING SPECIFIC LIKE "DRIBBLING SKILLS" OR "TACKLING DRILLS." IT JUST SAYS "SOCCER PRACTICE," AND IT WAS WRITTEN IN AFTER THE BROCHURE WAS PRINTED.
THAT'S BECAUSE THEY TRY TO PERSONALIZE THE PROGRAM FOR EACH CAMPER'S NEEDS.
DID YOU SEE THE HEAD SOCCER TRAINER USES JUST ONE NAME, LIKE PELE?
HEY, YOU THINK EMILIO KNOWS ANYTHING ABOUT SOCCER?
PROBABLY.
WHAT'S HIS LAST NAME?
I CAN'T REMEMBER.

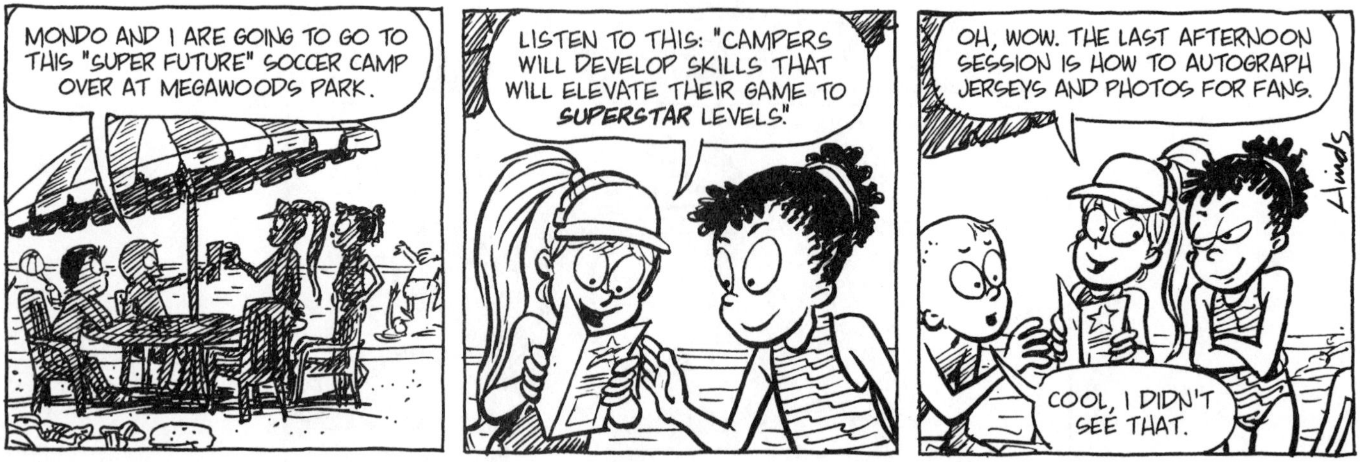
MONDO AND I ARE GOING TO GO TO THIS "SUPER FUTURE" SOCCER CAMP OVER AT MEGAWOODS PARK.
LISTEN TO THIS: "CAMPERS WILL DEVELOP SKILLS THAT WILL ELEVATE THEIR GAME TO SUPERSTAR LEVELS."
OH, WOW. THE LAST AFTERNOON SESSION IS HOW TO AUTOGRAPH JERSEYS AND PHOTOS FOR FANS.
COOL, I DIDN'T SEE THAT.

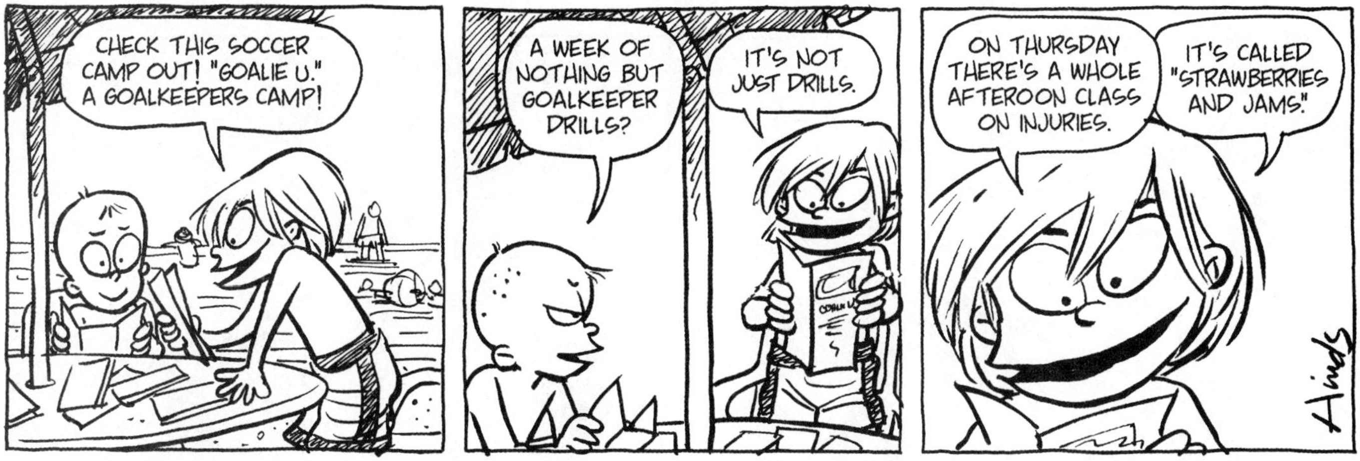
CHECK THIS SOCCER CAMP OUT! "GOALIE U." A GOALKEEPERS CAMP!
A WEEK OF NOTHING BUT GOALKEEPER DRILLS?
IT'S NOT JUST DRILLS.
ON THURSDAY THERE'S A WHOLE AFTEROON CLASS ON INJURIES.
IT'S CALLED "STRAWBERRIES AND JAMS."
Hinds

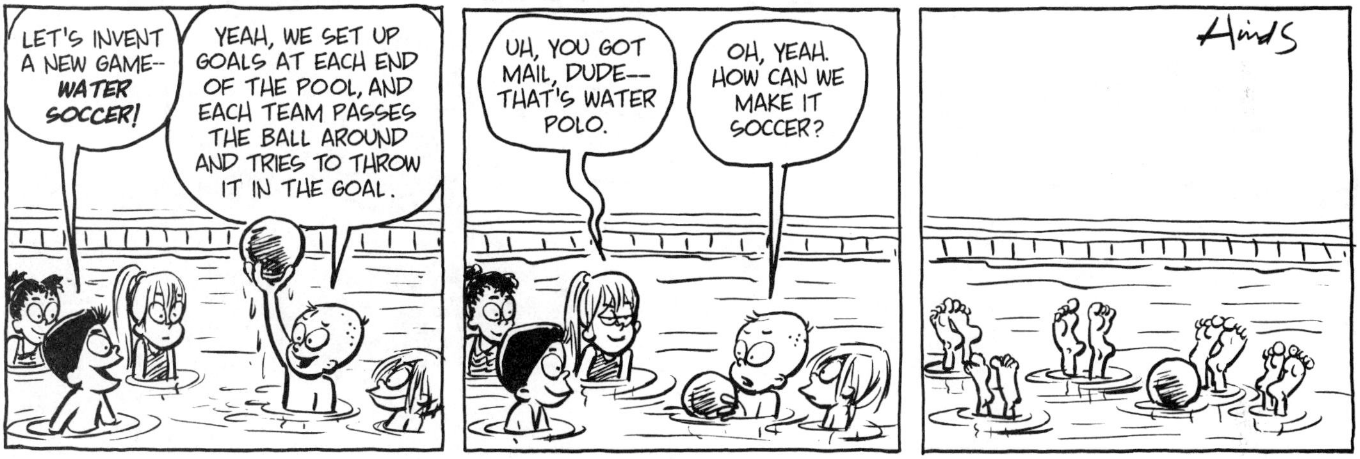
LET'S INVENT A NEW GAME-- **WATER SOCCER!**
YEAH, WE SET UP GOALS AT EACH END OF THE POOL, AND EACH TEAM PASSES THE BALL AROUND AND TRIES TO THROW IT IN THE GOAL.
UH, YOU GOT MAIL, DUDE-- THAT'S WATER POLO.
OH, YEAH. HOW CAN WE MAKE IT SOCCER?
Hinds

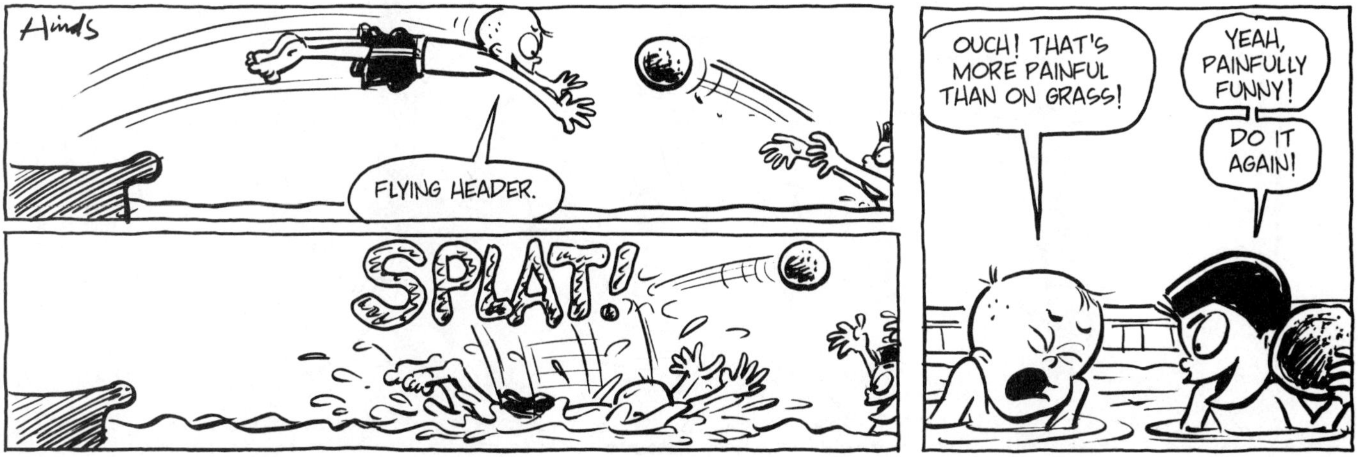
Hinds
FLYING HEADER.
SPLAT!
OUCH! THAT'S MORE PAINFUL THAN ON GRASS!
YEAH, PAINFULLY FUNNY!
DO IT AGAIN!

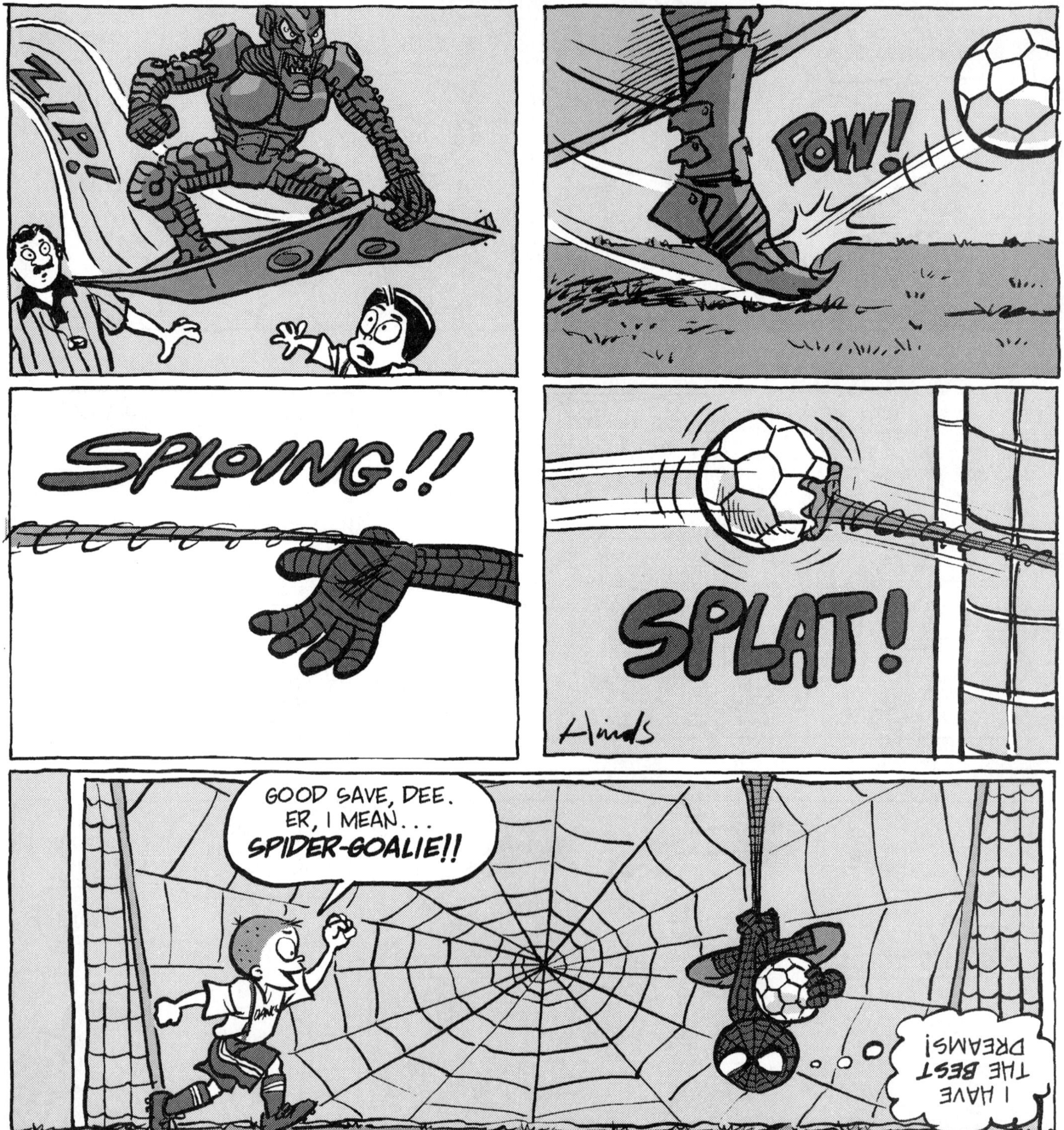

ZIP!
POW!
SPLOING!!
SPLAT!
Hinds
GOOD SAVE, DEE. ER, I MEAN... SPIDER-GOALIE!!
I HAVE THE BEST DREAMS!

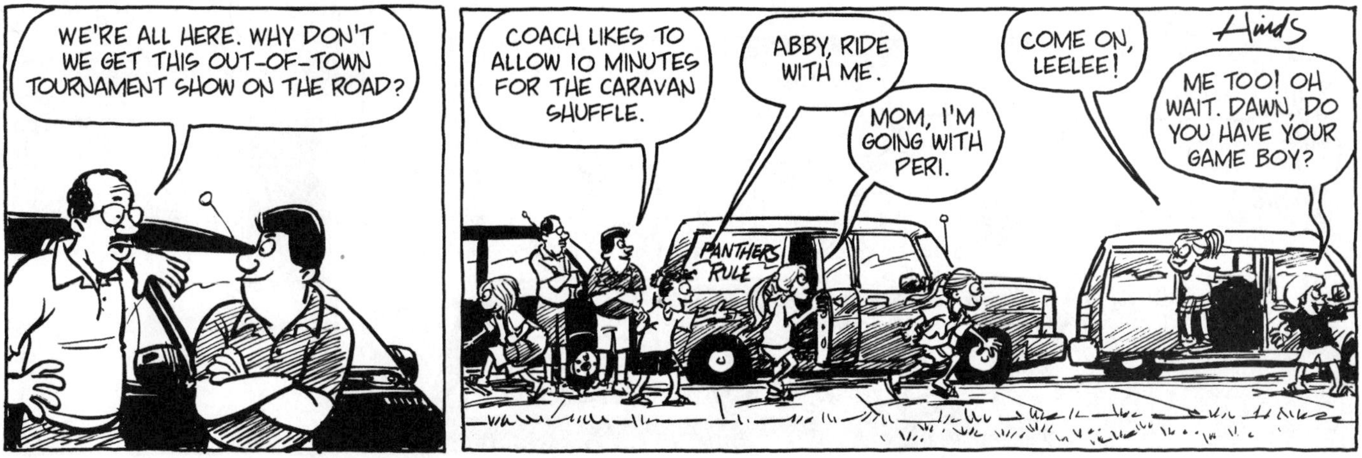
WE'RE ALL HERE. WHY DON'T WE GET THIS OUT-OF-TOWN TOURNAMENT SHOW ON THE ROAD?
COACH LIKES TO ALLOW 10 MINUTES FOR THE CARAVAN SHUFFLE.
ABBY, RIDE WITH ME.
MOM, I'M GOING WITH PERI.
PANTHERS RULE
COME ON, LEELEE!
ME TOO! OH WAIT. DAWN, DO YOU HAVE YOUR GAME BOY?

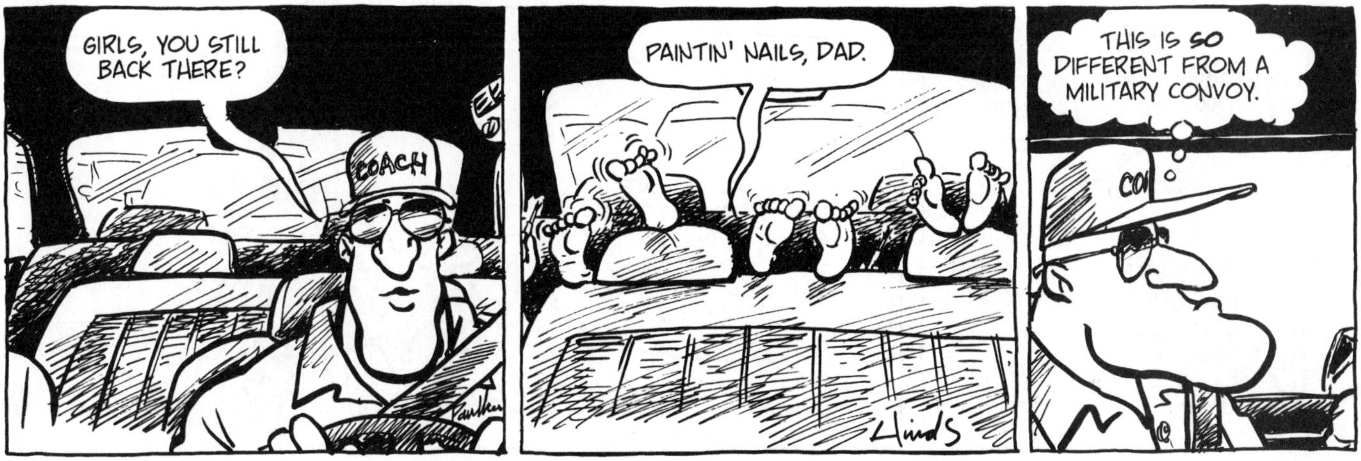
GIRLS, YOU STILL BACK THERE?
COACH
PAINTIN' NAILS, DAD.
THIS IS SO DIFFERENT FROM A MILITARY CONVOY.

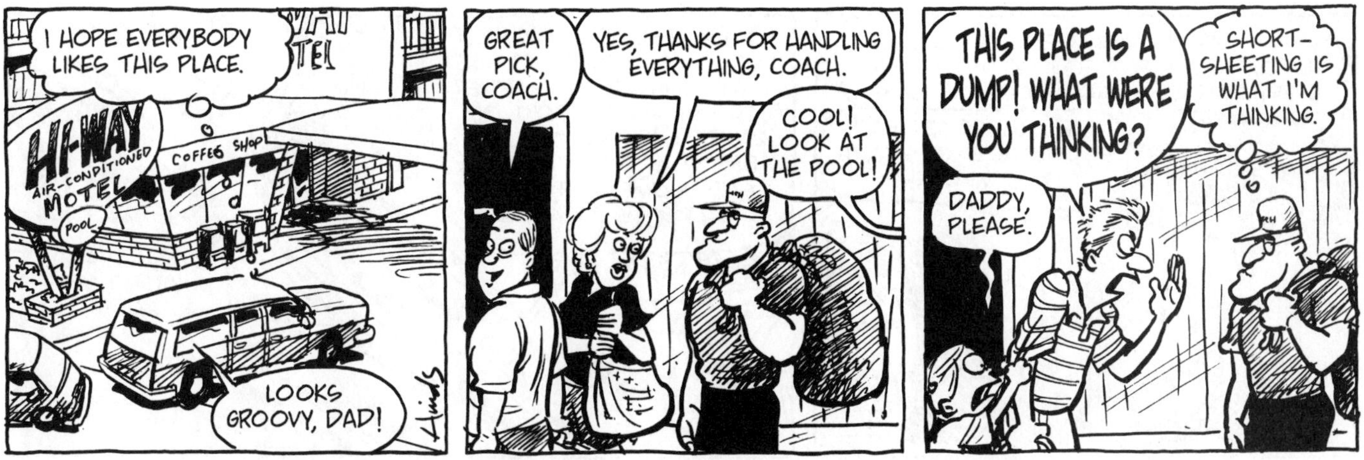
I HOPE EVERYBODY LIKES THIS PLACE.
HI-WAY
AIR-CONDITIONED
MOTEL
POOL
COFFEE SHOP
LOOKS GROOVY, DAD!
GREAT PICK, COACH.
YES, THANKS FOR HANDLING EVERYTHING, COACH.
COOL! LOOK AT THE POOL!
THIS PLACE IS A DUMP! WHAT WERE YOU THINKING?
SHORT-SHEETING IS WHAT I'M THINKING.
DADDY, PLEASE.

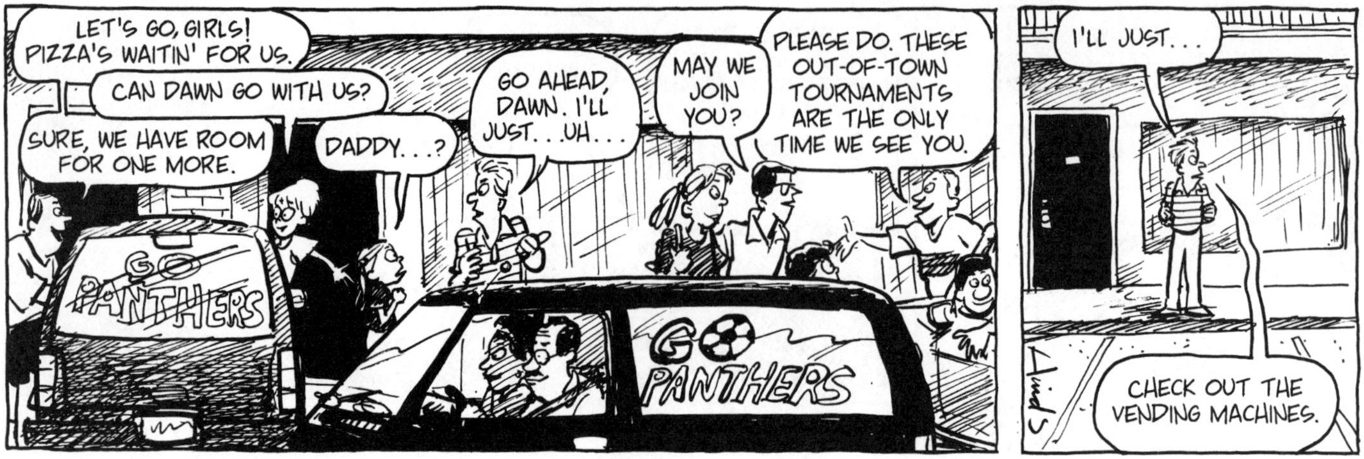
LET'S GO, GIRLS! PIZZA'S WAITIN' FOR US.
CAN DAWN GO WITH US?
SURE, WE HAVE ROOM FOR ONE MORE.
DADDY...?
GO AHEAD, DAWN. I'LL JUST...UH...
MAY WE JOIN YOU?
PLEASE DO. THESE OUT-OF-TOWN TOURNAMENTS ARE THE ONLY TIME WE SEE YOU.
GO PANTHERS
GO PANTHERS
I'LL JUST...
CHECK OUT THE VENDING MACHINES.

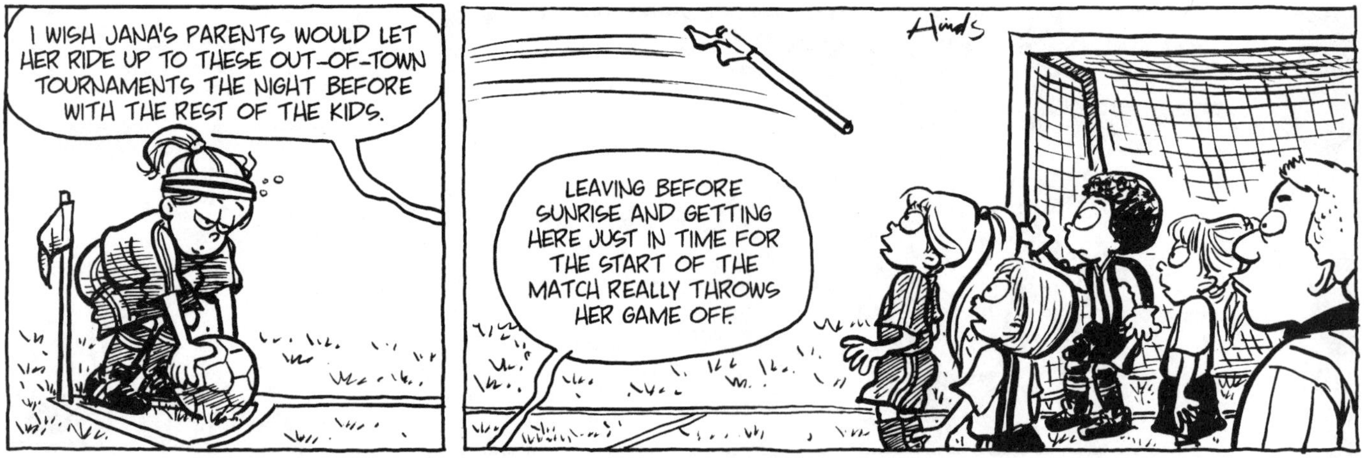
I WISH JANA'S PARENTS WOULD LET HER RIDE UP TO THESE OUT-OF-TOWN TOURNAMENTS THE NIGHT BEFORE WITH THE REST OF THE KIDS.
LEAVING BEFORE SUNRISE AND GETTING HERE JUST IN TIME FOR THE START OF THE MATCH REALLY THROWS HER GAME OFF.

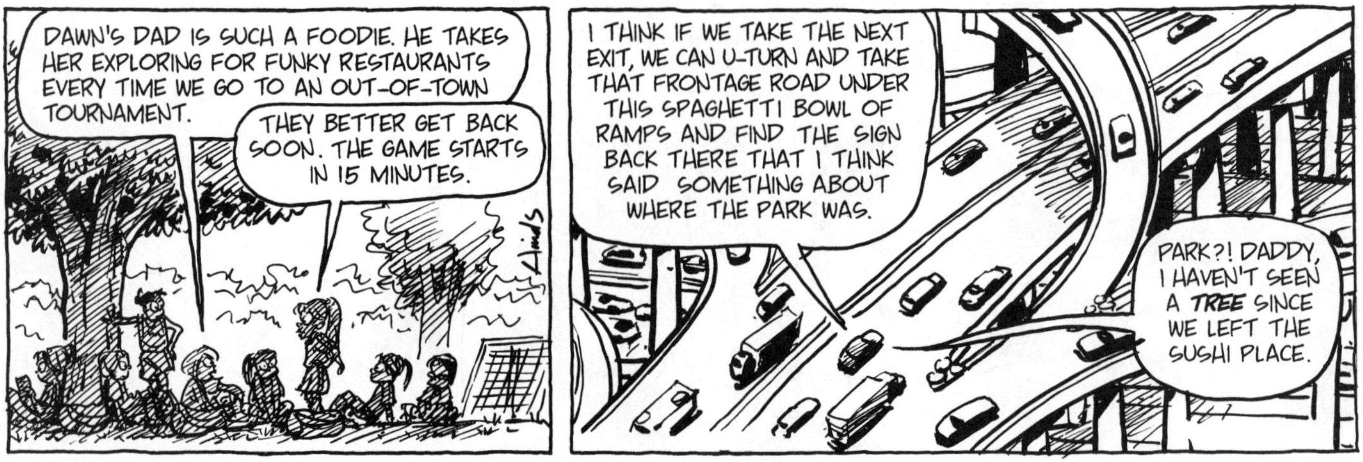
DAWN'S DAD IS SUCH A FOODIE. HE TAKES HER EXPLORING FOR FUNKY RESTAURANTS EVERY TIME WE GO TO AN OUT-OF-TOWN TOURNAMENT.
THEY BETTER GET BACK SOON. THE GAME STARTS IN 15 MINUTES.
I THINK IF WE TAKE THE NEXT EXIT, WE CAN U-TURN AND TAKE THAT FRONTAGE ROAD UNDER THIS SPAGHETTI BOWL OF RAMPS AND FIND THE SIGN BACK THERE THAT I THINK SAID SOMETHING ABOUT WHERE THE PARK WAS.
PARK?! DADDY, I HAVEN'T SEEN A TREE SINCE WE LEFT THE SUSHI PLACE.

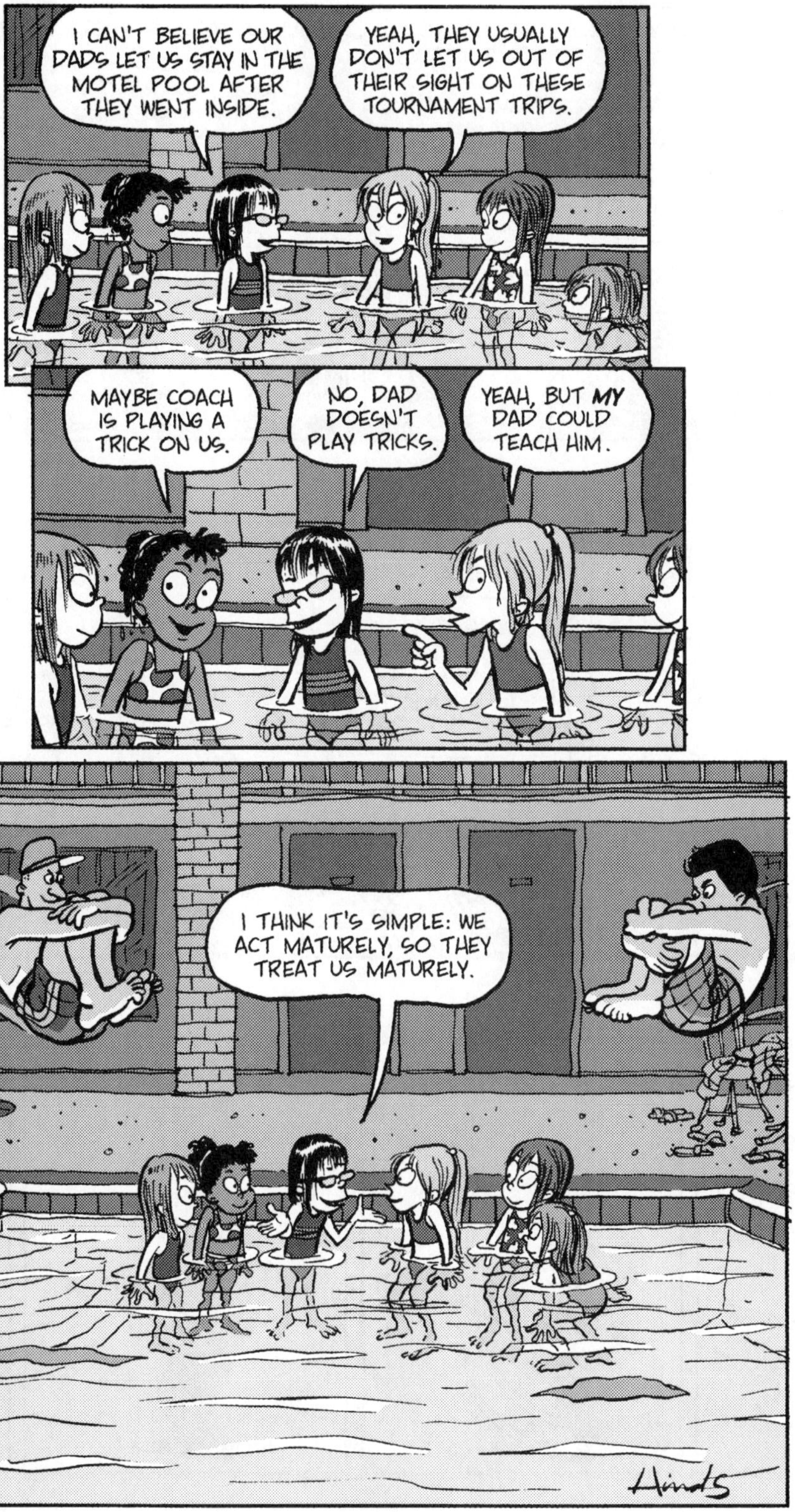
I CAN'T BELIEVE OUR DADS LET US STAY IN THE MOTEL POOL AFTER THEY WENT INSIDE.
YEAH, THEY USUALLY DON'T LET US OUT OF THEIR SIGHT ON THESE TOURNAMENT TRIPS.
MAYBE COACH IS PLAYING A TRICK ON US.
NO, DAD DOESN'T PLAY TRICKS.
YEAH, BUT **MY** DAD COULD TEACH HIM.
I THINK IT'S SIMPLE: WE ACT MATURELY, SO THEY TREAT US MATURELY.
Hinds

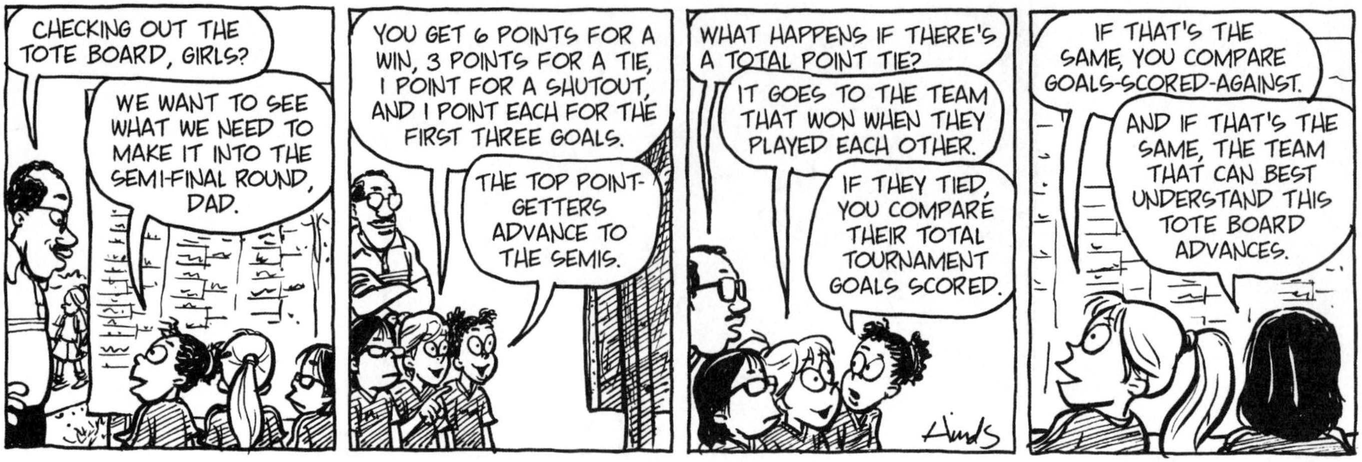
CHECKING OUT THE TOTE BOARD, GIRLS?
WE WANT TO SEE WHAT WE NEED TO MAKE IT INTO THE SEMI-FINAL ROUND, DAD.
YOU GET 6 POINTS FOR A WIN, 3 POINTS FOR A TIE, 1 POINT FOR A SHUTOUT, AND 1 POINT EACH FOR THE FIRST THREE GOALS.
THE TOP POINT-GETTERS ADVANCE TO THE SEMIS.
WHAT HAPPENS IF THERE'S A TOTAL POINT TIE?
IT GOES TO THE TEAM THAT WON WHEN THEY PLAYED EACH OTHER.
IF THEY TIED, YOU COMPARE THEIR TOTAL TOURNAMENT GOALS SCORED.
Hinds
IF THAT'S THE SAME, YOU COMPARE GOALS-SCORED-AGAINST.
AND IF THAT'S THE SAME, THE TEAM THAT CAN BEST UNDERSTAND THIS TOTE BOARD ADVANCES.

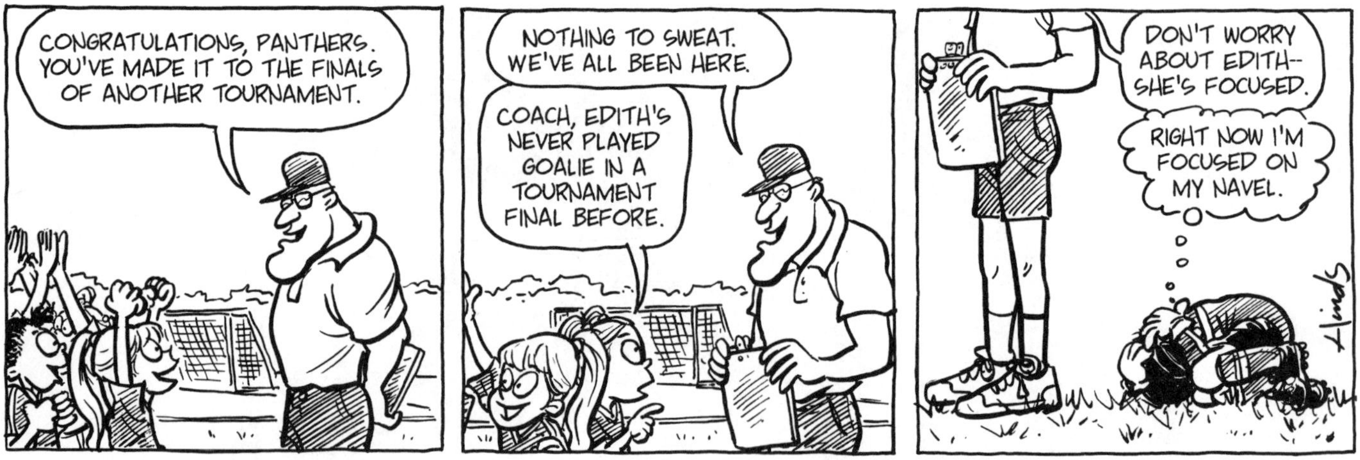
CONGRATULATIONS, PANTHERS. YOU'VE MADE IT TO THE FINALS OF ANOTHER TOURNAMENT.
COACH, EDITH'S NEVER PLAYED GOALIE IN A TOURNAMENT FINAL BEFORE.
NOTHING TO SWEAT. WE'VE ALL BEEN HERE.
DON'T WORRY ABOUT EDITH--SHE'S FOCUSED.
RIGHT NOW I'M FOCUSED ON MY NAVEL.
Hinds

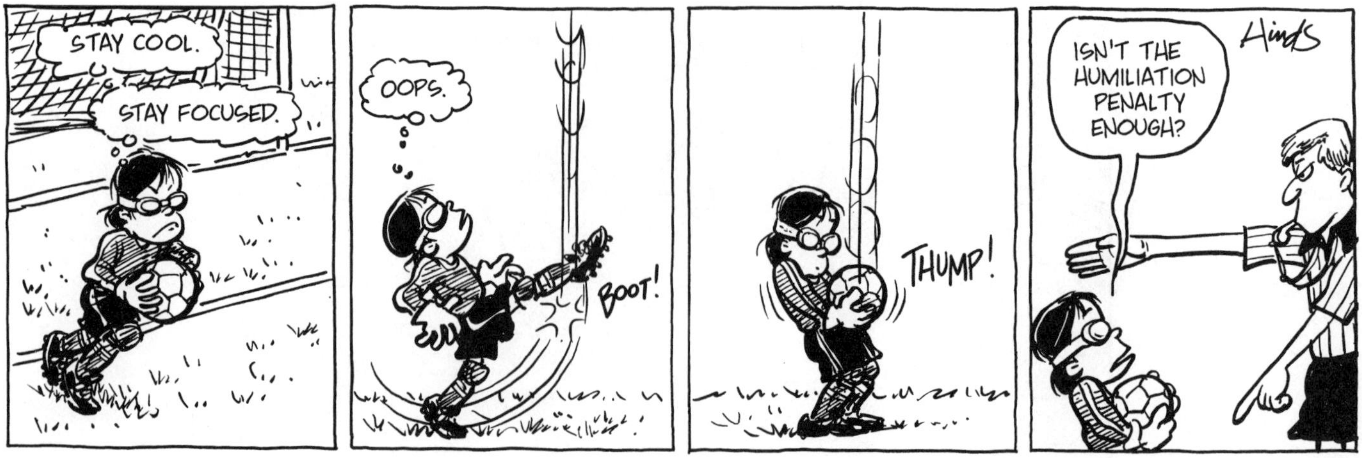
STAY COOL.
STAY FOCUSED.
OOPS.
BOOT!
THUMP!
Hinds
ISN'T THE HUMILIATION PENALTY ENOUGH?

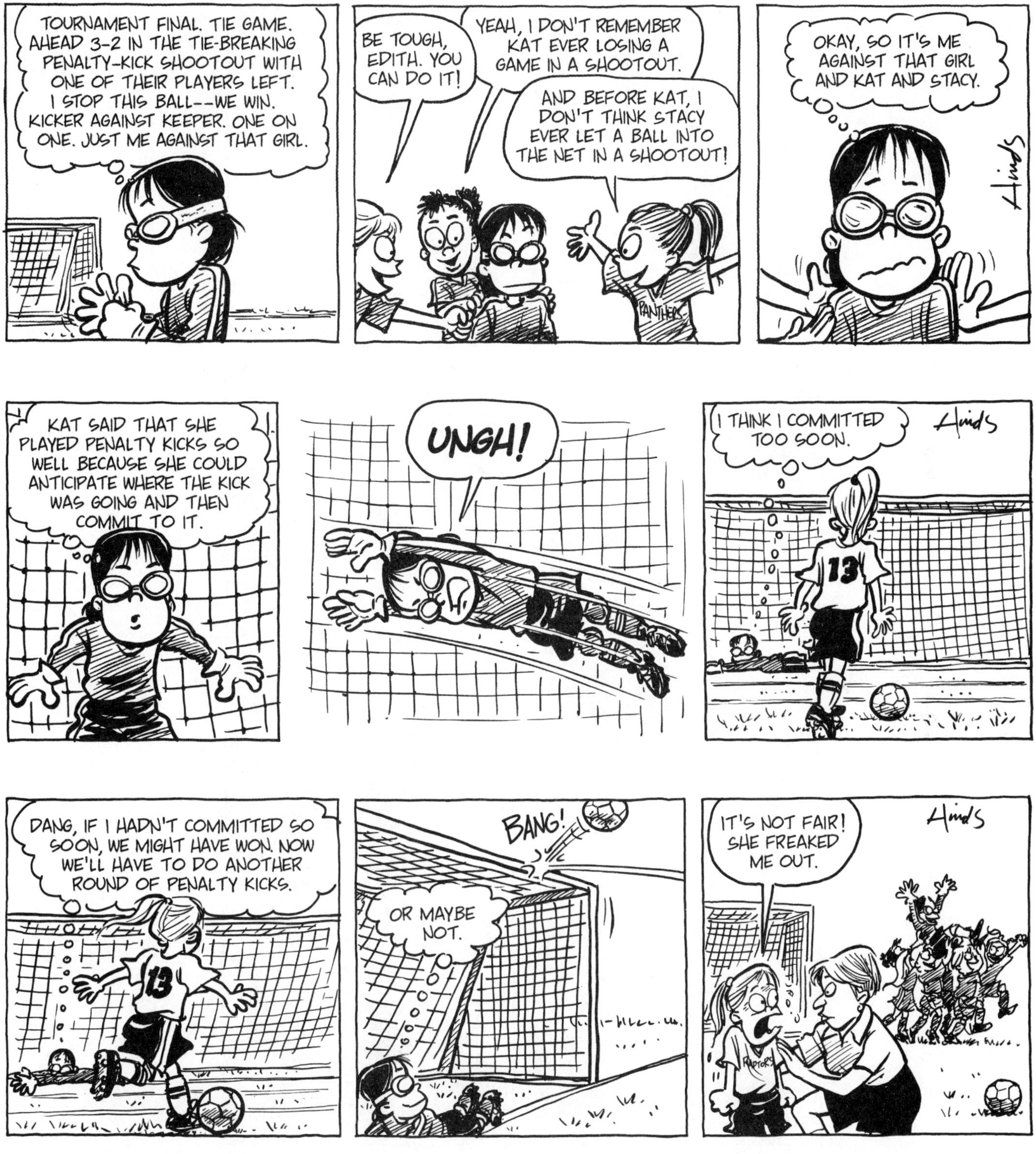
TOURNAMENT FINAL. TIE GAME. AHEAD 3-2 IN THE TIE-BREAKING PENALTY-KICK SHOOTOUT WITH ONE OF THEIR PLAYERS LEFT. I STOP THIS BALL--WE WIN. KICKER AGAINST KEEPER. ONE ON ONE. JUST ME AGAINST THAT GIRL.
BE TOUGH, EDITH. YOU CAN DO IT!
YEAH, I DON'T REMEMBER KAT EVER LOSING A GAME IN A SHOOTOUT.
AND BEFORE KAT, I DON'T THINK STACY EVER LET A BALL INTO THE NET IN A SHOOTOUT!
PANTHERS
OKAY, SO IT'S ME AGAINST THAT GIRL AND KAT AND STACY.
Hinds
KAT SAID THAT SHE PLAYED PENALTY KICKS SO WELL BECAUSE SHE COULD ANTICIPATE WHERE THE KICK WAS GOING AND THEN COMMIT TO IT.
UNGH!
I THINK I COMMITTED TOO SOON.
Hinds
13
DANG, IF I HADN'T COMMITTED SO SOON, WE MIGHT HAVE WON. NOW WE'LL HAVE TO DO ANOTHER ROUND OF PENALTY KICKS.
13
BANG!
OR MAYBE NOT.
IT'S NOT FAIR! SHE FREAKED ME OUT.
RAPTORS
Hinds

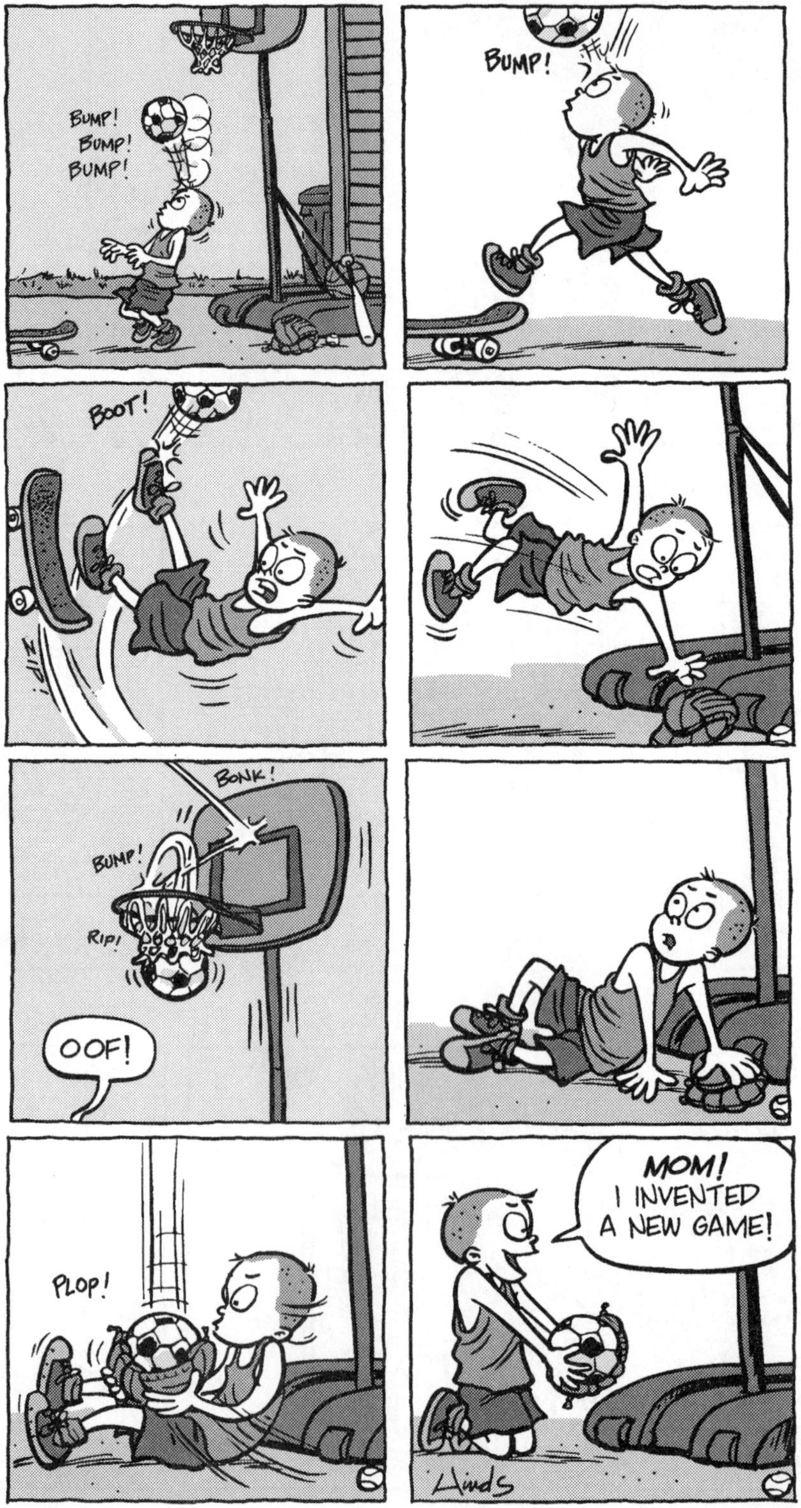
BUMP!
BUMP!
BUMP!
BUMP!
BOOT!
BONK!
BUMP!
RIP!
OOF!
PLOP!
MOM!
I INVENTED
A NEW GAME!
Hinds

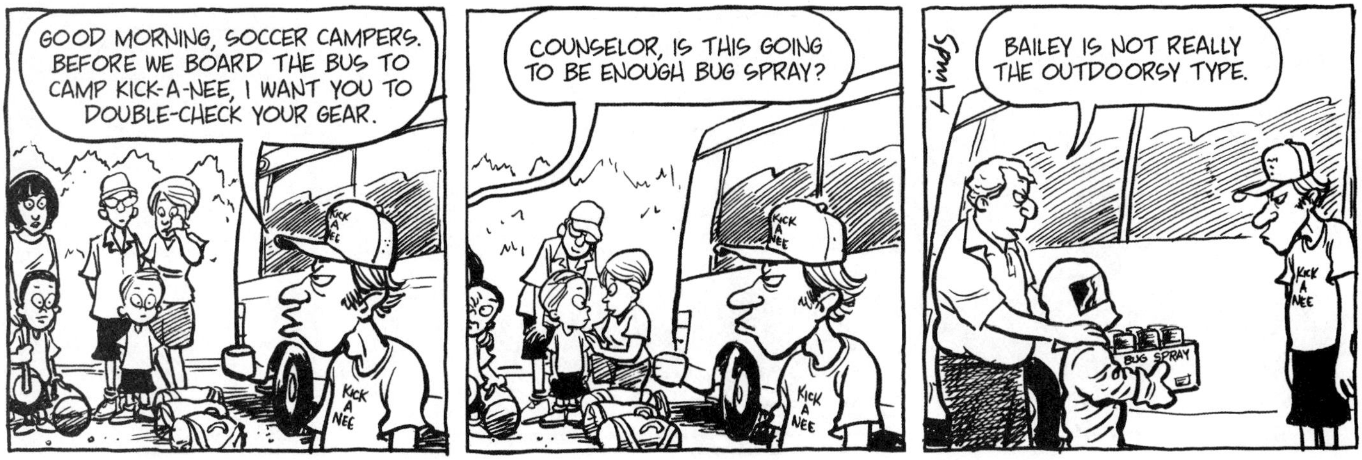
GOOD MORNING, SOCCER CAMPERS. BEFORE WE BOARD THE BUS TO CAMP KICK-A-NEE, I WANT YOU TO DOUBLE-CHECK YOUR GEAR.
COUNSELOR, IS THIS GOING TO BE ENOUGH BUG SPRAY?
BUG SPRAY
BAILEY IS NOT REALLY THE OUTDOORSY TYPE.

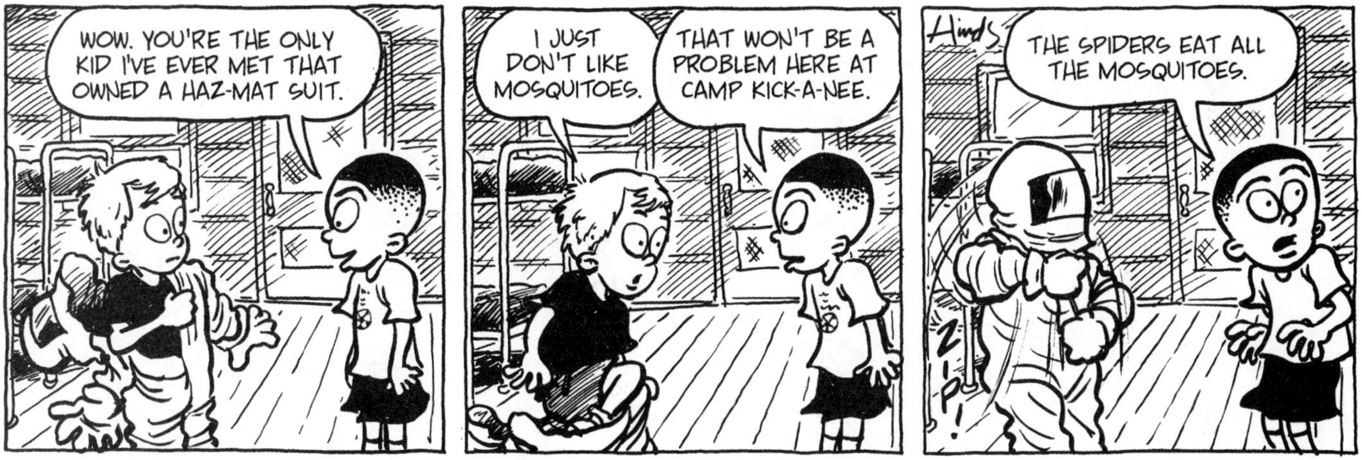
WOW. YOU'RE THE ONLY KID I'VE EVER MET THAT OWNED A HAZ-MAT SUIT.
I JUST DON'T LIKE MOSQUITOES.
THAT WON'T BE A PROBLEM HERE AT CAMP KICK-A-NEE.
THE SPIDERS EAT ALL THE MOSQUITOES.

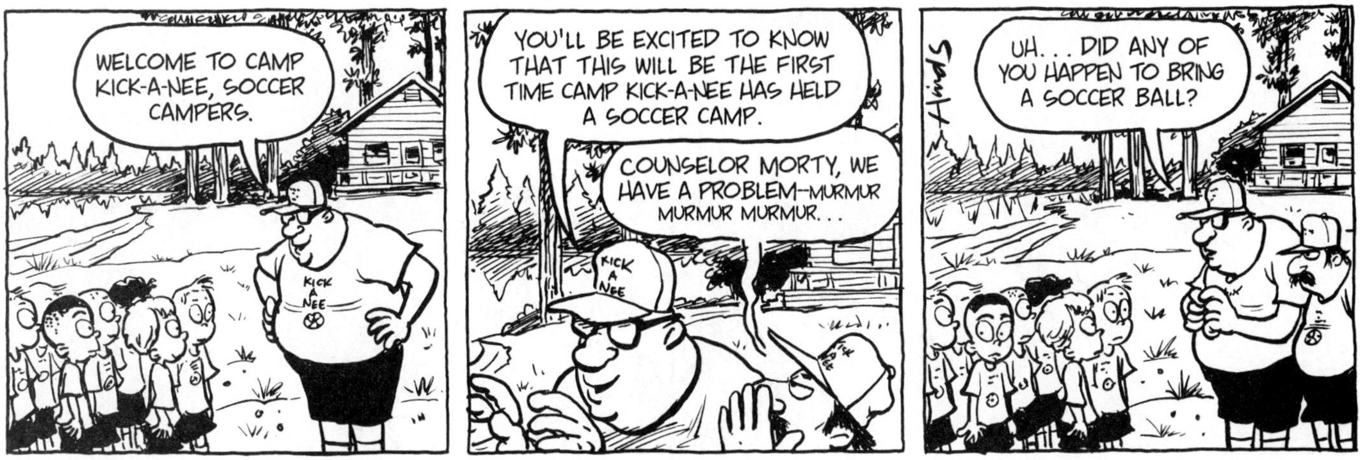
WELCOME TO CAMP KICK-A-NEE, SOCCER CAMPERS.
YOU'LL BE EXCITED TO KNOW THAT THIS WILL BE THE FIRST TIME CAMP KICK-A-NEE HAS HELD A SOCCER CAMP.
COUNSELOR MORTY, WE HAVE A PROBLEM—MURMUR MURMUR MURMUR. . .
UH. . . DID ANY OF YOU HAPPEN TO BRING A SOCCER BALL?

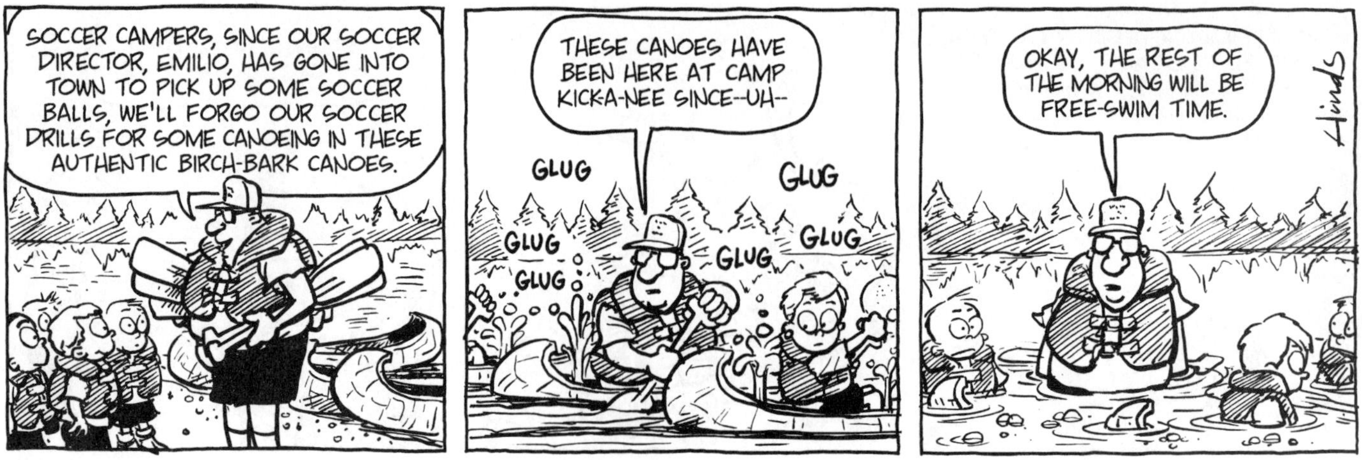
SOCCER CAMPERS, SINCE OUR SOCCER DIRECTOR, EMILIO, HAS GONE INTO TOWN TO PICK UP SOME SOCCER BALLS, WE'LL FORGO OUR SOCCER DRILLS FOR SOME CANOEING IN THESE AUTHENTIC BIRCH-BARK CANOES.
THESE CANOES HAVE BEEN HERE AT CAMP KICK-A-NEE SINCE--UH--
GLUG
GLUG
GLUG
GLUG
GLUG
GLUG
OKAY, THE REST OF THE MORNING WILL BE FREE-SWIM TIME.

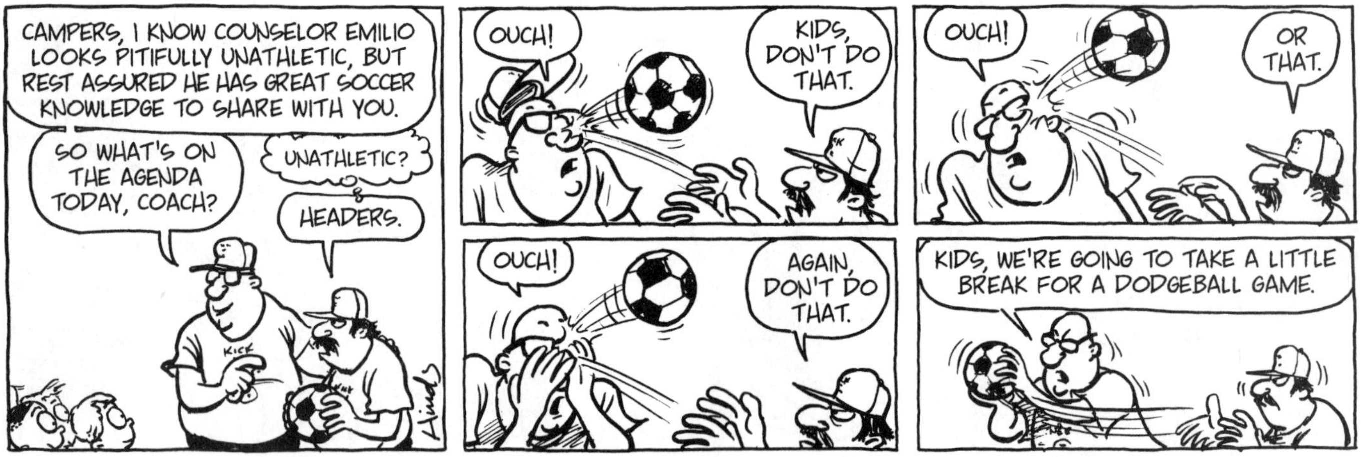
CAMPERS, I KNOW COUNSELOR EMILIO LOOKS PITIFULLY UNATHLETIC, BUT REST ASSURED HE HAS GREAT SOCCER KNOWLEDGE TO SHARE WITH YOU.
SO WHAT'S ON THE AGENDA TODAY, COACH?
UNATHLETIC?
HEADERS.
OUCH!
KIDS, DON'T DO THAT.
OUCH!
OR THAT.
OUCH!
AGAIN, DON'T DO THAT.
KIDS, WE'RE GOING TO TAKE A LITTLE BREAK FOR A DODGEBALL GAME.

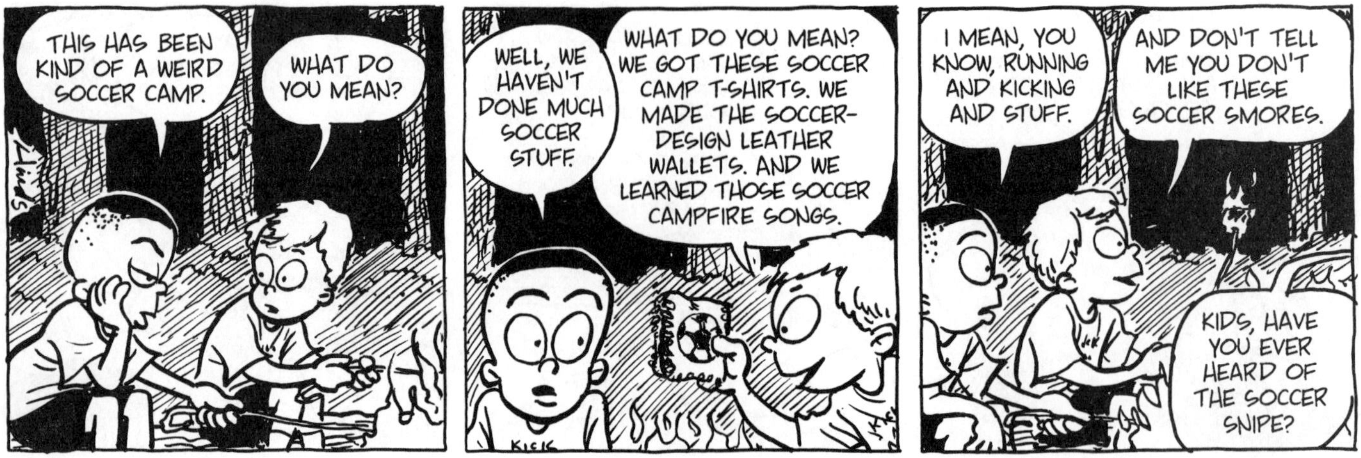
THIS HAS BEEN KIND OF A WEIRD SOCCER CAMP.
WHAT DO YOU MEAN?
WELL, WE HAVEN'T DONE MUCH SOCCER STUFF.
WHAT DO YOU MEAN? WE GOT THESE SOCCER CAMP T-SHIRTS. WE MADE THE SOCCER-DESIGN LEATHER WALLETS. AND WE LEARNED THOSE SOCCER CAMPFIRE SONGS.
I MEAN, YOU KNOW, RUNNING AND KICKING AND STUFF.
AND DON'T TELL ME YOU DON'T LIKE THESE SOCCER SMORES.
KIDS, HAVE YOU EVER HEARD OF THE SOCCER SNIPE?

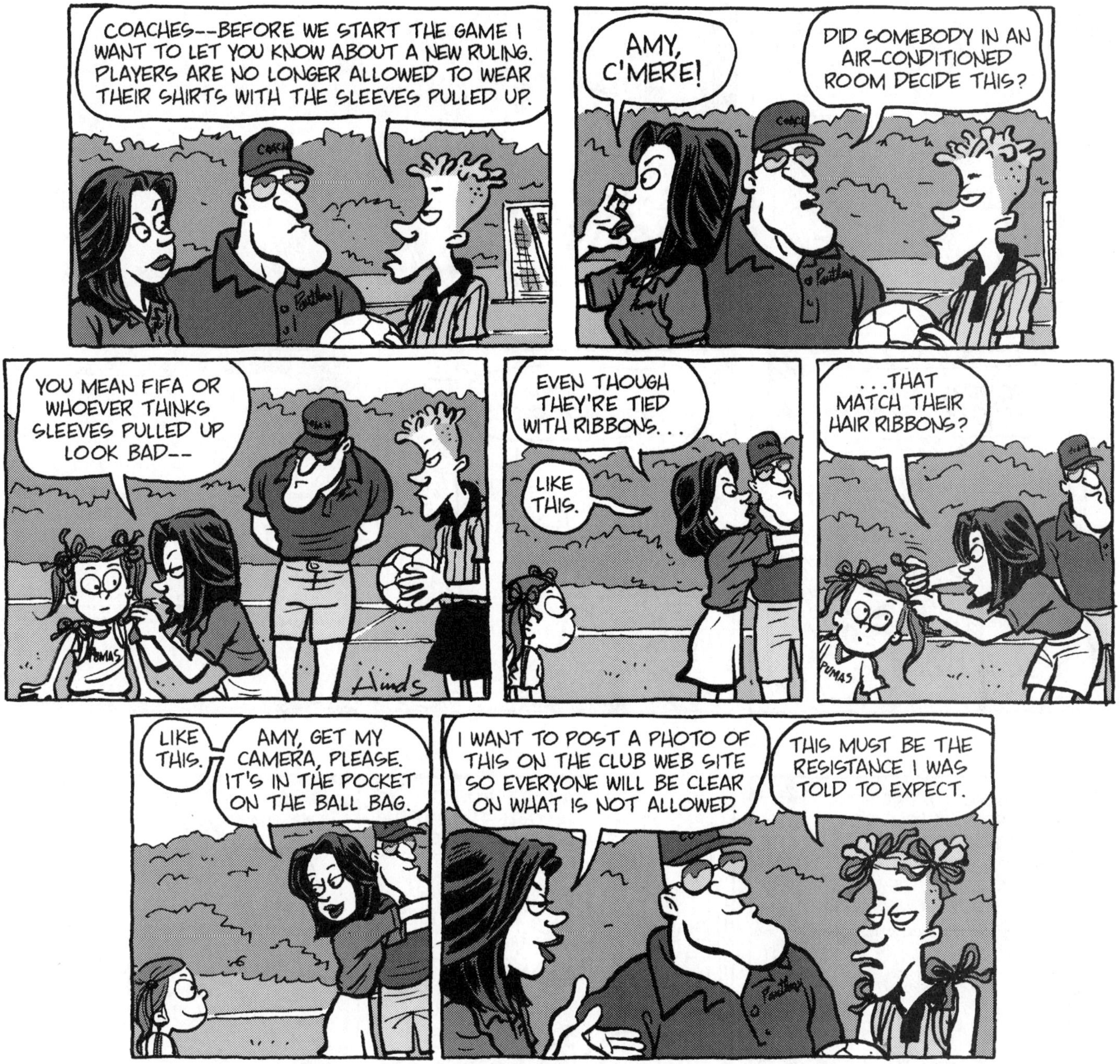
COACHES--BEFORE WE START THE GAME I WANT TO LET YOU KNOW ABOUT A NEW RULING. PLAYERS ARE NO LONGER ALLOWED TO WEAR THEIR SHIRTS WITH THE SLEEVES PULLED UP.
AMY, C'MERE!
DID SOMEBODY IN AN AIR-CONDITIONED ROOM DECIDE THIS?
YOU MEAN FIFA OR WHOEVER THINKS SLEEVES PULLED UP LOOK BAD--
EVEN THOUGH THEY'RE TIED WITH RIBBONS...
LIKE THIS.
...THAT MATCH THEIR HAIR RIBBONS?
LIKE THIS.
AMY, GET MY CAMERA, PLEASE. IT'S IN THE POCKET ON THE BALL BAG.
I WANT TO POST A PHOTO OF THIS ON THE CLUB WEB SITE SO EVERYONE WILL BE CLEAR ON WHAT IS NOT ALLOWED.
THIS MUST BE THE RESISTANCE I WAS TOLD TO EXPECT.

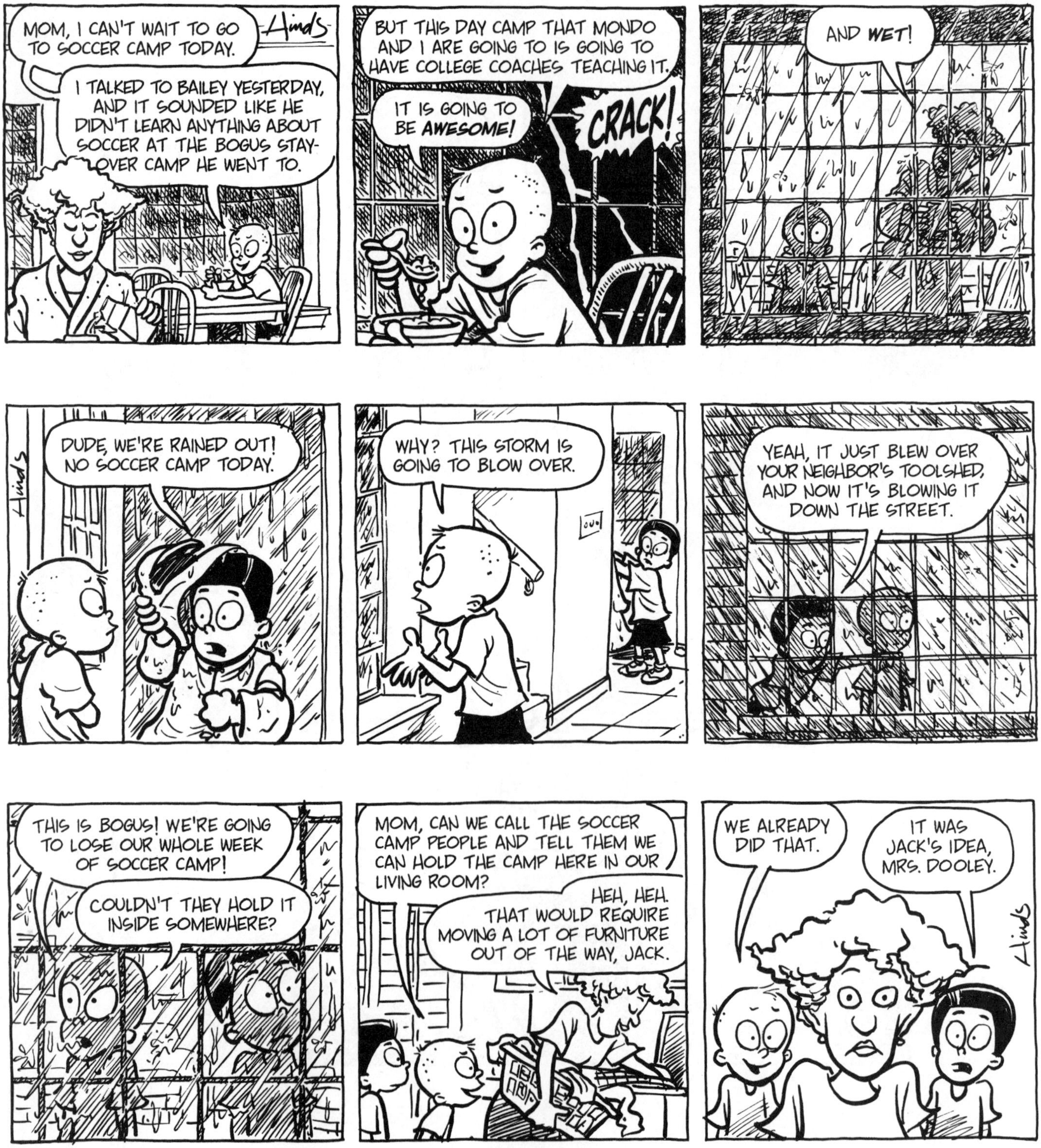

Hinds
MOM, I CAN'T WAIT TO GO TO SOCCER CAMP TODAY.
I TALKED TO BAILEY YESTERDAY, AND IT SOUNDED LIKE HE DIDN'T LEARN ANYTHING ABOUT SOCCER AT THE BOGUS STAY-OVER CAMP HE WENT TO.
BUT THIS DAY CAMP THAT MONDO AND I ARE GOING TO IS GOING TO HAVE COLLEGE COACHES TEACHING IT.
IT IS GOING TO BE **AWESOME!**
CRACK!
AND **WET!**
Hinds
DUDE, WE'RE RAINED OUT! NO SOCCER CAMP TODAY.
WHY? THIS STORM IS GOING TO BLOW OVER.
YEAH, IT JUST BLEW OVER YOUR NEIGHBOR'S TOOLSHED, AND NOW IT'S BLOWING IT DOWN THE STREET.
THIS IS BOGUS! WE'RE GOING TO LOSE OUR WHOLE WEEK OF SOCCER CAMP!
COULDN'T THEY HOLD IT INSIDE SOMEWHERE?
MOM, CAN WE CALL THE SOCCER CAMP PEOPLE AND TELL THEM WE CAN HOLD THE CAMP HERE IN OUR LIVING ROOM?
HEH, HEH. THAT WOULD REQUIRE MOVING A LOT OF FURNITURE OUT OF THE WAY, JACK.
WE ALREADY DID THAT.
IT WAS JACK'S IDEA, MRS. DOOLEY.
Hinds

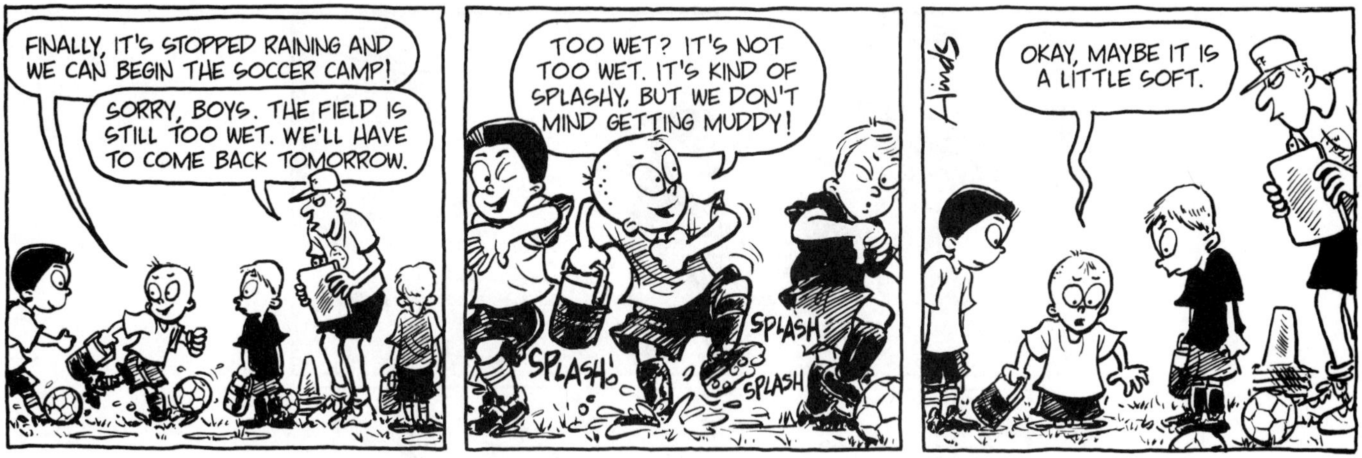
FINALLY, IT'S STOPPED RAINING AND WE CAN BEGIN THE SOCCER CAMP!
SORRY, BOYS. THE FIELD IS STILL TOO WET. WE'LL HAVE TO COME BACK TOMORROW.
TOO WET? IT'S NOT TOO WET. IT'S KIND OF SPLASHY, BUT WE DON'T MIND GETTING MUDDY!
SPLASH
SPLASH
SPLASH
Hinds
OKAY, MAYBE IT IS A LITTLE SOFT.

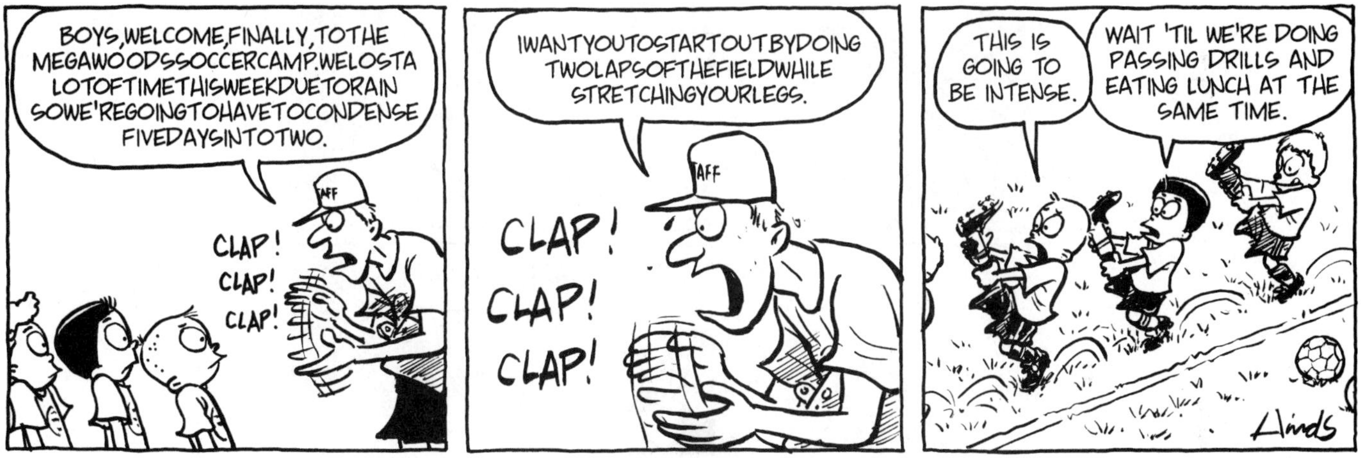
BOYS,WELCOME,FINALLY,TOTHE MEGAWOODSSOCCERCAMP.WELOSTA LOTOFTIMETHISWEEKDUETORAIN SOWE'REGOINGTOHAVETOCONDENSE FIVEDAYSINTOTWO.
CLAP! CLAP! CLAP!
IWANTYOUTOSTARTOUTBYDOING TWOLAPSOFTHEFIELDWHILE STRETCHINGYOURLEGS.
CLAP! CLAP! CLAP!
THIS IS GOING TO BE INTENSE.
WAIT 'TIL WE'RE DOING PASSING DRILLS AND EATING LUNCH AT THE SAME TIME.
Hinds

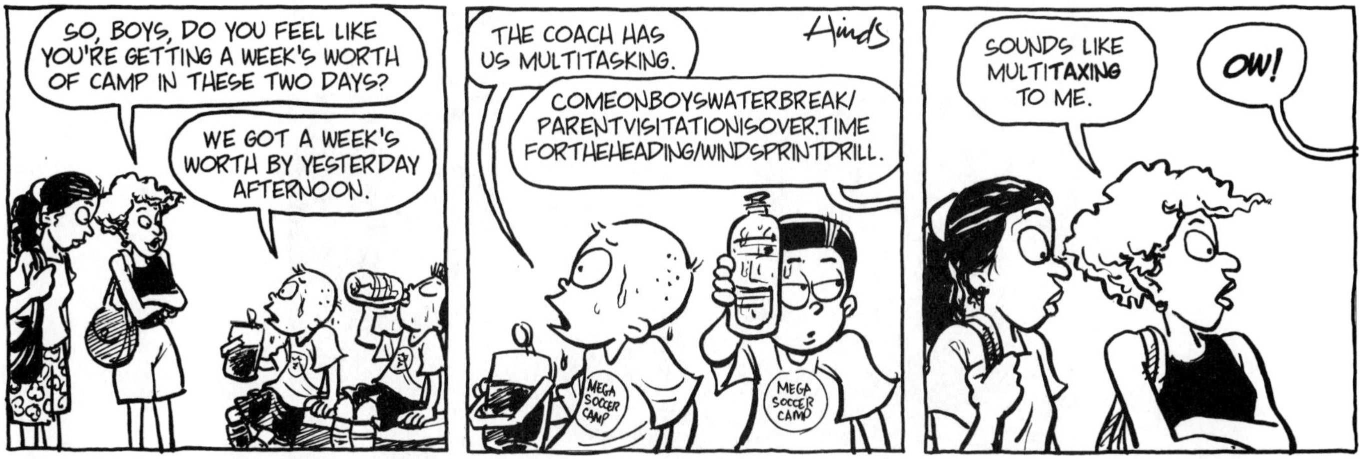
SO, BOYS, DO YOU FEEL LIKE YOU'RE GETTING A WEEK'S WORTH OF CAMP IN THESE TWO DAYS?
WE GOT A WEEK'S WORTH BY YESTERDAY AFTERNOON.
Hinds
THE COACH HAS US MULTITASKING.
COMEONBOYSWATERBREAK/ PARENTVISITATIONISOVER.TIME FORTHEHEADING/WINDSPRINTDRILL.
MEGA SOCCER CAMP
MEGA SOCCER CAMP
SOUNDS LIKE MULTI**TAXING** TO ME.
OW!

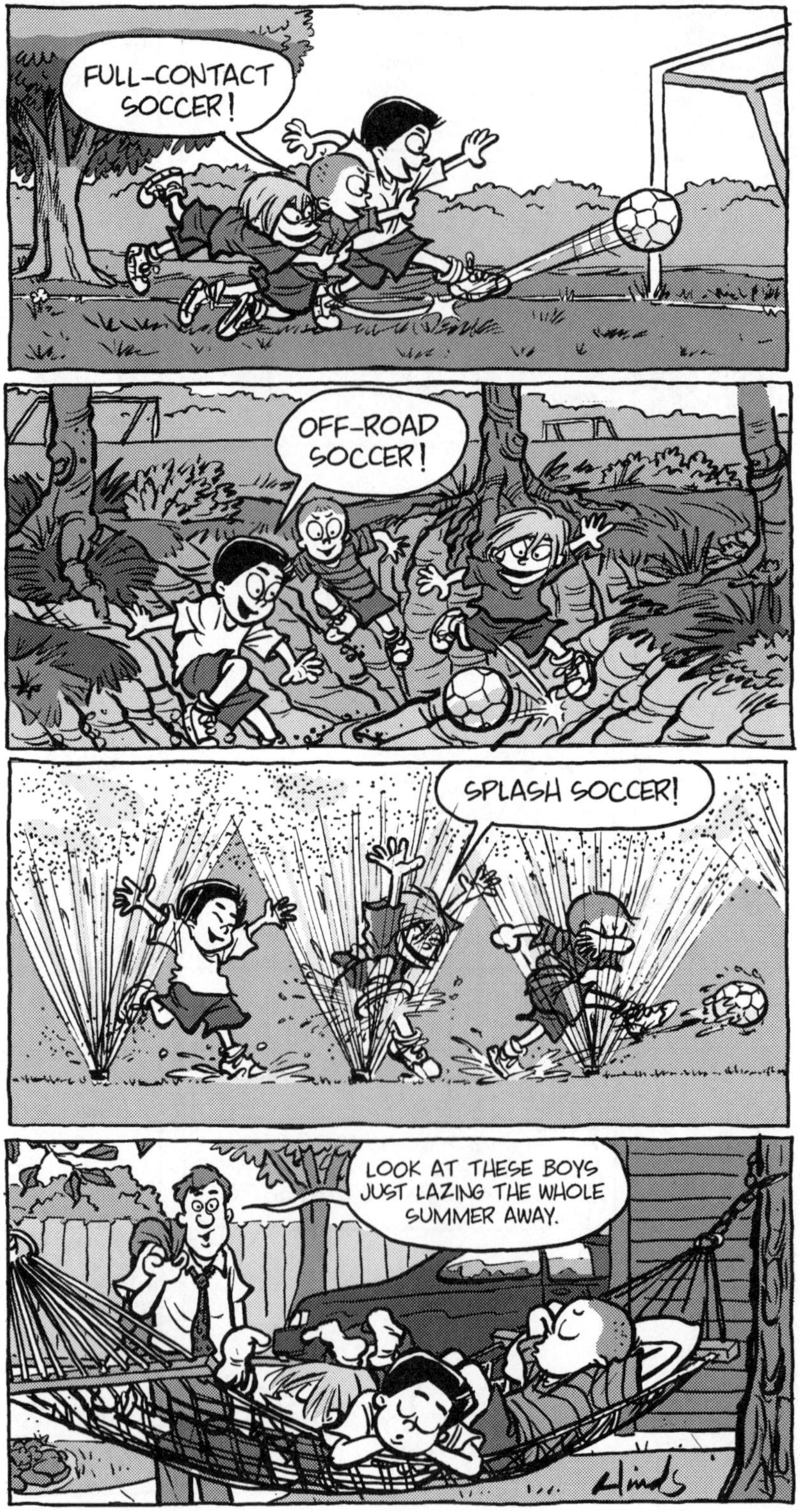
FULL-CONTACT SOCCER!
OFF-ROAD SOCCER!
SPLASH SOCCER!
LOOK AT THESE BOYS JUST LAZING THE WHOLE SUMMER AWAY.
Hinds

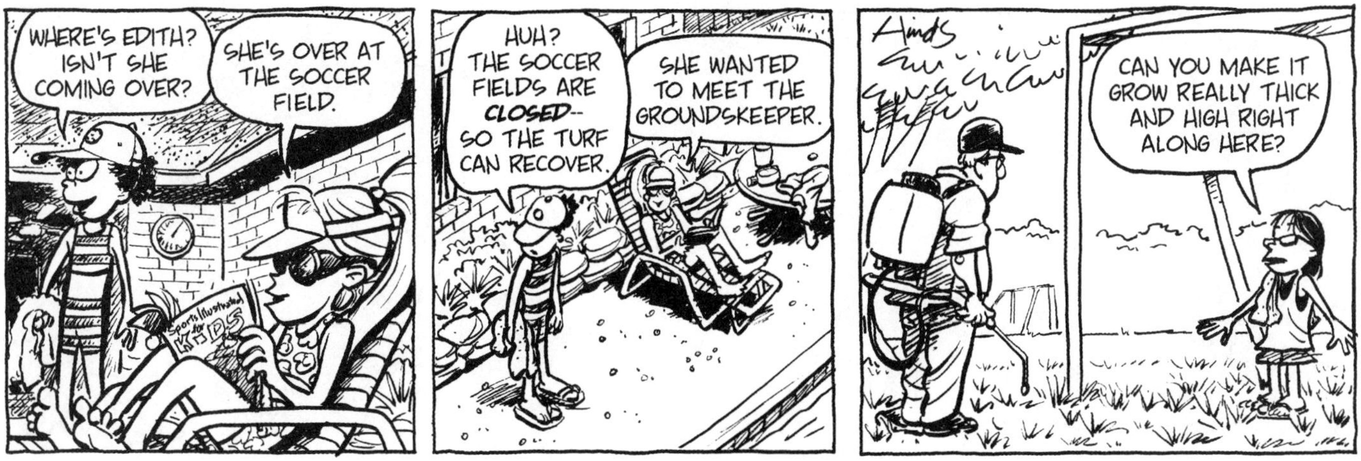
Hinds
WHERE'S EDITH? ISN'T SHE COMING OVER?
SHE'S OVER AT THE SOCCER FIELD.
Sports Illustrated for KIDS
HUH? THE SOCCER FIELDS ARE CLOSED-- SO THE TURF CAN RECOVER.
SHE WANTED TO MEET THE GROUNDSKEEPER.
CAN YOU MAKE IT GROW REALLY THICK AND HIGH RIGHT ALONG HERE?

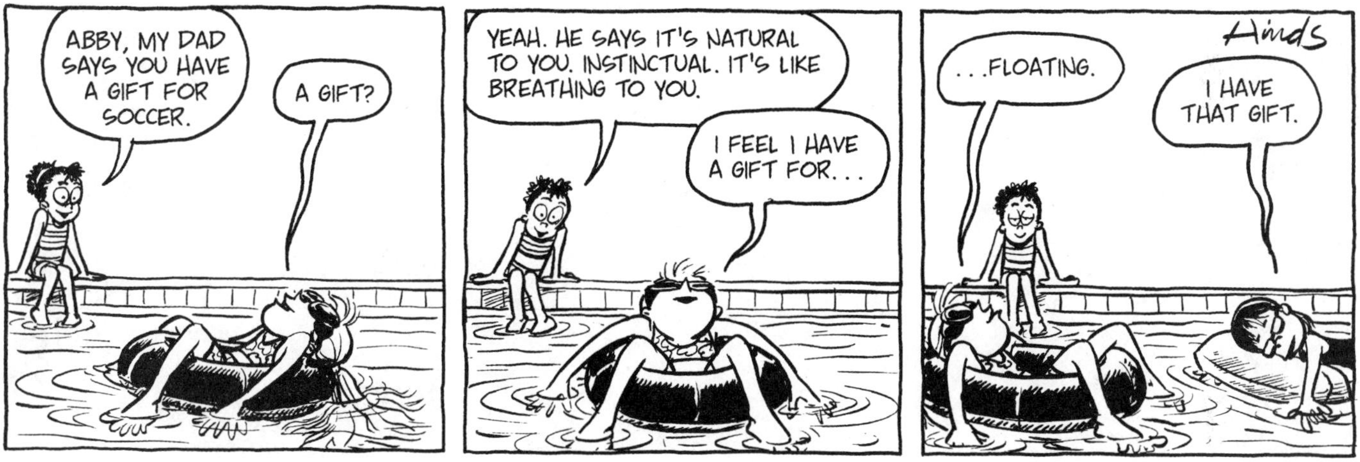
ABBY, MY DAD SAYS YOU HAVE A GIFT FOR SOCCER.
A GIFT?
YEAH. HE SAYS IT'S NATURAL TO YOU. INSTINCTUAL. IT'S LIKE BREATHING TO YOU.
I FEEL I HAVE A GIFT FOR...
Hinds
...FLOATING.
I HAVE THAT GIFT.

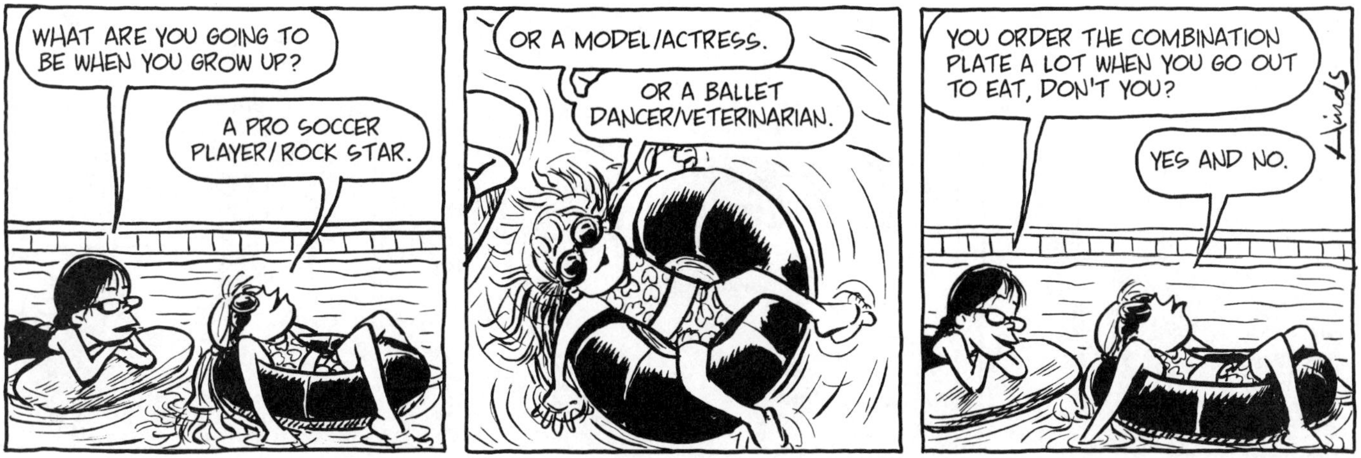
WHAT ARE YOU GOING TO BE WHEN YOU GROW UP?
A PRO SOCCER PLAYER/ROCK STAR.
OR A MODEL/ACTRESS.
OR A BALLET DANCER/VETERINARIAN.
YOU ORDER THE COMBINATION PLATE A LOT WHEN YOU GO OUT TO EAT, DON'T YOU?
YES AND NO.
Hinds

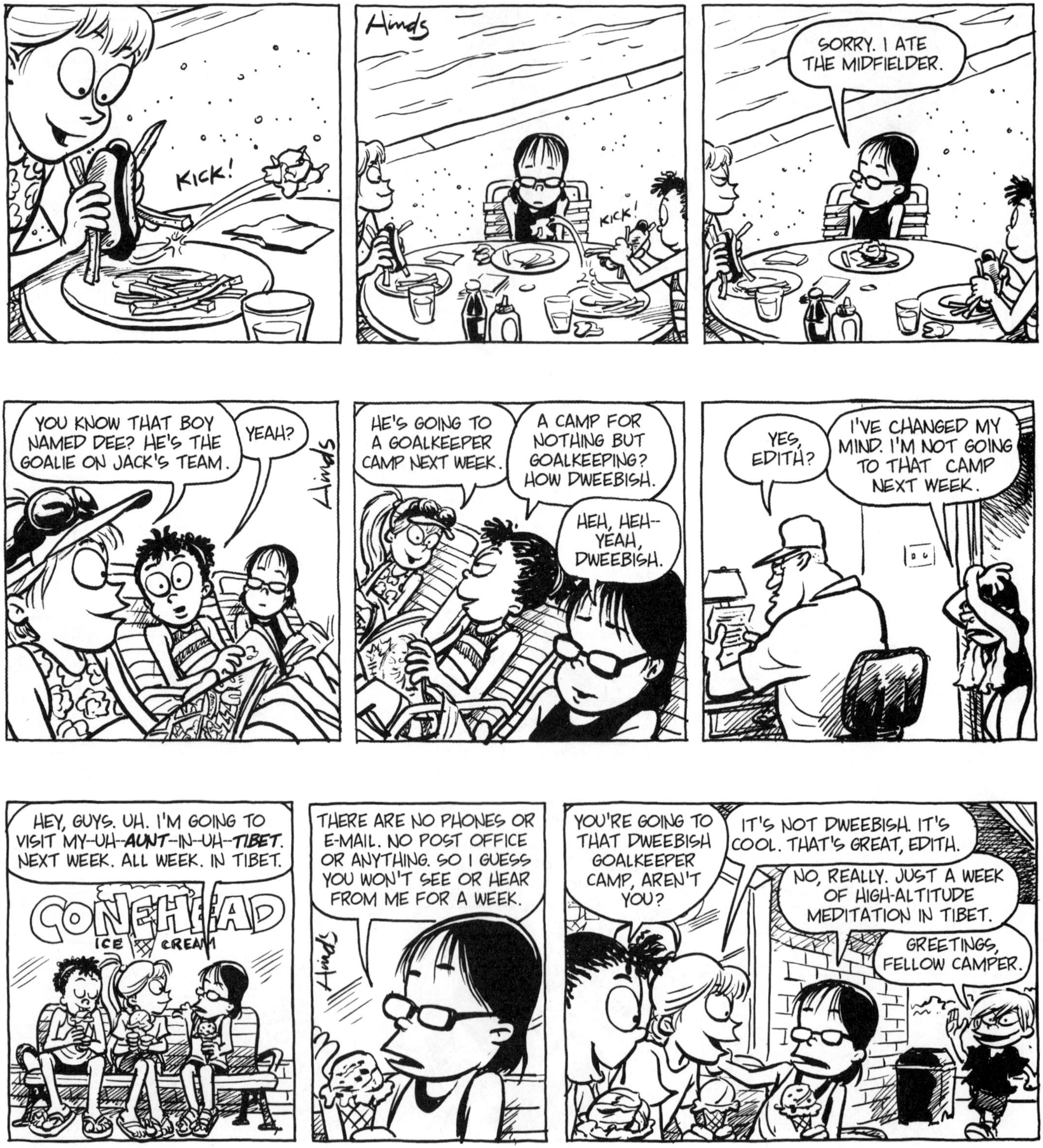

KICK!
Hinds
KICK!
SORRY. I ATE THE MIDFIELDER.
YOU KNOW THAT BOY NAMED DEE? HE'S THE GOALIE ON JACK'S TEAM.
YEAH?
Hinds
HE'S GOING TO A GOALKEEPER CAMP NEXT WEEK.
A CAMP FOR NOTHING BUT GOALKEEPING? HOW DWEEBISH.
HEH, HEH-- YEAH, DWEEBISH.
YES, EDITH?
I'VE CHANGED MY MIND. I'M NOT GOING TO THAT CAMP NEXT WEEK.
HEY, GUYS. UH. I'M GOING TO VISIT MY--UH--***AUNT***--IN--UH--***TIBET***. NEXT WEEK. ALL WEEK. IN TIBET.
CONEHEAD ICE CREAM
THERE ARE NO PHONES OR E-MAIL. NO POST OFFICE OR ANYTHING. SO I GUESS YOU WON'T SEE OR HEAR FROM ME FOR A WEEK.
Hinds
YOU'RE GOING TO THAT DWEEBISH GOALKEEPER CAMP, AREN'T YOU?
IT'S NOT DWEEBISH. IT'S COOL. THAT'S GREAT, EDITH.
NO, REALLY. JUST A WEEK OF HIGH-ALTITUDE MEDITATION IN TIBET.
GREETINGS, FELLOW CAMPER.

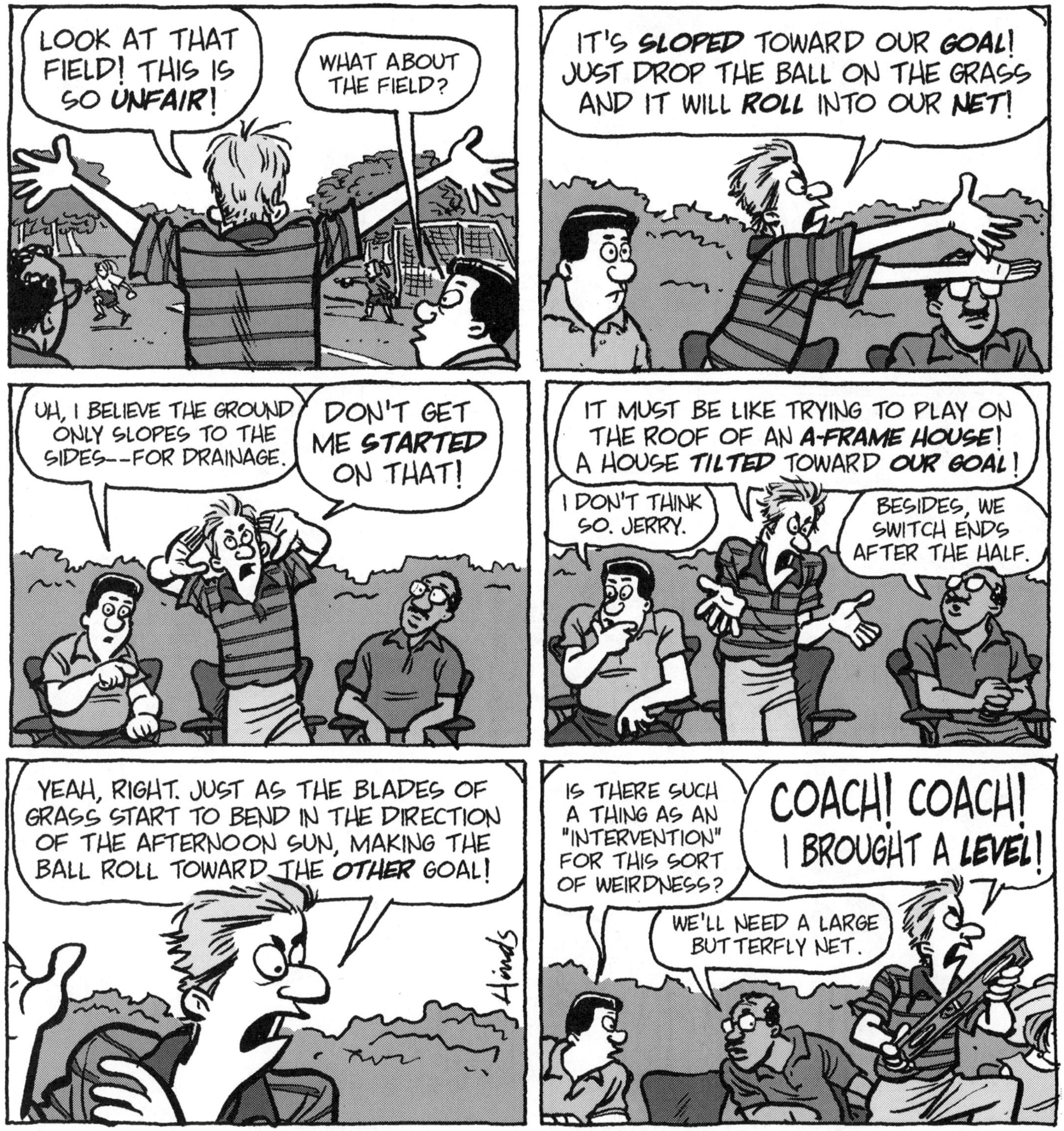
LOOK AT THAT FIELD! THIS IS SO UNFAIR!
WHAT ABOUT THE FIELD?
IT'S SLOPED TOWARD OUR GOAL! JUST DROP THE BALL ON THE GRASS AND IT WILL ROLL INTO OUR NET!
UH, I BELIEVE THE GROUND ONLY SLOPES TO THE SIDES--FOR DRAINAGE.
DON'T GET ME STARTED ON THAT!
IT MUST BE LIKE TRYING TO PLAY ON THE ROOF OF AN A-FRAME HOUSE! A HOUSE TILTED TOWARD OUR GOAL!
I DON'T THINK SO. JERRY.
BESIDES, WE SWITCH ENDS AFTER THE HALF.
YEAH, RIGHT. JUST AS THE BLADES OF GRASS START TO BEND IN THE DIRECTION OF THE AFTERNOON SUN, MAKING THE BALL ROLL TOWARD THE OTHER GOAL!
Hinds
IS THERE SUCH A THING AS AN "INTERVENTION" FOR THIS SORT OF WEIRDNESS?
COACH! COACH! I BROUGHT A LEVEL!
WE'LL NEED A LARGE BUTTERFLY NET.

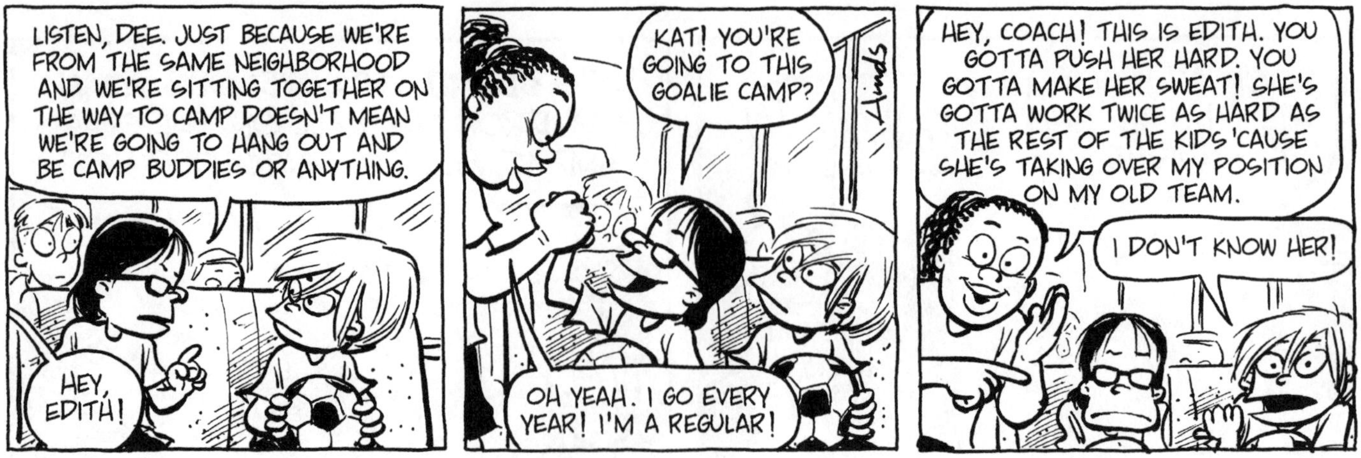
LISTEN, DEE. JUST BECAUSE WE'RE FROM THE SAME NEIGHBORHOOD AND WE'RE SITTING TOGETHER ON THE WAY TO CAMP DOESN'T MEAN WE'RE GOING TO HANG OUT AND BE CAMP BUDDIES OR ANYTHING.
HEY, EDITH!
KAT! YOU'RE GOING TO THIS GOALIE CAMP?
OH YEAH. I GO EVERY YEAR! I'M A REGULAR!
HEY, COACH! THIS IS EDITH. YOU GOTTA PUSH HER HARD. YOU GOTTA MAKE HER SWEAT! SHE'S GOTTA WORK TWICE AS HARD AS THE REST OF THE KIDS 'CAUSE SHE'S TAKING OVER MY POSITION ON MY OLD TEAM.
I DON'T KNOW HER!

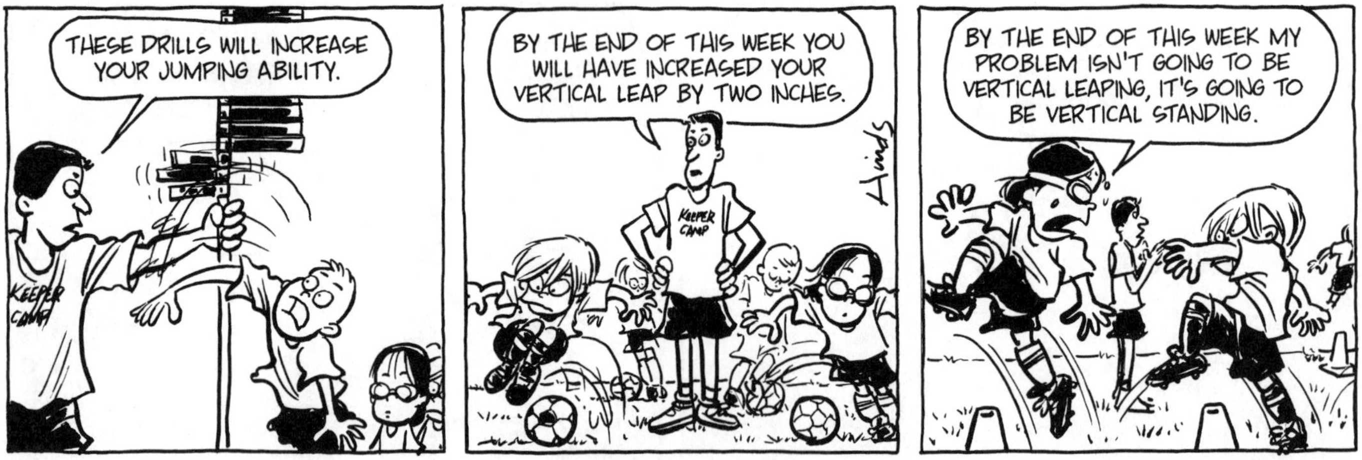
THESE DRILLS WILL INCREASE YOUR JUMPING ABILITY.
KEEPER CAMP
BY THE END OF THIS WEEK YOU WILL HAVE INCREASED YOUR VERTICAL LEAP BY TWO INCHES.
KEEPER CAMP
BY THE END OF THIS WEEK MY PROBLEM ISN'T GOING TO BE VERTICAL LEAPING, IT'S GOING TO BE VERTICAL STANDING.

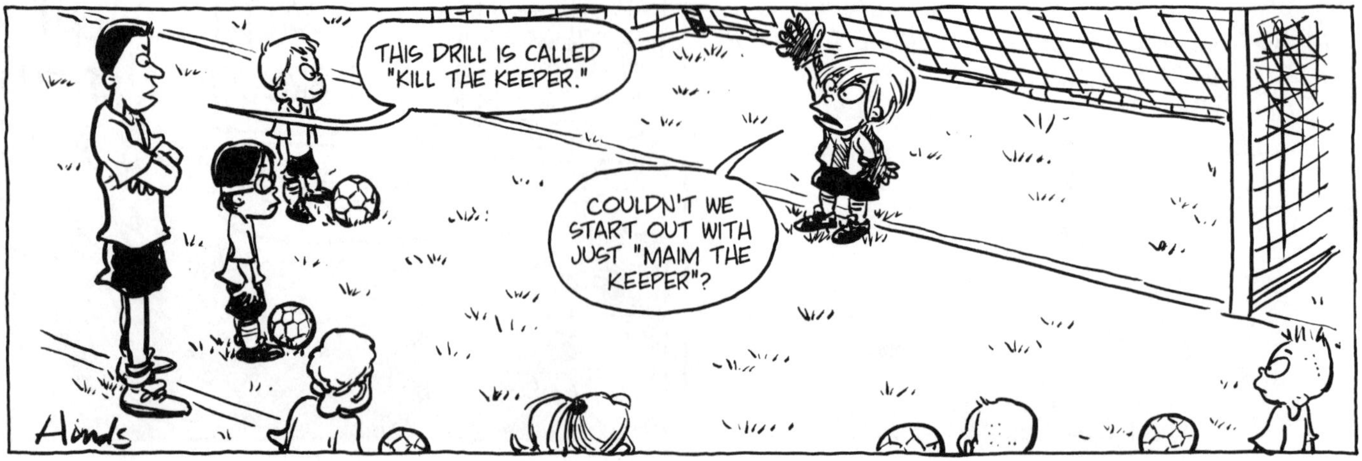
THIS DRILL IS CALLED "KILL THE KEEPER."
COULDN'T WE START OUT WITH JUST "MAIM THE KEEPER"?

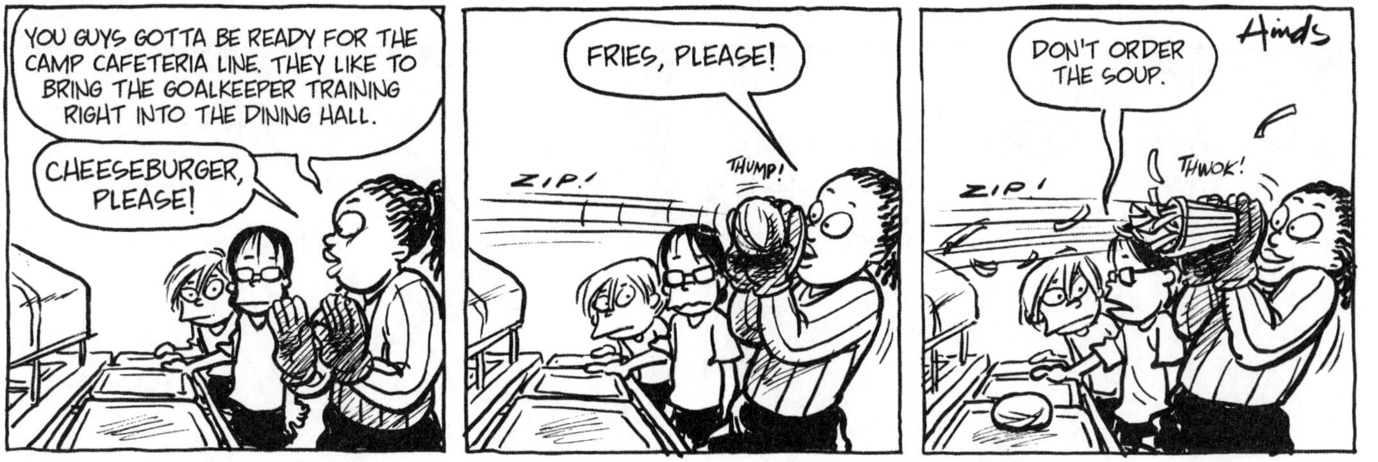
YOU GUYS GOTTA BE READY FOR THE CAMP CAFETERIA LINE. THEY LIKE TO BRING THE GOALKEEPER TRAINING RIGHT INTO THE DINING HALL.
CHEESEBURGER, PLEASE!
ZIP!
THUMP!
FRIES, PLEASE!
Hinds
DON'T ORDER THE SOUP.
ZIP!
THWOK!

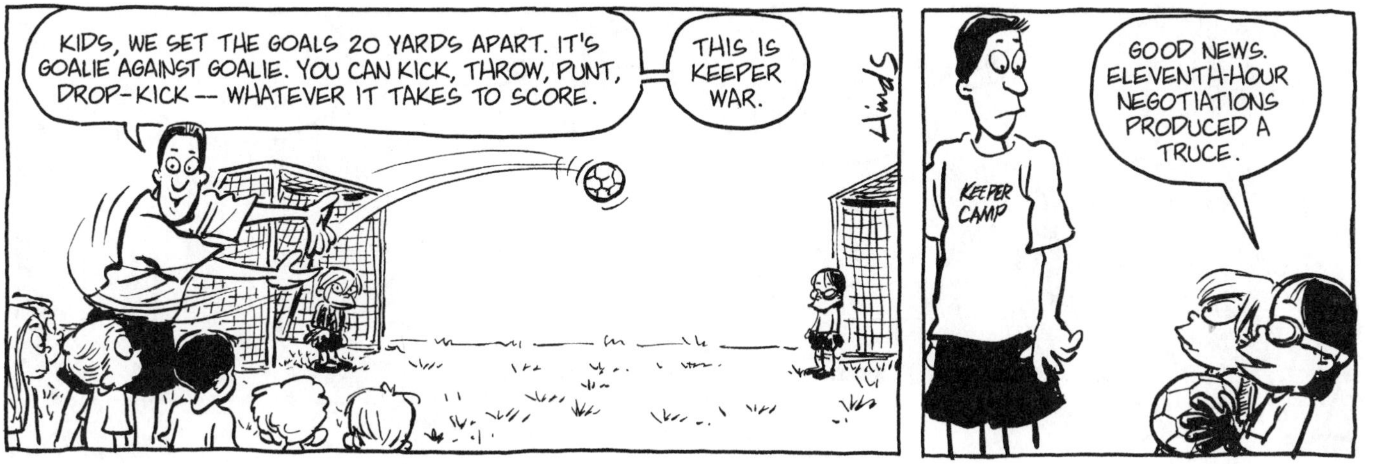
KIDS, WE SET THE GOALS 20 YARDS APART. IT'S GOALIE AGAINST GOALIE. YOU CAN KICK, THROW, PUNT, DROP-KICK -- WHATEVER IT TAKES TO SCORE.
THIS IS KEEPER WAR.
Hinds
KEEPER CAMP
GOOD NEWS. ELEVENTH-HOUR NEGOTIATIONS PRODUCED A TRUCE.

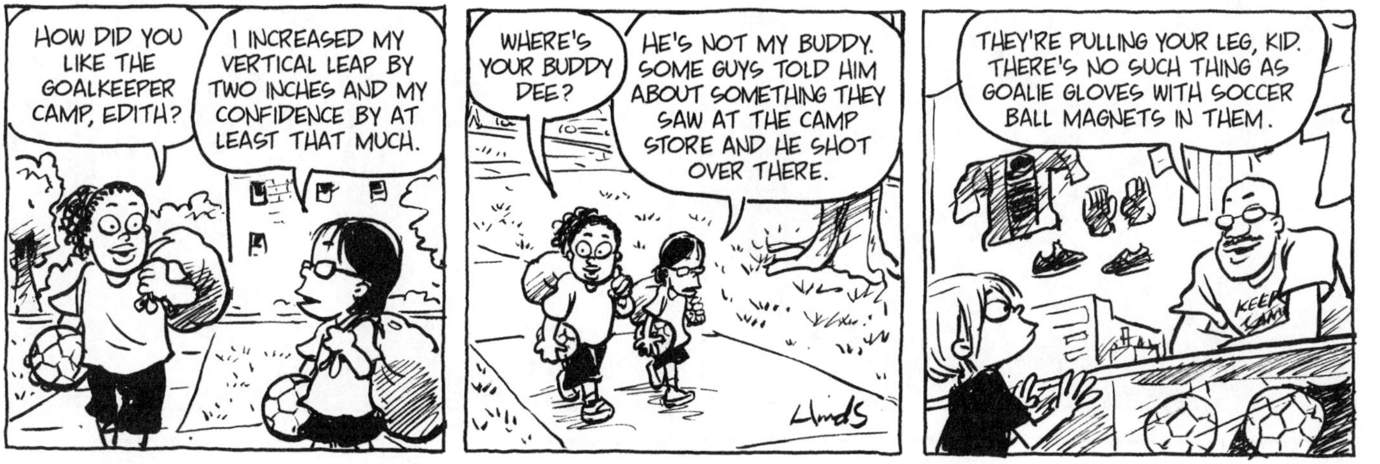
HOW DID YOU LIKE THE GOALKEEPER CAMP, EDITH?
I INCREASED MY VERTICAL LEAP BY TWO INCHES AND MY CONFIDENCE BY AT LEAST THAT MUCH.
WHERE'S YOUR BUDDY DEE?
HE'S NOT MY BUDDY. SOME GUYS TOLD HIM ABOUT SOMETHING THEY SAW AT THE CAMP STORE AND HE SHOT OVER THERE.
Hinds
THEY'RE PULLING YOUR LEG, KID. THERE'S NO SUCH THING AS GOALIE GLOVES WITH SOCCER BALL MAGNETS IN THEM.

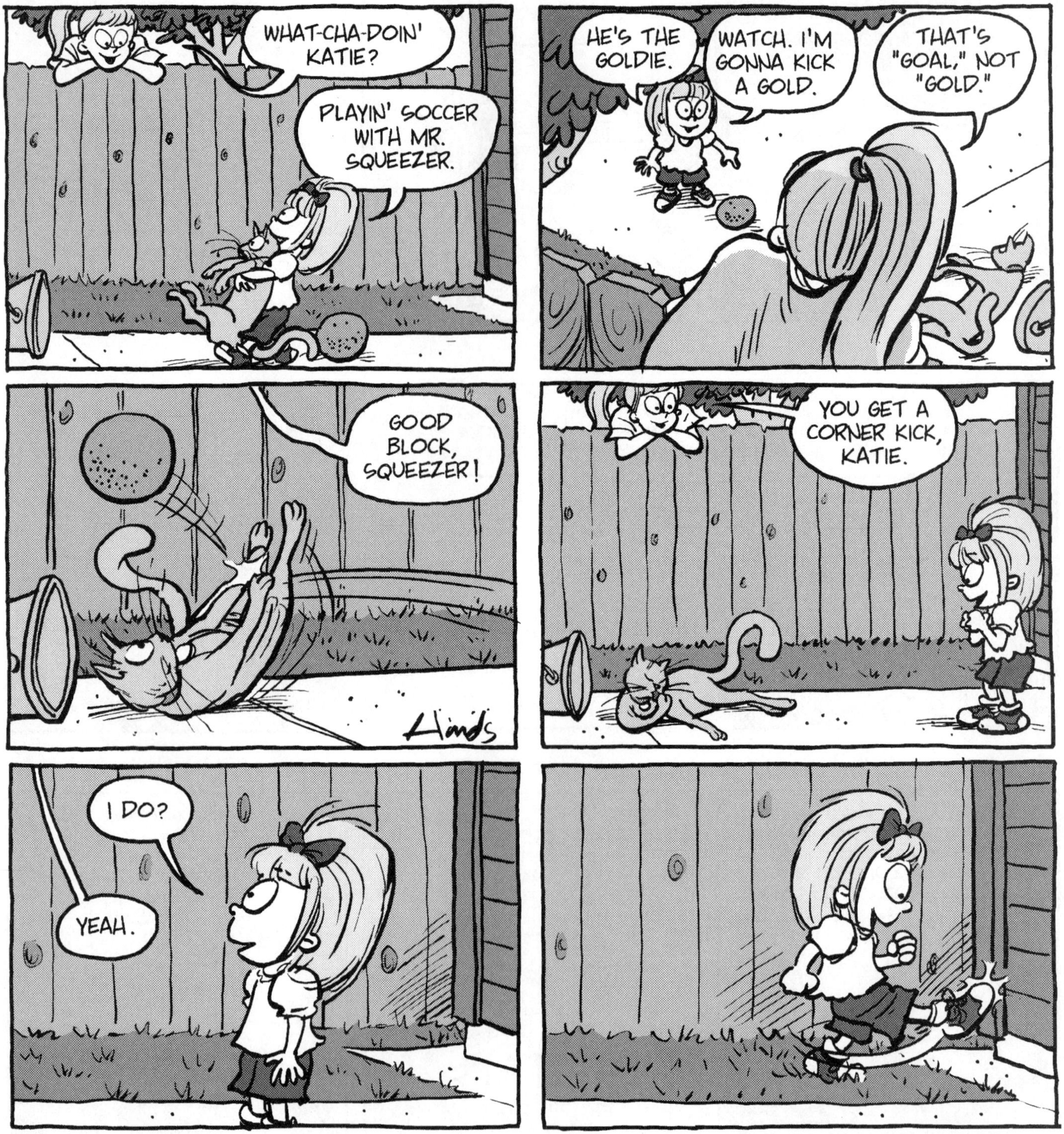
WHAT-CHA-DOIN' KATIE?
PLAYIN' SOCCER WITH MR. SQUEEZER.
HE'S THE GOLDIE.
WATCH. I'M GONNA KICK A GOLD.
THAT'S "GOAL," NOT "GOLD."
GOOD BLOCK, SQUEEZER!
Hinds
YOU GET A CORNER KICK, KATIE.
I DO?
YEAH.

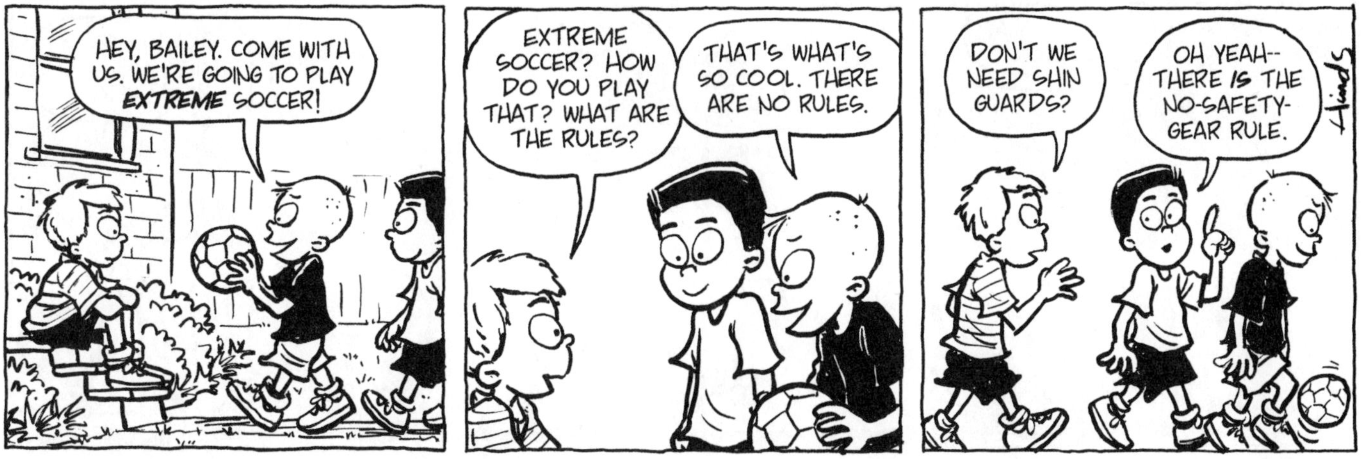
HEY, BAILEY. COME WITH US. WE'RE GOING TO PLAY **EXTREME** SOCCER!
EXTREME SOCCER? HOW DO YOU PLAY THAT? WHAT ARE THE RULES?
THAT'S WHAT'S SO COOL. THERE ARE NO RULES.
DON'T WE NEED SHIN GUARDS?
OH YEAH-- THERE **IS** THE NO-SAFETY-GEAR RULE.
Hinds

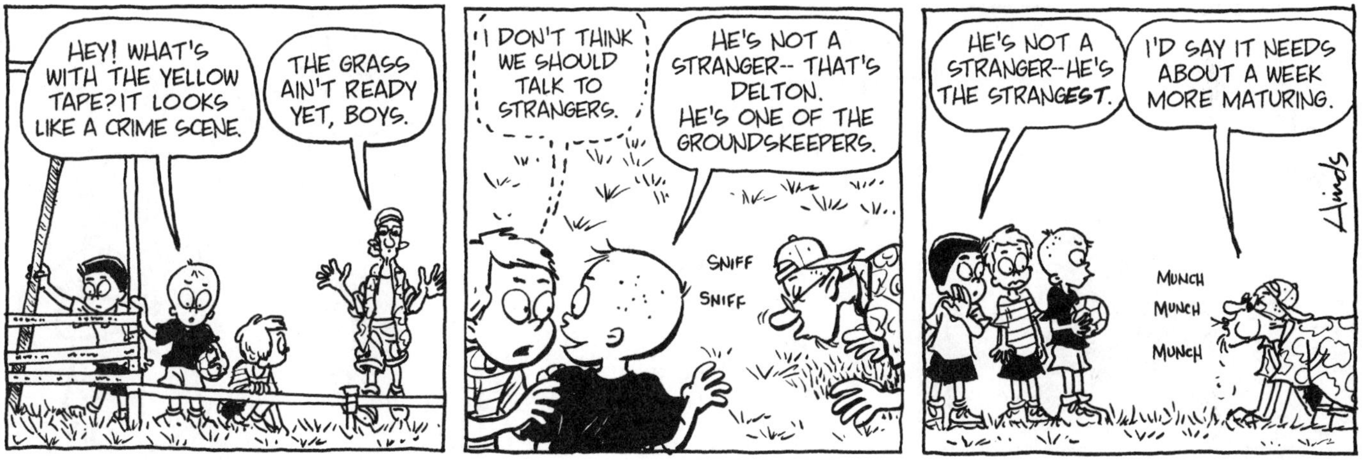
HEY! WHAT'S WITH THE YELLOW TAPE? IT LOOKS LIKE A CRIME SCENE.
THE GRASS AIN'T READY YET, BOYS.
I DON'T THINK WE SHOULD TALK TO STRANGERS.
HE'S NOT A STRANGER-- THAT'S DELTON. HE'S ONE OF THE GROUNDSKEEPERS.
SNIFF
SNIFF
HE'S NOT A STRANGER--HE'S THE STRANG**EST**.
I'D SAY IT NEEDS ABOUT A WEEK MORE MATURING.
MUNCH
MUNCH
MUNCH
Hinds

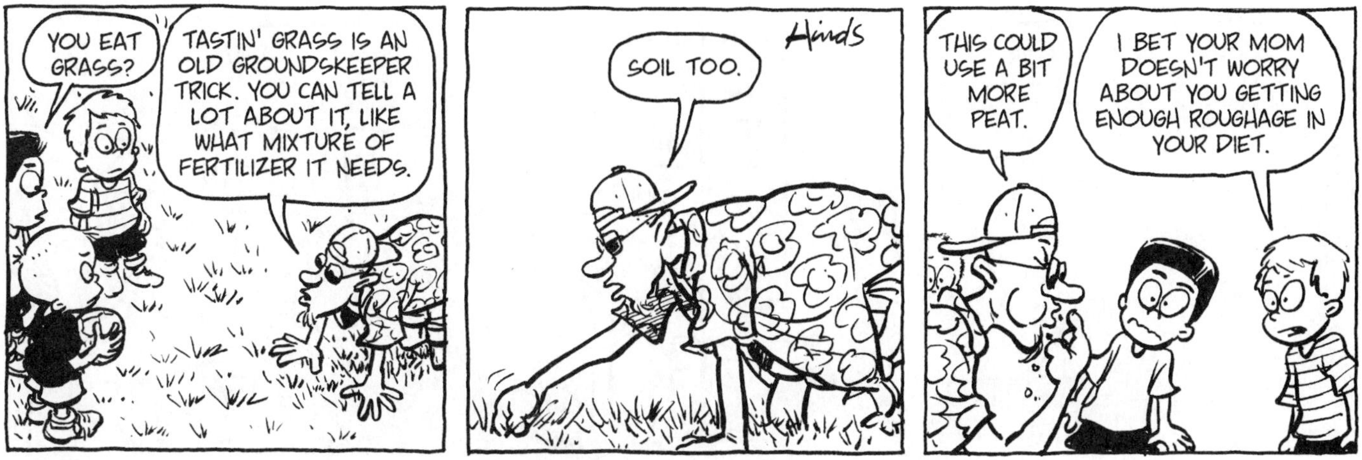
YOU EAT GRASS?
TASTIN' GRASS IS AN OLD GROUNDSKEEPER TRICK. YOU CAN TELL A LOT ABOUT IT, LIKE WHAT MIXTURE OF FERTILIZER IT NEEDS.
SOIL TOO.
Hinds
THIS COULD USE A BIT MORE PEAT.
I BET YOUR MOM DOESN'T WORRY ABOUT YOU GETTING ENOUGH ROUGHAGE IN YOUR DIET.

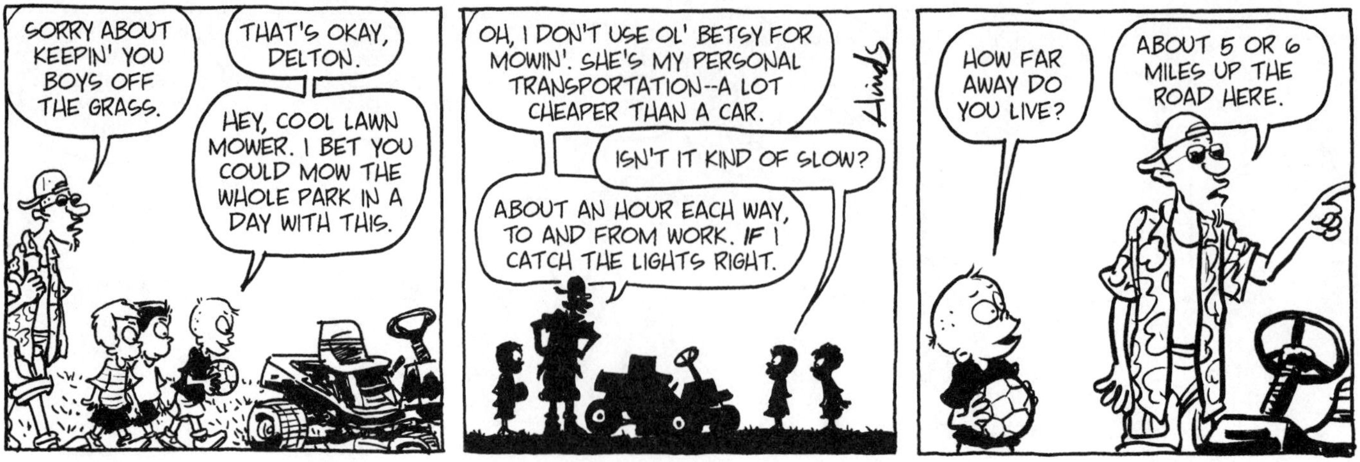
SORRY ABOUT KEEPIN' YOU BOYS OFF THE GRASS.
THAT'S OKAY, DELTON.
HEY, COOL LAWN MOWER. I BET YOU COULD MOW THE WHOLE PARK IN A DAY WITH THIS.
OH, I DON'T USE OL' BETSY FOR MOWIN'. SHE'S MY PERSONAL TRANSPORTATION--A LOT CHEAPER THAN A CAR.
ISN'T IT KIND OF SLOW?
ABOUT AN HOUR EACH WAY, TO AND FROM WORK. IF I CATCH THE LIGHTS RIGHT.
HOW FAR AWAY DO YOU LIVE?
ABOUT 5 OR 6 MILES UP THE ROAD HERE.

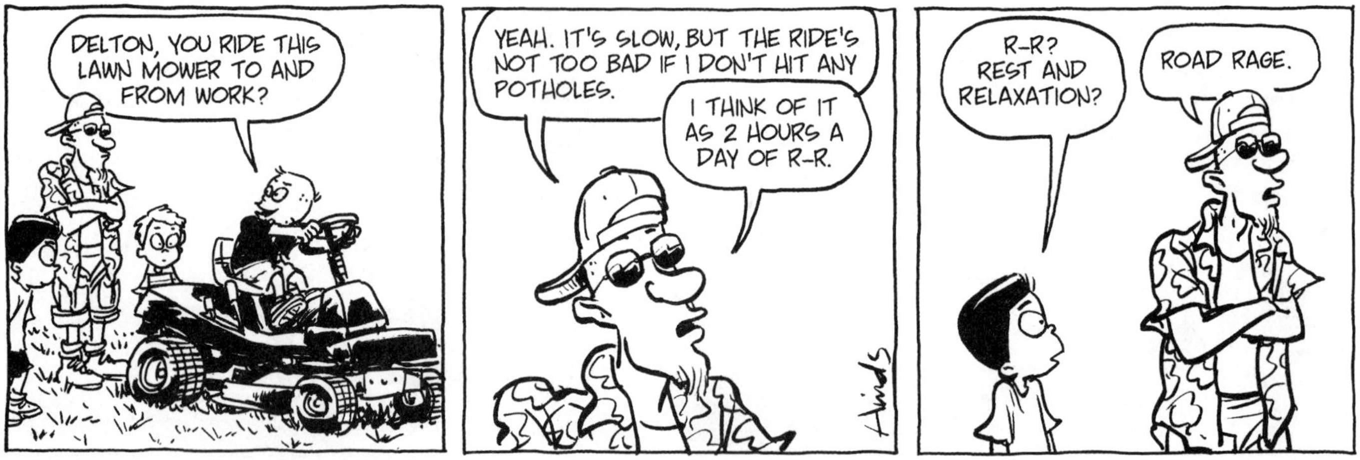
DELTON, YOU RIDE THIS LAWN MOWER TO AND FROM WORK?
YEAH. IT'S SLOW, BUT THE RIDE'S NOT TOO BAD IF I DON'T HIT ANY POTHOLES.
I THINK OF IT AS 2 HOURS A DAY OF R-R.
R-R? REST AND RELAXATION?
ROAD RAGE.

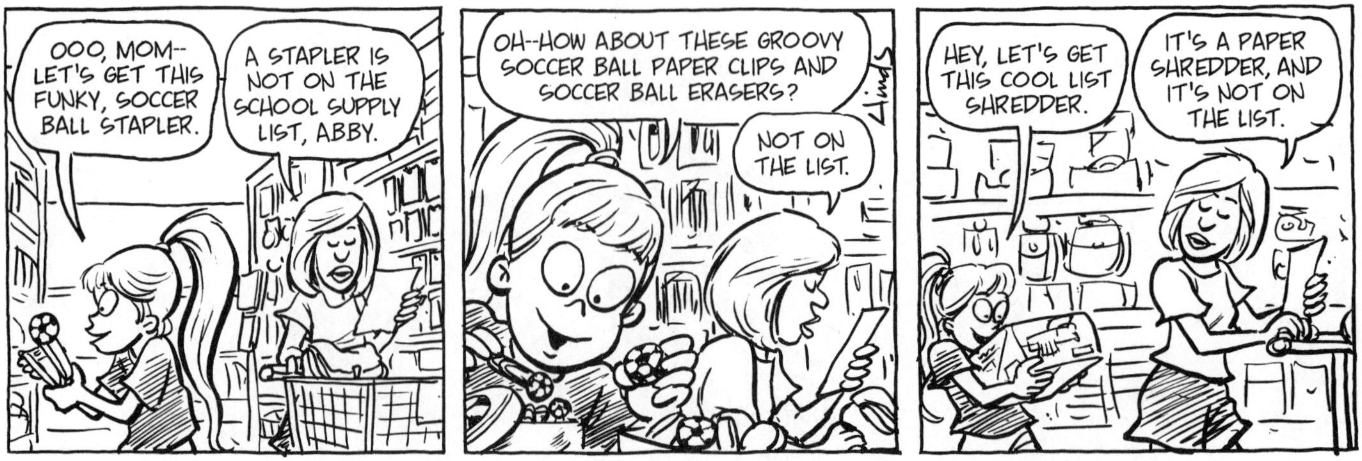
OOO, MOM-- LET'S GET THIS FUNKY, SOCCER BALL STAPLER.
A STAPLER IS NOT ON THE SCHOOL SUPPLY LIST, ABBY.
OH--HOW ABOUT THESE GROOVY SOCCER BALL PAPER CLIPS AND SOCCER BALL ERASERS?
NOT ON THE LIST.
HEY, LET'S GET THIS COOL LIST SHREDDER.
IT'S A PAPER SHREDDER, AND IT'S NOT ON THE LIST.

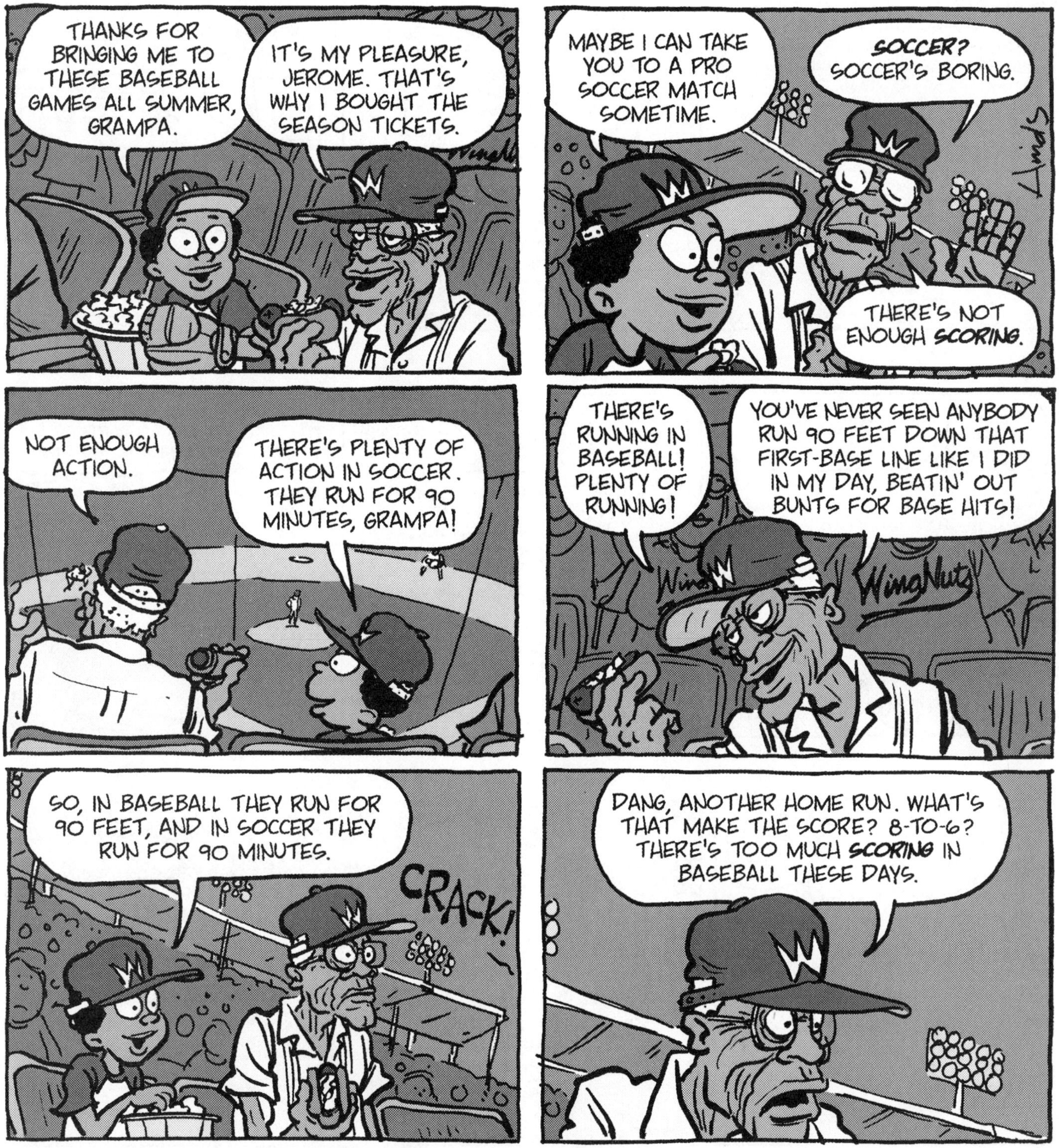
THANKS FOR BRINGING ME TO THESE BASEBALL GAMES ALL SUMMER, GRAMPA.
IT'S MY PLEASURE, JEROME. THAT'S WHY I BOUGHT THE SEASON TICKETS.
MAYBE I CAN TAKE YOU TO A PRO SOCCER MATCH SOMETIME.
SOCCER? SOCCER'S BORING.
THERE'S NOT ENOUGH SCORING.
NOT ENOUGH ACTION.
THERE'S PLENTY OF ACTION IN SOCCER. THEY RUN FOR 90 MINUTES, GRAMPA!
THERE'S RUNNING IN BASEBALL! PLENTY OF RUNNING!
YOU'VE NEVER SEEN ANYBODY RUN 90 FEET DOWN THAT FIRST-BASE LINE LIKE I DID IN MY DAY, BEATIN' OUT BUNTS FOR BASE HITS!
WingNuts
SO, IN BASEBALL THEY RUN FOR 90 FEET, AND IN SOCCER THEY RUN FOR 90 MINUTES.
CRACK!
DANG, ANOTHER HOME RUN. WHAT'S THAT MAKE THE SCORE? 8-TO-6? THERE'S TOO MUCH SCORING IN BASEBALL THESE DAYS.

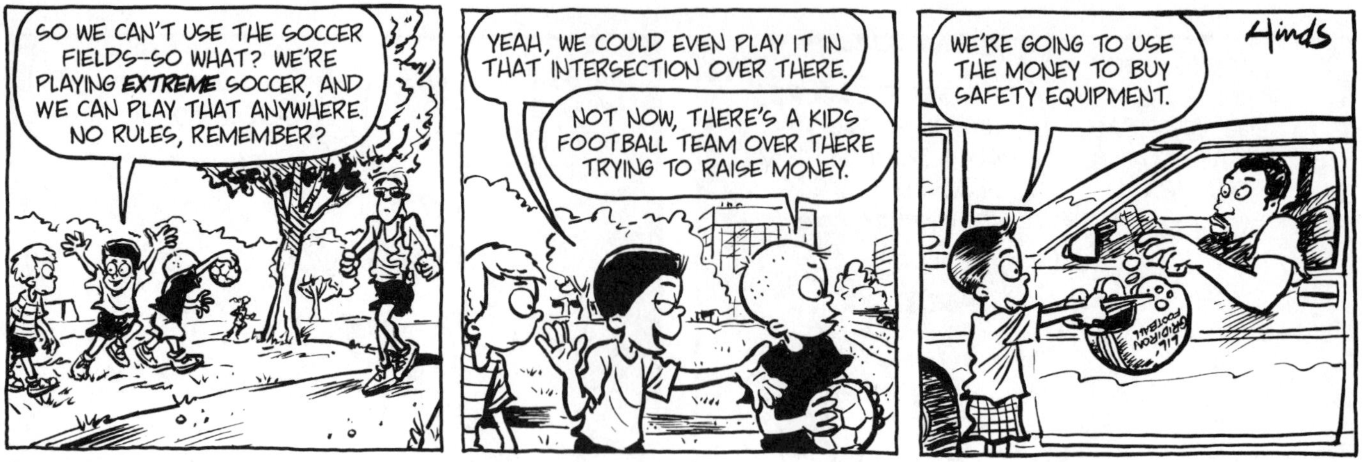
SO WE CAN'T USE THE SOCCER FIELDS--SO WHAT? WE'RE PLAYING **EXTREME** SOCCER, AND WE CAN PLAY THAT ANYWHERE. NO RULES, REMEMBER?
YEAH, WE COULD EVEN PLAY IT IN THAT INTERSECTION OVER THERE.
NOT NOW, THERE'S A KIDS FOOTBALL TEAM OVER THERE TRYING TO RAISE MONEY.
WE'RE GOING TO USE THE MONEY TO BUY SAFETY EQUIPMENT.

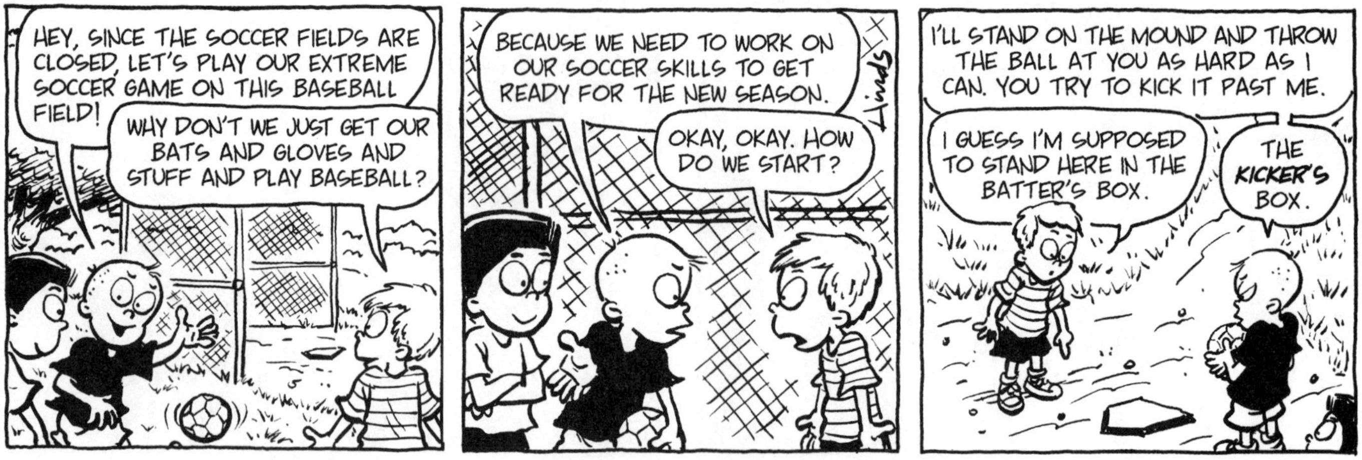
HEY, SINCE THE SOCCER FIELDS ARE CLOSED, LET'S PLAY OUR EXTREME SOCCER GAME ON THIS BASEBALL FIELD!
WHY DON'T WE JUST GET OUR BATS AND GLOVES AND STUFF AND PLAY BASEBALL?
BECAUSE WE NEED TO WORK ON OUR SOCCER SKILLS TO GET READY FOR THE NEW SEASON.
OKAY, OKAY. HOW DO WE START?
I'LL STAND ON THE MOUND AND THROW THE BALL AT YOU AS HARD AS I CAN. YOU TRY TO KICK IT PAST ME.
I GUESS I'M SUPPOSED TO STAND HERE IN THE BATTER'S BOX.
THE **KICKER'S** BOX.

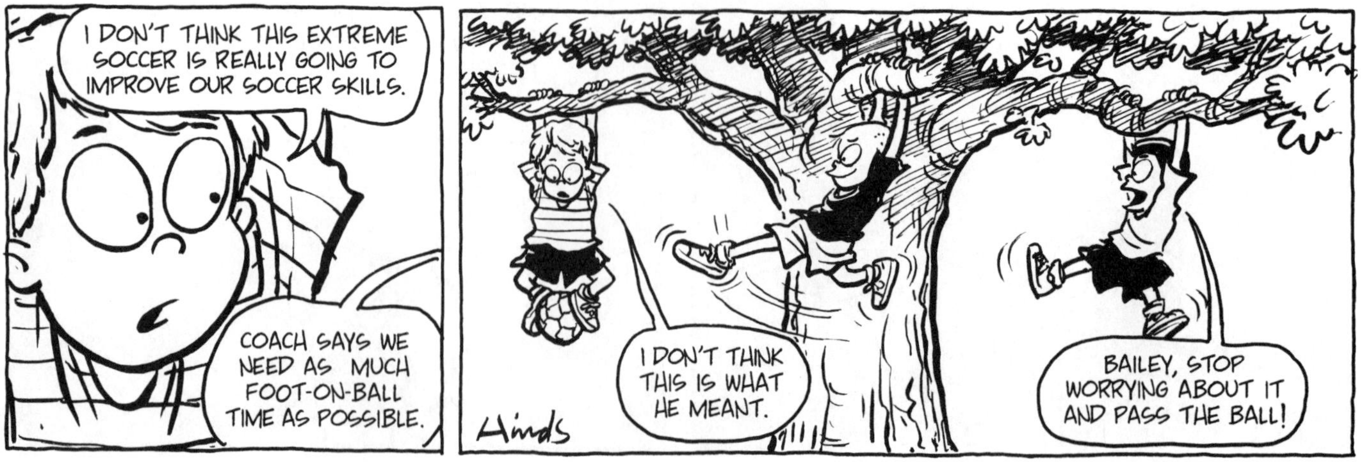
I DON'T THINK THIS EXTREME SOCCER IS REALLY GOING TO IMPROVE OUR SOCCER SKILLS.
COACH SAYS WE NEED AS MUCH FOOT-ON-BALL TIME AS POSSIBLE.
I DON'T THINK THIS IS WHAT HE MEANT.
BAILEY, STOP WORRYING ABOUT IT AND PASS THE BALL!

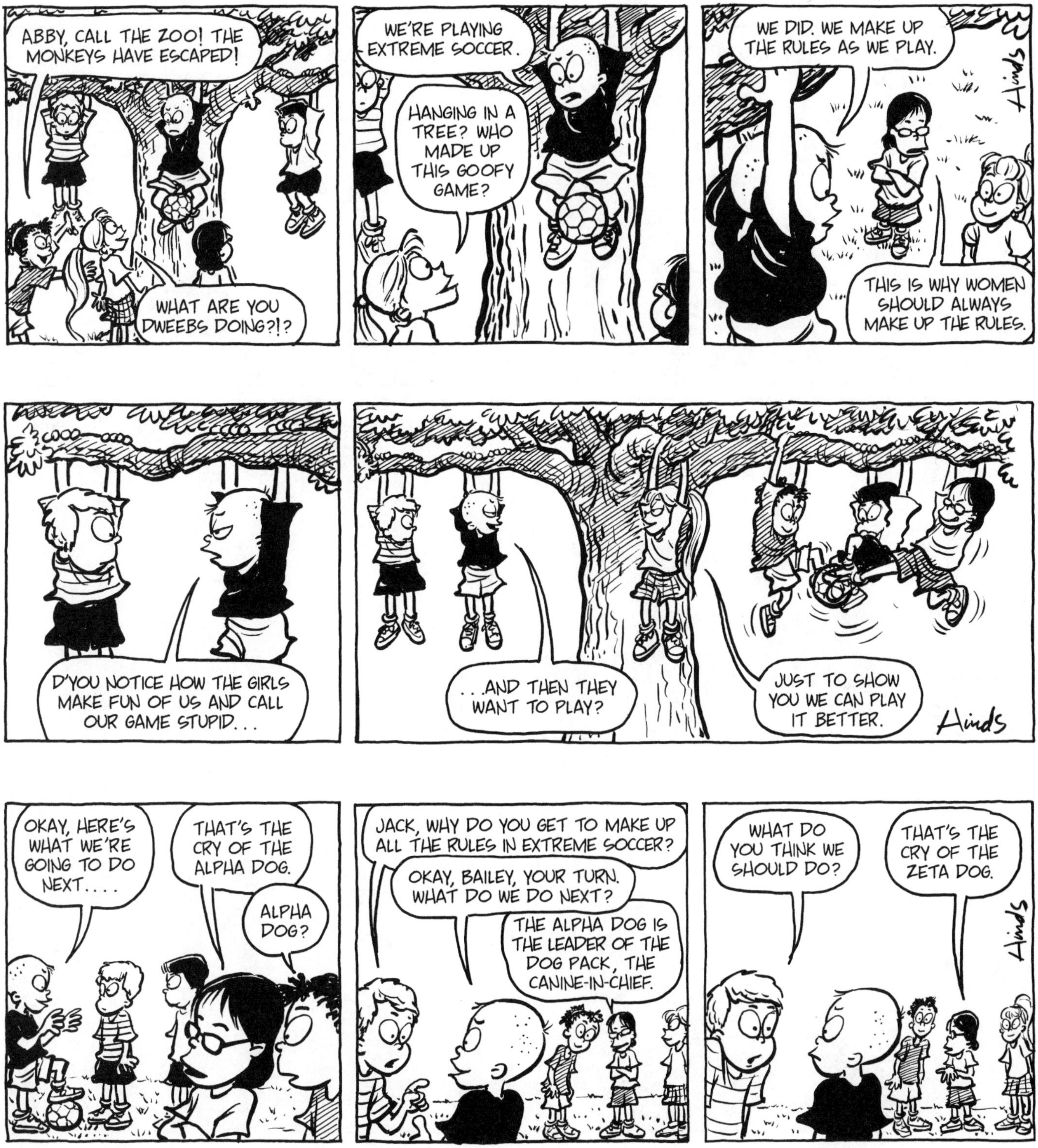
ABBY, CALL THE ZOO! THE MONKEYS HAVE ESCAPED!
WHAT ARE YOU DWEEBS DOING?!?
WE'RE PLAYING EXTREME SOCCER.
HANGING IN A TREE? WHO MADE UP THIS GOOFY GAME?
WE DID. WE MAKE UP THE RULES AS WE PLAY.
THIS IS WHY WOMEN SHOULD ALWAYS MAKE UP THE RULES.
Hinds
D'YOU NOTICE HOW THE GIRLS MAKE FUN OF US AND CALL OUR GAME STUPID...
...AND THEN THEY WANT TO PLAY?
JUST TO SHOW YOU WE CAN PLAY IT BETTER.
Hinds
OKAY, HERE'S WHAT WE'RE GOING TO DO NEXT....
THAT'S THE CRY OF THE ALPHA DOG.
ALPHA DOG?
JACK, WHY DO YOU GET TO MAKE UP ALL THE RULES IN EXTREME SOCCER?
OKAY, BAILEY, YOUR TURN. WHAT DO WE DO NEXT?
THE ALPHA DOG IS THE LEADER OF THE DOG PACK, THE CANINE-IN-CHIEF.
WHAT DO YOU THINK WE SHOULD DO?
THAT'S THE CRY OF THE ZETA DOG.
Hinds

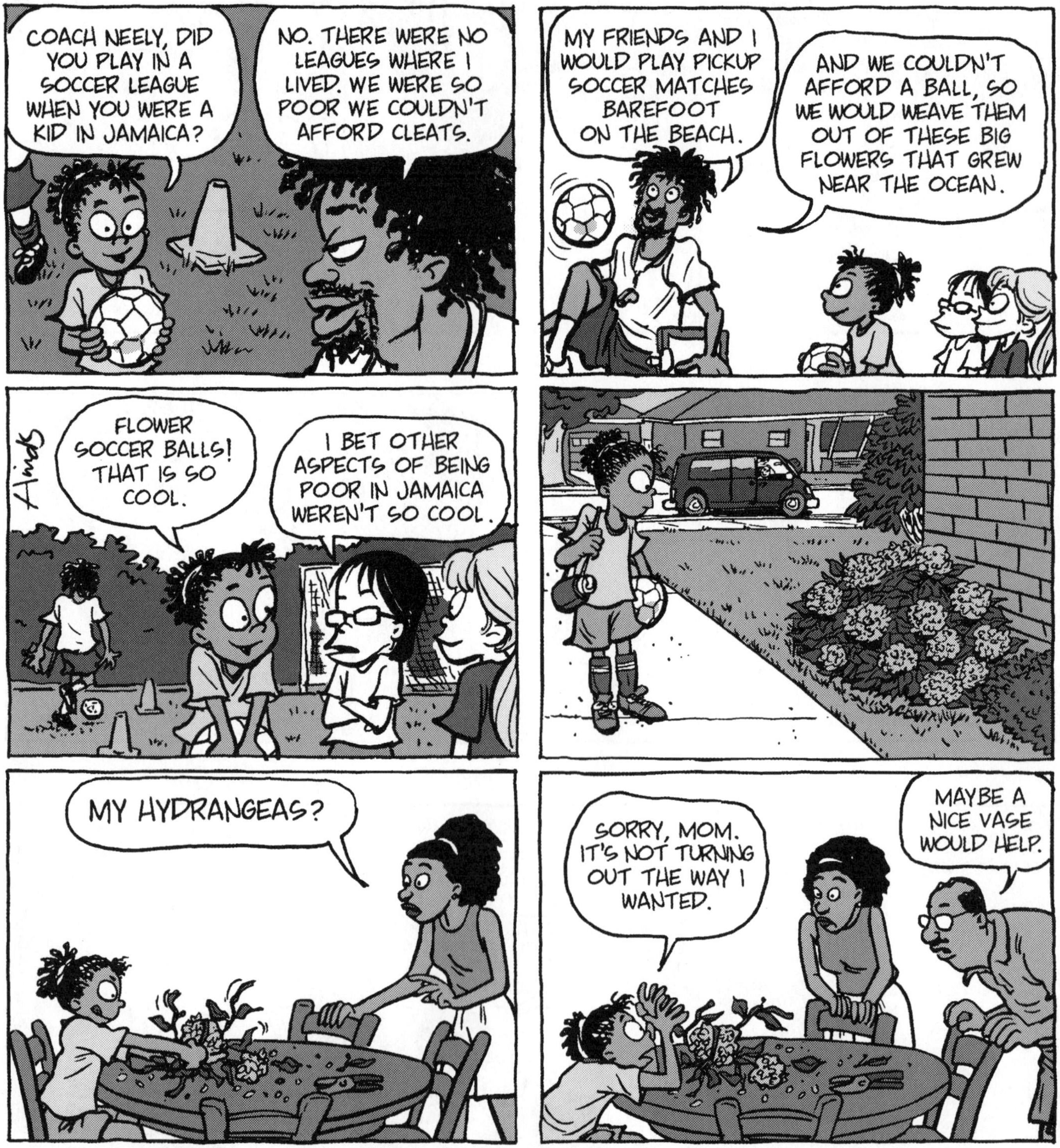
COACH NEELY, DID YOU PLAY IN A SOCCER LEAGUE WHEN YOU WERE A KID IN JAMAICA?
NO. THERE WERE NO LEAGUES WHERE I LIVED. WE WERE SO POOR WE COULDN'T AFFORD CLEATS.
MY FRIENDS AND I WOULD PLAY PICKUP SOCCER MATCHES BAREFOOT ON THE BEACH.
AND WE COULDN'T AFFORD A BALL, SO WE WOULD WEAVE THEM OUT OF THESE BIG FLOWERS THAT GREW NEAR THE OCEAN.
Hinds
FLOWER SOCCER BALLS! THAT IS SO COOL.
I BET OTHER ASPECTS OF BEING POOR IN JAMAICA WEREN'T SO COOL.
MY HYDRANGEAS?
SORRY, MOM. IT'S NOT TURNING OUT THE WAY I WANTED.
MAYBE A NICE VASE WOULD HELP.

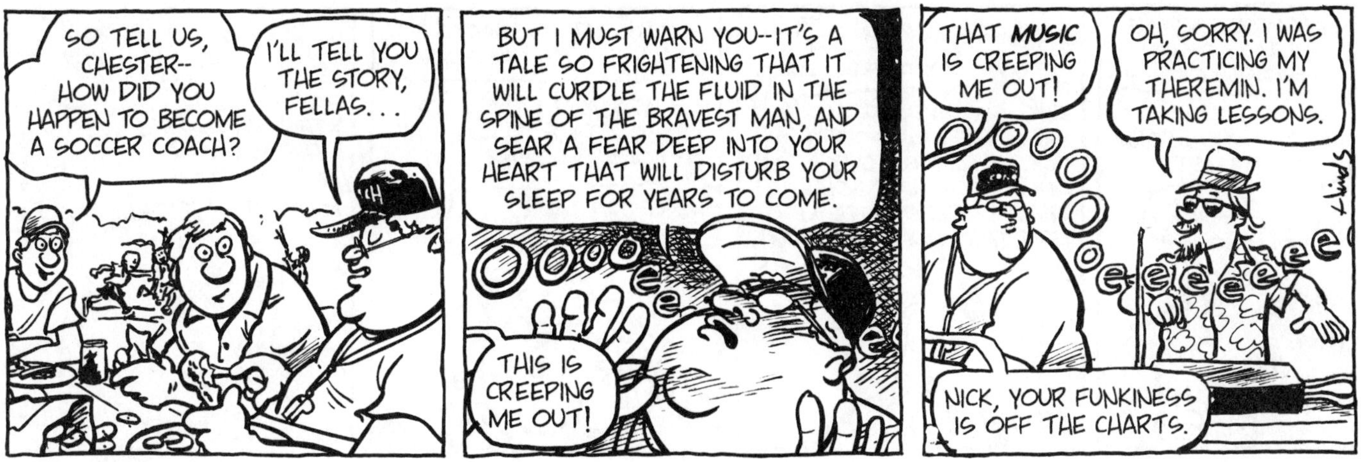
SO TELL US, CHESTER-- HOW DID YOU HAPPEN TO BECOME A SOCCER COACH?
I'LL TELL YOU THE STORY, FELLAS. . .
BUT I MUST WARN YOU--IT'S A TALE SO FRIGHTENING THAT IT WILL CURDLE THE FLUID IN THE SPINE OF THE BRAVEST MAN, AND SEAR A FEAR DEEP INTO YOUR HEART THAT WILL DISTURB YOUR SLEEP FOR YEARS TO COME.
OOOOOeee
THIS IS CREEPING ME OUT!
THAT MUSIC IS CREEPING ME OUT!
OH, SORRY. I WAS PRACTICING MY THEREMIN. I'M TAKING LESSONS.
OOOOOOOeeeeeee
NICK, YOUR FUNKINESS IS OFF THE CHARTS.
Hinds

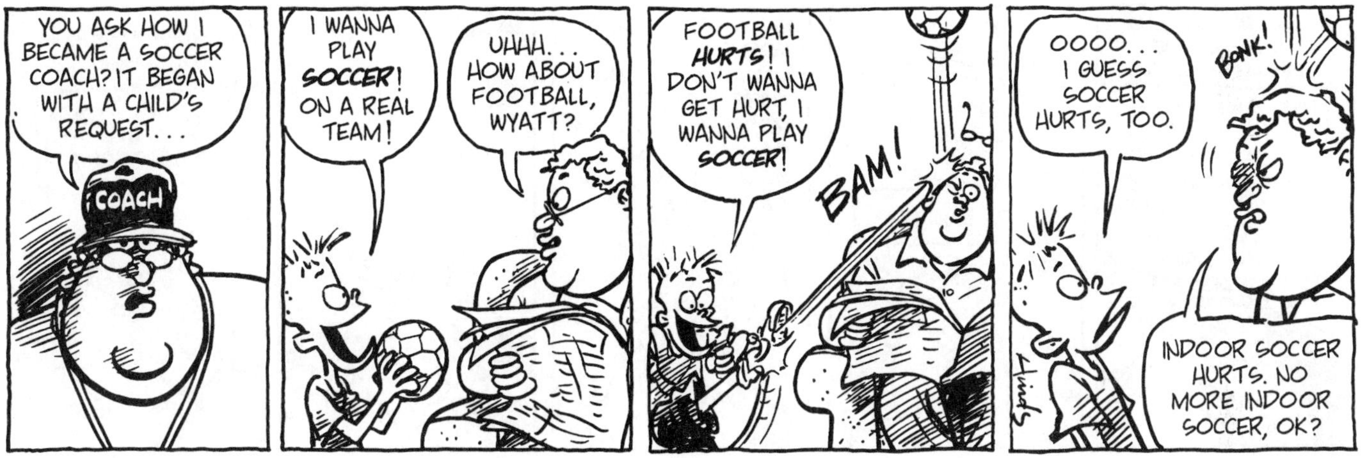
YOU ASK HOW I BECAME A SOCCER COACH? IT BEGAN WITH A CHILD'S REQUEST. . .
COACH
I WANNA PLAY SOCCER! ON A REAL TEAM!
UHHH. . . HOW ABOUT FOOTBALL, WYATT?
FOOTBALL HURTS! I DON'T WANNA GET HURT, I WANNA PLAY SOCCER!
BAM!
OOOO. . . I GUESS SOCCER HURTS, TOO.
BONK!
INDOOR SOCCER HURTS. NO MORE INDOOR SOCCER, OK?
Hinds

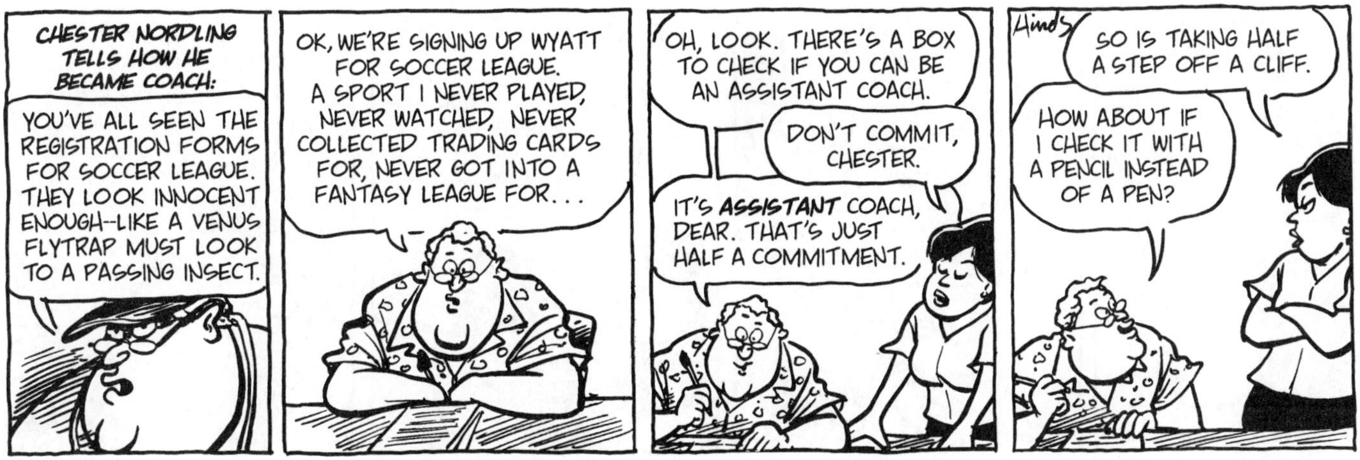
CHESTER NORDLING TELLS HOW HE BECAME COACH:
YOU'VE ALL SEEN THE REGISTRATION FORMS FOR SOCCER LEAGUE. THEY LOOK INNOCENT ENOUGH--LIKE A VENUS FLYTRAP MUST LOOK TO A PASSING INSECT.
OK, WE'RE SIGNING UP WYATT FOR SOCCER LEAGUE. A SPORT I NEVER PLAYED, NEVER WATCHED, NEVER COLLECTED TRADING CARDS FOR, NEVER GOT INTO A FANTASY LEAGUE FOR. . .
OH, LOOK. THERE'S A BOX TO CHECK IF YOU CAN BE AN ASSISTANT COACH.
DON'T COMMIT, CHESTER.
IT'S ASSISTANT COACH, DEAR. THAT'S JUST HALF A COMMITMENT.
Hinds
SO IS TAKING HALF A STEP OFF A CLIFF.
HOW ABOUT IF I CHECK IT WITH A PENCIL INSTEAD OF A PEN?

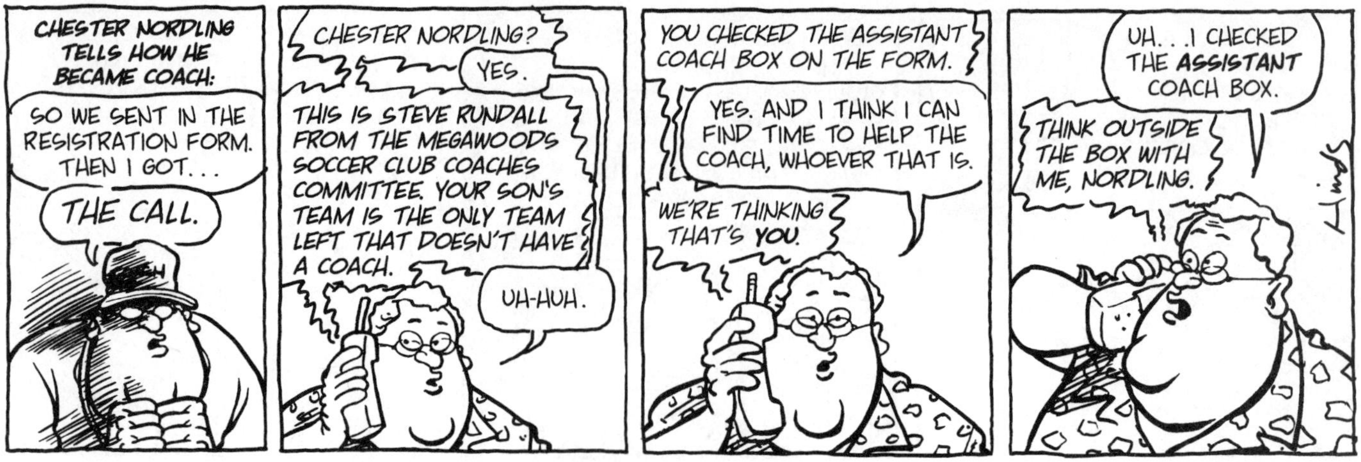
CHESTER NORDLING TELLS HOW HE BECAME COACH:
SO WE SENT IN THE REGISTRATION FORM. THEN I GOT...
THE CALL.
CHESTER NORDLING?
YES.
THIS IS STEVE RUNDALL FROM THE MEGAWOODS SOCCER CLUB COACHES COMMITTEE. YOUR SON'S TEAM IS THE ONLY TEAM LEFT THAT DOESN'T HAVE A COACH.
UH-HUH.
YOU CHECKED THE ASSISTANT COACH BOX ON THE FORM.
YES. AND I THINK I CAN FIND TIME TO HELP THE COACH, WHOEVER THAT IS.
WE'RE THINKING THAT'S YOU.
UH...I CHECKED THE ASSISTANT COACH BOX.
THINK OUTSIDE THE BOX WITH ME, NORDLING.
Hinds

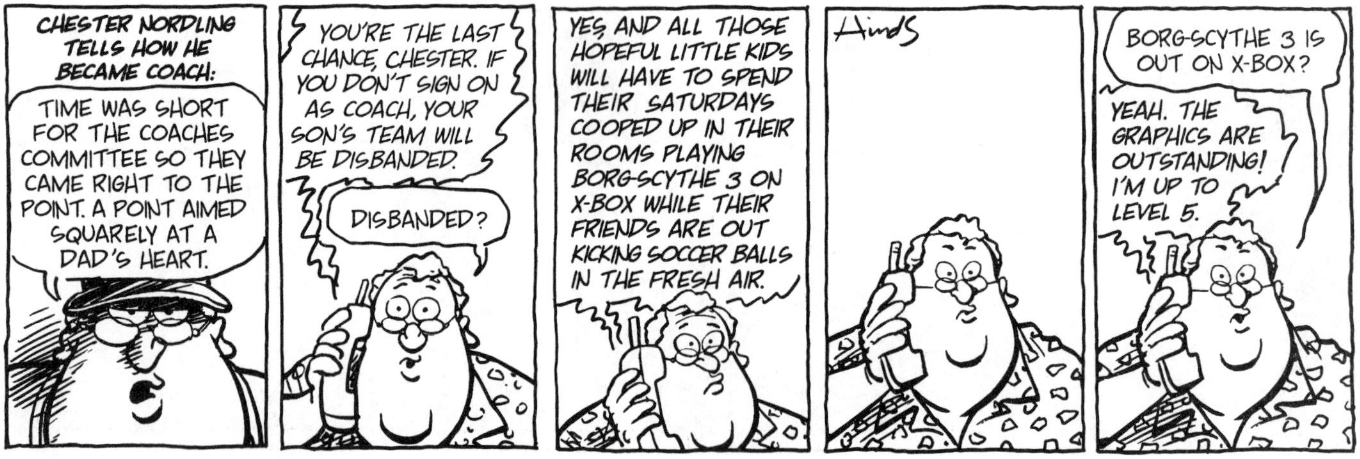
CHESTER NORDLING TELLS HOW HE BECAME COACH:
TIME WAS SHORT FOR THE COACHES COMMITTEE SO THEY CAME RIGHT TO THE POINT. A POINT AIMED SQUARELY AT A DAD'S HEART.
YOU'RE THE LAST CHANCE, CHESTER. IF YOU DON'T SIGN ON AS COACH, YOUR SON'S TEAM WILL BE DISBANDED.
DISBANDED?
YES, AND ALL THOSE HOPEFUL LITTLE KIDS WILL HAVE TO SPEND THEIR SATURDAYS COOPED UP IN THEIR ROOMS PLAYING BORG-SCYTHE 3 ON X-BOX WHILE THEIR FRIENDS ARE OUT KICKING SOCCER BALLS IN THE FRESH AIR.
Hinds
BORG-SCYTHE 3 IS OUT ON X-BOX?
YEAH. THE GRAPHICS ARE OUTSTANDING! I'M UP TO LEVEL 5.

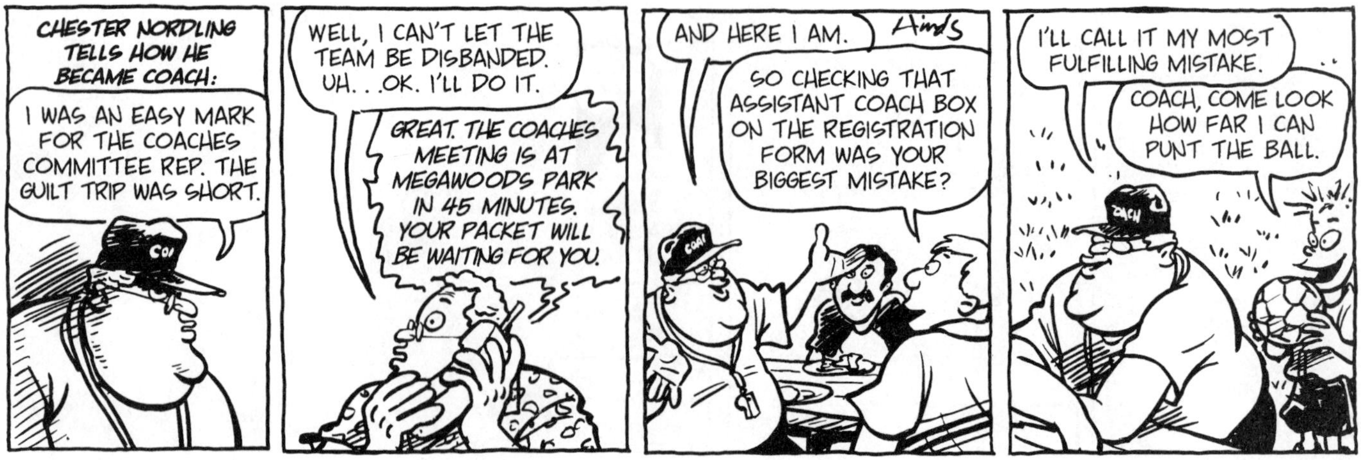
CHESTER NORDLING TELLS HOW HE BECAME COACH:
I WAS AN EASY MARK FOR THE COACHES COMMITTEE REP. THE GUILT TRIP WAS SHORT.
WELL, I CAN'T LET THE TEAM BE DISBANDED. UH...OK. I'LL DO IT.
GREAT. THE COACHES MEETING IS AT MEGAWOODS PARK IN 45 MINUTES. YOUR PACKET WILL BE WAITING FOR YOU.
AND HERE I AM.
Hinds
SO CHECKING THAT ASSISTANT COACH BOX ON THE REGISTRATION FORM WAS YOUR BIGGEST MISTAKE?
I'LL CALL IT MY MOST FULFILLING MISTAKE.
COACH, COME LOOK HOW FAR I CAN PUNT THE BALL.

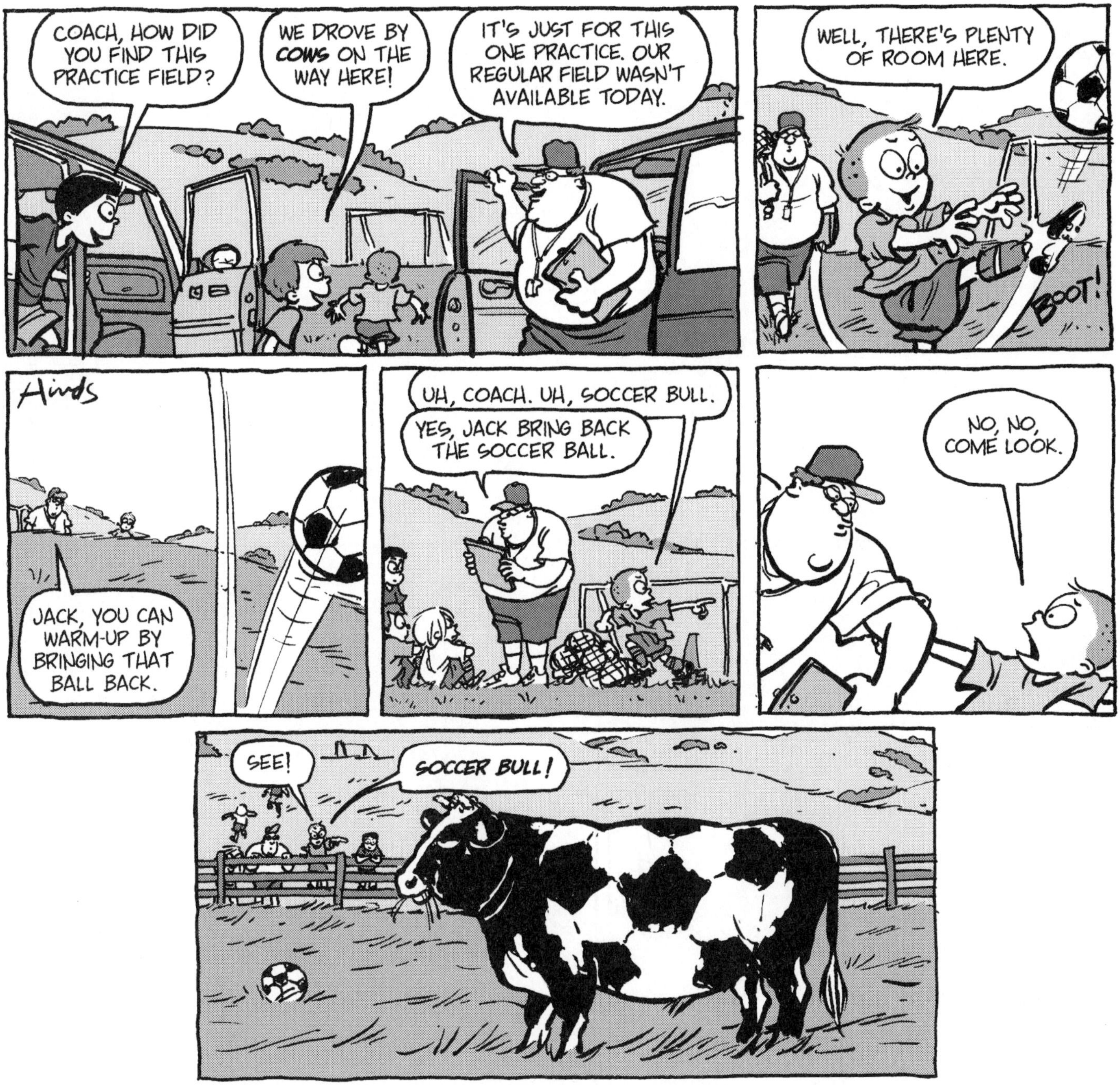

COACH, HOW DID YOU FIND THIS PRACTICE FIELD?
WE DROVE BY COWS ON THE WAY HERE!
IT'S JUST FOR THIS ONE PRACTICE. OUR REGULAR FIELD WASN'T AVAILABLE TODAY.
WELL, THERE'S PLENTY OF ROOM HERE.
BOOT!
Hinds
JACK, YOU CAN WARM-UP BY BRINGING THAT BALL BACK.
UH, COACH. UH, SOCCER BULL.
YES, JACK BRING BACK THE SOCCER BALL.
NO, NO, COME LOOK.
SEE!
SOCCER BULL!